Houghton
Mifflin

Spelling and Vocabulary

Scallop shells
from beaches
around the world

Senior Authors
Edmund H. Henderson
Shane Templeton

Consulting Authors
Barbara Coulter
Joyce A. M. Thomas

Consultants
Jane Adrian
Judith Pierce Jefferson
Catherine Leeker
Jane Ann Malakosky
Elisabeth L. Rowlands

Houghton Mifflin Company   **Boston**

Atlanta   Dallas   Geneva, Illinois   Palo Alto   Princeton   Toronto

Acknowledgments

Select definitions in the Spelling Dictionary are adapted and reprinted by permission from the following Houghton Mifflin Company publications. Copyright © 1986 *The Houghton Mifflin Intermediate Dictionary*. Copyright © 1986 *The Houghton Mifflin Student Dictionary*. Copyright © 1985 *The American Heritage Dictionary, Second College Edition*.

PASSWORD is the registered trademark of the Super Password Company. Used by permission.

Literature excerpts:
from ''The Adobe Way.'' Copyright © 1989. Reprinted by permission of Houghton Mifflin Company.

from *Charlotte's Web* by E. B. White. Copyright 1952 by E. B. White. Text copyright © renewed 1980 by E. B. White. Illustrations copyright © renewed 1980 by Garth Williams. Adapted and reprinted by permission of Harper & Row, Publishers, Inc. and Hamish Hamilton Ltd.

from ''Hurdles'' by Mary Blocksma with Esther Romero. Copyright © 1989. Reprinted by permission of Houghton Mifflin Company.

from *The Once-A-Year Day* by Eve Bunting. Copyright © 1974 by Eve Bunting. Reprinted by permission of the author.

from *Seven True Elephant Stories* by Barbara Williams. Copyright © 1978. Adapted and reprinted by permission of Hastings House Publishers, Inc.

ISBN: 0-395-62661-7

23456789-DP-97 96 95 94

How to Study a Word

1 **LOOK at the word.**
- What letters are in the word?
- What does the word mean? Does it have more than one meaning?

2 **SAY the word.**
- What are the consonant sounds?
- What are the vowel sounds?

3 **THINK about the word.**
- How is each sound spelled?
- Did you see any familiar spelling patterns?
- Did you note any prefixes, suffixes, or other word parts?

4 **WRITE the word.**
- Think about the sounds and the letters.
- Form the letters correctly.

5 **CHECK the spelling.**
- Did you spell the word the same way it is spelled in your word list?
- Do you need to write the word again in your Notebook for Writing?

Your Notebook for Writing

A Notebook for Writing is a good way to build your own personal word list. What words should you write in your notebook?

- new words from your reading and your school subjects
- words from your writing that you have trouble spelling
- spelling words that you need to study

When should you use your Notebook for Writing?

- when you are looking for exact or interesting words to use in your writing
- when you are proofreading your writing for misspelled words
- to help you study spelling

First, fold eight pieces of paper lengthwise. Also fold a cover sheet.

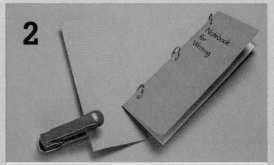

Staple the sheets, or punch holes and fasten with rings. Write **Notebook for Writing** and your name on the cover.

Beginning on the first page, write the numbers for the 36 units you will study. Write two numbers on each page.

As you begin a unit, use this part of your notebook to write the spelling words that you especially need to study.

Write **My Own Words** on the first page of the second part. Write two alphabet letters on each page.

In this part of your notebook, keep your own personal word list.

Contents
Cycle One

Cycle Two

Cycle Four

Cycle Six

Student's Handbook

1 Spelling |ă| and |ā|

A. _____

_____

_____

_____

_____

B. _____

_____

_____

_____

_____

_____

_____

_____

_____

_____

_____

_____

_____

■ Challenge

_____

_____

_____

_____

LOOK at each word.

SAY each word.

Basic Words		**■ Challenge**
1. skate	11. jail	21. champion
2. blade	12. shape	22. graceful
3. gain	13. plant	23. athletic
4. safe	14. hang	24. activity
5. drag	15. pray	25. relay
6. aid	16. pain	
7. past	17. glass	
8. gray	18. shall	
9. drain	19. sale	
🐘10. break	🐘20. steak	

THINK about the words.

Each word has the short *a* sound or the long *a* sound. The short *a* sound is usually spelled *a* followed by a consonant sound. The long *a* sound is often spelled *a*-consonant-*e* or with two letters.

|ă| dr**a**g |ā| sk**ate**, g**ai**n, gr**ay**

- What is one spelling pattern for the |ă| sound? What are three patterns for the |ā| sound? What is the spelling pattern for the |ā| sound in the Elephant Words?

WRITE the words.

Practice   **Write the Basic Words to answer the questions.**

A. Which **six** words have the |ă| sound?

B. Which **fourteen** words have the |ā| sound?

■ Now write the five Challenge Words. Underline the patterns that spell the |ă| and the |ā| sounds.

CHECK your spelling.

Spelling-Meaning Hint Can you see *safe* in these words: *safely, safety, unsafe*? These words are all related in spelling and meaning. **Think of this:** Following *safety* rules will keep you *safe*.

Independent Practice

Spelling-Meaning Look at the Spelling-Meaning Hint.

1-2. Write *safety*. Then write the Basic Word that you see in *safety*.

Word Analysis Complete the exercises with Basic Words.

3-4. The first sound in *ship* is shown as |sh|. Write the two words that begin with the |sh| sound.

5-7. Write the three words that rhyme with *train*.

Definitions Write the Basic Word that fits each meaning.

8. a piece of meat
9. to crack
10. gone by
11. to glide on ice
12. a color that mixes black and white
13. to hope very much
14. to pull along
15. to give help to

 plant

 safe

■ **Challenge Words** Write the Challenge Word that fits each meaning. Use your Spelling Dictionary.

16. a winner
17. good at sports
18. to pass along
19. showing beauty in movement
20. movement or action

1. _____
2. _____
3. _____
4. _____
5. _____
6. _____
7. _____
8. _____
9. _____
10. _____
11. _____
12. _____
13. _____
14. _____
15. _____
16. _____
17. _____
18. _____
19. _____
20. _____

Summing Up

The |ă| sound is usually spelled *a* followed by a consonant sound. The |ā| sound is often spelled with the pattern *a*-consonant-*e*, *ai*, or *ay*.

Basic

1. skate
2. blade
3. gain
4. safe
5. drag
6. aid
7. past
8. gray
9. drain
10. break
11. jail
12. shape
13. plant
14. hang
15. pray
16. pain
17. glass
18. shall
19. sale
20. steak

■ Challenge

21. champion
22. graceful
23. athletic
24. activity
25. relay

Review

1. last
2. stage
3. clay
4. face
5. paint

Proofreading Marks

¶ Indent
∧ Add something
℮ Take out something
≡ Capitalize
/ Make a small letter

Expanding Vocabulary

Using a Thesaurus   Where can you find words that say exactly what you mean? Look in a thesaurus. A **thesaurus** gives words that can be used in place of other words. This thesaurus entry gives *careful* and *protected* as words for *safe*.

> part of speech ⟶ | definition
> main entry word ⟶ **safe** *adj.* free from danger, risk, or harm.
> *This old bridge is not* **safe**.
> subentries ⟶ **careful** taking the necessary caution.
> *My mother is a* **careful** *driver.*
> **protected** covered or guarded from harm.
> sample sentence ⟶ *Wild animals are* **protected** *in this park.*

Practice   Read pages 253–254 to learn how to use your Thesaurus. Then look up the three words below in your Thesaurus. Write the two subentries listed for each word.

1. last   **2.** break   **3.** pull

1. _____   _____

2. _____   _____

3. _____   _____

Proofreading

End Marks   End every sentence with the correct mark.

    STATEMENT: Grandfather works at the Sports Center.
    COMMAND: Read this article about his store.
    QUESTION: Do famous players shop there?
    EXCLAMATION: What a great job that must be!

Practice   Proofread this ad. Find four misspelled words and two missing end marks. Use proofreading marks to correct the errors.

Example: Is this sled ~~save~~ *safe* ?

Are your skates old and out of shap

Do you have a dull skate blad?

Does your sled need a new coat of pant?

Visit the Sports Center during our winter sal

14

Review: Spelling Spree

Hidden Words Write the Basic or Review Word that you find in each row of letters. Do not let the other words fool you.

Example: l a p r a y a r d *pray*

1. l e s t a y s a f e e l
2. t r a s h o s t e a k
3. r i s k a t e a r
4. l e g a i n e a r l y
5. w a s h a l l e l s
6. l a s h a n g e r

7. f a l l a s t e l l
8. c a s t a g e a r
9. s o f a c e d a r
10. s a l e a p e d
11. w e b l a d e a r
12. g r a l s a i d o

Letter Math Write a Basic or Review Word by adding and subtracting letters from the words below.

Example: st + page − p = *stage*

13. br + steak − st =
14. gr + pray − pr =
15. cl + play − pl =
16. gl + class − cl =
17. pr + way − w =
18. j + pail − p =
19. p + train − tr =

20. p + fast − f =
21. p + faint − f =
22. pl + grant − gr =
23. sh + tape − t =
24. dr + main − m =
25. dr + sag − s =

¹r							
e							
l							
²a	t	h	l	e	t	i	c
y							

■ **Challenge Words** Make a crossword puzzle using the Challenge Words. Draw boxes down and across to fit the Challenge Words. Then write numbered clues or definitions for the words. Trade puzzles with a classmate.

📖 *Writing Application:* A Personal Story Write a paragraph telling about a fun time that you had outdoors during the winter. What was the weather like? Who was with you? Why was this experience special? Try to use five words from the list on page 14.

1. _____
2. _____
3. _____
4. _____
5. _____
6. _____
7. _____
8. _____
9. _____
10. _____
11. _____
12. _____
13. _____
14. _____
15. _____
16. _____
17. _____
18. _____
19. _____
20. _____
21. _____
22. _____
23. _____
24. _____
25. _____

1   Spelling Across the Curriculum

Recreation: *Winter Sports*

Theme Vocabulary

snowmobile
sledding
rink
toboggan
sleigh
parka
ski
gloves

Using Vocabulary   Write the Vocabulary Words to complete the paragraph. Use your Spelling Dictionary.

Every year our town has a Winter Weekend. Skiers from many towns __(1)__ in downhill races, and skaters perform in the ice __(2)__. You can hear the sounds of __(3)__ motors as people ride all over town. People also ride in a horse-drawn __(4)__. Everyone with a sled goes __(5)__. My brothers and I use a long, narrow sled called a __(6)__. I stay warm in my new red __(7)__ and matching __(8)__ for my hands. I love Winter Weekend!

Understanding Vocabulary   Write *yes* or *no* to answer each question.

9. Does a snowmobile go faster than a sleigh?
10. Can you go skiing in a rink?
11. Will a parka keep your head warm?
12. Does a toboggan use gasoline?

1. _____
2. _____
3. _____
4. _____
5. _____
6. _____
7. _____
8. _____
9. _____
10. _____
11. _____
12. _____

FACT FILE

A slalom is a ski race. In the slalom, skiers race downhill through a set of marked poles with flags on them. Skiers zigzag between the poles as fast as possible.

Enrichment

 **Writing**
An Emergency Plan

Pretend that you are in charge of the Winter Weekend for the town of Summerville. The visitors have begun to arrive, but there is one big problem. There is no snow! What can the town do? Can they make fake ice and snow? Can they use something else for sledding and skiing? Write a plan that tells what you will do to solve the problem. Your plan can be real or imaginary. Try to use words from the lists in this unit. Be sure to proofread your paper.

WINTER WEEKEND POSTERS

Draw a poster advertising a Winter Weekend. Draw a picture of one of the activities, such as skating or sledding. Then write several sentences telling about the Winter Weekend. What are the special events? What contests will be held? Make sure your poster will catch people's attention. Use as many list words as possible.

 Spelling Slalom

Players: 2   **You need:** a drawing like the one shown, game markers
How to play: One player gives a clue for a spelling word, such as "A square is one." *(shape)* If the other player guesses the spelling word and spells it correctly, he or she moves a marker to the first flag on the game board. Players take turns giving clues. The first player to reach FINISH wins.

2 Spelling |ĕ| and |ē|

A. _____

B. _____

C. _____

D. _____

■ **Challenge**

_____

LOOK at each word.

SAY each word.

Basic Words		■ **Challenge**
1. peach	11. desk	21. chef
2. sweet	12. least	22. yeast
3. feast	13. east	23. menu
4. cream	14. greed	24. restaurant
5. fresh	15. real	25. knead
6. free	16. dream	
7. reach	17. west	
8. kept	18. speed	
9. spent	19. cheap	
🐘10. field	🐘20. chief	

THINK about the words.

Each word has the short _e_ sound or the long _e_ sound. The short _e_ sound is usually spelled _e_ followed by a consonant sound. The long _e_ sound is often spelled with two vowels.

|ĕ| fr**e**sh |ē| p**ea**ch, sw**ee**t

- What is one spelling pattern for the |ĕ| sound? What are two patterns for the |ē| sound? What pattern spells the |ē| sound in the Elephant Words?

WRITE the words.

Practice **Write the Basic Words to answer the questions.**

A. Which **five** words have the |ĕ| sound?
B. Which **nine** words spell |ē| with the _ea_ pattern?
C. Which **four** words spell |ē| with the _ee_ pattern?
D. Which **two** words spell |ē| another way?

■ **Now write the five Challenge Words.** Underline the patterns that spell the |ĕ| and the |ē| sounds.

CHECK your spelling.

fresh
freshness
refresh
refreshments

> *Spelling-Meaning Hint* Can you see *fresh* in these words: *freshness, refresh, refreshments*? **Think of this:** The *refreshments* helped us feel *fresh* again.

Independent Practice

Spelling-Meaning Look at the Spelling-Meaning Hint.
   1-2. Write *refreshments*. Then write the Basic Word that is related to *refreshments* in spelling and meaning.

Word Analysis Complete the exercises with Basic Words.

   3-6. Write the four words that end with the cluster *st*.

7-10. Write the four words that begin or end with *ch*.

Analogies An **analogy** compares word pairs that are related in the same way. Write a Basic Word to complete each analogy.
Example: **Big** is to **small** as **loud** is to **quiet.**
   11. *Lemon* is to *sour*
       as *honey* is to ——.
   12. *Came* is to *went*
       as *saved* is to ——.
   13. *Kitchen* is to *table*
       as *classroom* is to ——.
   14. *Hockey* is to *rink*
       as *football* is to ——.
   15. *Sweep* is to *swept*
       as *keep* is to ——.

cream
|ē|

|ĕ|
desk

■ **Challenge Words** Write the Challenge Word that fits each meaning. Use your Spelling Dictionary.
   16. a list of foods   **19.** makes bread dough rise
   17. to mix, roll, or press   **20.** a place where meals
   18. a cook   are served

1. _____
2. _____
3. _____
4. _____
5. _____
6. _____
7. _____
8. _____
9. _____
10. _____
11. _____
12. _____
13. _____
14. _____
15. _____
16. _____
17. _____
18. _____
19. _____
20. _____

Summing Up

The |ĕ| sound is usually spelled *e* followed by a consonant sound.
The |ē| sound is often spelled with the pattern *ea* or *ee*.

Basic

1. peach
2. sweet
3. feast
4. cream
5. fresh
6. free
7. reach
8. kept
9. spent
10. field
11. desk
12. least
13. east
14. greed
15. real
16. dream
17. west
18. speed
19. cheap
20. chief

■ **Challenge**

21. chef
22. yeast
23. menu
24. restaurant
25. knead

Review

1. need
2. three
3. left
4. seem
5. speak

1. _____
2. _____
3. _____
4. _____
5. _____
6. _____
7. _____
8. _____

Expanding Vocabulary

Word Clues Can you figure out the meaning of *banquet*?

We all ate many delicious foods at the **banquet**.

Use other words in a sentence as clues to help you figure out the meaning of an unfamiliar word. The words *ate* and *foods* can help you figure out that a banquet is a feast.

Practice **Write the word that means the same as each underlined word. Use word clues to help you.**

real   need   hard   ripe   cheap

1. We saved money by buying <u>inexpensive</u> vegetables.
2. <u>Mellow</u> fruit that is ready for eating has the best flavor.
3. Kim makes <u>complicated</u> dishes look easy to prepare.
4. This imitation cheese is not made with <u>genuine</u> cream.
5. Some foods <u>require</u> salt and pepper to bring out flavor.

1. _____   4. _____

2. _____   5. _____

3. _____

Dictionary

Alphabetical Order How would you find *peach* quickly in a dictionary? The words in a dictionary are in alphabetical order. Turn to the part of the dictionary with the words beginning with *p*.

BEGINNING   MIDDLE   END

a b c d e f g   h i j k l m n o p   q r s t u v w x y z

Suppose you see *pear*. Does *peach* come before or after it? Look at the first letters that are different to alphabetize the words: peach, pear. *Peach* comes before *pear*.

Practice **1-8. Write these words in alphabetical order.**

spent   space
spell   speak
speed   speck
spare   sped

Review: Spelling Spree

Letter Swap Change the first letter of each word to make a Basic or Review Word. Write the words.

Example: wept *kept*

1. tweet
2. best
3. feast
4. tree
5. fast
6. cream
7. peach
8. seed
9. deal
10. breed
11. yield
12. reach
13. thief
14. deem
15. least
16. dream

Proofreading **17-25.** Find and cross out nine misspelled Basic or Review Words in this class story. Then write each word correctly.

> Mr. Chang came to our class to spek about cooking. He teaches cooking at thre schools. He told us that freash vegetables and sweet fruits keep us healthy. He put some vegetables on a dask. He said they were cheep! He had speant only a few dollars for them. Mr. Chang used a special pan to cook the vegetables with spead. He made a real feast! We cept the pan when he leaft to show the other classes.

■ **Challenge Words** What words do you think of when you hear *chef*? Do you think of a *skillet*? a *spatula*? an *apron*? Write each Challenge Word. Then write a word that has something to do with the Challenge Word. Use both words in a sentence.

Example: chef — spatula

The **chef** flipped the pancakes with a **spatula.**

Writing Application: A Review Write a review of your favorite place to eat. What food is served there? Is it good? Try to use five words from the list on page 20.

1. _____
2. _____
3. _____
4. _____
5. _____
6. _____
7. _____
8. _____
9. _____
10. _____
11. _____
12. _____
13. _____
14. _____
15. _____
16. _____
17. _____
18. _____
19. _____
20. _____
21. _____
22. _____
23. _____
24. _____
25. _____

2   Spelling Across the Curriculum

Home Economics: *Cooking*

Theme Vocabulary

sift
grate
measure
barbecue
simmer
fry
mince
poach

Using Vocabulary Write the Vocabulary Words to complete the paragraph. Use your Spelling Dictionary.

How do you cook fish? Many people like to __(1)__ it on a grill. Others heat water just below the boiling point and let it __(2)__ . Then they __(3)__ the fish in the water. Sometimes I make a batter for the fish. I use a measuring cup to __(4)__ the flour. Then I __(5)__ it to remove the lumps. Next, I shred or __(6)__ some cheese and use a sharp knife to __(7)__ some onion. Finally, I roll the fish in the batter and __(8)__ it in the pan.

Understanding Vocabulary   Write a Vocabulary Word to answer each question.

9. What can you do to flour but not to milk?
10. What can you do to water but not to bread?
11. What do you do with butter melted in a pan?
12. What do you do with a tablespoon?

1. _____
2. _____
3. _____
4. _____
5. _____
6. _____
7. _____
8. _____
9. _____
10. _____
11. _____
12. _____

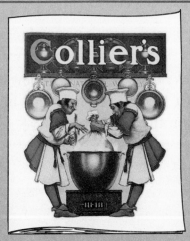

FACT FILE

Do you know the old saying "Too many cooks spoil the broth"? It means that too many helpers can lead to mistakes no matter what kind of task you are doing.

Enrichment

👥 *Cooking with Class*

Cooking Fun

Write and perform your own TV cooking show. Working with a partner, think of a food that you know how to make, or look up a new recipe in a cookbook. Write the script for your cooking show. Try to use some words from this unit in your script. Tell your audience what you are making, what the ingredients are, and how you put the ingredients together. Bring empty boxes or jars from home, or make props out of art materials in your classroom. Perform your cooking show in front of a small group of your classmates.

📖 *Writing*
A Royal Recipe

Pretend that you are the royal cook in the Kingdom of Dreary. King Sourpuss is in a bad mood and bored with his meals. Write a recipe for an exciting new dish that will cheer up the king. Try to use words from the lists in this unit. Be sure to proofread your paper.

MAGNIFICENT MENU

Create your dream menu. Fold a piece of construction paper in half. On the outside, draw a cover for the menu. On the inside, list your favorite foods and drinks. After each item, write a sentence describing the dish and its ingredients. Try to use list words. Add prices, if you wish. Decorate your menu with drawings or pictures.

3 Spelling |ĭ| and |ī|

A. _____

_____

_____

_____

_____

_____

_____

B. _____

_____

_____

_____

_____

_____

_____

_____

_____

_____

_____

_____

■ Challenge

_____

_____

_____

_____

_____

LOOK at each word.

SAY each word.

Basic Words		■ Challenge
1. brick	11. blind	21. inspect
2. skill	12. sting	22. polish
3. lift	13. fright	23. rigid
4. pride	14. wind	24. advice
5. grind	15. hint	25. recognize
6. still	16. ripe	
7. crime	17. shine	
8. flight	18. inch	
9. live	19. sigh	
🐘10. build	🐘20. built	

THINK about the words.

Each word has the short *i* sound or the long *i* sound. The short *i* sound is often spelled *i* followed by a consonant sound. The long *i* sound can be spelled *i*-consonant-*e* or with patterns of one or more letters.

|ĭ| br**i**ck |ī| pr**ide**, fl**igh**t, gr**i**nd

Live and *wind* can be pronounced with |ĭ| or |ī|.

• What is one pattern for the |ĭ| sound? What are three patterns for the |ī| sound? What pattern spells the |ĭ| sound in the Elephant Words?

WRITE the words.

Practice Write the Basic Words to answer the questions.

A. Which **nine** words have |ĭ|?
B. Which **eleven** words, including *live* and *wind*, have |ī|?

■ **Now write the five Challenge Words.** Underline the patterns that spell the |ĭ| and the |ī| sounds.

CHECK your spelling.

24

Spelling-Meaning Hint   *Crime* and *criminal* have different vowel sounds, but they are related in spelling and meaning. **Think of this:** A *criminal* commits a *crime*.

cri̯me
cri̯minal

Independent Practice

Spelling-Meaning   Look at the Spelling-Meaning Hint.

1-2. Write *criminal*. Then write the Basic Word that is related to *criminal* in spelling and meaning.

Word Analysis   Complete the exercises with Basic Words.

3-4. Write *build*. Then write its past tense.

5-8. Write the word that begins with each consonant cluster.
   5. pr
   6. bl
   7. fl
   8. fr

9-10. Write the two words that rhyme with *hill*.

Classifying   Write the Basic Word that belongs in each group.
11. rain, snow, _____
12. board, stone, _____
13. chop, slice, _____
14. foot, yard, _____
15. shout, whisper, _____

i–consonant–e

s t r i p e
|ī|

■ **Challenge Words**   Write the Challenge Word that fits each meaning. Use your Spelling Dictionary.
16. to look at carefully
17. stiff or not easily bent
18. to make shiny
19. to know from the past
20. a suggestion about how to solve a problem

1. _____
2. _____
3. _____
4. _____
5. _____
6. _____
7. _____
8. _____
9. _____
10. _____
11. _____
12. _____
13. _____
14. _____
15. _____
16. _____
17. _____
18. _____
19. _____
20. _____

Summing Up

The |ĭ| sound is often spelled *i* followed by a consonant sound. The |ī| sound is often spelled with the pattern *i*-consonant-*e*, *igh*, or *i*.

Basic

1. brick
2. skill
3. lift
4. pride
5. grind
6. still
7. crime
8. flight
9. live
10. build
11. blind
12. sting
13. fright
14. wind
15. hint
16. ripe
17. shine
18. inch
19. sigh
20. built

■ **Challenge**

21. inspect
22. polish
23. rigid
24. advice
25. recognize

Review

1. mix
2. tight
3. sight
4. mind
5. smile

Expanding Vocabulary

Words with the Same Spellings   Some words, such as *wind* and *wind*, are spelled the same but have different meanings. They may also be pronounced differently.

| I'll **wind** my watch. | |wīnd| to turn |
| A kite needs **wind** to fly. | |wĭnd| moving air |

Here are more pairs of words with different meanings and pronunciations:

lead	lēd		to direct
lead	lĕd		a metal
tear	tîr		a drop of water in the eye
tear	târ		to rip

Practice   **Write the letter of the correct pronunciation for each underlined word.**

1. Do not <u>tear</u> this piece of paper.   (**a.** |tîr| **b.** |târ|)
2. A <u>tear</u> rolled down her face.   (**a.** |tîr| **b.** |târ|)
3. This pipe is made of <u>lead</u>.   (**a.** |lēd| **b.** |lĕd|)
4. Ana will <u>lead</u> the parade.   (**a.** |lēd| **b.** |lĕd|)

1. _____   2. _____   3. _____   4. _____

Dictionary

Guide Words   To find an **entry word,** or main word, on a dictionary page, use the guide words. The **guide words** show the first and last entry words on the page. Why would *sting* be on the same page as these guide words?

---

sticky | stitch

stick·y |stĭk′ ē| *adj.* stickier, stickiest 1. Tending to stick.

Practice   **1-6. Write the six words below that would be on a dictionary page with the guide words *sift | sky*.**

| silver | still | six | shine |
| skip | skill | sight | silly |

1. _____   3. _____   5. _____

2. _____   4. _____   6. _____

Review: Spelling Spree

Word Addition Write a Basic or Review Word by adding the beginning of the first word to the middle and end of the second word.

Example: mend + right   *might*

1. seven + high
2. west + find
3. blade + kind
4. hang + print
5. flood + night
6. steal + hill
7. magic + six
8. lamb + gift
9. free + might
10. rang + wipe
11. stare + king
12. lazy + give
13. cream + time
14. group + find
15. safe + light
16. brush + thick
17. tape + fight

Proofreading **18-25.** Find and cross out eight misspelled Basic or Review Words in this paragraph. Then write each word correctly.

> My cousin Alex likes to bild dollhouses. The furniture he makes is often less than an intch tall. He does not minde spending hours carving little brick fireplaces and trying to shin tiny brass doorknobs. In fact, he takes great pried in it. Once I asked him why he has not bilt any houses for people to live in. He said that he likes using his skil to make children smil.

■ **Challenge Words** Make a mini-thesaurus. Staple five half sheets of paper. On each one, write a Challenge Word and a word that could replace it. Write a definition and a sample sentence for each word. Use your Spelling Dictionary and a class dictionary.

Writing Application: An Article Pretend that a new skyscraper is being built in your town. How tall is it? What will it look like? Write a newspaper article about the building. Try to use five words from the list on page 26.

1. _____
2. _____
3. _____
4. _____
5. _____
6. _____
7. _____
8. _____
9. _____
10. _____
11. _____
12. _____
13. _____
14. _____
15. _____
16. _____
17. _____
18. _____
19. _____
20. _____
21. _____
22. _____
23. _____
24. _____
25. _____

3   Spelling Across the Curriculum

Industrial Arts: *Construction*

Theme Vocabulary

plank
hammer
clamp
screwdriver
wrench
drill
pliers
handsaw

Using Vocabulary   Write the Vocabulary Words to complete the paragraph. Use your Spelling Dictionary.

To build a birdhouse, start by using a __(1)__ to hold a long __(2)__ of wood in place. Then cut the wood into pieces with a __(3)__. After you nail the pieces together with a __(4)__, use screws and a __(5)__ to attach hinges to the top. Make a hole for the perch with a __(6)__. Then use nuts and bolts to attach a handle. Be sure to tighten the bolts with a __(7)__. Finally, with a pair of __(8)__, twist some wire into a loop and hang the birdhouse.

Understanding Vocabulary   Write *yes* if the underlined word is used correctly. Write *no* if it is not.

9. Liz used her <u>handsaw</u> to tighten the bolt.
10. A <u>clamp</u> would hold these two boards together.
11. Which <u>drill</u> did you use to make this hole?
12. The <u>wrench</u> cut completely through the wood.

1. _____
2. _____
3. _____
4. _____
5. _____
6. _____
7. _____
8. _____
9. _____
10. _____
11. _____
12. _____

FACT FILE

People often build things from the materials that are most available. The Inuit of Alaska and Canada built shelters called igloos from blocks of hard-packed snow and ice.

Enrichment

👪 *Letter by Letter*

With a partner, build Word Houses using the vowel *i*. Start by drawing a pyramid of squares like the one shown. Write the letter *i* in the top square. Below it, have your partner write a two-letter word containing an *i*. Then add a letter to make a new word in the third row. Take turns adding letters to make new words. See how many Word Houses you can build together. Try to use words from the lists in this unit.

YOUR DREAM HOUSE

Draw a plan for your dream house. Use a ruler, a pencil, and graph paper. Label each room, and give its measurements. Below the plan, write a short description of the outside of the house. Try to use some list words.

📖 *Writing*
Construction Instructions

Have you ever made a tree house, created a water dam, or built a sand castle? Think about something you have built or made. What was the first step? What tools did you use? What other steps did you follow? Write instructions to a friend explaining how to build your project. Try to use words from the lists in this unit. Be sure to proofread your paper.

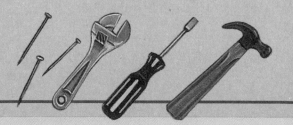

Theme: Exploration

4 Spelling |ŏ| and |ō|

A. _____

_____

_____

_____

B. _____

_____

_____

_____

_____

_____

_____

_____

_____

_____

_____

_____

_____

■ **Challenge**

_____

_____

_____

LOOK at each word.

SAY each word.

Basic Words		■ Challenge
1. globe	11. crow	21. continent
2. coast	12. stock	22. longitude
3. goal	13. chose	23. approach
4. spoke	14. folk	24. motion
5. odd	15. coal	25. accomplish
6. shown	16. host	
7. gold	17. bowl	
8. wrote	18. grown	
9. snow	19. shock	
10. block	20. broke	

THINK about the words.

Each word has the short *o* or the long *o* sound. The short *o* sound is usually spelled *o* followed by a consonant sound. The long *o* sound is often spelled *o*-consonant-*e* or with patterns of one or more letters.

|ŏ| bl**o**ck |ō| gl**o**be, g**oa**l, sh**ow**n, g**o**ld

- What is one spelling pattern for the |ŏ| sound? What are four patterns for the |ō| sound?

WRITE the words.

Practice   Write the Basic Words to answer the questions.

A. Which **four** words have the |ŏ| sound?

B. Which **sixteen** words have the |ō| sound?

■ **Now write the five Challenge Words.** Underline the patterns that spell the |ŏ| and the |ō| sounds.

CHECK your spelling.

coast
coast*al*
coast*line*
sea**coast**

Spelling-Meaning Hint   Can you see *coast* in these words: *coastal, seacoast, coastline*? These words are related in spelling and meaning. **Think of this:** The *Coast* Guard sailed along the *coastline*.

Independent Practice

Spelling-Meaning   Look at the Spelling-Meaning Hint.
1-2. Write *coastal*. Then write the Basic Word that you see in *coastal*.

Word Analysis   Complete the exercises with Basic Words.

3. Write the word that has a double consonant.

4-7. Write the past tense of each word below.
   4. break   6. write
   5. speak   7. choose

Making Inferences   Write the Basic Word that fits each clue.
8. Soup is served in it.
9. It's burned for heat.
10. Jewelry is made from it.
11. It falls in winter.
12. A scarecrow will scare it.
13. Electricity can give you one.
14. It can be a cube with letters.
15. It is shaped like a ball.

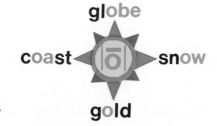

■ **Challenge Words**   Write the Challenge Word that fits each meaning. Use your Spelling Dictionary.
16. to carry out or achieve
17. a main land mass
18. movement
19. to come near
20. distance measured in degrees east or west of the meridian at Greenwich, England

1. _____
2. _____
3. _____
4. _____
5. _____
6. _____
7. _____
8. _____
9. _____
10. _____
11. _____
12. _____
13. _____
14. _____
15. _____
16. _____
17. _____
18. _____
19. _____
20. _____

Summing Up

The |ŏ| sound is usually spelled *o* followed by a consonant sound.
The |ō| sound is often spelled *o*-consonant-*e, oa, ow,* or *o.*

Basic

1. globe
2. coast
3. goal
4. spoke
5. odd
6. shown
7. gold
8. wrote
9. snow
10. block
11. crow
12. stock
13. chose
14. folk
15. coal
16. host
17. bowl
18. grown
19. shock
20. broke

■ Challenge

21. continent
22. longitude
23. approach
24. motion
25. accomplish

Review

1. know
2. most
3. smoke
4. drop
5. soap

Proofreading Marks

¶ Indent
∧ Add
    something
ℓ Take out
    something
≡ Capitalize
/ Make a small
    letter

Expanding Vocabulary

Exact Words for *show* Read these sentences. Why is *revealed* a better verb to use than *showed*?

    I **showed** the secret room.   I **revealed** the secret room.

Revealed is more exact than *showed*. It makes you think of a secret. Exact words make your writing clear and interesting.

Practice **Write the best word below to replace *show* in each sentence. Use your Thesaurus.**

    demonstrate   reveal   guide   display

1. We <u>show</u> our flag on the Fourth of July.
2. Ms. Sims will <u>show</u> the hikers through the woods.
3. Don't <u>show</u> where the gifts are hidden!
4. Will you <u>show</u> the experiment to the class?

1. _____   3. _____

2. _____   4. _____

Proofreading

Proper Nouns A **proper noun** names a particular person, place, or thing. Capitalize proper nouns.

    Aunt Mary   Chicago   Fourth of July

Practice **Proofread this post card. Find four misspelled words and three missing capital letters. Use proofreading marks to correct the errors.**

              spoke
Example: Maria s̶p̶o̶k̶ Spanish when she visited peru.

     Dear Kate,
       Did you no that I am in south america with Dad? We are exploring the cost. He has shown me many odd sights. What a shok it was to see sno here when it is summer at home!
             maria

Review: Spelling Spree

Finding Words   Write the Basic or Review Word in each word below.

1. unblock
2. oddness
3. spoken
4. bowls
5. chosen
6. restock
7. broken
8. knowing
9. rewrote
10. soapy
11. crowed
12. coastal
13. golden

Puzzle Play   Write a Basic or Review Word to fit each clue. Circle the letter that would appear in the box. Write these letters in order to spell three mystery words that name a place.

Example: a round dish _ _ _ □   bow(l)

14. one who has guests _ _ _ □
15. a bad surprise _ □ _ _ _
16. comes from fires _ _ _ _ □
17. white ice crystals _ □ _ _
18. black lumps that burn _ □ _ _
19. form of *grow* _ □ _ _ _

20. greatest number _ _ _ _ □
21. form of *show* _ □ _ _ _
22. to let fall _ _ _ □
23. people _ □ _ _
24. purpose or aim _ _ _ _ □
25. earth _ _ _ _ _ □

Mystery Words: _ _ _   _ _ _ _ _   _ _ _ _

■ **Challenge Words**   Create your own Puzzle Play. Think of a five-letter mystery word that can be made by combining one letter from each Challenge Word. Write a clue for each Challenge Word. Then draw blanks for the letters, and add boxes to show the letters in the mystery word. Arrange the clues so that the boxed letters will spell the mystery word. Write the answers on the back of your paper. Trade puzzles with a classmate.

Writing Application: Creative Writing   Pretend that you are the captain of one of Christopher Columbus's ships. You have sighted land! Write an entry in your ship's log. Try to use five words from the list on page 32.

1. _____
2. _____
3. _____
4. _____
5. _____
6. _____
7. _____
8. _____
9. _____
10. _____
11. _____
12. _____
13. _____
14. _____
15. _____
16. _____
17. _____
18. _____
19. _____
20. _____
21. _____
22. _____
23. _____
24. _____
25. _____

4 Spelling Across the Curriculum

Social Studies: *Exploration*

Theme Vocabulary

explore
cavern
jungle
equator
desert
route
map
compass

Using Vocabulary Write the Vocabulary Words to complete the paragraph. Use your Spelling Dictionary.

Did you ever try to __(1)__ a dark cave or __(2)__? How did you know which __(3)__ or path to follow? The early explorers did not have a written __(4)__ that told which way to go. In Africa, how did David Livingstone get through the steamy, overgrown __(5)__ near the __(6)__? How did Heinrich Barth cross the hot, dry __(7)__? A simple tool called the __(8)__ helped explorers tell direction long ago. We use that same tool today.

Understanding Vocabulary Write a Vocabulary Word to match each clue.

9. It always points to the north.
10. You must bring extra water if you explore there.
11. It shows you where Africa is.
12. You will need a flashlight if you explore there.

1. _____
2. _____
3. _____
4. _____
5. _____
6. _____
7. _____
8. _____
9. _____
10. _____
11. _____
12. _____

FACT FILE

In 1513 Juan Ponce de León, a Spanish explorer, searched for a fountain of youth. In his search, he discovered land. He named it Florida, or "full of flowers."

Enrichment

Long o Bingo

Players: 3 or more **You need:** paper, pencils
How to play: Each player draws a card with nine squares and writes a spelling for the |ō| sound in each square. One player is the announcer, who reads aloud a spelling word with the |ō| sound. Players who have a square with that spelling for the |ō| sound write the given word in the square and cover the square with a marker. Play continues until one player covers three spellings across, down, or at an angle. (Note: The announcer cannot use a word more than once during the game.)

o-consonant-e globe	ow	oa
ow	oa	ow
o	oa	o-consonant-e

EXPLORER'S PUZZLE

Make an explorer's jigsaw puzzle. Use an atlas to help you draw a map of Africa. Label parts of Africa that you would like to explore, such as the Sahara Desert or the jungle. Cut the map into puzzle pieces, and let a friend complete it.

Writing
Shipwrecked

Pretend that you were on an explorer's ship. You were thrown overboard during a storm and were washed up on an island. Write a story for *True Adventures* magazine, telling how you survived. What did you eat? Did you build a hut? Try to use words from the lists in this unit. Be sure to proofread your paper.

5 Homophones

A. _____

_____

_____

_____

_____

_____

_____

_____

_____

B. _____

_____

C. _____

_____

D. _____

_____

E. _____

_____

_____

_____

■ **Challenge**

_____

_____

_____

_____

_____

> **LOOK** at each word.
>
> **SAY** each word.

Basic Words		■ Challenge
1. steel	11. beet	21. vain
2. steal	12. beat	22. vein
3. lead	13. meet	23. vane
4. led	14. meat	24. ore
5. wait	15. peek	25. oar
6. weight	16. peak	
7. wear	17. deer	
8. ware	18. dear	
9. creak	19. ring	
10. creek	20. wring	

> **THINK** about the words.

Homophones are words that sound alike but have different meanings and spellings.

|stēl| st**eel**   a metal made from iron and carbon
|stēl| st**eal**   to take without being allowed

- Does each pair of homophones have the same vowel and consonant sounds? How are the spellings of the words in each pair different? What does each word mean?

> **WRITE** the words.

Practice   Write the Basic Words to answer the questions.

A. Which **ten** homophones have the |ē| sound?
B. Which **two** homophones have the |ĕ| sound?
C. Which **two** homophones have the |ā| sound?
D. Which **two** homophones rhyme with *sing*?
E. Which **four** homophones have a vowel sound + *r*?

■ **Now write the five Challenge Words.**

> **CHECK** your spelling.

> *Spelling-Meaning Hint* Can you see *creak* in these words: *creaky, creaking, creakiness*? **Think of this:** I heard a *creak* in the *creaky* old house.

creak
creaky
creaking
creakiness

Independent Practice

Spelling-Meaning Look at the Spelling-Meaning Hint.

  1-2. Write *creaky*. Then write the Basic Word that is related to *creaky* and means "a squeaking sound."

  3. Write the Basic Word that is a homophone for *creak* and means "a small stream."

Context Sentences Write Basic Words to complete the sentences.

  4-5. We climbed to the __(4)__ to __(5)__ at the eagle's nest.

  6-7. I can __(6)__ you at the __(7)__ counter in the market.

  8-9. Sal was as red as a __(8)__ after he __(9)__ David at tennis.

  10-11. Please __(10)__ in line for the nurse to check your __(11)__.

  12-13. Niki __(12)__ me to the pencil sharpener so that I could sharpen my __(13)__ pencil.

  14-15. I had to __(14)__ out my clothes after I jumped in the pool to find my __(15)__.

ring

wring

■ **Challenge Words** Write the Challenge Word that fits each meaning. Use your Spelling Dictionary.

  16. a mineral from which a metal, such as gold, can be mined

  17. a long, narrow deposit of a mineral in rock

  18. having no success

  19. used to row a boat

  20. a piece of wood or metal that shows wind direction

1. _____
2. _____
3. _____
4. _____
5. _____
6. _____
7. _____
8. _____
9. _____
10. _____
11. _____
12. _____
13. _____
14. _____
15. _____
16. _____
17. _____
18. _____
19. _____
20. _____

Summing Up

Homophones are words that sound alike but have different meanings and spellings.

Basic

1. steel
2. steal
3. lead
4. led
5. wait
6. weight
7. wear
8. ware
9. creak
10. creek
11. beet
12. beat
13. meet
14. meat
15. peek
16. peak
17. deer
18. dear
19. ring
20. wring

■ Challenge

21. vain
22. vein
23. vane
24. ore
25. oar

Review

1. its
2. it's
3. there
4. their
5. they're

Expanding Vocabulary

Homophones   Can you finish this nursery rhyme? "Says Simple Simon to the pieman, /Let me taste your ____ ."

ware: goods for sale   **wear:** to have on one's body

The meaning of a sentence helps you know which homophone to use. Why is *ware* the correct homophone?

Practice   Write the correct homophone to complete each sentence. Use your Spelling Dictionary.

| heal | through | peace |
| heel | threw | piece |

1. This ____ of paper is very important.
2. It says that the enemies want to make ____ .
3. I hurt my ____ when I stepped on a tack.
4. I bandaged the sore so that it would ____ quickly.
5. Rhonda ____ the ball too hard.
6. It went ____ the neighbor's window!

1. _____   4. _____

2. _____   5. _____

3. _____   6. _____

Dictionary

Homophones   A dictionary entry shows homophones.

> **peak** |pēk| *n., pl.* **peaks** The top of a mountain.
>   ♦ *These sound alike* **peak, peek.**

Practice   Write the answers to these questions. Use your Spelling Dictionary.

1. Look up *hall.* What word is a homophone for *hall?*
2. Which spelling of |hôl| means "to pull or carry"?
3. Which spelling of |hôl| means "a passageway"?

Write the spelling for |hôl| that fits each sentence.

4. You are not allowed to run in the ____ .
5. We need to ____ this heavy trash to the dump.

1. _____

2. _____

3. _____

4. _____

5. _____

Review: Spelling Spree

Homophone Riddles   Write a pair of Basic Words to answer each silly riddle.

Example: What do thieves do when they take a piece of metal?
   steal steel

1-2.   What do you call a squeaky sound made by a stream?
3-4.   What did the parade leader do to a float made of pencils?
5-6.   What is a drum noise made by a purplish-red vegetable?
7-8.   What do you call clothes for sale?
9-10.   What is a circle of people twisting their clothes dry?
11-12.   How did the fork introduce the peas to the steak?
13-14.   What is a quick look at a mountain from behind a tree?
15-16.   What do you call a lovable fawn?

Proofreading   17-25. Find and cross out nine misspelled Basic or Review Words in this conversation. Then write each word correctly.

My Visit to a Factory

GUIDE: Hello. You must weight here before we go in, but you may steel a peek through the window.
MARY: Why do the workers wear masks?
GUIDE: You have to heat steal to work with it. The masks there wearing protect they're faces. Look at that huge machine in their. Can you guess it's wait? Well, its over two thousand pounds.

■ **Challenge Words**   Look at the Homophone Riddles activity. Write homophone riddles, using all of the Challenge Word homophones. Draw pictures to illustrate your riddles.

📖 *Writing Application:* A Paragraph   What does it mean to have "nerves of steel"? Are you a brave person? Write a paragraph describing some times when you might need "nerves of steel." Try to use five words from the list on page 38.

1. _____
2. _____
3. _____
4. _____
5. _____
6. _____
7. _____
8. _____
9. _____
10. _____
11. _____
12. _____
13. _____
14. _____
15. _____
16. _____
17. _____
18. _____
19. _____
20. _____
21. _____
22. _____
23. _____
24. _____
25. _____

5   Spelling Across the Curriculum

Science: *Metals*

Theme Vocabulary

iron
copper
zinc
mercury
tin
bronze
calcium
aluminum

Using Vocabulary   Write the Vocabulary Words to complete the paragraph. Use your Spelling Dictionary.

Metals have many forms and uses. The liquid in a thermometer is the metal __(1)__ . Your teeth and bones are made of __(2)__ . A reddish-brown metal that conducts heat is __(3)__ . A blue-white metal used in batteries is __(4)__ . Steel is made from a mixture of __(5)__ and carbon. Another combination, copper and tin, creates the metal— and color— __(6)__ . Pots and pans are often made of __(7)__ , while cans made of __(8)__ won't rust.

Understanding Vocabulary   Write *T* if the sentence is true. Write *F* if it is false.

9. Mercury is a liquid at room temperature.
10. You use iron when you cover a bowl with foil.
11. You cut through tin when you open a can of soup.
12. A penny is made of calcium.

1. _____
2. _____
3. _____
4. _____
5. _____
6. _____
7. _____
8. _____
9. _____
10. _____
11. _____
12. _____

FACT FILE

When two or more metals are melted and mixed together, they form a stronger metal called an alloy. Bronze is an alloy made by mixing together copper and tin.

Enrichment

HOMOPHONE BOOK

Fold six sheets of white drawing paper in half. Punch two holes along the fold, and tie a string through the holes to keep the pages together. On each page write a pair of homophones from the lists in this unit. Draw a picture, or paste a magazine photograph that shows the meaning of each word. After you have finished, draw a cover for your Homophone Book.

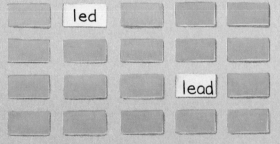

Match Game

Players: 2-4 **You need:** 20 word cards with one Basic Word on each card

How to play: Spread the cards face down on a desk or a table. Players take turns turning over two cards at a time. If a player turns over matching homophones, he or she must use each word correctly in a sentence to keep the cards. The player with the most pairs wins.

Writing
As Good As Gold

Have you ever heard of the metal pyrite, or "fool's gold"? Use an encyclopedia or other resources to find information about pyrite. Why is it called fool's gold? How is it different from real gold? Write a short report about the difference between fool's gold and real gold. Try to use words from the lists in this unit. Be sure to proofread your paper.

6 Review: Units 1–5

Unit 1   Spelling |ă| and |ā| pp. 12-17

skate	aid	gray	past	break
pain	hang	shape	pray	steak

Remember: The |ă| sound is usually spelled **a** followed by a consonant sound. The |ā| sound is often spelled **a**-consonant-**e**, **ai**, or **ay**.

 plant

 safe

Write the word that fits each clue.
1. help   3. something to eat
2. rhymes with *rain*   4. a time before the present

Write six words by adding the missing letters. Circle the word with the |ă| sound.
5. br _ _ k   7. gr _ _   9. h _ _ _
6. pr _ _   8. sk _ _ _   10. sh _ _ _

Unit 2   Spelling |ĕ| and |ē| pp. 18-23

kept	reach	spent	sweet	field
least	cheap	greed	west	chief

Remember: The |ĕ| sound is usually spelled **e** followed by a consonant sound. The |ē| sound is often spelled **ea** or **ee**.

cream

desk

Write the word that rhymes with each word below.
11. speed   13. yield
12. teach   14. leap

Write the word that means the opposite of each word or phrase below. Circle the words with the |ē| sound.
15. east   18. sour
16. most   19. given away
17. saved   20. lowest in rank

1. _____
2. _____
3. _____
4. _____
5. _____
6. _____
7. _____
8. _____
9. _____
10. _____

11. _____
12. _____
13. _____
14. _____
15. _____
16. _____
17. _____
18. _____
19. _____
20. _____

Half of the words from each unit are reviewed on these pages.
The rest are reviewed on pages 229–231.

Unit 3   Spelling |ĭ| and |ī| pp. 24-29

live	grind	flight	still	build
hint	fright	shine	blind	built

Remember: The |ĭ| sound is often spelled **i** followed by a consonant sound. The |ī| sound is often spelled **i-consonant-e**, **igh**, or **i**.

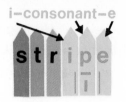

i-consonant-e

Write the word that fits each meaning.

21. not able to see
22. to give off light
23. a useful clue
24. calm
25. to crush or pound
26. act of flying
27. to be alive
28. strong fear

Write an Elephant Word to complete each sentence.

29. Did you ____ the new clubhouse?
30. Was the clubhouse ____ quickly?

21. _____
22. _____
23. _____
24. _____
25. _____
26. _____
27. _____
28. _____
29. _____
30. _____

Unit 4   Spelling |ŏ| and |ō| pp. 30-35

block	shown	wrote	coast	gold
grown	stock	crow	broke	coal

Remember: The |ŏ| sound is usually spelled **o** followed by a consonant sound. The |ō| sound is often spelled **o-consonant-e**, **oa**, **ow**, or **o**.

globe
coast |ō| snow
gold

Change a vowel in each word below to write a spelling word. Circle the words with the |ō| sound.

31. gild   34. stick
32. cool   35. black
33. crew   36. write

Write the word that fits each clue.

37. shattered into pieces
38. not hidden
39. a form of *grow*
40. near the sea

31. _____
32. _____
33. _____
34. _____
35. _____
36. _____
37. _____
38. _____
39. _____
40. _____

Unit 5 Homophones pp. 36-41

wait	wear	steel	meet	ring
weight	ware	steal	meat	wring

Remember: **Homophones** are words that sound alike but have different meanings and spellings.

ring

wring

Write the word that completes each analogy.
41. *Drink* is to *water* as *chew* is to ____.
42. *Good-by* is to *leave* as *hello* is to ____.
43. *House* is to *wood* as *bridge* is to ____.
44. *Give* is to *provide* as *rob* is to ____.

Write the word that fits each clue.
45. to put on   47. stop for a time   49. a bell's sound
46. goods for sale   48. heaviness   50. to twist

■ Challenge Words Units 1-5 pp. 12-41

knead	ore	continent	polish	approach
chef	oar	graceful	inspect	athletic

Write the word that completes each analogy.
51. *Artist* is to *artistic* as *athlete* is to ____.
52. *Wood* is to *carpenter* as *food* is to ____.
53. *Soup* is to *stir* as *dough* is to ____.
54. *Boring* is to *interesting* as *clumsy* is to ____.
55. *Car* is to *wax* as *shoe* is to ____.
56. *Water* is to *ocean* as *land* is to ____.

Write the word that fits each clue.
57. to come toward
58. to examine
59. a paddle
60. a mineral containing metal

41. _____
42. _____
43. _____
44. _____
45. _____
46. _____
47. _____
48. _____
49. _____
50. _____

51. _____
52. _____
53. _____
54. _____
55. _____
56. _____
57. _____
58. _____
59. _____
60. _____

Spelling-Meaning Strategy

Vowel Changes: Long to Short Vowel Sound

You know that words, like people, can be related to each other. Look at the related words *steal* and *stealth*.

> If you leave money lying around, someone might **steal** it. A thief can move with such **stealth** that your money will be gone without your knowing it.

steal
stealth

Think
- How are *steal* and *stealth* related in meaning?
- What vowel sound do you hear in each word? How is each vowel sound spelled?

Here are more related words with the *ea* spelling pattern and the same change from the |ē| sound to the |ĕ| sound.

heal	please	breathe
health	pleasant	breath

Apply and Extend

Complete these activities on a separate piece of paper.

1. Look up the words in the Word Box above in the Spelling Dictionary, and write their meanings. Then write a short paragraph, using one pair of words.

2. With a partner list as many words as you can that are related to *steal, heal, please,* and *breathe.* Then look on page 273 of your Spelling-Meaning Index. Add any other words that you find in these families to your list.

Summing Up Words that are related in meaning are often related in spelling, even though one word has a long vowel sound and the other word has a short vowel sound.

A Story About Yourself

Who is telling this story about a class race?

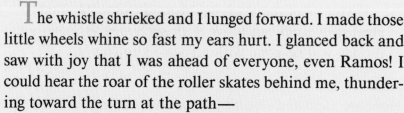

The whistle shrieked and I lunged forward. I made those little wheels whine so fast my ears hurt. I glanced back and saw with joy that I was ahead of everyone, even Ramos! I could hear the roar of the roller skates behind me, thundering toward the turn at the path—

The sharp turn! I had misjudged the sharp turn! I came up on it too fast to slow down. I tried crossing my right foot over my left foot for one of those smooth turns, but my legs twisted like pretzels. Still in full view of the crowd, I bounced off a tree and into the bushes.

I heard the skates spin by me, but I couldn't move. I couldn't face it. I was going to stay there forever when I felt a tug on my skates. "Come on, Vicente!"

It was Ramos. Painfully I got up.

"Move!" shouted Ramos.

"I'll be last!" I could barely whisper.

"Try!" begged Ramos. "Please!" Then he was gone.

Trying to feel grateful, I wobbled off behind him.

from "Hurdles" by Mary Blocksma with Esther Romero

Think and Discuss

1. Through whose eyes, or **point of view,** is this story told? How do you know who is telling the story?

2. What **details** let you see and hear the race?

The Writing Process

The passage from the story "Hurdles" on page 46 lets you see and feel the action from the main character's **point of view**. You too can write a story about yourself.

Write a **beginning** that will make your readers want to read more. Use **dialogue** to make the characters come to life. Include **details** to make your story more interesting.

Assignment: Write a Story About Yourself

Step One: Prewriting

1. List some interesting times you have had. Discuss them with a classmate. Choose one idea to write about.
2. Write two beginnings. Choose the one you like.

Step Two: Write a First Draft

1. Think about your purpose and your audience.
2. Do not worry about mistakes—just write!

Step Three: Revise

1. Could you make your beginning even better? Where could you add details and dialogue in your story?
2. Use your Thesaurus to find exact words.
3. Read your story to a classmate or to your teacher. Did you think of more ideas? Make your changes.

Step Four: Proofread

1. Did you use correct end marks?
2. Did you spell all words correctly? Copy any words you misspelled into your Notebook for Writing.

Step Five: Publish

1. Copy your story neatly. Add an interesting title.
2. Share your story by acting it out with friends.

Composition Words

skate
tease
spent
dream
hint
sigh
peek
goal

Proofreading Marks

¶ Indent
∧ Add something
ℓ Take out something
≡ Capitalize
/ Make a small letter

7 Spelling |ŭ|, |yo͞o|, and |o͞o|

A. _____

_____

_____

_____

_____

_____

B. _____

_____

_____

_____

_____

_____

_____

_____

_____

_____

_____

■ **Challenge**

_____

_____

_____

_____

LOOK at each word.

SAY each word.

Basic Words		■ Challenge
1. brush	11. suit	21. newscast
2. juice	12. pump	22. commute
3. fruit	13. due	23. tissue
4. tube	14. dull	24. attitude
5. lunch	15. tune	25. slumber
6. crumb	16. blew	
7. few	17. trunk	
8. true	18. sum	
🐘 9. truth	19. glue	
🐘 10. done	20. threw	

THINK about the words.

Each word has the |ŭ|, the |yo͞o|, or the |o͞o| sound. The |ŭ| sound is usually spelled _u_ followed by a consonant sound. The |yo͞o| and the |o͞o| sounds can be spelled _u_-consonant-_e_ or with two letters.

|ŭ| br**u**sh |yo͞o| and |o͞o| t**u**b**e**, f**ew**, tr**ue**, j**ui**ce

• What is one spelling pattern for the |ŭ| sound? What are four spelling patterns for the |yo͞o| and the |o͞o| sounds? How are these sounds spelled in the Elephant Words? Why does _truth_ sound like _true_?

WRITE the words.

Practice Write the Basic Words to answer the questions.

A. Which **eight** words have the |ŭ| sound?

B. Which **twelve** words have the |yo͞o| or the |o͞o| sound?

■ **Now write the five Challenge Words.** Underline the patterns that spell the |ŭ|, the |yo͞o|, and the |o͞o| sounds.

CHECK your spelling.

crum**b**
crum**b**le

> *Spelling-Meaning Hint*   How can you remember that *crumb* ends with a *b*? Think of the related word *crumble* in which the *b* is pronounced.

Independent Practice

Spelling-Meaning   Look at the Spelling-Meaning Hint.

1-2. Write *crumb* and *crumble*. Underline the letter that is silent in one word and pronounced in the other.

Word Analysis   Complete the exercises with Basic Words.

3. Write the word that has the |s| sound spelled *ce*.

4-5. Write *tune*. Then change one letter and write another word.

6-7. Write the two words that are homophones for these words.
6. dew   **7.** through

Word Clues   Write the Basic Word that fits each clue.
8. opposite of *false*
9. the whole amount
10. not a lie
11. form of *do*
12. means the same as *boring*
13. opposite of *many*
14. form of *blow*
15. a set of clothes

■ **Challenge Words**   Write the Challenge Word that fits each meaning. Use your Spelling Dictionary.
16. sleep   **19.** soft paper
17. state of mind   **20.** a broadcast of information about
18. to travel to work   recent events

1.	
2.	
3.	
4.	
5.	
6.	
7.	
8.	
9.	
10.	
11.	
12.	
13.	
14.	
15.	
16.	
17.	
18.	
19.	
20.	

Summing Up

The |ŭ| sound is usually spelled *u* followed by a consonant sound. The |yo͞o| and the |o͞o| sounds can be spelled with the pattern *u*-consonant-*e, ew, ue,* or *ui.*

Basic

1. brush
2. juice
3. fruit
4. tube
5. lunch
6. crumb
7. few
8. true
9. truth
10. done
11. suit
12. pump
13. due
14. dull
15. tune
16. blew
17. trunk
18. sum
19. glue
20. threw

■ Challenge

21. newscast
22. commute
23. tissue
24. attitude
25. slumber

Review

1. chew
2. blue
3. rub
4. shut
5. June

Expanding Vocabulary

Exact Words for *throw* Which sentence better describes how a basketball player throws the ball through a hoop?

Willy **throws** the basketball.　Willy **shoots** the basketball.

Shoots describes the action more exactly than *throws*. Always try to use exact words.

Practice Write the best word to replace *throw* in each sentence. Use your Thesaurus.

pitch　　toss　　hurl　　cast　　pass

1. Please <u>throw</u> three balls to each batter.
2. Let's <u>throw</u> our fishing lines into the water here.
3. Watch the player <u>throw</u> the football to the halfback.
4. Did you see Anne <u>throw</u> herself over the high jump?
5. I might as well <u>throw</u> this old paper into the trash.

1. _____　　4. _____

2. _____　　5. _____

3. _____

Dictionary

Spelling Table How can you look up *juice* in a dictionary if you do not know how to spell the |s| sound? Turn to the **spelling table**, which lists the different ways a sound can be spelled. Begin with the first spelling for the |s| sound, and look up *juic*. Check each spelling until you find *juice*.

SOUND	SPELLINGS	SAMPLE WORDS
|s|	**c, ce, ps, s, sc, ss**	city, fence, **ps**ychology, same, **sc**ent, lesson

Practice Write the correct spelling for each of these words with the |ē| sound. Use the spelling table on page 277 and your Spelling Dictionary.

1. |fēld|　　4. |spēk|
2. |rēf|　　5. |ēl|
3. |skē|　　6. |yēst|

1. _____　　3. _____　　5. _____

2. _____　　4. _____　　6. _____

Review: Spelling Spree

Hink Pinks   Write a Basic or Review Word that answers the question and rhymes with the given word.

Example: What makes the best fires?   good ____   *wood*

1. What is a boring seabird called?   ____ gull
2. What do you call a nice set of clothes?   cute ____
3. What is a sad math problem called?   glum ____
4. What is a true statement for a child?   youth ____
5. What is a stupid piece of bread called?   dumb ____
6. What is a container for a square object?   cube ____
7. What is a group that eats at noon?   ____ bunch
8. What do you call a fresh bite?   new ____
9. What do you call a round water faucet?   plump ____
10. What is a song that is sung at lunchtime?   noon ____
11. What do you call a shriveled tree part?   shrunk ____
12. What did the wind do to the window?   ____ through
13. What is cutting bushes in late spring called?   ____ prune
14. What is a hint about something sticky called?   ____ clue

Proofreading   15-25.   Find and cross out eleven misspelled Basic or Review Words in this story. Then write each word correctly.

I shot my eyes and gave them a rob. Was it really troo? My report was dew today on June 1! I through on my blew gym suit and ran to bruch my teeth. I took a fue gulps of frute juise and ran to the library. How would I get the report dun on time?

■ **Challenge Words**   Write five song titles about morning, using the Challenge Words. Capitalize the first, last, and each important word in each title. Write a sentence to describe each song.

Writing Application: A Personal Story   Have you had a morning when things went wrong? Write a paragraph about it. Try to use five words from the list on page 50.

1. _____
2. _____
3. _____
4. _____
5. _____
6. _____
7. _____
8. _____
9. _____
10. _____
11. _____
12. _____
13. _____
14. _____
15. _____
16. _____
17. _____
18. _____
19. _____
20. _____
21. _____
22. _____
23. _____
24. _____
25. _____

7 Spelling Across the Curriculum

Health: *Morning Activities*

Theme Vocabulary

radio
awake
mirror
cereal
muffin
cupboard
routine
comb

Using Vocabulary Write the Vocabulary Words to complete the paragraph. Use your Spelling Dictionary.

Every morning when I get ready for school, I follow my morning __(1)__ . Music on the __(2)__ wakes me at 6:30 A.M. I listen for thirty minutes before I am really __(3)__ . I take another half hour to __(4)__ my hair in front of the __(5)__ . In the kitchen, I open the food __(6)__ and take out my usual box of __(7)__ . Then I eat a corn __(8)__ . I drink some juice, and then I'm out the door!

Understanding Vocabulary Write the Vocabulary Word that fits each clue.

9. It can be sliced in half and toasted.
10. Dishes are often stored in it.
11. This is often used with a brush.
12. It is a standard set of actions.

1. _____
2. _____
3. _____
4. _____
5. _____
6. _____
7. _____
8. _____
9. _____
10. _____
11. _____
12. _____

FACT FILE

Do you know why we say a grouchy person "got up on the wrong side of the bed"? Long ago people thought that the left side brought bad luck. They always tried to get up on the right side.

Enrichment

👪 *Breakfast Survey*

With a partner survey the students in your class to find out their favorite breakfast foods. List the different foods that the students name, such as cereal, juice, fruit, milk, toast, or eggs. Then count the number of times each food was mentioned. Draw a graph that shows how many people like each kind of food.

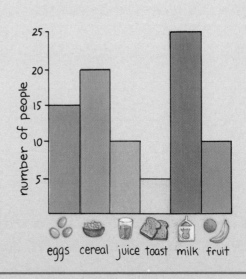

📖 *Writing*
Sell a Cereal

Write a television ad for a new breakfast cereal. Why is the cereal good? Why should people buy it? At the end of your ad, write a clever slogan for the cereal that will help people remember it. Try to use words from the lists in this unit. Be sure to proofread your paper.

RISE AND SHINE

Draw a four-frame comic strip of yourself on a school morning. What do you do each morning? Do you lie awake in bed for a while? Do you help in the kitchen or feed your pets? Write a brief explanation of your pictures. Try to use words from the lists in this unit.

Theme: Camping

8 Spelling |o͞o| and |o͝o|

A. _____

_____

_____

_____

_____

_____

_____

_____

_____

_____

B. _____

_____

_____

_____

_____

_____

_____

_____

_____

_____

■ **Challenge**

_____

_____

_____

_____

_____

LOOK at each word.

SAY each word.

Basic Words		■ Challenge
1. wood	11. stood	21. soot
2. brook	12. stool	22. marooned
3. tool	13. hook	23. bulletin
4. put	14. smooth	24. cocoon
5. wool	15. shoot	25. superb
6. push	16. bush	
7. full	17. fool	
8. roof	18. pull	
🐘 9. group	🐘 19. soup	
🐘 10. prove	🐘 20. move	

THINK about the words.

Each word has the |o͞o| or the |o͝o| sound. The |o͞o| sound is often spelled *oo*. The |o͝o| sound is often spelled *oo* or *u* followed by a consonant sound.

|o͞o| **too**l |o͝o| **woo**d, p**u**t

• What is one spelling pattern for the |o͞o| sound? How is the |o͞o| sound spelled in the Elephant Words? What are two spelling patterns for the |o͝o| sound?

WRITE the words.

Practice   Write the Basic Words to answer the questions.

A. Which **ten** words, including *roof*, have the |o͞o| sound?

B. Which **ten** words have the |o͝o| sound?

■ **Now write the five Challenge Words.** Underline the patterns that spell the |o͞o| and the |o͝o| sounds.

CHECK your spelling.

Spelling-Meaning Hint Can you see *wool* in these words: *woolly*, *woolen*? These words are all related in spelling and meaning. **Think of this:** My *woolen* jacket is made of lamb's *wool*.

wool
woolly
woolen

Independent Practice

Spelling-Meaning Look at the Spelling-Meaning Hint.
1-2. Write *woolen* and the Basic Word that you see in *woolen*.

Word Analysis Complete the exercises with Basic Words.

3-4. Write *full*. Change one letter, and write another word.

5-7. Write three words by adding the missing letters.
    5. pr _ _ _   **7.** gr _ _ p
    6. m _ _ _

8-10. Write the three words that begin or end with *sh*.

Making Inferences Write a Basic Word that fits each clue.
11. It often flows in the woods.
12. It is often found on the end of a fishing pole.
13. It is often found in a pot, and it is good to eat.
14. It is often found in a fireplace.
15. It is often used to help you reach things in high places.

■ **Challenge Words** Write the Challenge Word that fits each meaning. Use your Spelling Dictionary.
16. short announcement   **19.** abandoned on an island
17. excellent   **20.** fine, black powder produced
18. caterpillar's covering   by burning wood or coal

1. _____
2. _____
3. _____
4. _____
5. _____
6. _____
7. _____
8. _____
9. _____
10. _____
11. _____
12. _____
13. _____
14. _____
15. _____
16. _____
17. _____
18. _____
19. _____
20. _____

Summing Up

The |o͞o| sound is often spelled with the *oo* pattern.
The |o͝o| sound is often spelled *oo* or *u* followed by a consonant or a cluster.

Basic

1. wood
2. brook
3. tool
4. put
5. wool
6. push
7. full
8. roof
9. group
10. prove
11. stood
12. stool
13. hook
14. smooth
15. shoot
16. bush
17. fool
18. pull
19. soup
20. move

■ Challenge

21. soot
22. marooned
23. bulletin
24. cocoon
25. superb

Review

1. cook
2. spoon
3. shook
4. school
5. tooth

Proofreading Marks

¶ Indent
∧ Add something
℮ Take out something
≡ Capitalize
/ Make a small letter

Expanding Vocabulary

The Suffix -y A **suffix** is a word part added to the end of a base word. A suffix can add meaning to the word. The suffix -y can mean "like a" or "full of." Notice that words ending with e drop the e when -y is added.

BASE WORD	SUFFIX	NEW WORD	MEANING
bush	+ y	= bushy	like a bush
juice	+ y	= juicy	full of juice

Practice Write a word that ends with the suffix -y to match each meaning.

1. full of salt
2. full of spice
3. full of hair
4. like frost
5. full of stones
6. like wood

1. _____
2. _____
3. _____
4. _____
5. _____
6. _____

Proofreading

Singular Possessive Nouns To make a singular noun show ownership, add an apostrophe and s ('s).

the teacher's note   Gus's lunch

Practice Proofread the teacher's note. Find four misspelled words and two incorrect possessive nouns. Use proofreading marks to correct the errors.

Example: Mr. Tilden ~~pot~~ ^put the note on Ana's desk.

> Dear Parents,
>
>   On the last day of scool, our class will go to Pride Park in the principals van. Marys father will kook lunch for the groupe over a wod fire. The day should be full of fun!
>
>   Sincerely,
>
>   Mr. Tilden

Review: Spelling Spree

Phrases   Write Basic or Review Words to finish the phrases.

1. lamb's ____
2. ____ and pull
3. fork and ____
4. a loose front ____
5. a yellow ____ bus
6. chicken noodle ____

7. a ____ of people
8. to sit on a three-legged ____
9. trembled and ____ like a leaf
10. to ____ a hot meal
11. carved out of ____
12. the ____ of a house

Word Search   Write the Basic Word that is hidden in each sentence below.

Example: The kang<u>aroo f</u>ollowed us home.   *roof*

13. The bus had a flat tire.
14. The farmer tried to shoo the cows out of the corn.
15. Did you hear the cows moo this morning?
16. This shirt is too dirty to wear.
17. The puppies were too little to be taken from their mother.
18. Amy is putting another log on the fire.
19. We saw some brookweed on our walk.
20. The worker used a rope and pulley to raise the box.
21. Don't be foolish. Study for the test.
22. I am overjoyed at the news.
23. Timmy tied the fishhook onto the fishing line.
24. The helpful lady gave us directions.
25. The teacher approved the students' plans.

■ **Challenge Words**   Write each Challenge Word in a phrase. Then write a sentence, using the phrase.

Example: bulletin — bulletin board
　　　　　We put our stories on the bulletin board.

> 📖 *Writing Application:* A Letter   Pretend that last night was your first night at camp. Write a letter to your family, telling them about strange noises you heard during the night. Try to use five words from the list on page 56.

1. _____
2. _____
3. _____
4. _____
5. _____
6. _____
7. _____
8. _____
9. _____
10. _____
11. _____
12. _____
13. _____
14. _____
15. _____
16. _____
17. _____
18. _____
19. _____
20. _____
21. _____
22. _____
23. _____
24. _____
25. _____

8 Spelling Across the Curriculum

Recreation: *Camping*

Theme Vocabulary

lantern
kindling
canteen
backpack
tent
campsite
waterproof
poncho

Using Vocabulary Write the Vocabulary Words to complete the paragraph. Use your Spelling Dictionary.

I'll never forget my last camping trip. After we hiked to our __(1)__ and I took off my heavy __(2)__ that held my gear, it began to rain. My father and I lit a __(3)__ and went off to search for __(4)__ for a fire and for water to fill our __(5)__ . We came back to pitch the __(6)__ and discovered we had forgotten it! Dad took off his long __(7)__ and tied it to some branches to make a shelter. Because it was __(8)__ , we stayed dry all night.

Understanding Vocabulary Write the Vocabulary Word that answers each question.

9. Which is used to carry food: a canteen or a backpack?
10. Which keeps you drier: a backpack or a poncho?
11. Which helps you see: a canteen or a lantern?
12. Which needs a match: a campsite or kindling?

1. _____
2. _____
3. _____
4. _____
5. _____
6. _____
7. _____
8. _____
9. _____
10. _____
11. _____
12. _____

FACT FILE

The Great Smoky Mountains National Park was once wilderness that was settled by Cherokee Indians and pioneers. It lies on the border of North Carolina and Tennessee.

Enrichment

8

👥 *Twenty Questions*

Players: 3-5 **You need:** a list of the Basic and Review Words in this unit

How to play: Players take turns thinking of a word on the list. The other players take turns asking questions to help them guess the word. Players can ask questions such as "Does it begin with two consonants?" "Does it have the |o͞o| sound?" or "Is it something to eat?" A player can ask a question and make a guess in the same turn. The player must then spell the word correctly to score a point. If the player spells the word incorrectly, the next player may try to score a point by spelling it correctly.

CAMPERS' CATALOG

Make a catalog for camping equipment. Staple together sheets of drawing paper. On each page, draw or paste magazine pictures of camping gear and outdoor equipment. Under each picture, write a short description of the item. Try to use words from the lists in this unit.

📖 *Writing*
A Campfire Tale

Pretend that you are sitting around a campfire and telling scary stories. Write a scary story to tell. What makes your story scary? Will your story have a surprise ending? Try to use words from the lists in this unit. Be sure to proofread your paper.

(Theme: Dogs)

9 Spelling |ou| and |ô|

A. _____
_____
_____
_____
_____
_____
_____
_____
_____
_____

B. _____
_____
_____
_____
_____
_____
_____
_____

C. _____

■ **Challenge**
_____
_____
_____
_____
_____

LOOK   at each word.

SAY   each word.

Basic Words		■ **Challenge**
1. pound	11. drawn	21. gnaw
2. howl	12. scout	22. prowl
3. jaw	13. false	23. pounce
4. bounce	14. proud	24. doubt
5. cause	15. frown	25. scrawny
6. always	16. sauce	
7. shout	17. gown	
8. aloud	18. couch	
9. south	19. dawn	
🐘10. couple	20. mount	

THINK   about the words.

Each word has the |ou| or the |ô| sound. These sounds are usually spelled with two letters. The *ou* and the *au* patterns are usually followed by a consonant sound.

|ou| **h**ow**l, p**ou**nd** |ô| **j**aw, **c**au**se, **a**l**ways**

• What are two spelling patterns for the |ou| sound? What are three patterns for the |ô| sound? What consonant follows *a* when it spells the |ô| sound? What is different about the Elephant Word?

WRITE   the words.

Practice   Write the Basic Words to answer the questions.

A. Which **twelve** words have the |ou| sound?
B. Which **seven** words have the |ô| sound?
C. Which word has the *ou* pattern without the |ou| sound?

■ **Now write the five Challenge Words.** Underline the patterns that spell the |ou| and the |ô| sounds.

CHECK   your spelling.

> *Spelling-Meaning Hint*   Can you see *south* in the word *southern*? These words are related in spelling and meaning, even though they have different vowel sounds.

so**u**th
so**u**thern

Independent Practice

Spelling-Meaning   Look at the Spelling-Meaning Hint.

1-2. Write *south* and *southern*. Then, in each word, underline the two letters that spell different vowel sounds.

Word Analysis   Complete the exercises with Basic Words.

3-4. Write the two words that have the |s| sound spelled *ce*.

5-6. Write the two words that have the |z| sound.

7. Write the word that rhymes with *paw*.

Word Clues   Write the Basic Word that fits each clue.

8. means the same as *sunrise*
9. often found in a living room
10. a good place to find a dog
11. two people
12. worn at a ball or a party
13. sound made by a wolf
14. an unhappy look
15. a loud cry

|ou||ou|
howl

■ **Challenge Words**   Write the Challenge Words to complete the paragraph. Use your Spelling Dictionary.

   Stray dogs and cats __(16)__ through streets at night. Cats __(17)__ on mice and catch them. Today a hungry, __(18)__ dog followed me home from school. I gave him a bone to __(19)__ on. I want to keep him, but I __(20)__ that my parents will let me.

1. _____
2. _____
3. _____
4. _____
5. _____
6. _____
7. _____
8. _____
9. _____
10. _____
11. _____
12. _____
13. _____
14. _____
15. _____
16. _____
17. _____
18. _____
19. _____
20. _____

Summing Up

The |ou| sound is often spelled with the pattern *ou* or *ow*.
The |ô| sound is often spelled with the pattern *aw*, *au*, or *a* before *l*.
A consonant sound usually follows the *ou* or the *au* pattern.

Basic

1. pound
2. howl
3. jaw
4. bounce
5. cause
6. always
7. shout
8. aloud
9. south
10. couple
11. drawn
12. scout
13. false
14. proud
15. frown
16. sauce
17. gown
18. couch
19. dawn
20. mount

■ **Challenge**

21. gnaw
22. prowl
23. pounce
24. doubt
25. scrawny

Review

1. walk
2. lawn
3. loud
4. sound
5. clown

Expanding Vocabulary

Exact Words for *shout*   Read each sentence, and imagine the sound Marcy made.

Marcy let out a **shout** when I stepped on her foot.
Marcy let out a **howl** when I stepped on her foot.

Howl is another word for *shout*, but it is more exact and describes a special kind of loud cry. Use exact words to make your speaking and writing more interesting.

Practice   Write the best word to replace *shout* in each sentence. Use your Thesaurus.

bellow   cheer   scream   yell

1. The children on the roller coaster shout with fright.
2. The coaches shout instructions in deep voices.
3. The fans shout each time their team scores.
4. Never shout "fire" unless there really is danger.

1. _____   3. _____

2. _____   4. _____

Dictionary

Entry Words and Their Meanings   A dictionary may list several meanings for an entry word. A **sample sentence** or **phrase** may be given to help make a meaning clear.

sample phrase   sample sentence

false | fôls | *adj.* **falser, falsest. 1.** Not true, real, honest, or correct: *a false statement.* **2.** Lacking loyalty: *They turned out to be false friends.*

Practice   Look up *always* in your Spelling Dictionary. Write the sample sentence given for each meaning below.
1. at all times
2. for as long as one can imagine

1. _____

2. _____

Review: Spelling Spree

Code Breaker   Some Basic and Review Words have been written in the code below. Use the code to figure out each word. Write the words correctly.

CODE:	z	y	x	w	v	u	t	s	q	o	n	m	l	k	i	h	g	f	d	b
LETTER:	a	b	c	d	e	f	g	h	j	l	m	n	o	p	r	s	t	u	w	y

Example: hlfgs   *south*

1. xoldm
2. uzohv
3. xlfxs
4. uildm
5. zolfw
6. hlfmw
7. hzfxv
8. hxlfg
9. nlfmg
10. qzd
11. wzdm
12. tldm
13. wizdm
14. xlfkov
15. sldo

Proofreading   **16-25.** Find and cross out ten misspelled Basic or Review Words in this story. Then write each word correctly.

Alex had allways wanted to enter his dog Rags in the Dog Show. Every day he and Rags were up at dawn to practice. Now the prowd moment had come. Alex and Rags began to wok past the judges. Then Rags let out a lowd howl. With one big bonce, Rags jumped over the judges' table and raced across the soth lown. People began to showt. A tiny chipmunk weighing little more than a pond was the couse of poor Rags's downfall.

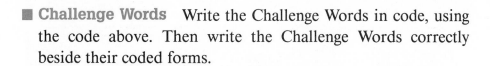

■ **Challenge Words**   Write the Challenge Words in code, using the code above. Then write the Challenge Words correctly beside their coded forms.

📖 *Writing Application:* An Ad   Pretend that you train dogs. Write an ad to tell what you can teach dogs to do. Try to use five words from the list on page 62.

1. _____
2. _____
3. _____
4. _____
5. _____
6. _____
7. _____
8. _____
9. _____
10. _____
11. _____
12. _____
13. _____
14. _____
15. _____
16. _____
17. _____
18. _____
19. _____
20. _____
21. _____
22. _____
23. _____
24. _____
25. _____

9 Spelling Across the Curriculum

Science: *Dogs*

Theme Vocabulary

spaniel
collie
greyhound
Saint Bernard
terrier
husky
poodle
basset hound

Using Vocabulary Write the Vocabulary Words to complete the paragraph. Use your Spelling Dictionary.

There are many kinds of dogs. The long-haired __(1)__ is often used to herd sheep. In the far north, a __(2)__ pulls sleds. In Switzerland the __(3)__ was used to rescue people in the mountains. Two hunting dogs are the small, short-haired __(4)__ and the __(5)__, which has a long body, short legs, and long, drooping ears. Two show dogs are the curly-haired __(6)__ and the __(7)__, which has long ears and a silky coat. The __(8)__ is a fast runner.

Understanding Vocabulary Write *T* if the sentence is true. Write *F* if it is false.

9. The collie has a curly coat.
10. The greyhound has short legs.
11. The Saint Bernard is bigger than the terrier.
12. The basset hound is shorter than the greyhound.

1. _____
2. _____
3. _____
4. _____
5. _____
6. _____
7. _____
8. _____
9. _____
10. _____
11. _____
12. _____

FACT FILE

The saying "His bark is worse than his bite" comes from a thirteenth century proverb. It describes a person who may frighten you with loud talk but never really hurt you.

Enrichment

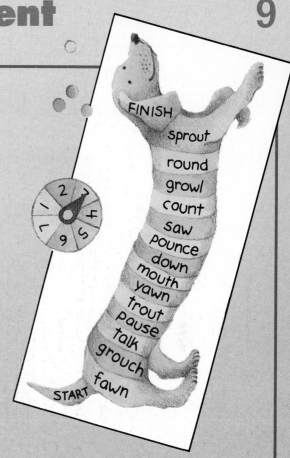

👪 Hot Dog

Players: 2-4 **You need:** a game board like the one shown, a spinner, game markers
How to play: The first player spins the spinner and moves a marker. He or she must think of and correctly spell a spelling word that rhymes with the word written on the space. If the word is incorrectly spelled, the marker must go back to its previous position. Players may help each other think of rhyming spelling words but may not help with the spelling. The first player to reach the head of the dog wins.

📖 Writing
B Is for Buster

Imagine that you have a very special pet dog. Write the letters of your dog's name down the side of a piece of paper. Beside each letter, write a sentence that begins with that letter. In each sentence, describe one special quality of your dog. Try to use words from the lists in this unit. Be sure to proofread your paper.

Sam wags his tail.
a
m

CANINE CARTOON

Draw a cartoon that has a dog as its main character. First, think of a situation that a dog might think is funny or strange from its point of view. Then draw a series of pictures that show the situation. Write speech balloons for the people and thought balloons for the dog. Try to use words from the lists in this unit.

10 Spelling |îr|, |är|, and |âr|

A. _____

_____

_____

_____

_____

B. _____

_____

_____

_____

_____

_____

C. _____

_____

_____

_____

_____

_____

D. _____

_____

_____

■ Challenge

_____

_____

_____

_____

LOOK at each word.

SAY each word.

Basic Words   ■ Challenge

1. gear   11. starve   21. barnacle
2. spear   12. charm   22. awareness
3. sharp   13. beard   23. startle
4. stare   14. scarf   24. marvel
5. alarm   15. spare   25. weary
6. cheer   16. stairs
7. square   17. year
8. hairy   18. charge
🐘 9. heart   19. dairy
🐘 10. weird   🐘 20. scarce

THINK about the words.

Each word has a vowel sound + *r*. The |îr| sounds are close to the |ē| sound. The |är| sounds are close to the |ă| sound. The |âr| sounds are close to the |ā| sound.

|îr| g**ear**, ch**eer** |är| sh**ar**p |âr| st**are**, h**air**y

• What are two patterns for the |îr| sounds? What is one pattern for the |är| sounds? What are two patterns for the |âr| sounds? How are the Elephant Words different?

WRITE the words.

Practice Write the Basic Words to answer the questions.

A. Which **five** words spell |îr| with the *ear* or *eer* pattern?
B. Which **six** words spell |är| with the *ar* pattern?
C. Which **six** words spell |âr| with the *are* or *air* pattern?
D. Which **three** words spell these sounds other ways?

■ Now write the five Challenge Words. Underline the patterns that spell the |îr|, the |är|, and the |âr| sounds.

CHECK your spelling.

Spelling-Meaning Hint Can you see *cheer* in these words: *cheerful, cheerless, cheery*? **Think of this:** A *cheerful* smile makes you feel *cheery*.

cheer
cheerful
cheerless
cheery

Independent Practice

Spelling-Meaning Look at the Spelling-Meaning Hint.
1-2. Write *cheerful*. Then write the Basic Word that is related to *cheerful* in spelling and meaning.

Word Analysis Complete the exercises with Basic Words.

3-5. Write the three words that have the consonant cluster *st*.

6-7. Write the two words that end with the |ē| sound.

8-9. Write two words by adding the missing letters.
   8. w _ _ _ d
   9. sc _ _ ce

Classifying Write the Basic Word that fits with each group.
10. brain, lung, ____
11. hat, mittens, ____
12. siren, bell, ____
13. week, month, ____
14. arrow, harpoon, ____
15. circle, triangle, ____

■ **Challenge Words** Write the Challenge Word that completes each sentence. Use your Spelling Dictionary.
16. Scuba diving can give you a new ____ of sea life.
17. You should rest for a while if you become ____.
18. The fish often dart away when you ____ them.
19. Have you ever seen a ____ attached to a rock?
20. Most people ____ at the beauty of the underwater world.

1. _____
2. _____
3. _____
4. _____
5. _____
6. _____
7. _____
8. _____
9. _____
10. _____
11. _____
12. _____
13. _____
14. _____
15. _____
16. _____
17. _____
18. _____
19. _____
20. _____

Summing Up

The |îr| sounds are often spelled with the pattern *ear* or *eer*.
The |är| sounds are often spelled with the pattern *ar*.
The |âr| sounds are often spelled with the pattern *are* or *air*.

Basic

1. gear
2. spear
3. sharp
4. stare
5. alarm
6. cheer
7. square
8. hairy
9. heart
10. weird
11. starve
12. charm
13. beard
14. scarf
15. spare
16. stairs
17. year
18. charge
19. dairy
20. scarce

■ Challenge

21. barnacle
22. awareness
23. startle
24. marvel
25. weary

Review

1. air
2. near
3. large
4. scare
5. chair

Proofreading Marks

¶   Indent
∧   Add something
℘   Take out something
≡   Capitalize
/   Make a small letter

Expanding Vocabulary

Easily Confused Words   Which word below would complete this sentence: *Have you ever seen a cow being milked in a ___?*

> **dairy**: a farm where milk is produced
>
> **diary**: a daily written record

Some words are easily confused because they look similar. How do *dairy* and *diary* look similar?

Practice   Write *dairy* or *diary* to complete each sentence correctly. Use your Spelling Dictionary.

1. Our class visited a ___ and saw cows being milked.
2. I wrote about the field trip in my ___ .
3. I learned that cheese is a ___ product.
4. Soon my ___ will be filled with things I have learned.

1. _____   3. _____

2. _____   4. _____

Proofreading

Plural Possessive Nouns   To form the possessive of a plural noun that ends with *s*, add an apostrophe. If the word does not end with *s*, add an apostrophe and *s*.

> spears' points   men's classes

Practice   Proofread this ad. Find four misspelled words and two incorrect plural possessive nouns. Use proofreading marks to correct the errors.

Example: Do you sell swimmers's geer at the school?

• Does water skare you? • Do big fish alarm you?

Take our divers's classes!

Learn how to dive in your spair time.

Discover the charm of the wierd, wonderful sea.

The charj for childrens' lessons is half price.

Review: Spelling Spree

Word Addition   Write a Basic or Review Word by adding the beginning of the first word to the end of the second word.

Example: chill + start   *chart*

1. scale + dare
2. dive + fairy
3. check + barge
4. step + carve
5. yes + dear
6. chin + flair
7. spot + fear
8. stone + care
9. chop + steer
10. new + hear
11. show + harp
12. still + pairs
13. give + rear
14. spend + share
15. choose + farm
16. alert + harm
17. help + dairy
18. squirm + bare

Questions   Write a Basic or Review Word to answer each question.

19. What keeps your neck warm in winter?
20. What can we breathe but not see?
21. If an ant is small, what is an elephant?
22. What is a valentine often shaped like?
23. What might grow on a man's face?
24. If you saw something strange, what would you call it?
25. What adjective describes water in the desert?

a	w	a	r	e	n	e	s	s	
					t				
					a				
					r				
					t				
					l	s			
					e	t	b		
						a	o		
						r	q		
						e	q		

■ **Challenge Words**   Make a Word Square puzzle with ten squares across and ten squares down. Write each Challenge Word across or down. Then fill in Basic Words or other letters to complete the square. (Part of a Word Square is shown.) Trade puzzles with a partner.

📖 *Writing Application:* Creative Writing Write a paragraph describing an imaginary underwater creature that is half plant and half animal. What does it eat? Can it move? Try to use five words from the list on page 68.

1. _____
2. _____
3. _____
4. _____
5. _____
6. _____
7. _____
8. _____
9. _____
10. _____
11. _____
12. _____
13. _____
14. _____
15. _____
16. _____
17. _____
18. _____
19. _____
20. _____
21. _____
22. _____
23. _____
24. _____
25. _____

10 Spelling Across the Curriculum

Recreation: *Scuba Diving*

Theme Vocabulary

scuba diver
tank
mask
flippers
shipwreck
island
lagoon
reef

Using Vocabulary Write the Vocabulary Words to complete the paragraph. Use your Spelling Dictionary.

From the boat Alice could see a tree-covered __(1)__. She knew that just beyond it was a shallow, sandy __(2)__ where the __(3)__ of the *Maria* lay. Many years ago the ship had run aground on a coral __(4)__ and sunk. Now the spot was Alice's favorite place to dive. Alice was a skilled __(5)__. Carefully she checked her air __(6)__, the face of her __(7)__, and the heel straps of her __(8)__. With a splash, she was off!

Understanding Vocabulary Write *yes* if the underlined word is used correctly. Write *no* if it is not.

9. The <u>flippers</u> kept my hands dry.
10. The <u>mask</u> will protect your feet from the sharp coral.
11. The <u>reef</u> scratched the bottom of the boat.
12. We could reach the <u>island</u> only by boat.

1. _____
2. _____
3. _____
4. _____
5. _____
6. _____
7. _____
8. _____
9. _____
10. _____
11. _____
12. _____

FACT FILE

Jacques Cousteau helped invent the aqualung and other diving equipment. He is also an expert underwater explorer and photographer. His best-known film is *The Silent World*.

Enrichment

👪 *Wall-to-Wall Water*

With your class, draw a mural of the underwater world. Use an encyclopedia or resource books to find pictures of sea animals and plants. Draw them in their natural surroundings. Include a picture of a scuba diver and the different kinds of diving equipment. Label the equipment, as well as each plant and animal. Use markers, crayons, or paints to color the mural. Try to use words from the unit lists.

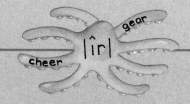

WORD OCTOPUSES

Draw three large octopuses. Write |îr| on the body of the first octopus. Write |är| on the second and |âr| on the third. For each octopus, write eight words—one on each arm—that have the same vowel + |r| sounds that are written on the octopus's body. Use Basic Words, Review Words, and other words with the correct vowel + |r| sounds.

📖 *Writing*
Underwater Tours

Pretend that you are a scuba diver who leads people on dives to famous shipwrecks. Write a brochure for your diving trips. Describe three different wrecks. What is each one like? What are its unique features? Try to use words from the lists in this unit. Be sure to proofread your paper.

Theme: Horses

11 Spelling |ôr|, |ûr|, and |yŏŏr|

A. _____

_____

_____

_____

_____

_____

B. _____

LOOK at each word.

SAY each word.

Basic Words		■ Challenge
1. horse	11. earn	21. thoroughbred
2. chore	12. burn	22. enormous
3. firm	13. cure	23. hurdle
4. learn	14. score	24. foreign
5. dirty	15. worm	25. earnest
6. curve	16. thirteen	
7. world	17. worn	
8. pure	18. curl	
🐘 9. board	19. shirt	
🐘10. course	20. search	

THINK about the words.

Each word has a vowel sound + *r*. The |ôr| sounds are close to the |ō| sound. The |yŏŏr| sounds are close to the |yōō| sound. The |ûr| sounds have a weak vowel sound.

|ôr|	horse, chore	|yŏŏr|	pure
|ûr|	firm, curve, learn, worm		

• What are two patterns for the |ôr| sounds? How are the Elephant Words different? What are four patterns for the |ûr| sounds? What is one pattern for the |yŏŏr| sounds?

WRITE the words.

Practice Write the Basic Words to answer the questions.

A. Which **six** words have the |ôr| sounds?
B. Which **twelve** words have the |ûr| sounds?
C. Which **two** words have the |yŏŏr| sounds?

■ **Now write the five Challenge Words.** Underline the patterns that spell the |ôr| and the |ûr| sounds.

CHECK your spelling.

C. _____

_____

■ Challenge

_____

_____

_____

_____

Spelling-Meaning Hint   Can you see *learn* in these words: *learner, learned, unlearn*? These words are all related in spelling and meaning. **Think of this:** If you *learn* a bad habit, you can *unlearn* it.

learn
learner
learned
unlearn

Independent Practice

Spelling-Meaning   Look at the Spelling-Meaning Hint.
1-2. Write *learner* and the Basic Word that you see in *learner*.

Word Analysis   Complete the exercises with Basic Words.

  3. Write the word that begins with the |th| sound.

4-5. Write the two words that rhyme with *tore*.

6-9. Write a homophone for each word below.
      6. hoarse   **7.** coarse   **8.** bored   **9.** urn

Synonyms   A **synonym** is a word that means the same or nearly the same as another word. Write the Basic Word that is a synonym for each word below.
10. scorch
11. seek
12. hard
13. unclean
14. heal
15. earth

|ôr|

h ors**e**
ch or**e**

■ **Challenge Words**   Write the Challenge Word that fits each meaning. Use your Spelling Dictionary.
16. from another country   **19.** a barrier to jump over
17. huge   **20.** sincere
18. an animal of pure stock

Summing Up

The |ôr| sounds are often spelled with the patterns *or* and *ore*.
The |ûr| sounds are often spelled with the patterns *ur, ear, ir,*
   and *or*.
The |yŏŏr| sounds are often spelled with the pattern *ure*.

1. _____
2. _____
3. _____
4. _____
5. _____
6. _____
7. _____
8. _____
9. _____
10. _____
11. _____
12. _____
13. _____
14. _____
15. _____
16. _____
17. _____
18. _____
19. _____
20. _____

Basic

1. horse
2. chore
3. firm
4. learn
5. dirty
6. curve
7. world
8. pure
9. board
10. course
11. earn
12. burn
13. cure
14. score
15. worm
16. thirteen
17. worn
18. curl
19. shirt
20. search

■ **Challenge**

21. thoroughbred
22. enormous
23. hurdle
24. foreign
25. earnest

Review

1. first
2. hurt
3. work
4. third
5. storm

Expanding Vocabulary

Antonyms   Would you be *dirty* or *clean* after working in a barn all day? *Dirty* and *clean* are **antonyms**, or words with opposite meanings.

Practice   **Write the word below that is an antonym for each underlined word. Use your Spelling Dictionary.**

> dirty   firm   fancy   forget

1. The ground was <u>soft</u> beneath the horse's hooves.
2. Did you <u>remember</u> to lock the stable door?
3. The rodeo rider did some <u>simple</u> tricks on his horse.
4. I am surprised at how <u>clean</u> this stall is.

1. _____   3. _____

2. _____   4. _____

Dictionary

Pronunciation Key   A **pronunciation key** helps you understand the symbols in the pronunciation given after an entry word. Look at the pronunciation for *search*. How do you pronounce the |û| sound? The pronunciation key shows that the *u* in *fur* has the |û| sound. Say *fur*. Listen for |û|.

pronunciation   part of a pronunciation key

search |sûrch|

ā pay	ē be	ŏ pot	ô paw, for
â care	î near	ō go	û fur

Practice   **Write the word from the second column that matches each pronunciation. Use the pronunciation key above. Check your answers in your Spelling Dictionary.**

1. |chîr| chore
2. |skôr| chair
3. |chôr| cheer
4. |skâr| score
5. |châr| scare

1. _____   3. _____   5. _____

2. _____   4. _____

Review: Spelling Spree

Letter Math   Write a Basic or Review Word by solving each word problem.

Example: first − st + m = *firm*

1. s + tore − e + m =
2. worry − ry + k =
3. c + sure − s =
4. curb − b + l =
5. third − d + teen =
6. p + sure − s =
7. l + earth − th + n =
8. horn − n + se =
9. sh + dirt − d =
10. thirst − st + d =
11. s + earn − n + ch =
12. b + turn − t =
13. world − ld + m =
14. sc + store − st =
15. curl − l + ve =
16. ch + shore − sh =
17. b + soar − s + d =

Proofreading   **18-25.** Find and cross out eight misspelled Basic or Review Words in this journal entry. Then write each word correctly.

Saturday, May 12
   Today I went to Cobb Stables. Mrs. Cobb is letting me ern money by helping with a chore or two. The work is hard and durty, but it is worth it. Someday I will be allowed to take a horse around the coarse. However, frist I must learn to be a ferm and skillful rider. Right now I feel warn out and my muscles hirt, but I wouldn't trade this job for the wold!

■ **Challenge Words**   Look at the Letter Math activity. Write two problems for each Challenge Word. Think of a complete word. Then add and subtract letters to write the Challenge Word.

📖 *Writing Application:* Comparison and Contrast
The pictures show a Clydesdale and a pinto. Write a paragraph about the horses, describing how they are alike and different. Try to use five words from the list on page 74.

1. _____
2. _____
3. _____
4. _____
5. _____
6. _____
7. _____
8. _____
9. _____
10. _____
11. _____
12. _____
13. _____
14. _____
15. _____
16. _____
17. _____
18. _____
19. _____
20. _____
21. _____
22. _____
23. _____
24. _____
25. _____

pinto

Clydesdale

11 Spelling Across the Curriculum

Science: *Horses*

Theme Vocabulary

colt
mustang
filly
saddle
reins
bridle
stirrups
mare

Using Vocabulary Write the Vocabulary Words to complete the paragraph. Use your Spelling Dictionary.

Tim swung the __(1)__ onto the horse's back and put the __(2)__ over her head. After mounting, he checked his feet in the __(3)__ and loosely held the __(4)__ in his hands. He wished that instead of riding old Nell he could ride a wild __(5)__ . He knew that a __(6)__ nearby had just given birth. He did not know if the young horse was a __(7)__ , a male, or a __(8)__ , a female. He just hoped that someday the horse would be his.

Understanding Vocabulary Write *yes* or *no* to answer each question.

 9. Do you need a saddle to have stirrups on a horse?
10. Do you need a bridle to have reins on a horse?
11. Can a colt give birth to a filly?
12. Can a horse be both a mare and a mustang?

1. _____
2. _____
3. _____
4. _____
5. _____
6. _____
7. _____
8. _____
9. _____
10. _____
11. _____
12. _____

FACT FILE

In 1860 the pony express brought mail from Missouri to California. Riders carried the mail on horseback, stopping only to change horses at stations along the way.

Enrichment

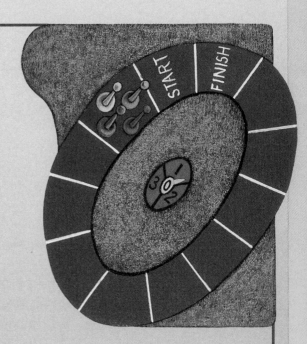

👪 *A Horse Race*

Players: 2-4 **You need:** a game board like the one shown, game markers, a spinner

How to play: Player 1 chooses a Basic Word for Player 2 to spell and use in a sentence. If Player 2 gives correct answers, he or she spins the spinner and moves that number of spaces. Players continue to take turns giving each other words and spinning the spinner until someone crosses the finish line.

📖 *Writing*
Small Talk

Many tales have been written about animals with amazing powers. Write a tale about a horse that can talk. What kinds of things might a talking horse be able to do? How could he or she help solve a problem or come to someone's aid? Try to use words from the lists in this unit. Be sure to proofread your paper.

HORSING AROUND

Make a picture dictionary of compound words that contain the word *horse*, such as *horsepower* and *sea horse*. Illustrate each word with a silly picture. For example, to illustrate the word *horsepower*, you might show a horse lifting weights. Next to each picture, write the correct definition of the word. Use your dictionary to help you find compound "horse" words.

12 Review: Units 7–11

Unit 7 Spelling |ŭ|, |yōō|, and |ōō| pp. 48-53

tube	lunch	fruit	truth	done
suit	threw	trunk	tune	glue

Remember:

|ŭ| → **u** followed by a consonant sound

|yōō| or |ōō| → **u**-consonant-**e**,

ew, ue, ui

Write the word that belongs in each group.

1. song, melody, ____
2. dress, slacks, ____
3. paste, tape, ____
4. breakfast, dinner, ____
5. vegetables, bread, ____

Write the word that fits each clue.

6. past tense of *throw*
7. opposite of *not finished*
8. Toothpaste comes in one.
9. storage space in a car
10. something that is true

Unit 8 Spelling |ōō| and |ŏŏ| pp. 54-59

tool	push	wood	group	prove
pull	hook	stool	soup	move

Remember: |ōō| → **oo**

|ŏŏ| → **oo** or **u** followed

by a consonant sound

Write a spelling word by changing one letter in each word below.

11. stoop   13. fool   15. good
12. bush   14. look   16. bull

Write the Elephant Words that complete these sentences.

17. Can you ____ that your statement is true?
18. We will ____ into another house next summer.
19. Please have another bowl of hot ____.
20. The play was put on by a small ____ of students.

1. _____
2. _____
3. _____
4. _____
5. _____
6. _____
7. _____
8. _____
9. _____
10. _____
11. _____
12. _____
13. _____
14. _____
15. _____
16. _____
17. _____
18. _____
19. _____
20. _____

Half of the words from each unit are reviewed on these pages.
The rest are reviewed on pages 232–234.

Unit 9   Spelling |ou| and |ô| pp. 60-65

howl	cause	always	pound	couple
dawn	couch	sauce	false	frown

Remember: |ou| → **ou, ow**

　　　　|ô| → **aw, au, a before l**

Write the word that rhymes with each word below.

21. gown   **24.** lawn

22. pause   **25.** sound

23. growl   **26.** pouch

Write the words that complete these sentences.

27. Last night we had spaghetti with tomato _____ .

28. You should _____ tell the truth.

29. Is the answer to this question true or _____ ?

30. I wrote a _____ of letters to two friends.

21. _____

22. _____

23. _____

24. _____

25. _____

26. _____

27. _____

28. _____

29. _____

30. _____

Unit 10   Spelling |îr|, |är|, and |âr| pp. 66-71

cheer	alarm	square	heart	weird
charm	beard	dairy	spare	scarce

Remember: |îr| → **ear, eer**

　　　　|är| → **ar**

　　　　|âr| → **are, air**

Write the word that completes each analogy.

31. *Air* is to *lungs* as *blood* is to _____ .

32. *Head* is to *hair* as *chin* is to _____ .

33. *Ball* is to *circle* as *cube* is to _____ .

34. *Wheat* is to *mill* as *milk* is to _____ .

Write the word that fits each meaning.

35. strange   **37.** rare   **39.** shout

36. warning   **38.** to delight   **40.** extra

31. _____

32. _____

33. _____

34. _____

35. _____

36. _____

37. _____

38. _____

39. _____

40. _____

12 Review

41. _____

42. _____

43. _____

44. _____

45. _____

46. _____

47. _____

48. _____

49. _____

50. _____

Unit 11   Spelling |ôr|, |ûr|, and |yŏŏr| pp. 72-77

| horse | curve | learn | board | course |
| cure | worm | score | search | thirteen |

Remember: |ôr| → **or, ore**

|ûr| → **ir, ur, ear, or**

|yŏŏr| → **ure**

h **or** se
ch **ore**

Write six words. Add letters that spell the vowel + |r| sounds.
41. c _ _ ve   43. c _ _ _   45. b _ _ _ d
42. h _ _ se   44. s _ _ _ ch   46. w _ _ m

Write the words that complete these sentences.
47. Did you ____ about fractions in your math lesson today?
48. Did you have a high or a low ____ on your math test?
49. I answered ____ out of fifteen questions correctly.
50. I am going to take a special math ____ next year.

51. _____

52. _____

53. _____

54. _____

55. _____

56. _____

57. _____

58. _____

59. _____

60. _____

■ Challenge Words   Units 7-11   pp. 48-77

| commute | scrawny | marooned | bulletin | thoroughbred |
| pounce | barnacle | newscast | enormous | awareness |

Write the word that belongs in each group.
51. giant, huge, ____
52. clam, snail, ____
53. memo, notice, ____
54. stranded, deserted, ____
55. knowledge, understanding, ____

Write the word that fits each clue.
56. It describes a chicken without much meat on it.
57. Many working people do this Monday through Friday.
58. It describes an animal from good stock.
59. Kittens do this when they play with a ball of yarn.
60. You watch this to find out about world events.

Spelling-Meaning Strategy

Consonant Changes: Silent to Sounded

Sometimes you can remember how to spell a word by thinking of a word that is related in spelling and meaning. Read this paragraph.

These muffins are messy to eat because they **crumble** easily. Fortunately, the pigeons are happy to eat every **crumb** that we drop.

crumb
crumble

Think

- How are *crumb* and *crumble* related in meaning?
- Which letter is silent in *crumb* but pronounced in *crumble*?

Here are more related words in which a consonant is silent in one word and pronounced in the other.

soften	fasten	hasten
soft	fast	haste

Apply and Extend

Complete these activities on a separate piece of paper.

1. Look up the words in the Word Box above in the Spelling Dictionary, and write a sentence for each word. Can you make the words' meanings clear?

2. With a partner list as many words as you can that are related to *crumb, soften, fasten,* and *hasten*. Then look on page 271 of your Spelling-Meaning Index. Add any other words that you find in these families to your list.

Summing Up Sometimes you can remember how to spell a word with a silent consonant by thinking of a related word in which the letter is pronounced.

Comparison and Contrast

If you think that there is only one kind of elephant, this article will surprise you. How many kinds of elephants does it compare and contrast?

There are two kinds of elephants. One kind comes from Asia; the other comes from Africa.

It is not hard to tell the difference between Asian and African elephants. African elephants have big ears that look like the two sides of a giant valentine heart. Asian elephants' ears are smaller and shaped more like a triangle. African elephants have sloping foreheads and sway backs. Asian elephants have foreheads that go straight up and down. Their backs are rounded at the top.

Among both Asian and African elephants, males are called bulls. Females are called cows. Babies are called calves. In Asia, only bulls grow tusks. In Africa, both bulls and cows grow tusks. African elephants have rings around their trunks and two "fingers" at the tips. Asian elephants have smoother trunks and one "finger" at the tips.

from Seven True Elephant Stories *by Barbara Williams*

Think and Discuss

1. What are the two kinds of elephants?
2. What is the **topic sentence** of the second paragraph?
3. What **supporting details** in the second paragraph tell how Asian and African elephants are **different**?
4. How are Asian and African elephants **alike**?

The Writing Process

The paragraphs on page 82 compare and contrast two kinds of elephants. To compare and contrast two things, tell how they are **alike** in one paragraph and how they are **different** in another paragraph. Begin each paragraph with a **topic sentence** that tells the **main idea**. Then give **supporting details** that tell how the two things are alike and different.

Assignment: Write to Compare and Contrast

Step One: Prewriting

1. List pairs of things you can compare and contrast. Discuss your ideas with a classmate. Choose one.
2. List the ways your subjects are alike and different.

Step Two: Write a First Draft

1. Think about your purpose and your audience.
2. Do not worry about mistakes—just write!

Step Three: Revise

1. Does each paragraph have a topic sentence?
2. Where can you add more supporting details?
3. Use your Thesaurus to find exact words.
4. Read your paragraphs to a classmate. Make any changes.

Step Four: Proofread

1. Did you capitalize proper nouns?
2. Did you spell all words correctly? Copy any words that you misspelled into your Notebook for Writing.

Step Five: Publish

1. Copy your work neatly. Add an interesting title.
2. Add pictures, and display them with your paragraphs.

Composition Words

few
dull
smooth
prove
always
weird
sharp
firm

Proofreading Marks

¶ Indent
∧ Add something
ℓ Take out something
≡ Capitalize
/ Make a small letter

Theme: Travel

13 Compound Words

A. _____

_____

_____

_____

_____

_____

_____

_____

_____

_____

_____

_____

_____

_____

_____

B. _____

_____

C. _____

_____

■ **Challenge**

_____

_____

_____

_____

_____

LOOK at each word.

SAY each word.

Basic Words   ■ Challenge

1. railroad   11. fireplace   21. landmark
2. airport   12. ourselves   22. nationwide
3. seat belt   13. all right   23. postscript
4. everywhere   14. forever   24. motorcycle
5. homesick   15. breakfast   25. handkerchief
6. understand   16. whenever
7. background   17. everything
8. anything   18. meanwhile
9. ninety-nine   19. afternoon
🐘10. already   20. make-believe

THINK about the words.

Each word is a compound word. A **compound word** is made up of two or more smaller words.

    rail + **road**   = railroad   **seat** + **belt** = seat belt
    ninety + **nine** = ninety-nine

• What three ways can a compound word be written? What words make up each compound word? What is unusual about the spelling of the Elephant Word?

WRITE the words.

Practice   **Write the Basic Words to answer these questions about compound words.**

A. Which **sixteen** words are written as one word?
B. Which **two** words are written with a hyphen?
C. Which **two** words are written as two separate words?

■ **Now write the five Challenge Words.** Draw a line between the two words that make up each compound word.

CHECK your spelling.

Spelling-Meaning Hint *Any* means "one or some, no matter which kind." Can you see how the meaning of *any* is included in *anything, anyplace,* and *anybody*?

any
any*thing*
any*place*
any*body*

Independent Practice

Spelling-Meaning   Look at the Spelling-Meaning Hint.
1-2. Write *anybody*. Then write the Basic Word that contains one of the words that make up *anybody*.

Word Analysis   Complete the exercise with Basic Words.
3-10. Write the word that contains each word below.

3. place	**7.** where
4. after	**8.** believe
5. nine	**9.** our
6. ready	**10.** mean

Context Sentences   Write the Basic Word that completes each sentence.
11. We waved good-by as the train left the _____ station.
12. In the dining car, we ate juice and cereal for _____ .
13. Traveling was fun, but I felt a little _____ at first.
14. We went to the _____ to get on a plane to fly home.
15. Before takeoff, I fastened my _____ .

■ **Challenge Words**   Write the Challenge Word that fits each meaning. Use your Spelling Dictionary.
16. small square of cloth
17. throughout the country
18. a two-wheeled vehicle that is driven by an engine
19. familiar object or building
20. message added at the end of a letter

1. _____
2. _____
3. _____
4. _____
5. _____
6. _____
7. _____
8. _____
9. _____
10. _____
11. _____
12. _____
13. _____
14. _____
15. _____
16. _____
17. _____
18. _____
19. _____
20. _____

Summing Up

A **compound word** is made up of two or more smaller words. A compound word may be written as one word, as two words joined by a hyphen, or as two separate words.

Basic

1. railroad
2. airport
3. seat belt
4. everywhere
5. homesick
6. understand
7. background
8. anything
9. ninety-nine
10. already
11. fireplace
12. ourselves
13. all right
14. forever
15. breakfast
16. whenever
17. everything
18. meanwhile
19. afternoon
20. make-believe

■ Challenge

21. landmark
22. nationwide
23. postscript
24. motorcycle
25. handkerchief

Review

1. inside
2. outside
3. birthday
4. baseball
5. sometimes

1. _____
2. _____
3. _____
4. _____
5. _____
6. _____
7. _____
8. _____

Expanding Vocabulary

Blending Word Parts   What would you call a meal that is part breakfast and part lunch?

breakfast + l**unch** = **brunch**

Compound words are formed by joining two or more words. **Blended words**, such as *brunch*, are formed by blending parts of well-known words.

Practice   **Write blended words by joining the underlined word parts.**

Example: helicopter + airport = *heliport*

1. motor + hotel =
2. smoke + fog =
3. motorbike + pedals =
4. cheese + hamburger =
5. smack + crash =
6. twist + whirl =
7. splash + spatter =
8. flutter + hurry =

1. _____   5. _____
2. _____   6. _____
3. _____   7. _____
4. _____   8. _____

Dictionary

Dividing Words into Syllables   A **syllable** is a word part that has one vowel sound. Some entry words have more than one syllable. In your Spelling Dictionary, the syllables in a word are divided by black dots.

un•der•stand |ŭn dər stănd′| v. **understood, understanding 1.** To get the meaning of: *Do you understand my question?* **2.** To be familiar with; know well: *I wish I could understand Spanish.*

Between which letters can you divide the word *understand*?

Practice   **Look up each word in your Spelling Dictionary. Write the word, and draw a line between the syllables.**

1. always
2. dairy
3. couple
4. already
5. anything
6. thirteen
7. homesick
8. afternoon

Review: Spelling Spree

Silly Rhymes   Write the Basic or Review Word that rhymes with each pair of words.

Example: rafter spoon   *afternoon*

1. then never
2. clean smile
3. wire space
4. thunder grand
5. heat melt
6. chase call
7. or never
8. many sing
9. shout hide
10. hair sort
11. thin slide
12. tall sight
13. crack sound
14. dome pick
15. pail load
16. come dimes

Proofreading   **17–25.** Find and cross out nine misspelled Basic or Review Words in this story. Then write each word correctly.

My grandmother turned nintynine yesterday. For her brithday she wanted to take a make believe trip. Whenever Grandma and I play pretend, she takes care of everthing. After brekfast she had all ready set up our pretend railroad car. Maps were everwhere. We sat down to enjoy ourselfs. Grandma told me about places she had been. In the afternon, we took our pretend train home.

■ **Challenge Words**   Write the Challenge Words across the top of a sheet of paper. Underneath each word, write as many new compound words as you can that have one part of the Challenge Word in them. For example, for *landmark*, you could write *landslide* and *markdown*. Use a class dictionary to help you.

Writing Application: A Post Card   What place would you most like to visit? Pretend that you are there. Write a post card to a friend. Describe things you have seen or done. Try to use five words from the list on page 86.

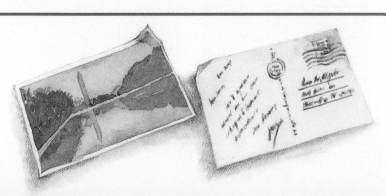

1. _____
2. _____
3. _____
4. _____
5. _____
6. _____
7. _____
8. _____
9. _____
10. _____
11. _____
12. _____
13. _____
14. _____
15. _____
16. _____
17. _____
18. _____
19. _____
20. _____
21. _____
22. _____
23. _____
24. _____
25. _____

13   Spelling Across the Curriculum

Social Studies: *Travel*

Theme Vocabulary

Augusta
Topeka
Austin
Olympia
Sacramento
Columbia
Trenton
Madison

Using Vocabulary   Write the Vocabulary Words to complete the paragraph. Use your Spelling Dictionary.

One summer my family drove from __(1)__ , Maine, to __(2)__ , California. First, we drove through New England and New York to __(3)__ , New Jersey. We saw Civil War battlefields on our way to __(4)__ , South Carolina. We crossed the plains to __(5)__ , Kansas, and visited friends who raise cattle near __(6)__ , Texas. On our return trip, we camped in the rain forests near __(7)__ , Washington, and toured dairy farms outside of __(8)__ , Wisconsin.

Understanding Vocabulary   Write a Vocabulary Word to answer each question.

9. Which city is the state capital of Washington?
10. Which city is the state capital of Texas?
11. Which city is the state capital of Maine?
12. Which city is the state capital of Wisconsin?

1. _____
2. _____
3. _____
4. _____
5. _____
6. _____
7. _____
8. _____
9. _____
10. _____
11. _____
12. _____

FACT FILE

Washington, D.C., is the capital of the United States. The President lives in the White House. Other sights to see are the Lincoln Memorial and the Washington Monument.

Enrichment

Railroad Tickets

Players: 2-4 **You need:** 40 word cards with one part of a Basic Word on each card

How to play: Players try to match cards to make Basic Words. Deal five cards to each player. Place the remaining cards face down in the "ticket office." Player 1 asks another player for a card to match a word in his or her hand. If the other player does not have the card, Player 1 draws a card from the "ticket office." When a player makes a match, either by asking or by drawing, that player lays down those cards and takes another turn. The player with the most pairs of "tickets" at the end of the game wins.

WORD TRAIN

Make a compound word train. Cut five or more train cars out of construction paper. Write a compound word on each car. The last part of the word on one car should be the same as the first part of the word on the next car. Try to use words from this unit.

Writing
A Travel Brochure

Write a travel brochure for a real or make-believe country. Write information about the country. What does the land look like? What are some things to see or do there? Add pictures. Try to use words from the lists in this unit. Be sure to proofread your brochure.

Theme: Sailing

14 Final |ər|

A. _____

_____

_____

_____

_____

_____

_____

_____

B. _____

_____

_____

_____

_____

_____

_____

C. _____

_____

_____

_____

■ Challenge

_____

_____

_____

_____

_____

LOOK at each word.

SAY each word.

Basic Words		■ Challenge
1. sailor	11. collar	21. schooner
2. harbor	12. proper	22. anchor
3. enter	13. motor	23. stellar
4. weather	14. favor	24. lunar
5. labor	15. bitter	25. solar
6. ladder	16. beggar	
7. cellar	17. shower	
8. chapter	18. temper	
9. sugar	19. feather	
10. suffer	20. doctor	

THINK about the words.

Each word has two syllables. A syllable is a word or a word part that has one vowel sound. The final syllable of each word ends with a weak vowel sound + *r*. The vowel sound is called the **schwa** sound. The schwa sound is shown as |ə|.

|ər| sounds   ent**er**, sail**or**, sug**ar**

• What sounds do you hear at the end of each word? What three patterns may spell the final |ər| sounds?

WRITE the words.

Practice   Write the Basic Words to answer the questions.

A. Which **ten** words have the final |ər| sounds spelled *er*?
B. Which **six** words have the final |ər| sounds spelled *or*?
C. Which **four** words have the final |ər| sounds spelled *ar*?

■ **Now write the five Challenge Words.** Underline the patterns that spell the final |ər| sounds.

CHECK your spelling.

> *Spelling-Meaning Hint* Can you see the word *labor* in *laboratory*? These two words are related in spelling and meaning. **Think of this:** Scientists *labor* in the *laboratory*.

labor
laboratory

Independent Practice

Spelling-Meaning   Look at the Spelling-Meaning Hint.

1-2. Write *laboratory*. Then write the Basic Word that is related to *laboratory* in spelling and meaning.

Word Analysis   Complete the exercises with Basic Words.

3-4. Write the two words that begin with the |sh| sound spelled *s* or *sh*.

5-10. Write the six words that have double consonants.

Making Inferences   Write the Basic Word that fits each clue below.

11. It is part of a book.

12. It can be a command to "come in."

13. This person is trained to work on a boat.

14. Without this, a boat has no power.

15. This person often works in a hospital.

■ Challenge Words   Write the Challenge Word that fits each clue. Use your Spelling Dictionary.

16. keeps a ship in place

17. has masts and sails

18. relating to a star

19. relating to the sun

20. having to do with the moon

| 1. |
| 2. |
| 3. |
| 4. |
| 5. |
| 6. |
| 7. |
| 8. |
| 9. |
| 10. |
| 11. |
| 12. |
| 13. |
| 14. |
| 15. |
| 16. |
| 17. |
| 18. |
| 19. |
| 20. |

Summing Up

The final |ər| sounds in a two-syllable word are often spelled with the patterns *er*, *or*, and *ar*.

Basic

1. sailor
2. harbor
3. enter
4. weather
5. labor
6. ladder
7. cellar
8. chapter
9. sugar
10. suffer
11. collar
12. proper
13. motor
14. favor
15. bitter
16. beggar
17. shower
18. temper
19. feather
20. doctor

■ **Challenge**

21. schooner
22. anchor
23. stellar
24. lunar
25. solar

Review

1. summer
2. center
3. neighbor
4. dollar
5. daughter

Proofreading Marks

¶ Indent
∧ Add something
℮ Take out something
≡ Capitalize
/ Make a small letter

Expanding Vocabulary

The Suffixes -or and -er   The suffixes -or and -er can be added to verbs to form nouns. These suffixes mean "something or someone who does" whatever the verb says. Notice what happens to a final e when the suffix is added.

BASE WORD	SUFFIX		MEANING
sail	+ **or**	= sail**or**	someone who sails
write	+ **er**	= writ**er**	someone who writes

Practice   **Add -or or -er to each underlined verb to write a noun that fits each meaning.**

1. one who <u>acts</u> (-or)
2. one who <u>bakes</u> (-er)
3. one who <u>dances</u> (-er)
4. one who <u>directs</u> (-or)
5. something that <u>broils</u> (-er)
6. something that <u>grinds</u> (-er)

1. _____
2. _____
3. _____
4. _____
5. _____
6. _____

Proofreading

Comparing with *good* and *bad*   When you compare with *good* and *bad,* remember to change their forms.

	good	**bad**
COMPARING TWO:	better	worse
COMPARING THREE OR MORE:	best	worst

Practice   **Proofread part of Pedro's book report. Find four misspelled words and two incorrect forms of *good* or *bad*. Use proofreading marks to correct the errors.**

Example: Was Tina a ~~worst~~ *worse* ~~sailer~~ *sailor* than Gary?

> *Trouble at Sea by May Eng was best than her first book. Tina, the dauter of a sailer, is caught in a storm at sea. The wether is the worse of the year. She tries to enter a harbor, but the boat's moter stops. What will Tina do?*

Review: Spelling Spree

Jobs Match   Look at the list of workers. Write a Basic or Review Word that names something each worker makes, uses, or deals with on the job.

Example: nurse   *doctor*

1. baker
2. writer
3. banker
4. carpenter
5. auto mechanic
6. forecaster
7. bird watcher
8. tailor

Hidden Words   Write the Basic or Review Word that you find in each row of letters. Don't let the other words fool you.

Example: m o t o r o o s t e r   *motor*

9. p e n e i g h b o r e d
10. d e c e n t e r r o r
11. b e g g a r d e n
12. r a s h o w e r r o r
13. r o o f a v o r i t e
14. d o c t o r d e r
15. b u s u f f e r r y
16. e n t e r r a c e
17. e a r t h a r b o r
18. l a b o r d e r
19. l a d a u g h t e r
20. a s u m m e r c y
21. t e m p e r s o n
22. c r i b i t t e r
23. i m p r o p e r k
24. c e l l o c e l l a r
25. e a r s a i l o r a l

■ **Challenge Words**   Write five questions that can be answered with the Challenge Words. Then write the answers on the back of your paper. Trade papers with a classmate, and answer each other's questions.

Example: What kind of heat can heat a house?   *solar*

📖 *Writing Application:* An Explanation Pretend that you are sailing alone across the Atlantic Ocean. The trip will take a long time. You take a break to read. What books have you brought on your journey? Why did you choose those books? Write a paragraph, describing your choices. Try to use five words from the list on page 92.

1. _____
2. _____
3. _____
4. _____
5. _____
6. _____
7. _____
8. _____
9. _____
10. _____
11. _____
12. _____
13. _____
14. _____
15. _____
16. _____
17. _____
18. _____
19. _____
20. _____
21. _____
22. _____
23. _____
24. _____
25. _____

14 Spelling Across the Curriculum

Recreation: *Sailing*

Theme Vocabulary

mast
galley
stern
hull
deck
port
captain
rigging

Using Vocabulary Write the Vocabulary Words to complete the paragraph. Use your Spelling Dictionary.

Sid, a new sailor, had just eaten his first meal in the __(1)__ . His job was interesting. The ship's __(2)__ had taught Sid how to repair the outer frame, or __(3)__ , of the ship. Now Sid looked at the sea as he walked on the top __(4)__ toward the rear part, or __(5)__ , of the ship. Sid gazed up at the tall, thin __(6)__ looming overhead and the mass of ropes that made up the __(7)__ . If only they would leave this sheltered __(8)__ and sail out to sea!

Understanding Vocabulary Write a Vocabulary Word to answer each question.

9. Where on a ship would you find a stove?
10. What has ropes and knots to support the sails?
11. Where should a ship go in a bad storm?
12. What is the tallest part of a ship?

1. _____
2. _____
3. _____
4. _____
5. _____
6. _____
7. _____
8. _____
9. _____
10. _____
11. _____
12. _____

FACT FILE

Vikings lived long ago in northern Europe. In their ships with one square sail and a row of oars on each side, they sailed to North America before Columbus did.

Enrichment

👪 *Climb the Mast*

Players: 2, a caller   **You need:** a yardstick, a broom handle, or any other long stick for the "mast"

How to play: The caller says a Basic or Review Word. If the first player spells it correctly, he or she grabs the bottom of the mast with one hand. If the second player spells the next word correctly, he or she grabs the mast just above the first player's hand. As players spell words, they move their hands one over the other up the mast. If they spell the word incorrectly, they cannot move. The player who reaches the top of the mast first wins.

SAILING SHIPS

Find pictures of sailing ships in an encyclopedia or resource book. Make a poster showing ships from different periods in history. Label the parts of the ships, and write a few sentences to describe each drawing. When was the ship built? Who built it? How big was it? Try to use words from the lists in this unit.

📖 *Writing*
Old Man and the Sea

Pretend that you are a reporter. Interview a famous sea captain. What dangers has the captain faced? What is it like to spend months at a time at sea? Write your questions and the captain's answers. Try to use words from the lists in this unit.

Be sure to proofread your paper.

(Theme: Money)

15 Final |l| or |əl|

A. _____

_____

_____

B. _____

_____

_____

_____

C. _____

_____

_____

_____

_____

_____

_____

_____

_____

_____

■ Challenge

_____

_____

_____

_____

_____

LOOK at each word.

SAY each word.

Basic Words   ■ Challenge

1. nickel	11. towel	21. decimal
2. metal	12. medal	22. financial
3. total	13. battle	23. trifle
4. eagle	14. candle	24. cancel
5. middle	15. trouble	25. industrial
6. special	16. handle	
7. final	17. simple	
8. model	18. uncle	
9. bottle	19. title	
10. double	20. cattle	

THINK about the words.

Each two-syllable word has the final |l| or |əl| sounds:

|l| or |əl| nick**el**, fin**al**, midd**le**

• What are three spelling patterns for the final |l| or |əl| sounds?

WRITE the words.

Practice   Write the Basic Words to answer the questions about the final |l| and |əl| sounds.

A. Which **three** words have these sounds spelled *el*?
B. Which **five** words have these sounds spelled *al*?
C. Which **twelve** words have these sounds spelled *le*?

■ **Now write the five Challenge Words.** Underline the patterns that spell the final |l| and |əl| sounds.

CHECK your spelling.

Spelling-Meaning Hint   How can you remember how to spell the schwa sound in *final*? Think of the |ă| sound in the related word *finality*.

**fin[a]l
fin[a]lity**

Independent Practice

Spelling-Meaning   Look at the Spelling-Meaning Hint.

1-2. Write *final* and *finality*. Underline the letter that has the schwa sound in one word and the |ă| sound in the other word.

Word Analysis   Complete the exercises with Basic Words.

3-6. Write the word that rhymes with each word below.

   3. riddle
   4. pedal
   5. dimple
   6. petal

|ə|
nick**e**l
tot**a**l
eag**le**

7-10. Write the four words that have a long vowel sound.

Analogies   Write the Basic Word that completes each analogy.

11. *Tin* is to *can* as *glass* is to ____ .
12. *Niece* is to *nephew* as *aunt* is to ____ .
13. *Bulb* is to *lamp* as *wick* is to ____ .
14. *Once* is to *twice* as *single* is to ____ .
15. *Dollar* is to *five dollars* as *penny* is to ____ .

■ **Challenge Words**   Write the Challenge Word that fits each meaning. Use your Spelling Dictionary.

16. something unimportant
17. having to do with industry
18. to call off
19. of or based on ten
20. having to do with the management of money

1. _____
2. _____
3. _____
4. _____
5. _____
6. _____
7. _____
8. _____
9. _____
10. _____
11. _____
12. _____
13. _____
14. _____
15. _____
16. _____
17. _____
18. _____
19. _____
20. _____

Summing Up

The final |l| or |əl| sounds are often spelled with the pattern *el*, *al*, or *le* in a two-syllable word.

Basic

1. nickel
2. metal
3. total
4. eagle
5. middle
6. special
7. final
8. model
9. bottle
10. double
11. towel
12. medal
13. battle
14. candle
15. trouble
16. handle
17. simple
18. uncle
19. title
20. cattle

■ Challenge

21. decimal
22. financial
23. trifle
24. cancel
25. industrial

Review

1. little
2. able
3. circle
4. purple
5. apple

1. _____
2. _____
3. _____
4. _____
5. _____
6. _____

Expanding Vocabulary

The Suffix -al Sometimes the final letters *al* are a suffix meaning "having to do with." When this suffix is added to a noun, it forms an adjective. Notice that when a word ends with *e*, the *e* is dropped before *-al* is added.

BASE WORD	SUFFIX			MEANING
coast	+ **al**	=	coast**al**	having to do with the coast
tide	+ **al**	=	tid**al**	having to do with the tide

Practice Add *-al* to the noun in parentheses to write an adjective that fits each sentence.

1. Many countries work together on _____ projects. (globe)
2. The flight of geese marks a _____ change. (season)
3. "The Star-Spangled Banner" is our _____ song. (nation)
4. These books are my _____ property. (person)
5. Her painting is a beautiful example of _____ art. (tribe)

1. _____   4. _____

2. _____   5. _____

3. _____

Dictionary

The Schwa Sound The **schwa** sound is the weak vowel sound you hear in the last syllable of *final*. The dictionary shows this sound as |ə|. The pronunciation key shows words with different vowel letters that spell the schwa sound.

PART OF A PRONUNCIATION KEY

final |fī′nəl| |ə| **ago, item, pencil, atom, circus**

Practice Each word below has been divided into syllables. Compare each word with its pronunciation. Then write the word, and underline the letter that spells the |ə| sound.

1. al·bum |ăl′ bəm|
2. com·pass |kŭm′ pəs|
3. lev·el |lĕv′ əl|
4. po·lite |pə līt′|
5. nick·el |nĭk′ əl|
6. fos·sil |fŏs′ əl|

Review: Spelling Spree

Syllable Addition   Combine the underlined syllables in each pair of words to write a Basic or Review Word.

Example: <u>mod</u>ern + lev<u>el</u>   *model*

1. <u>cir</u>cus + un<u>cle</u>
2. <u>lit</u>ter + rat<u>tle</u>
3. <u>bat</u>ter + tat<u>tle</u>
4. <u>sim</u>mer + rip<u>ple</u>
5. <u>can</u>dy + bun<u>dle</u>
6. <u>pur</u>pose + dim<u>ple</u>
7. <u>mid</u>day + rid<u>dle</u>
8. <u>to</u>ken + men<u>tal</u>

9. <u>a</u>cre + bub<u>ble</u>
10. <u>tow</u>er + cha<u>pel</u>
11. <u>un</u>til + cir<u>cle</u>
12. <u>cat</u>bird + set<u>tle</u>
13. <u>ti</u>ger + gen<u>tle</u>
14. <u>fi</u>ber + spi<u>nal</u>
15. <u>ea</u>ger + wig<u>gle</u>
16. <u>bot</u>tom + man<u>tle</u>

Proofreading   17-25. Find and cross out nine misspelled Basic or Review Words in this sign. Then write each word correctly.

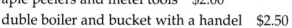

Yard Sale Today

Come and buy lots of speshel items at low prices!

It's no troble to discuss prices!

modle ship in a bottle $5.00

eagle medel   50¢

aple peelers and metel tools $2.00

duble boiler and bucket with a handel $2.50

Try some juice while you look. It's only a nickle!

■ **Challenge Words**   Look at the Syllable Addition activity. Divide the Challenge Words into syllables. Then find other words with those syllables. Write the words and the Challenge Words as addition problems.

Example: <u>dec</u>orate + <u>it</u>em + an<u>imal</u> = *decimal*

📖 *Writing Application:* A Paragraph   Write a paragraph about ways you have earned an allowance or extra money. Try to use five words from the list on page 98.

1. _____
2. _____
3. _____
4. _____
5. _____
6. _____
7. _____
8. _____
9. _____
10. _____
11. _____
12. _____
13. _____
14. _____
15. _____
16. _____
17. _____
18. _____
19. _____
20. _____
21. _____
22. _____
23. _____
24. _____
25. _____

15 Spelling Across the Curriculum

Math: *Money*

Theme Vocabulary

money
bank
cent
quarter
deposit
withdraw
savings
passbook

Using Vocabulary Write the Vocabulary Words to complete the paragraph. Use your Spelling Dictionary.

Last Thursday I opened my first account at a __(1)__ . I wanted to start a __(2)__ account in order to save for a bike. I had to __(3)__ at least ten dollars into the account. The teller said my account would earn money four times a year and would be worth the most at the end of the fourth __(4)__ . The teller handed me a __(5)__ to keep track of the __(6)__ in the account. I will not __(7)__ a penny because I need every __(8)__ to buy a bike.

Understanding Vocabulary Write *yes* or *no* to answer each question.

9. Is money kept in a passbook?
10. Do you take out money when you withdraw it?
11. Could you get change for a cent?
12. Do you deposit money to add it to your account?

1. _____
2. _____
3. _____
4. _____
5. _____
6. _____
7. _____
8. _____
9. _____
10. _____
11. _____
12. _____

FACT FILE

When you put your money in a bank, the bank pays you for keeping your money there. The money the bank pays you is called interest. Interest is added to your savings during the year.

Enrichment

Spelling Savings

Players: 2-4 **You need:** 25 cards with a Basic or Review Word on each card. Write *$1.00* on 5 cards and *$5.00* on 20 cards.

How to play: On the back of each $1.00 "bill," write a meaning or a clue for a Review Word. Write meanings or clues for the Basic Words on the $5.00 bills. Stack the bills clue-side up. Players take turns choosing a bill and then naming and spelling the word that fits the clue. If the word is spelled correctly, the player keeps the bill. If not, the bill is returned to the stack. The player with the most "money" at the end of the game wins.

Writing
A Dollar's Life

Pretend that you are a dollar bill. Where were you made? Who has owned you? Where have you been? Have your looks changed over the years? Write your autobiography. Try to use words from the lists in this unit. Be sure to proofread your paper.

DOLLAR DESIGNS

If you could design your own money, what would it look like? What kinds of pictures would it have on it? Design three bills or coins. Draw both the front and the back. Then write several sentences for each bill or coin. Tell why you chose each design. Try to use words from the lists in this unit.

Theme: Exercise

16 Words with -ed and -ing

A. _____

_____

_____

_____

B. _____

_____

_____

_____

_____

_____

_____

_____

_____

_____

_____

_____

_____

■ Challenge

_____

_____

_____

_____

_____

LOOK at each word.

SAY each word.

Basic Words		■ Challenge
1. dancing	11. dimmed	21. breathing
2. skipped	12. rubbing	22. tiring
3. hiking	13. striped	23. urged
4. flipped	14. wasting	24. scarred
5. snapping	15. traced	25. striving
6. raced	16. stripped	
7. landed	17. tanning	
8. pleasing	18. smelling	
9. checking	19. phoning	
10. dared	20. fainted	

THINK about the words.

Each word has a base word and an ending. A **base word** is a word to which a beginning or an ending can be added.

race + **ed** = rac**ed**   land + **ed** = land**ed**
sna**p** + **ing** = sna**pping**

- Look at the examples. Which letter was dropped when the ending was added to *race*? Which word, *land* or *snap*, ends with one vowel and one consonant? How does the spelling of that word change when the ending is added?

WRITE the words.

Practice   Write the Basic Words to answer the questions.

A. Which **four** words did not have a spelling change when *-ed* or *-ing* was added?

B. Which **sixteen** words did have a spelling change?

■ **Now write the five Challenge Words.** Underline the words that drop a final *e* when *-ed* or *-ing* is added.

CHECK your spelling.

> *Spelling-Meaning Hint* *Please* and *pleasing* have different vowel sounds than *pleasant* and *pleasure*. **Think of this:** A *pleasing* gift gives *pleasure*.

ple a se
ple a sing
ple a sant
ple a sure

Independent Practice

Spelling-Meaning Look at the Spelling-Meaning Hint.

1-2. Write *pleasing* and *pleasant*. Underline the letters that spell the |ĕ| sound in one word and the |ē| sound in the other word.

Word Analysis Complete the exercises with Basic Words.

3. Write the word that has the |f| sound spelled *ph*.

4-7. Write the four words with the |ă| sound.

8-10. Write the three words that rhyme with *shipped*.

Word Clues Write the Basic Word that fits each clue.
11. synonym for *sniffing*
12. People often carry a backpack when they are doing this.
13. past tense of *faint*
14. having long, narrow lines of different colors
15. copied by following lines seen through a sheet of paper

■ **Challenge Words** Write the Challenge Word that fits each meaning. Use your Spelling Dictionary.
16. convinced or pleaded with
17. becoming weak or weary
18. reaching toward a goal
19. taking air into the lungs
20. left with a mark from a healed wound

1. _____
2. _____
3. _____
4. _____
5. _____
6. _____
7. _____
8. _____
9. _____
10. _____
11. _____
12. _____
13. _____
14. _____
15. _____
16. _____
17. _____
18. _____
19. _____
20. _____

Summing Up

If a word ends with *e*, drop the *e* before adding *-ed* or *-ing*.
If a one-syllable word ends with one vowel followed by a single consonant, double the consonant before adding *-ed* or *-ing*.

Basic

1. dancing
2. skipped
3. hiking
4. flipped
5. snapping
6. raced
7. landed
8. pleasing
9. checking
10. dared
11. dimmed
12. rubbing
13. striped
14. wasting
15. traced
16. stripped
17. tanning
18. smelling
19. phoning
20. fainted

■ **Challenge**

21. breathing
22. tiring
23. urged
24. scarred
25. striving

Review

1. cared
2. joking
3. tapping
4. wrapped
5. fixing

Expanding Vocabulary

Meanings for *check* The word *check* has more than one meaning. The dictionary entry below gives four meanings.

> **check** |chĕk| *n., pl.* **checks** **1.** Something that restrains or controls. **2.** Examination to be sure something is as it should be. **3.** A mark made to show that something has been noted. **4.** A restaurant bill.

Practice **Write the number of the definition of *check* that fits each sentence. Use the dictionary entry above.**
1. Please put a check next to your name.
2. Try to keep a check on your enthusiasm.
3. I did a complete check of my homework.
4. When we had finished the meal, we asked for the check.

1. _____ 2. _____ 3. _____ 4. _____

Dictionary

Entry Words as Base Words If you want to know if *dimmed* has one or two *m*'s, look up the base word *dim*. The dictionary entry shows forms of *dim*.

> **dim** |dĭm| *adj.* **dimmer, dimmest 1.** Somewhat dark. **2.** Giving off little light: *a dim lamp.* **3.** Not clearly seen: *a dim shape.* *v.* **dimmed, dimming** To make or become dim.

Adjectives and verbs with the endings *-er, -est, -ed,* and *-ing* are usually listed with their base words.

Practice **Write the answer to each question.**
1. What are the *-er* and *-est* forms of the word *dim*?
2. Which two words are the verb forms of *dim*?

1. _____ _____

2. _____ _____

Write the entry word you would look up to find each word.
3. flipped   5. joking
4. phoning   6. wrapped

3. _____ 5. _____

4. _____ 6. _____

Review: Spelling Spree

Adding Endings   Write the Basic or Review Word that combines each base word and ending.

1. land + ed
2. trace + ed
3. faint + ed
4. fix + ing
5. please + ing
6. stripe + ed
7. dare + ed
8. smell + ing
9. hike + ing
10. tan + ing
11. dim + ed
12. wrap + ed
13. care + ed
14. phone + ing
15. strip + ed
16. joke + ing
17. flip + ed

Proofreading   **18-25.** Find and cross out eight misspelled Basic or Review Words in this story. Then write each word correctly.

Hank walked into the new health club and saw a big room with brightly striped wallpaper. A man at a desk was cheking membership cards. Beyond him people were danceing and snaping their fingers to music. A group of men skiped rope. An instructor was fixing some weights for a woman. The woman was rubing white chalk on her hands. Hank began taping his feet to the music. Without waisting a moment, he rased to sign up.

■ **Challenge Words**   Write each Challenge Word and its base word. Then write two sentences for each pair. Use the base word in the first sentence. Then use the Challenge Word in the second sentence.

📖 *Writing Application:* An Ad   Pretend you are the owner of a new health club. Write an ad to make people want to join. What kinds of activities are there? How much does it cost? Try to use five words from the list on page 104.

1. _____
2. _____
3. _____
4. _____
5. _____
6. _____
7. _____
8. _____
9. _____
10. _____
11. _____
12. _____
13. _____
14. _____
15. _____
16. _____
17. _____
18. _____
19. _____
20. _____
21. _____
22. _____
23. _____
24. _____
25. _____

16 Spelling Across the Curriculum

Health: *Exercise*

Theme Vocabulary

exercise
energy
fitness
athlete
stretch
strengthen
balance
workout

Using Vocabulary Write the Vocabulary Words to complete the paragraph. Use your Spelling Dictionary.

Elena took her mark at the starting line. As she leaned forward, she felt her muscles pull and __(1)__. Elena was in top form. She knew that health and total __(2)__ were important to a trained __(3)__. She ate well to give her body lots of __(4)__. She got plenty of __(5)__ by jogging and going to the gym for a daily __(6)__. She even took skating lessons to improve her sense of __(7)__ and to help build and __(8)__ her leg muscles. Elena was ready for this race!

Understanding Vocabulary Write *yes* if the underlined word is used correctly. Write *no* if it is not.

9. The diver lost his <u>balance</u> and fell into the water.
10. Watching the movie was a tough <u>workout</u>.
11. I have lots of <u>energy</u> after a good night's sleep.
12. Part of my <u>exercise</u> routine is napping every day.

1. _____
2. _____
3. _____
4. _____
5. _____
6. _____
7. _____
8. _____
9. _____
10. _____
11. _____
12. _____

FACT FILE

When you breathe, your body takes in oxygen to give you energy. Aerobic exercises such as jogging, biking, and fast walking help your body do a better job of using oxygen.

Enrichment

KEEPING FIT

Make a collage about exercise. Cut out magazine pictures that show people exercising in different ways. Paste the pictures on a piece of heavy construction paper. Add cut-out words, phrases, and sentences that have to do with exercise. Try to use words from the lists in this unit. Arrange the cutouts in interesting ways, and fill the entire paper.

Charades

Players: Teams of 2 or more
You need: 25 word cards with a Basic or Review Word on each card, a clock
How to play: A player from one team picks a word card and acts out the word for his or her teammates, who have one minute to guess the word and spell it correctly. If they do, the team gets a point. If not, another team may guess. The team with the most points at the end wins.

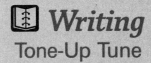 ## Writing
Tone-Up Tune

You have been hired to write the theme song for a new exercise show. Write the lyrics for your song, using a familiar tune to go along with the words. Try to make the song lively and interesting so that people watching the show will want to exercise. Try to use words from the lists in this unit. Be sure to proofread your paper.

Lift up your arms. Stretch to the sky...

17 Final |ē|

A.

LOOK at each word.

SAY each word.

Basic Words   ■ Challenge

1. beauty	11. duty	21. fiery
2. ugly	12. hungry	22. envy
3. lazy	13. lonely	23. mercy
4. marry	14. alley	24. medley
5. ready	15. body	25. imaginary
6. sorry	16. plenty	
7. empty	17. turkey	
8. honey	18. hockey	
9. valley	19. fifty	
10. movie	20. monkey	

THINK about the words.

Each word has two syllables and ends with the final |ē| sound:

final |ē| beaut**y**, hon**ey**

• What are two spelling patterns for the final |ē| sound? What pattern spells the final |ē| sound in the Elephant Word?

B.

WRITE the words.

Practice   Write the Basic Words to answer the questions.

A. Which **thirteen** words have the final |ē| sound spelled *y*?
B. Which **six** words have the final |ē| sound spelled *ey*?
C. Which **one** word has the final |ē| sound spelled another way?

C.

■ Challenge

■ **Now write the five Challenge Words.** Underline the patterns that spell the final |ē| sound.

CHECK your spelling.

movie
moving

> *Spelling-Meaning Hint* Did you know that the word *movie* comes from the words *moving picture*? *Movie* is related in spelling and meaning to *moving*. **Think of this:** A *movie* shows people *moving*.

Independent Practice

Spelling-Meaning Look at the Spelling-Meaning Hint.

1-2. Write *moving*. Then write the Basic Word that is related to *moving* in spelling and meaning.

Word Analysis Complete the exercises with Basic Words.

3. Write the word with the |yo͞o| sound spelled *eau*.

4-6. Write the three words that have the |ĕ| sound.

7-10. Write the four words that have double consonants.

Analogies Write the Basic Word that completes each analogy.

11. *Silkworm* is to *silk* as *bee* is to ____.

12. *Water* is to *thirsty* as *food* is to ____.

13. *Desert* is to *camel* as *jungle* is to ____.

14. *Moo* is to *cow* as *gobble* is to ____.

15. *Ball* is to *soccer* as *puck* is to ____.

/ē/ **honey**
beauty

■ **Challenge Words** Write the Challenge Word that fits each clue. Use your Spelling Dictionary.

16. synonym for *jealousy*

17. describes a dragon's breath

18. kindness a knight would show

19. not real

20. music made up of different songs

1. _____
2. _____
3. _____
4. _____
5. _____
6. _____
7. _____
8. _____
9. _____
10. _____
11. _____
12. _____
13. _____
14. _____
15. _____
16. _____
17. _____
18. _____
19. _____
20. _____

Summing Up

The final |ē| sound is often spelled *y* or *ey* in a two-syllable word.

Basic

1. beauty
2. ugly
3. lazy
4. marry
5. ready
6. sorry
7. empty
8. honey
9. valley
10. movie
11. duty
12. hungry
13. lonely
14. alley
15. body
16. plenty
17. turkey
18. hockey
19. fifty
20. monkey

■ **Challenge**

21. fiery
22. envy
23. mercy
24. medley
25. imaginary

Review

1. pretty
2. sadly
3. friendly
4. city
5. slowly

Proofreading Marks

¶ Indent
∧ Add something
ℯ Take out something
≡ Capitalize
/ Make a small letter

Expanding Vocabulary

Exact Words How would you describe an unused lot that is overgrown with weeds? Would you call it an *empty* lot or a *vacant* lot? *Vacant* is more exact because it describes a place that has been deserted. Use exact words to make your writing clearer.

Practice **Write the best word to replace *empty* or *dark* in each sentence. Use your Thesaurus.**

| **empty** blank, vacant | **dark** murky, shady |

1. The house was <u>empty</u> long after we moved.
2. I have only three more <u>empty</u> pages to fill in my diary.
3. A frog disappeared into the <u>dark</u> water of the pond.
4. I found relief from the hot sun in the cool, <u>dark</u> forest.

1. _____   3. _____

2. _____   4. _____

Proofreading

Abbreviations Each abbreviation for the name of a month begins with a capital letter and ends with a period. (See page 247 for abbreviations of other months.)

April Apr.   January Jan.   September Sept.

Practice **Proofread the Beast's diary. Find four misspelled words and three incorrect abbreviations. Use proofreading marks to correct the errors.**

Example: jan. 4   A witch turned me into an ~~uglie~~ *ugly* beast.

Mar. 23 Everyone screams at me in horror. I walk the streets slowley and sadly.

aug. 6 I have plenny of gold but no friends.

Sept 9 A girl named Beauty was friendly to me.

oct 26 Beauty wants to marrie me!

Dec. 14 Thanks to Beauty, I am no longer a lonly beast.

Review: Spelling Spree

Riddles   Write a Basic or Review Word to answer each riddle.

Example: What kind of "T" is nice to look at?   *pretty*

1. What kind of "Z" does not like to work?
2. What kind of "T" has streets and buildings?
3. What kind of "T" is half of one hundred?
4. What kind of "D" has arms and legs?
5. What kind of "V" do you watch in a theater?
6. What kind of "T" has nothing in it?
7. What kind of "T" is something you are supposed to do?
8. What kind of "D" is always prepared?
9. What kind of "T" is a lot of something?

Syllable Scramble   Two of the three syllables in each item below form a Basic or Review Word. Write the words correctly.

Example: ty ug emp   *empty*

10. ly eve slow
11. sad fif ly
12. ley hon al
13. lone read ly
14. ley fif val
15. mon slow key
16. ry mov mar
17. ty tur beau

18. laz friend ly
19. ty lone pret
20. sor ug ry
21. hock gry hun
22. hon plen ey
23. key beau tur
24. ug cit ly
25. tur ey hock

■ **Challenge Words**   Look at the Riddles activity. Write a riddle for each Challenge Word. On the back of your paper, write the answers. Then have a classmate try to solve your riddles.

Example: What kind of "E" can be played on the piano? *medley*

📖 *Writing Application:* Creative Writing   Think of a familiar fairy tale. Write a new ending for it. For example, what might have happened if Little Red Riding Hood had made friends with the wolf? Try to use five words from the list on page 110.

1. _____
2. _____
3. _____
4. _____
5. _____
6. _____
7. _____
8. _____
9. _____
10. _____
11. _____
12. _____
13. _____
14. _____
15. _____
16. _____
17. _____
18. _____
19. _____
20. _____
21. _____
22. _____
23. _____
24. _____
25. _____

17 Spelling Across the Curriculum

Language Arts: *Fairy Tales*

Theme Vocabulary

dungeon
princess
elf
prince
dragon
wicked
wizard
enchanted

Using Vocabulary Write the Vocabulary Words to complete the paragraph. Use your Spelling Dictionary.

The king's daughter Lilla, the __(1)__ of Trinia, quickly followed her tiny fairylike friend, the __(2)__. They had been searching for her brother, the __(3)__, for days. A fire-breathing __(4)__ had locked him in a cold, dark __(5)__ in a faraway castle. This castle had become __(6)__ after an evil __(7)__ named Zin had placed it under a spell. Zin was so __(8)__ that Lilla feared she might never see her brother again if she did not hurry.

Understanding Vocabulary Write a Vocabulary Word to match each clue.

9. It could stand underneath a mushroom.
10. It is a home for prisoners.
11. He wears a crown.
12. It would be a good pet to have at a barbecue.

1. _____
2. _____
3. _____
4. _____
5. _____
6. _____
7. _____
8. _____
9. _____
10. _____
11. _____
12. _____

FACT FILE

Hans Christian Andersen wrote fairy tales based on real feelings. In "The Ugly Duckling," a story of a lonely young swan, Andersen may have been writing about his own life.

Enrichment

Ready, Set, Go!

Players: 2, a caller **You need:** 6 cards—two labeled *ey*, two labeled *y*, and two labeled *ie* **How to play:** The two players are each given a set of the three endings to place in front of them. The caller calls out a Basic or Review Word. Each player tries to be the first to hold up the card with the correct ending. The first player to do so and spell the word correctly wins a point. The player with the most points at the end wins the game.

Writing
An Enchanting Letter

Write a fan letter to your favorite fairy tale character. What do you like most about this person? What did he or she do in the story that you admired? Try to use words from the lists in this unit. Be sure to proofread your paper.

FAIRY TALE PUPPETS

Make finger puppets for a puppet show based on a fairy tale. Draw the characters from a famous fairy tale on stiff paper. Cut out each puppet, and paste a paper ring on the back of it for your finger to fit through. Then act out the fairy tale. Try to use words from this unit in your play.

18 Review: Units 13-17

Unit 13   Compound Words   pp. 84-89

seat belt	everywhere	anything	already
background	breakfast	meanwhile	ourselves
forever	make-believe		

Remember: A compound word may be written as one word, as two words joined by a hyphen, or as two separate words.

rail road

Write the compound word that contains each word below.
 1. mean   **2.** for   **3.** ready   **4.** our   **5.** any   **6.** back
Write the compound word that completes each analogy.
 7. *Nothing* is to *everything* as *nowhere* is to ____.
 8. *Nonfiction* is to *real* as *fiction* is to ____.
 9. *Sandwich* is to *lunch* as *cereal* is to ____.
 10. *Boat* is to *life jacket* as *car* is to ____.

1. _____
2. _____
3. _____
4. _____
5. _____
6. _____
7. _____
8. _____
9. _____
10. _____

Unit 14   Final |ər| pp. 90-95

sailor	cellar	chapter	harbor	sugar
beggar	doctor	feather	collar	motor

Remember: The final |ər| sounds are spelled **er, or,** or **ar** in two-syllable words.

|ər| enter |ər| harbor |ər| sugar

Write a spelling word by adding the second syllable.
 11. sail | ____   **14.** doc | ____
 12. har | ____   **15.** mo | ____
 13. beg | ____
Write the word that fits each clue.
 16. found in a book   **19.** found on a bird
 17. found in some foods   **20.** part of some buildings
 18. found on some shirts

11. _____
12. _____
13. _____
14. _____
15. _____
16. _____
17. _____
18. _____
19. _____
20. _____

Half of the words from each unit are reviewed on these pages.
The rest are reviewed on pages 235–237.

Unit 15   Final |l| or |əl| pp. 96-101

double	special	final	model	eagle
towel	candle	medal	trouble	cattle

Remember: The final |l| or |əl| sounds are often spelled **el, al,** or **le** in two-syllable words.

nick**el**
tot**al**
eag**le**

Write the word that belongs in each group.

21. hawk, owl, _____   24. sheep, horses, _____
22. single, _____, triple   25. example, copy, _____
23. lantern, torch, _____

Write the word that matches each meaning below.

26. last   29. difficulty
27. an award   30. cloth used for wiping
28. not common   something wet

21. _____
22. _____
23. _____
24. _____
25. _____
26. _____
27. _____
28. _____
29. _____
30. _____

Unit 16   Words with *-ed* and *-ing*   pp. 102-107

skipped	snapping	checking	pleasing	raced
fainted	stripped	phoning	striped	rubbing

Remember: check + **ing** = check**ing**
race − e + **ed** = rac**ed**
snap + p + **ing** = sna**pping**

Write the word that rhymes with each word below.

31. painted   33. teasing
32. paced   34. tapping

Write a spelling word by adding *-ed* or *-ing* to each word.

35. phone   38. strip
36. skip   39. check
37. rub   40. stripe

31. _____
32. _____
33. _____
34. _____
35. _____
36. _____
37. _____
38. _____
39. _____
40. _____

18 Review

| ready | valley | beauty | honey | movie |
| hockey | lonely | fifty | alley | hungry |

Remember: final |ē| → **y, ey**

/ē/ hon**ey**
be**auty**

Write the word that completes each sentence.

41. Snow falls more often in the mountains than in the ____ .
42. We took a shortcut through the narrow ____ .
43. The queen had great charm and ____ .
44. Are you ____ to take the test today?

Write the word that completes each phrase.

45. ____ theater   48. thirsty and ____
46. ____ puck   49. sad and ____
47. ____ dollars   50. as sweet as ____

41. _____
42. _____
43. _____
44. _____
45. _____
46. _____
47. _____
48. _____
49. _____
50. _____

■ Challenge Words   Units 13-17   pp. 84-113

| imaginary | striving | trifle | financial | handkerchief |
| schooner | medley | tiring | stellar | nationwide |

Write the word that fits each clue.

51. has to do with money
52. used when you sneeze
53. has to do with stars
54. something that is sung
55. throughout a whole nation
56. exists only in your mind

Write the word that rhymes with the underlined word.

57. The exercise was ____ , and we were all <u>perspiring</u>.
58. I could go on a ____ , but a bus would arrive <u>sooner</u>.
59. Open the window a ____ , or I will surely <u>stifle</u>.
60. Every swimmer was ____ to win first place in <u>diving</u>.

51. _____
52. _____
53. _____
54. _____
55. _____
56. _____
57. _____
58. _____
59. _____
60. _____

Vowel Changes: Schwa to Short Vowel Sound

Words from the same word families are often related in both spelling and meaning. Knowing how to spell one word may help you spell other, related words. Read this paragraph.

> Jeremy wore a knight's costume that looked like real **metal**. However, it was really made from stiff silver cloth that looked **metallic** in the light.

Think
- How are *metal* and *metallic* related in meaning?
- What vowel sound does the letter *a* spell in each word?

Here are more related words with the same change in vowel sounds as *metal* and *metallic*. Note that the spelling of the vowel sounds remains the same in each pair.

total	medal	formal
totality	medallion	formality

metal
metallic

Apply and Extend

Complete these activities on a separate sheet of paper.

1. Look up the words in the Word Box above in the Spelling Dictionary. Write a short paragraph, using one word pair.

2. With a partner list as many words as you can that are related to *metal, total, medal,* and *formal*. Then look on page 275 of your Spelling-Meaning Index. Add any other words that you find in these families to your list.

Summing Up You can remember how to spell the schwa sound in some words by thinking of a related word with a short vowel sound spelled the same way.

Story

Characters can be people or animals, real or make-believe. What do you learn about a pig named Wilbur in this passage?

One afternoon in June, when Wilbur was almost two months old, he wandered out into his small yard outside the barn. Fern had not arrived for her usual visit. Wilbur stood in the sun feeling lonely and bored.

"There's never anything to do around here," he thought. He walked slowly to his food trough and sniffed to see if anything had been overlooked at lunch. He found a small strip of potato skin and ate it. His back itched, so he leaned against the fence and rubbed against the boards. When he tired of this, he walked indoors and sat down. He didn't feel like going to sleep, he didn't feel like digging, he was tired of standing still, tired of lying down. "I'm less than two months old, and I'm tired of living," he said. He walked out to the yard again.

"When I'm out here," he said, "there's no place to go but in. When I'm indoors, there's no place to go but out in the yard."

"That's where you're wrong, my friend, my friend," said a voice.

from Charlotte's Web *by E. B. White*

Think and Discuss

1. What does this passage tell you about Wilbur, the main **character**? What is Wilbur's problem?
2. **Where** and **when** does this part of the story take place?
3. What do you think will happen next in the **plot**?

The Writing Process

The passage on page 118 is from the story *Charlotte's Web*. Every story has a beginning, a middle, and an end, which make up the **plot**. The beginning introduces the main **characters** and gives the **setting**, which tells where and when the story takes place. The middle tells how the characters face a problem and gives the main events. The end wraps up the story events in a way that makes sense.

Assignment: Write a Story

Step One: Prewriting

1. Make a list of story ideas. Discuss them with a classmate. Choose one to write about.
2. Write ideas for the beginning, the middle, and the end.

Step Two: Write a First Draft

1. Think about your purpose and your audience.
2. Do not worry about mistakes—just write!

Step Three: Revise

1. Does your story have a beginning, a middle, and an end? Does the ending make sense?
2. Use your Thesaurus to find exact words.
3. Read your story to a classmate. Make your changes.

Step Four: Proofread

1. Did you capitalize and punctuate quotations correctly?
2. Did you spell all words correctly? Copy any words that you misspelled into your Notebook for Writing.

Step Five: Publish

1. Copy your story neatly. Add a title, and draw a cover.
2. Share your story by adding it to the class library.

Composition Words

railroad
trouble
afternoon
skipped
weather
raced
special
sorry

Proofreading Marks

¶   Indent
∧   Add something
℘   Take out something
≡   Capitalize
/   Make a small letter

(Theme: Sea Life)

19 Spelling |k|, |ng|, and |kw|

A. _____

_____

_____

B. _____

_____

_____

_____

_____

_____

_____

_____

_____

_____

C. _____

_____

D. _____

_____

■ Challenge

_____

_____

_____

_____

_____

_____

LOOK at each word.

SAY each word.

Basic Words   ■ Challenge

1. shark	11. crooked	21. aquatic
2. attack	12. drink	22. squid
3. risk	13. topic	23. barracuda
4. public	14. track	24. speckled
5. sink	15. blanket	25. peculiar
6. question	16. struck	
7. electric	17. mistake	
8. jacket	18. junk	
9. blank	19. squirrel	
🐘 10. ache	🐘 20. stomach	

THINK about the words.

Each word has one of these sounds:

|k|	shar**k**, atta**ck**, publi**c**	|kw|	**qu**estion
|ng|	si**n**k		

• What are three spellings for the |k| sound? What letter spells the |ng| sound before a *k*? What is one spelling for the |kw| sounds? How are the Elephant Words different?

WRITE the words.

Practice **Write the Basic Words to answer the questions.**

A. Which **four** words have the |k| sound spelled *ck*?
B. Which **twelve** words have the |k| sound spelled *k* or *c*? Circle the five words with the |ng| sound.
C. Which **two** words have the |k| sound spelled other ways?
D. Which **two** words have the |kw| sounds?

■ **Now write the five Challenge Words.** Underline the letters that spell the |k| and the |kw| sounds.

CHECK your spelling.

electric
electricity

> *Spelling-Meaning Hint* How can you remember to spell the |s| sound in *electricity* with a *c*? Think of the related word *electric*. The sound of the *c* changes, but the spelling remains the same.

Independent Practice

Spelling-Meaning Look at the Spelling-Meaning Hint.
1-2. Write *electricity*. Then write the Basic Word that is related to *electricity* in spelling and meaning.

Word Analysis Complete the exercises with Basic Words.

3-4. Write the present tense of *sank* and *drank*.

5-8. Write the word that rhymes with each word below.
   5. dark   6. luck   7. skunk   8. racket

9-10. Write *blank*. Then write another Basic Word that contains *blank*.

Word Clues Write the Basic Word that fits each clue.
11. It eats nuts.
12. opposite of *answer*
13. where your food goes
14. synonym for *pain*
15. A train needs one.

■ **Challenge Words** Write the Challenge Word that fits each meaning. Use your Spelling Dictionary.
16. not usual
17. a long, narrow fish
18. living in water
19. spotted
20. a sea animal related to the octopus

1. _____
2. _____
3. _____
4. _____
5. _____
6. _____
7. _____
8. _____
9. _____
10. _____
11. _____
12. _____
13. _____
14. _____
15. _____
16. _____
17. _____
18. _____
19. _____
20. _____

Summing Up

The |k| sound is often spelled *k*, *ck*, or *c*.
The |ng| sound before *k* is spelled *n*.
The |kw| sounds are spelled *qu*.

Basic

1. shark
2. attack
3. risk
4. public
5. sink
6. question
7. electric
8. jacket
9. blank
10. ache
11. crooked
12. drink
13. topic
14. track
15. blanket
16. struck
17. mistake
18. junk
19. squirrel
20. stomach

■ **Challenge**

21. aquatic
22. squid
23. barracuda
24. speckled
25. peculiar

Review

1. quick
2. luck
3. picnic
4. week
5. sock

1. _____

2. _____

3. _____

4. _____

5. _____

6. _____

Expanding Vocabulary

The Suffixes -et and -let The suffixes -et and -let add the meaning "small" when they are added to the end of nouns. At one time a *jack* was a coat. What is a small or short coat?

jack + **et** = jack**et**

Practice Write a new word by adding the suffix shown to each noun below.

1. book + let
2. drop + let
3. pack + et
4. wave + let
5. pig + let
6. lock + et

1. _____ 4. _____

2. _____ 5. _____

3. _____ 6. _____

For each definition, write a word with -et or -let from the exercise above.

7. a small drop
8. a small package
9. a small pig
10. a short book
11. a small wave or ripple
12. a small metal case for a picture

7. _____ 10. _____

8. _____ 11. _____

9. _____ 12. _____

Dictionary

Stressed Syllables When you say the word *attack* aloud, which syllable do you stress, or say more strongly? The pronunciation shows the stressed syllable in dark print followed by an **accent mark (′)**.

at·tack ǀə **tăck′**ǀ

Practice Write each word below. Underline the stressed syllable in each word. Use the dictionary pronunciation.

1. public ǀ**pŭb′** lĭkǀ
2. doctor ǀ**dŏk′** tərǀ
3. unpack ǀŭn **păk′**ǀ
4. stomach ǀ**stŭm′** əkǀ
5. blanket ǀ**blăng′** kĭtǀ
6. agree ǀə **grē′**ǀ

Review: Spelling Spree

Familiar Phrases Write a Basic or Review Word to complete each phrase.

1. shoe and ___
2. a wish for good ___
3. pile of useless ___
4. bushy-tailed ___
5. sheets, pillow, and ___
6. kitchen ___
7. railroad ___
8. days of the ___
9. a bent and ___ stick
10. an ___ in a tooth
11. fill in the ___
12. ask a ___
13. a ___ basket
14. sleeves of a ___
15. the main ___ of a paragraph

Proofreading 16–25. Find and cross out ten misspelled Basic or Review Words in this movie review. Then write each word correctly.

The movie *Troubled Waters* opened with a quik shot of a publick beach. Then the camera focused on Sue and Lena as they spread their blanket on the sand. Sue lay on her stomack, while Lena reached into the picnic basket for some juice to drik. Suddenly someone yelled that there had been a sharck attach! Panic struk the beach. The air became electrik with fear. Was it a misstake? Was there really a resk of danger?

■ **Challenge Words** Write five newspaper headlines about exciting events that might happen in or near the ocean. Use one Challenge Word in each headline. Capitalize the first, the last, and each important word in your headlines.

📖 *Writing Application:* A Letter Pretend that you are entering your pet shark in a contest for the Pet of the Year. Write a letter to the judges telling them why your shark should be chosen Pet of the Year. Try to use five words from the list on page 122.

1. _____
2. _____
3. _____
4. _____
5. _____
6. _____
7. _____
8. _____
9. _____
10. _____
11. _____
12. _____
13. _____
14. _____
15. _____
16. _____
17. _____
18. _____
19. _____
20. _____
21. _____
22. _____
23. _____
24. _____
25. _____

19   Spelling Across the Curriculum

Science: *Sea Life*

Theme Vocabulary

dolphin
octopus
sponge
eel
whale
oyster
clam
coral

Using Vocabulary Write the Vocabulary Words to complete the paragraph. Use your Spelling Dictionary.

Sea animals, like land animals, live in different surroundings. The __(1)__, with its hundreds of tiny holes, and the __(2)__, known for its pearls, attach themselves to __(3)__ reefs in warm seas. The hard-shell or soft-shell __(4)__ burrows in mud. The snakelike __(5)__ and the eight-armed __(6)__ search for food along the ocean floor. Sea mammals, such as the giant blue __(7)__ and the smaller __(8)__, use the sea as their playground.

Understanding Vocabulary Write a Vocabulary Word to answer each riddle.

9. The skeletons of what sea creatures look like rocks?
10. The skeleton of what sea creature absorbs water?
11. What sea creature is long and slippery?
12. What sea creature is the largest in the sea?

1. _____
2. _____
3. _____
4. _____
5. _____
6. _____
7. _____
8. _____
9. _____
10. _____
11. _____
12. _____

FACT FILE

Coral reefs are formed from the skeletons of millions of tiny sea creatures. The largest coral reef is the Great Barrier Reef in Australia. It is about 1,250 miles long.

Enrichment

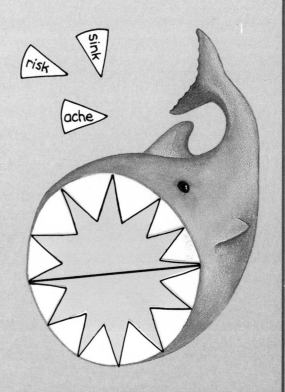

Shark's Teeth

Players: 2   **You need:** a game board like the one shown, 25 paper shark's teeth with a Basic or Review Word on each tooth

How to play: One player uses the top half of the mouth; the other uses the bottom half. Players place the teeth face down on a table. Player 1 draws a tooth and gives it to Player 2 to read aloud. Player 1 tries to spell the word correctly. If correct, Player 1 puts the tooth on his or her part of the shark's mouth. Then Player 2 takes a turn. The first player to cover his or her side of the game board wins.

Writing
Sea Similes

Have you ever heard the expression "as happy as a clam"? Writers use expressions like this, called similes, to describe people and things. Use the phrase "as ___ as a ___" to write five new similes. Then use each simile in a sentence. Try to use words from the lists in this unit. Be sure to proofread your paper.

WARNING SIGNS

Many signs use pictures to warn people about dangers or to give people information. For example, a "No Swimming" sign might show a swimmer with an X through the picture. Draw five signs that you might see at a beach. Beneath each sign, write sentences that tell what the sign means. Try to use words from the lists in this unit.

Theme: Villages

20 Final |j| and |s|

A. _____

_____

_____

_____

_____

_____

_____

B. _____

_____

_____

_____

_____

_____

_____

C. _____

_____

_____

_____

_____

_____

■ **Challenge**

_____

_____

_____

_____

_____

LOOK   at each word.

SAY   each word.

Basic Words		■ Challenge
1. village	11. glance	21. fleece
2. cottage	12. ridge	22. fragrance
3. bridge	13. manage	23. average
4. fence	14. damage	24. fringe
5. strange	15. since	25. excellence
6. chance	16. marriage	
7. twice	17. edge	
8. cage	18. lodge	
9. change	19. cabbage	
10. carriage	20. dodge	

THINK   about the words.

Each word has a final |j| or |s| sound. Words with more than one syllable, such as *village*, end with the |ĭj| sounds.

|j| bri**dge**, stran**ge** |ĭj| vill**age** |s| fen**ce**

• What are two spelling patterns for the |j| sound? Does a long or a short vowel sound come before the *dge* pattern? What is one spelling pattern for the final |ĭj| sounds in words with more than one syllable? What is one spelling pattern for the final |s| sound?

WRITE   the words.

Practice   Write the Basic Words to answer the questions.

A. Which **eight** one-syllable words end with |j|?

B. Which **seven** two-syllable words end with |ĭj|?

C. Which **five** words have the final |s| sound spelled *ce*?

■ **Now write the five Challenge Words.** Underline the patterns that spell the final |j|, |ĭj|, and |s| sounds.

CHECK   your spelling.

> *Spelling-Meaning Hint*   Did you know that *carriage* comes from *carry*? These words are related in spelling and meaning. **Think of this:** The *carriage* will *carry* the people into town.

carry
carriage

Independent Practice

Spelling-Meaning   Look at the Spelling-Meaning Hint.
  1-2. Write *carry*. Then write the Basic Word that comes from *carry*.

Word Analysis   Complete the exercises with Basic Words.

  3-4. Write *chance*. Then change one letter in *chance* to write another word.

  5-7. Write the three words that have the |ŏ| sound.

  8-10. Write the word that begins with each consonant cluster.
    8. str   **9.** br   **10.** tw

Classifying   Write the Basic Word that fits with each group.
  11. city, town, ____
  12. lettuce, carrots, ____
  13. rim, border, ____
  14. peak, slope, ____
  15. coop, pen, ____

strange
edge
|j|

■ **Challenge Words**   Write the Challenge Word that fits each meaning. Use your Spelling Dictionary.
  16. usual or ordinary   **19.** high quality
  17. a sheep's wool   **20.** shaggy border
  18. pleasant scent

Summing Up

The final |j| sound in a one-syllable word is usually spelled with the pattern *dge* or *ge*.
The final |ĭj| sounds in a word of more than one syllable are usually spelled with the pattern *age*.
The final |s| sound is often spelled with the pattern *ce*.

1. _____
2. _____
3. _____
4. _____
5. _____
6. _____
7. _____
8. _____
9. _____
10. _____
11. _____
12. _____
13. _____
14. _____
15. _____
16. _____
17. _____
18. _____
19. _____
20. _____

Basic

1. village
2. cottage
3. bridge
4. fence
5. strange
6. chance
7. twice
8. cage
9. change
10. carriage
11. glance
12. ridge
13. manage
14. damage
15. since
16. marriage
17. edge
18. lodge
19. cabbage
20. dodge

■ **Challenge**

21. fleece
22. fragrance
23. average
24. fringe
25. excellence

Review

1. nice
2. place
3. huge
4. judge
5. page

Proofreading Marks

¶ Indent
∧ Add something
ℓ Take out something
≡ Capitalize
/ Make a small letter

Expanding Vocabulary

Meanings for *change* Like many words, *change* has more than one meaning. The dictionary entry below gives three meanings. Suppose the weather report says "No change." Which of the three definitions of *change* is meant?

> **change** |chānj| *n., pl.* **changes 1.** The act or result of becoming different. **2.** The money returned when the amount given to pay for something is more than what is owed. **3.** Coins.

Practice **Write the number of the definition of *change* that goes with each sentence. Use the dictionary entry.**

1. We had a change of plans.
2. You will need change to use the public telephone.
3. There will be a change in the weather by Saturday.
4. I counted the change that I got back from the clerk.
5. I put my loose change in a big jar at the end of the week.

1. _____   3. _____   5. _____

2. _____   4. _____

Proofreading

Commas in a Series A **series** is a list of three or more items in a sentence. Use a comma after each item except the last.

The houses were made of wood, brick, or stone.

Practice **Proofread this travel guide. Find four misspelled words and two missing commas. Use proofreading marks to correct the errors.**

Example: You can see corn, beans, and ~~cabbge~~ *cabbage* in the fields.

Welcome to the villige of Harbor Town. Each cotage, shop and warehouse looks just as it did in the 1800s. Walk across the bridge to the docks to see where merchants traded food cloth, and spices. Take a carriage ride along the ege of the harbor. You'll love this special plase.

Part D   Unit Review   20

Review: Spelling Spree

Puzzle Play   Write a Basic or Review Word to fit each clue. Circle the letter that would appear in the box. Write these letters in order to spell three mystery words that name a building in a village.

Example: part of a book _ _ _ □   *pag(e)*

1. two times □ _ _ _ _
2. possibility _ □ _ _ _ _
3. marks off areas _ _ _ _ _ □
4. rim or border _ _ □ _
5. giant _ _ _ □
6. quick look _ _ _ □ _ _
7. pleasant _ _ _ □
8. built above rivers
    _ □ _ _ _

9. coins _ _ □ _ _ _
10. to put _ □ _ _ _
11. before now □ _ _ _ _
12. odd _ □ _ _ _ _ _
13. cabin _ □ _ _ _
14. narrow peak □ _ _ _ _
15. jump aside _ _ _ _ □
16. person in a
    courtroom _ _ _ _ _ _

Mystery Words: _ _ _   _ _ _ _ _ _ _ _   _ _ _ _

Using Clues   Write a Basic Word that fits each clue.
Example: This *age* is round and red, white, or green.   *cabbage*

17. This *age* is in a book.
18. This *age* is in control.
19. This *age* is hurt.
20. This *age* is a small house.
21. This *age* is a vegetable.
22. This *age* carries people.
23. This *age* can keep birds.
24. This *age* is a small town.
25. This *age* joins husband and wife.

■ **Challenge Words**   Write a riddle for each Challenge Word. Write a clue for each word, and follow the clue with the question "What is it?" Write the answers to your riddles on the back of your paper. Trade riddles with a classmate.
Example: It is always in the middle. What is it?   *average*

📖 *Writing Application:* An Opinion   Would you rather live in a small village or a big city? Write a paragraph about your choice, giving reasons to support it. Try to use five words from the list on page 128.

1.
2.
3.
4.
5.
6.
7.
8.
9.
10.
11.
12.
13.
14.
15.
16.
17.
18.
19.
20.
21.
22.
23.
24.
25.

129

20 Spelling Across the Curriculum

Social Studies: *Villages*

Theme Vocabulary

cobblestones
thatched
steeple
hearth
pasture
ivy
country
latch

Using Vocabulary Write the Vocabulary Words to complete the paragraph. Use your Spelling Dictionary.

Rob lifted the __(1)__ on the wooden gate and left the __(2)__ where the family's cows grazed. He walked quickly along the village path paved with __(3)__. The clock in the church __(4)__ struck six. Already it was getting dark. Autumn came early in this part of the __(5)__. The __(6)__ climbing on the cottage walls had already turned red. Rob could see the __(7)__ roof of his cottage. How he longed for its warm and cozy __(8)__!

Understanding Vocabulary Write *yes* or *no* to answer each question.

9. Could a roof be made of cobblestones?
10. Should a hearth be made of wood?
11. Could you find a pasture in the country?
12. Could a thatched roof catch on fire?

1. _____
2. _____
3. _____
4. _____
5. _____
6. _____
7. _____
8. _____
9. _____
10. _____
11. _____
12. _____

FACT FILE

Old Sturbridge Village in Massachusetts shows how people lived and worked between 1790 and 1840. It includes homes, shops, a school, farmland, and other features of village life.

Enrichment
20

👥 *School Days*

With a small group of students, find out what school was like in an early American village. Use an encyclopedia or other resource book. Then write a script for a skit, showing what a school day was like in colonial times. Make costumes or any props that you need. Perform your skit in front of a group of your classmates.

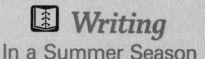

VILLAGE GUIDEPOST

Make a map of an imaginary village. Give your village a name. Then fill in your map with streets, buildings, and parks. Label the places on your map. Try to use words from the lists in this unit.

📖 *Writing*
In a Summer Season

Imagine that you live in a village. The time may be the present or the past. Write a poem that describes what it is like to live there during one of the four seasons. Is your house cozy in the winter? Are there flowers and birds in the summer? Try to use words from the lists in this unit. Be sure to proofread your poem.

(Theme: Crafts)

21 Words with Prefixes

A. _____
_____
_____
_____
_____
_____

B. _____
_____
_____

C. _____
_____
_____
_____
_____
_____
_____

■ Challenge

_____
_____
_____
_____
_____

LOOK at each word.

SAY each word.

Basic Words ■ Challenge

1. repaint	11. reread	21. redecorate
2. redo	12. unsure	22. unfamiliar
3. refill	13. reheat	23. unusual
4. rebuild	14. unpack	24. rearrange
5. discolor	15. unpaid	25. discontinue
6. untidy	16. distrust	
7. dislike	17. recount	
8. uneven	18. displease	
9. rewind	19. unload	
10. unlucky	20. disorder	

THINK about the words.

Each word has a prefix. A **prefix** is a word part added to the beginning of a base word. It adds meaning to the word.

PREFIX		BASE WORD		NEW WORD	MEANING
re	+	paint	=	**re**paint	paint again
dis	+	like	=	**dis**like	not like
un	+	even	=	**un**even	not even
un	+	pack	=	**un**pack	opposite of *pack*

• What three prefixes do you see? What do they mean?

WRITE the words.

Practice Write the Basic Words to answer the questions.

A. Which **eight** words have the prefix *re-*?
B. Which **five** words have the prefix *dis-*?
C. Which **seven** words have the prefix *un-*?

■ **Now write the five Challenge Words.** Underline the prefix in each word.

CHECK your spelling.

Spelling-Meaning Hint   Did you know that different prefixes can be added to the same base word to form new words that are related in spelling and meaning? **Think of this:** Please *undo* the knot, and *redo* it more tightly.

Independent Practice

Spelling-Meaning   Look at the Spelling-Meaning Hint.

1-2. Write *undo* and *redo*. Then circle the base word that appears in both words.

Word Analysis   Complete the exercises with Basic Words.

3-5. Write the three words with the |ē| sound spelled *ea*.

6-9. Write a Basic Word by adding a prefix.
   6. trust   **7.** lucky   **8.** like   **9.** fill

Synonyms   Write the Basic Word that means the same as each word below.

10. crooked
11. messy
12. confusion
13. stain
14. uncertain
15. reconstruct

■ **Challenge Words**   Write the Challenge Words to complete the paragraph. Use your Spelling Dictionary.

When we decided to __(16)__ our living room, we hired a decorator to help us choose the wallpaper. However, she was __(17)__ with our tastes. She put up wallpaper so __(18)__ that even the factory wants to __(19)__ it. Next time we will just __(20)__ the furniture!

Summing Up

A **prefix** is a word part added to the beginning of a base word. It adds meaning to the word. *Un-, re-,* and *dis-* are prefixes. Find the prefix and the base word, and spell the word by parts.

1. _____
2. _____
3. _____
4. _____
5. _____
6. _____
7. _____
8. _____
9. _____
10. _____
11. _____
12. _____
13. _____
14. _____
15. _____
16. _____
17. _____
18. _____
19. _____
20. _____

Basic

1. repaint
2. redo
3. refill
4. rebuild
5. discolor
6. untidy
7. dislike
8. uneven
9. rewind
10. unlucky
11. reread
12. unsure
13. reheat
14. unpack
15. unpaid
16. distrust
17. recount
18. displease
19. unload
20. disorder

■ Challenge

21. redecorate
22. unfamiliar
23. unusual
24. rearrange
25. discontinue

Review

1. remake
2. unclear
3. rewrite
4. unfair
5. unkind

3. _____

4. _____

5. _____

6. _____

7. _____

8. _____

9. _____

10. _____

Expanding Vocabulary

The Suffix -able The suffix -able can be added to a word to form an adjective. It means "capable of" or "able to."

refill + able = refill**able**   "capable of being refilled"

Practice   Add -able to the underlined word to write an adjective that fits each meaning.

1. capable of being reheated
2. capable of being enjoyed
3. capable of being depended on
4. able to be reached
5. able to be allowed
6. able to be questioned

1. _____   4. _____

2. _____   5. _____

3. _____   6. _____

Dictionary

Prefixes Where can you find the meaning of *unafraid*? Some words with prefixes are not listed as entry words in the dictionary. However, prefixes have separate entries. Look up the prefix and the base word, and combine the two meanings.

> **un-** A prefix that means: **1.** Not: *unable; unbecoming.* **2.** Lack of: *unemployment.* **3.** To do the opposite of: *unlock.*

Which meaning of *un-* is used in the word *unafraid*?

Practice   Write the answer to each question.
1. What is the first meaning of *un-*?
2. What sample word is given in the third meaning?

1. _____   2. _____

Write the prefix and the base word you would look up to find the meaning of each word below.

3-4. untrue   7-8. reopen
5-6. rewrite   9-10. unbutton

Review: Spelling Spree

Base Word Hunt   Write a Basic or Review Word that has the same base word as each word below.

1. kindness	**7.** luckily	**13.** pleased
2. writer	**8.** filling	**14.** reader
3. reorder	**9.** trusted	**15.** building
4. repack	**10.** fairness	**16.** unlike
5. prepaid	**11.** colorful	**17.** clearly
6. discount	**12.** loading	**18.** surely

Proofreading   19-25. Find and cross out seven misspelled Basic or Review Words in this list. Then write each word correctly.

Things to Do Today

- Take out and redoo hem on Nikki's skirt.
- Buy more clay, and remak pot to enter in crafts show.
- Rebuild unevin bookshelf, and repant it.
- Straighten out untidie sewing box. Untangle balls of yarn, and rewinde them.
- Reread instructions on how to reheet wax to make candles.

■ **Challenge Words**   Look at the Base Word Hunt activity. Write each Challenge Word and its base word. Then write one other word by adding an ending to the base word.

 Writing Application: A Personal Story   Did you ever try to learn a new craft? Did you ever make an art project that did not come out right? How did you fix it? Write a paragraph about a project you have made. Try to use five words from the list on page 134.

1. _____
2. _____
3. _____
4. _____
5. _____
6. _____
7. _____
8. _____
9. _____
10. _____
11. _____
12. _____
13. _____
14. _____
15. _____
16. _____
17. _____
18. _____
19. _____
20. _____
21. _____
22. _____
23. _____
24. _____
25. _____

21   Spelling Across the Curriculum

Art: *Crafts*

Theme Vocabulary

whittling
pottery
collage
quilting
embroidery
weaving
stenciling
batik

Using Vocabulary Write the Vocabulary Words to complete the paragraph. Use your Spelling Dictionary.

Last week my art class held a crafts fair in the gym. We set up a loom for __(1)__. Kim brought in some clay to make __(2)__. We had materials for pasting together a __(3)__. Joe displayed cutouts for __(4)__ letters and designs with ink. We also provided carving tools and wood for __(5)__. I sewed together padded squares of cloth to show how __(6)__ is done. Jane used tiny stitches to make an __(7)__ of a house. Cara used melted wax and colorful dyes to show the art of __(8)__.

Understanding Vocabulary Write the Vocabulary Word that names the craft in which each tool or material is used.

9. wax   **11.** paste
10. wood   **12.** kiln or oven

1. _____
2. _____
3. _____
4. _____
5. _____
6. _____
7. _____
8. _____
9. _____
10. _____
11. _____
12. _____

FACT FILE

The Pennsylvania Dutch are a group of people known for their simple way of life and fine crafts. Colorful designs of birds, hearts, and tulips decorate their barns and handicrafts.

Enrichment

WORD WEAVING

Near the left side of a wide piece of paper, write the prefix *re* in large letters. Cut two slits in the paper, as shown. Then cut a long strip of construction paper one inch wide. On the strip, write as many base words as you can think of that can be used with the prefix *re*. Weave the strip through the slits so that each time you move the strip, a new word appears. Make word weavers for the other prefixes in this unit.

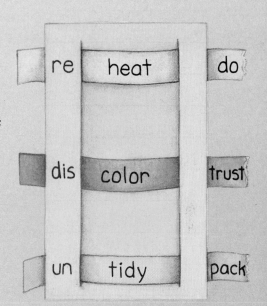

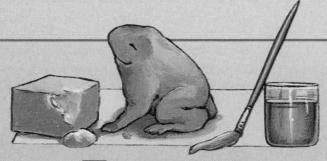

👪 Craft Class

Do you know how to whittle? Have you ever made a quilt? With a partner choose a craft that you both enjoy. Teach it to a group of your classmates. Set up the materials you need, and provide pictures or samples of the finished product. Show your classmates how to do the craft. Then give them a chance to try.

📖 Writing
Crafts Comments

Pretend that a new crafts exhibit has just opened at the art museum. Write a review of the exhibit for the newspaper. How many different kinds of crafts were shown? Describe some of the pieces on display. Which one was your favorite? Try to use words from the lists in this unit. Be sure to proofread your paper.

Theme: Photography

22 VCCV Pattern

A. _____

_____

_____

_____

_____

B. _____

_____

_____

_____

_____

_____

_____

_____

_____

_____

_____

_____

■ **Challenge**

_____

_____

_____

_____

_____

LOOK at each word.

SAY each word.

Basic Words   ■ Challenge

1. picture   11. harvest   21. filter
2. person   12. survive   22. candid
3. perfect   13. suppose   23. disturb
4. attend   14. perform   24. narrate
5. number   15. escape   25. rascal
6. support   16. helmet
7. common   17. allow
8. welcome   18. fellow
9. offer   19. barber
10. expert   20. tender

THINK about the words.

Each word has two syllables and the vowel-consonant-consonant-vowel (VCCV) pattern. Divide between the consonants to find the syllables. Look for familiar patterns.

VC | CV	VC | CV
per | son	**at | tend**

• Where is each word in the list divided into syllables?

WRITE the words.

Practice   Write the Basic Words to answer the questions. Draw a line between the syllables in each word.

A. Which **seven** words are divided into syllables between double consonants?

B. Which **thirteen** words are divided into syllables between two different consonants?

■ **Now write the five Challenge Words.** Draw a line between the syllables in each word.

CHECK your spelling.

> *Spelling-Meaning Hint*   How can you remember how to spell the |ĭ| sound in *perfect*? Think of the |ĕ| sound in the related word *perfection*.

**perfe⬛ct
perfe⬛ction**

Independent Practice

Spelling-Meaning   Look at the Spelling-Meaning Hint.
1-2. Write *perfect* and *perfection*. Then underline the letter in *perfection* that helps you spell the |ĭ| sound in *perfect*.

Word Analysis   Complete the exercises with Basic Words.

3-4. Write the two words that have a double *l*.

5-7. Write the three words that have a long vowel sound spelled vowel-consonant-*e*.

Definitions   Write the Basic Word that fits each meaning.
  8. usual or ordinary
  9. a human being
  10. to bring in crops
  11. a numeral
  12. a photograph or drawing
  13. to hold something up
  14. someone who cuts hair
  15. something worn to protect the head

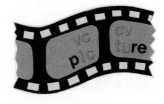

■ **Challenge Words**   Write the Challenge Word that completes each sentence. Use your Spelling Dictionary.
  16. Do not ____ me while I am taking the picture.
  17. Look at the pictures as I ____ the story.
  18. Your surprise is really captured in this ____ picture.
  19. You looked like such a ____ when you made that face!
  20. I used a red ____ to block out red light waves.

1. _____
2. _____
3. _____
4. _____
5. _____
6. _____
7. _____
8. _____
9. _____
10. _____
11. _____
12. _____
13. _____
14. _____
15. _____
16. _____
17. _____
18. _____
19. _____
20. _____

Summing Up

To find the syllables of a VCCV word, divide the word between the consonants. Look for patterns you have learned. Spell the word by syllables.

Basic

1. picture
2. person
3. perfect
4. attend
5. number
6. support
7. common
8. welcome
9. offer
10. expert
11. harvest
12. survive
13. suppose
14. perform
15. escape
16. helmet
17. allow
18. fellow
19. barber
20. tender

■ Challenge

21. filter
22. candid
23. disturb
24. narrate
25. rascal

Review

1. lesson
2. until
3. yellow
4. hello
5. garden

Proofreading Marks

⁋ Indent
∧ Add something
ℰ Take out something
≡ Capitalize
/ Make a small letter

Expanding Vocabulary

Meanings for *tender*   The word *tender* has more than one meaning. The definition of *tender* depends on the way it is used in a sentence. Which meaning would a cook be using if he tells you that the meat is *tender*?

> **ten·der** |tĕn′dər| *adj.* **tenderer, tenderest** **1.** Fragile. **2.** Not tough. **3.** Painful; sore. **4.** Gentle; loving.

Practice   Write the definition for *tender* that is used in each sentence.

1. The scrape on my knee is still <u>tender</u>.
2. This restaurant always serves <u>tender</u> meat.
3. The nurse at the hospital had a <u>tender</u> touch.
4. The flowerpot fell and crushed the <u>tender</u> plants.

1. _____   3. _____

2. _____   4. _____

Proofreading

Commas with Introductory Words   Use a comma to set off *yes, no,* and *well* at the beginning of a sentence. Otherwise, the meaning of the sentence may change.

No, photos should be saved.   No photos should be saved.

Practice   Proofread Andy's note. Find four misspelled words and two missing commas. Use proofreading marks to correct the errors.

Example: Yes, each ~~persen~~ *person* can enter only one photo.

> Dear Tom,
>
>   Yes I finally entered a picher in the photo contest. The prize is a lessen with an exspert. Well I suppose that I would welcome the advice. My photos are hardly perfict!
>
>   Your friend,
>   Andy

Review: Spelling Spree

Syllable Addition   Write a Basic or Review Word by combining the underlined syllables in each pair of words.

Example: a<u>tt</u>ack + pr<u>etend</u>   *attend*

1. <u>sup</u>ply + re<u>port</u>
2. <u>sur</u>face + re<u>vive</u>
3. per<u>fume</u> + in<u>fect</u>
4. <u>per</u>mit + in<u>form</u>
5. <u>gar</u>lic + sud<u>den</u>
6. <u>office</u> + pre<u>fer</u>
7. <u>tennis</u> + <u>under</u>
8. <u>pic</u>nic + na<u>ture</u>

Code Breaker   Some Basic and Review Words are written in code. Use the code shown below to write the words correctly.

CODE:	b	c	d	e	f	g	i	j	m	n	o	p	q	s	t	u	v	w	x	y	z
LETTER:	a	b	c	d	e	f	h	i	l	m	n	o	p	r	s	t	u	v	w	x	y

Example: ftdbqf   *escape*

9. ifmmp
10. voujm
11. gfmmpx
12. tvqqptf
13. ibswftu
14. ovncfs
15. dpnnpo
16. buufoe
17. qfstpo
18. zfmmpx
19. cbscfs
20. ifmnfu
21. bmmpx
22. fyqfsu
23. xfmdpnf
24. ftdbqf
25. mfttpo

■ **Challenge Words**   Create your own Code Breaker activity. Make each code letter stand for a different letter. Write each Challenge Word in code. Then write it correctly on the back of the paper. Trade puzzles with a classmate.

📖 *Writing Application:* A Description   Pretend you are a judge in a photo contest. Write a paragraph describing the winning photo. What is it a picture of? Why did it win? Try to use five words from the list on page 140.

1. _____
2. _____
3. _____
4. _____
5. _____
6. _____
7. _____
8. _____
9. _____
10. _____
11. _____
12. _____
13. _____
14. _____
15. _____
16. _____
17. _____
18. _____
19. _____
20. _____
21. _____
22. _____
23. _____
24. _____
25. _____

22 Spelling Across the Curriculum

Art: *Photography*

Theme Vocabulary

portrait
lens
shutter
film
pose
flash
develop
darkroom

Using Vocabulary Write the Vocabulary Words to complete the paragraph. Use your Spelling Dictionary.

My uncle is a professional photographer. I like to watch him work. First, he tells his customer to sit in a natural __(1)__. Then he winds a roll of __(2)__ into the camera. He focuses the __(3)__ and adjusts how quickly the __(4)__ will open and close. As he takes the __(5)__, a bright __(6)__ goes off. Then I go with him to the __(7)__, where he must __(8)__ the film in total darkness. Suddenly, like magic, images appear before my eyes!

Understanding Vocabulary Write *yes* if the underlined word is used correctly. Write *no* if it is not.

9. My father <u>lens</u> me his camera sometimes.
10. Brett mixed chemicals to <u>develop</u> the film.
11. My mother bought a pretty frame for my <u>pose</u>.
12. The wrong <u>shutter</u> speed may let in too much light.

1. _____

2. _____

3. _____

4. _____

5. _____

6. _____

7. _____

8. _____

9. _____

10. _____

11. _____

12. _____

FACT FILE

Dorothea Lange was a photographer who became famous for her pictures of people. Her photos showed the problems of the poor and the hardships of wartime.

Enrichment

👪 *Password*

What is the password?

Players: 4   **You need:** a word card for each Basic and Review Word, a clock

How to play: Divide into two teams. The first player draws a card and gives his or her partner a one-word clue for the word. The partner has one minute to guess the word and spell it correctly. During that minute, the first player may give more one-word clues, if necessary. Teams take turns giving and responding to clues. Each correct answer is worth one point. The first team to get five points wins.

Photo Album

PICTURE THIS

Make a photo album of your life. Fold four pieces of drawing paper together to make a book. Fill in the pages with drawings or photographs of special events in your life. Put the events in order, starting with your earliest memories. Below each picture, write a sentence about the event. Try to use list words.

📖 Writing
Faces of Photography

Write a research report about a person who has done something important for photography. You might choose an inventor, such as Louis Daguerre or George Eastman, or a photographer, such as Margaret Bourke-White or Ansel Adams. Try to use words from the lists in this unit. Be sure to proofread your paper.

Theme: White-Water Rafting

23 VCCV Pattern

A. _____

_____

_____

_____

_____

_____

B. _____

_____

_____

_____

_____

_____

_____

_____

_____

_____

_____

_____

_____

_____

■ **Challenge**

_____

_____

_____

_____

_____

LOOK at each word.

SAY each word.

Basic Words		■ Challenge
1. current	11. lumber	21. challenge
2. danger	12. seldom	22. vessel
3. canyon	13. engine	23. submerge
4. plastic	14. pillow	24. eddy
5. bottom	15. carpet	25. venture
6. hollow	16. garbage	
7. member	17. master	
8. borrow	18. arrow	
9. organ	19. army	
10. compose	20. thirty	

THINK about the words.

Each two-syllable word has the VCCV pattern. Divide each word into syllables between the consonants. Look for patterns you have learned. Spell the words by syllables.

VC I CV	VC I CV
cur I rent	**dan I ger**

• Where is each word in the list divided into syllables?

WRITE the words.

Practice **Write the Basic Words to answer the questions.** Draw a line between the syllables in each word.

A. Which **six** words are divided into syllables between double consonants?

B. Which **fourteen** words are divided into syllables between two different consonants?

■ **Now write the five Challenge Words.** Draw a line between the syllables in each word.

CHECK your spelling.

> **Spelling-Meaning Hint**   How can you remember that the first schwa sound in *composition* is spelled with an *o*? Think of the |ō| sound in the related word *compose*.

compo|se
compo|sition

Independent Practice

Spelling-Meaning   Look at the Spelling-Meaning Hint.

1-2. Write *composition*. Then write the Basic Word that is related to *composition* in spelling and meaning.

Word Analysis   Complete the exercises with Basic Words.

3-6. Write the four words that end with the |ər| sounds spelled *er*.

7-10. Write the word that rhymes with each word below.

   7. follow
   8. narrow
   9. willow
   10. sorrow

vc   cv

can   yon

Analogies   Write the Basic Word that completes each analogy.

11. *Always* is to *never* as *often* is to ____.
12. *Sailors* are to *navy* as *soldiers* are to ____.
13. *Table* is to *tablecloth* as *floor* is to ____.
14. *Nine* is to *ten* as *twenty-nine* is to ____.
15. *Attic* is to *top* as *basement* is to ____.

■ **Challenge Words**   Write the Challenge Word that fits each meaning. Use your Spelling Dictionary.

16. a task that is risky
17. to cover with water
18. a large boat
19. a current of water or air
20. a call to take part in a contest

1. _____
2. _____
3. _____
4. _____
5. _____
6. _____
7. _____
8. _____
9. _____
10. _____
11. _____
12. _____
13. _____
14. _____
15. _____
16. _____
17. _____
18. _____
19. _____
20. _____

Summing Up

To find the syllables of a VCCV word, divide the word between the consonants. Look for patterns you have learned. Spell the word by syllables.

Basic

1. current
2. danger
3. canyon
4. plastic
5. bottom
6. hollow
7. member
8. borrow
9. organ
10. compose
11. lumber
12. seldom
13. engine
14. pillow
15. carpet
16. garbage
17. master
18. arrow
19. army
20. thirty

■ Challenge

21. challenge
22. vessel
23. submerge
24. eddy
25. venture

Review

1. sudden
2. follow
3. enjoy
4. happen
5. forget

Expanding Vocabulary

Words from Spanish Do you know where the word *canyon* comes from? Many English words were borrowed from Spanish.

English word: **canyon**   Spanish word: **cañon**

Practice   Write the word below that matches each meaning. The Spanish word is given in parentheses.

alligator   ranch   vanilla   lasso   hurricane   burro

1. It means "a long rope." (*el lazo*)
2. It means "a special kind of farm." (*el rancho*)
3. It means "a large reptile." (*el lagarto*)
4. It means "a strong windstorm." (*el huracán*)
5. It means "a small donkey." (*el borrico*)
6. It means "a flavoring." (*la vainilla*)

1. _____   4. _____

2. _____   5. _____

3. _____   6. _____

Dictionary

Word Histories How can you find out where a word comes from? A dictionary may give a **word history** that tells what language or languages a word comes from and what it originally meant.

Current comes from a Latin word meaning "running." A current is something that runs or flows, such as a river current.

Practice   Write the answer to each question.
1. What language did the word *current* come from?
2. What did the word originally mean?

1. _____   2. _____

Look up each word below in your Spelling Dictionary. Read the word history. First, write the language the word comes from. Then write the original meaning of the word.

3. magazine   4. porcupine

3. _____

_____

4. _____

_____

Review: Spelling Spree

Alphabet Puzzler Write the Basic or Review Word that would appear alphabetically between each pair of words below.

1. both, ____, bought
2. swap, ____, under
3. arrive, ____, art
4. found, ____, hair
5. sand, ____, submarine
6. know, ____, lump
7. never, ____, person
8. camp, ____, cap
9. pile, ____, pilot
10. folder, ____, fool
11. armor, ____, arrange
12. many, ____, match
13. cape, ____, cat
14. end, ____, engulf
15. collar, ____, cost
16. holiday, ____, icy
17. border, ____, boss
18. plain, ____, platter

Proofreading **19-25.** Find and cross out seven misspelled Basic or Review Words in this journal entry. Then write each word correctly.

June 27 I will never ferget today. I have seldom had more fun. I went rafting on Big River. First, each group membor put on a life jacket. Our guide told us to follow her directions to avoid danjer. She said to hold on and injoy what was about to hapen. All of a suddin, the curent pulled us into white water. I was soaked!

■ **Challenge Words** Look at the Alphabet Puzzler activity. Write the Challenge Words in alphabetical order. Then, for each one, write a word that comes before it and one that comes after it alphabetically. Try to use words with the same first two letters.

📖 *Writing Application:* Creative Writing Imagine you are a branch floating down a churning, rushing river. How does it feel to be in the swirling water? What happens to you? Write a paragraph about being the branch. Try to use five words from the list on page 146.

1. _____
2. _____
3. _____
4. _____
5. _____
6. _____
7. _____
8. _____
9. _____
10. _____
11. _____
12. _____
13. _____
14. _____
15. _____
16. _____
17. _____
18. _____
19. _____
20. _____
21. _____
22. _____
23. _____
24. _____
25. _____

23 Spelling Across the Curriculum

Recreation: *White-Water Rafting*

Theme Vocabulary

raft
rapids
paddle
whirlpool
swift
gorge
steer
launch

Using Vocabulary Write the Vocabulary Words to complete the paragraph. Use your Spelling Dictionary.

With a shove of his long plastic __(1)__ , Phil helped his teammates move the large rubber __(2)__ into the water to __(3)__ it. He jumped in and began to guide and __(4)__ the boat into the __(5)__ current. He pulled quickly to the left to avoid a spinning __(6)__ . Up ahead, the river rounded a bend and entered a narrow __(7)__ . Beyond the bend were the biggest __(8)__ his team had ever faced. Phil braced himself for the rough ride.

Understanding Vocabulary Write a Vocabulary Word to match each clue.

9. If a rowboat needs oars, a canoe needs this.
10. It has high walls on both sides.
11. Its rotating water could make you dizzy.
12. If you do not do this, your boat will stay on land.

1. _____
2. _____
3. _____
4. _____
5. _____
6. _____
7. _____
8. _____
9. _____
10. _____
11. _____
12. _____

FACT FILE

The Colorado River is a popular river for white-water rafting, especially through the Grand Canyon. Its big rapids have such names as Last Chance Rapid.

Enrichment

 Raft Race

Players: 2   **You need:** 40 ice cream sticks or strips cut out of tag board

How to play: Use two ice cream sticks for each Basic Word. Write the first syllable of the word on one stick and the last syllable on the other. Place the sticks face down on a table. Players take turns turning over two sticks. If a player turns over a matching pair, he or she keeps the sticks and places them side by side to build a "raft." The player with the largest raft at the end of the game wins.

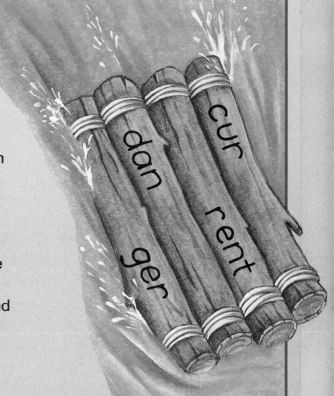

WORD WATERFALL

Cut seven strips of blue paper. On each strip, write at least three words. The last letter of each word must be the same as the first letter of the next word, such as *carpet*, *thirty*, and *yellow*. Use at least two words from this unit on each strip. Do not use the same word twice. Paste your strips on a big piece of paper to make a "waterfall."

Writing
Rapids Rap

Pretend that you are filming a TV show about outdoor sports. Interview a white-water rafter. What are some things this person might say about the sport? Is it scary? What does he or she enjoy most about it? Write the interview questions and answers. Try to use words from the lists in this unit. Be sure to proofread your paper.

24 Review: Units 19–23

Unit 19   Spelling |k|, |ng|, and |kw| pp. 120-125

electric	question	jacket	sink	ache
blanket	mistake	squirrel	track	stomach

Remember: |k| → **k, ck, c**

|ng| → **n** before **k**

|kw| → **qu**

Write the word that fits each clue below.
1. something asked   3. climbs trees   5. rhymes with *rink*
2. used on a bed   4. a short coat   6. rhymes with *stack*
Write the word that completes each sentence.
7. Joshua ate apples until his ____ was full.
8. Did your legs ____ after all that walking?
9. Our kitchen has an ____ stove instead of a gas stove.
10. I made a careless ____ on my homework.

1. _____
2. _____
3. _____
4. _____
5. _____
6. _____
7. _____
8. _____
9. _____
10. _____

Unit 20   Final |j| and |s| pp. 126-131

change	bridge	twice	strange	carriage
damage	edge	glance	since	lodge

Remember: |j| → **dge, ge** (one-syllable words)

|ĭj| → **age** (two-syllable words)

|s| → **ce**

Write the word that rhymes with each word below.
11. hedge   12. mice   13. mince   14. dodge   15. chance
Write the word that fits each meaning.
16. to make different
17. to harm
18. a vehicle with wheels that is used for carrying passengers
19. unfamiliar
20. a structure built over a river so that people or cars can cross from one side to another

11. _____
12. _____
13. _____
14. _____
15. _____
16. _____
17. _____
18. _____
19. _____
20. _____

Half of the words from each unit are reviewed on these pages.
The rest are reviewed on pages 238–240.

Unit 21   Words with Prefixes   pp. 132-137

| unlucky | uneven | rebuild | dislike | repaint |
| recount | unload | disorder | unsure | displease |

Remember: A **prefix** is a word part added to the beginning of a base word to form a new word. **Un-**, **re-**, and **dis-** are prefixes.

Write a word by changing the underlined prefix.

21. <u>re</u>order   **22.** <u>un</u>like   **23.** <u>mis</u>count   **24.** <u>re</u>load

Write a word by adding a prefix to each base word.

25. lucky   **26.** sure   **27.** please

Write the word that completes each sentence.

28. Those pieces of lumber are rough and ____.

29. We will ____ the porch so that it will be sturdy.

30. Can you ____ the woodwork to match the wallpaper?

21. _____

22. _____

23. _____

24. _____

25. _____

26. _____

27. _____

28. _____

29. _____

30. _____

Unit 22   VCCV Pattern   pp. 138-143

| expert | common | picture | welcome | perfect |
| barber | allow | escape | perform | survive |

Remember: To find the syllables of a word with the VCCV pattern, divide the word between the consonants.

Write the word that completes each analogy.

31. *Teeth* is to *dentist* as *hair* is to ____.

32. *Writer* is to *story* as *artist* is to ____.

33. *Appearance* is to *appear* as *performance* is to ____.

34. *Rough* is to *smooth* as *unusual* is to ____.

Write the word that matches each meaning.

35. to stay alive   **37.** to permit   **39.** having no mistakes

36. to get free   **38.** to greet   **40.** having special skills

31. _____

32. _____

33. _____

34. _____

35. _____

36. _____

37. _____

38. _____

39. _____

40. _____

Unit 23   VCCV Pattern   pp. 144-149

canyon	organ	compose	danger	borrow
army	carpet	garbage	seldom	arrow

Remember: To find the syllables of a word with the VCCV pattern, divide the word between the consonants.

VC   CV

can   yon

Write the word that completes each phrase.

41. to take out the ____
42. a bow and ____
43. lend and ____
44. a soldier in the ____
45. the steep walls of a ____

Write the word that belongs in each group.

46. write, create, ____
47. often, ____, never
48. risk, hazard, ____
49. trumpet, piano, ____
50. tile, rug, ____

41. _____
42. _____
43. _____
44. _____
45. _____
46. _____
47. _____
48. _____
49. _____
50. _____

■ Challenge Words   Units 19-23   pp. 120-149

unfamiliar	redecorate	challenge	average	narrate
excellence	barracuda	speckled	submerge	disturb

Write the word that means the opposite of each phrase.

51. well known
52. to leave in peace
53. not ordinary
54. to surface
55. a task of little difficulty

Write the word that fits each clue.

56. It is a way to tell a story.
57. It stands for the highest quality.
58. It describes a sparrow's spotted feathers.
59. It has sharp teeth.
60. It is something you do to a room.

51. _____
52. _____
53. _____
54. _____
55. _____
56. _____
57. _____
58. _____
59. _____
60. _____

Spelling-Meaning Strategy

Vowel Changes: Schwa to Long Vowel Sound

Unfamiliar words that at first seem difficult to spell may seem easier if you think about related words that you already know. Read this paragraph.

Let's **suppose** that each child in the school will bring two people to the fair. Based on that **supposition**, how many people should we expect?

supp**o**sition
supp**o**se

Think

- What does *suppose* mean? What does *supposition* mean? How are they related in meaning?
- What vowel sound does the letter *o* spell in each word?

Here are more related words in which the same letter spells a schwa sound in one word and a long vowel sound in the other.

admiration	relative	definition
admire	relate	define

Apply and Extend

Complete these activities on a separate piece of paper.

1. Look up the words in the Word Box above in the Spelling Dictionary. Write six sentences, using each word.

2. With a partner list as many words as you can that are related to *suppose, admire, relate*, and *define*. Then look on page 274 of your Spelling-Meaning Index. Add any other words that you find in these families to your list.

Summing Up   You can remember how to spell the schwa sound in some words by thinking of a related word with a long vowel sound spelled the same way.

Description

Annie could have an orange only once a year—on the special day when supplies came to her Alaskan village. What did the orange taste like to Annie?

Annie cradled the orange in her hands. She walked slowly behind the store and sat facing the bay. Then she closed her eyes, lifted the orange to her nose, and breathed of it. "California," she thought. In her hands, she held the sunshine, the warmth, the groves of orange trees, the blue of the ocean, and the wonder of the land she had learned of in school but might never see.

The day was shimmering to an end, the special day. She bit into the peel, tasting the first bitter oil, feeling it sting her tongue. She nibbled at the white beneath the peel and then placed the piece of skin carefully in her pocket. Later, she could take it out, smell, and remember. Little by little, she peeled the orange till its pale, tender roundness lay free in her hand. She pulled off one section and sank her teeth in. Oh, it was good. It was good beyond believing! Drops stung her chin, stickied her fingers. It was like eating summer.

from The Once-A-Year Day *by Eve Bunting*

Think and Discuss

1. **Sense words** appeal to the five senses. What sense words help you taste the orange? feel the juice?
2. What **exact words** tell you that Annie did not hurry to eat the orange?

The Writing Process

The description of Annie and the orange on page 154 is from *The Once-A-Year Day*. It uses **sense words** to describe how an orange smells, looks, tastes, and feels to a girl who can eat one only once a year. Use **sense words, exact words,** and **details** in your own description.

Assignment: Write a Description

Step One: Prewriting

1. List some topics for a description. Discuss them with a classmate. Choose a topic.
2. List sense words that describe your topic. Include words for sight, sound, smell, taste, and touch.

Step Two: Write a First Draft

1. Think about your purpose and audience.
2. Do not worry about mistakes—just write!

Step Three: Revise

1. Have you used sense words that appeal to at least three senses? Where could you add details?
2. Use your Thesaurus to find exact words.
3. Read your description to a classmate or to your teacher. Make any other changes you want.

Step Four: Proofread

1. Have you used commas in a series correctly?
2. Did you spell all words correctly? Copy any words that you misspelled into your Notebook for Writing.

Step Five: Publish

1. Copy your description neatly, and add a title.
2. Share your description. Record it with sound effects.

Composition Words

crooked
picture
mistake
number
uneven
hollow
untidy
perfect

Proofreading Marks

¶   Indent
∧   Add something
ℓ   Take out something
≡   Capitalize
/   Make a small letter

Theme: Weather

25   Changing Final y to i

A. _____

_____

_____

_____

_____

_____

_____

B. _____

_____

_____

_____

_____

_____

_____

_____

_____

_____

_____

■ Challenge

_____

_____

_____

_____

_____

LOOK   at each word.

SAY   each word.

Basic Words		■ Challenge
1. sunnier	11. ferries	21. iciest
2. cloudier	12. crazier	22. hazier
3. windier	13. funnier	23. breezier
4. cities	14. earlier	24. categories
5. heaviest	15. copied	25. qualities
6. prettiest	16. hobbies	
7. studied	17. angriest	
8. easier	18. emptied	
9. noisier	19. worried	
10. families	20. happiest	

THINK   about the words.

Each word has the ending -*es*, -*ed*, -*er*, or -*est*. The spelling of each base word changes when an ending is added.

city + es = cit**ies**		study + ed = stud**ied**
sunny + er = sunn**ier**		heavy + est = heav**iest**

• Does a vowel or a consonant come before the final *y* in each base word? How does the spelling of the base word change when an ending is added?

WRITE   the words.

Practice   **Write the Basic Words to answer the questions.**

A. In which **eight** words was the final *y* changed to *i* when -*es* or -*ed* was added?

B. In which **twelve** words was the final *y* changed to *i* when -*er* or -*est* was added?

■ Now write the five Challenge Words. Underline the letter that replaced *y* when the ending was added.

CHECK   your spelling.

> *Spelling-Meaning Hint*   Endings can be added to *easy* to form *easier*, *easiest*, and *easily*. These new words are related to *easy* in spelling and meaning. **Think of this:** You can complete an *easy* chore *easily*.

easy
easier
easiest
easily

Independent Practice

Spelling-Meaning   Look at the Spelling-Meaning Hint.
1-2. Write *easy*. Then write the Basic Word that is related to *easy* in spelling and meaning.

Word Analysis   Complete the exercises with Basic Words.

3-5. Write the past tense of each word below.
   3. study   4. copy   5. worry

6-9. Write the plural of each word below.
   6. city   8. family
   7. ferry   9. hobby

Opposites   Write the Basic Word that means the opposite of each word below.
10. filled
11. quieter
12. lightest
13. ugliest
14. saddest
15. harder

cloud   y   ier

■ **Challenge Words**   Write the Challenge Word that completes each sentence. Use your Spelling Dictionary.
16. Because of the sea winds, it is _____ near the ocean.
17. The fog from the sea made the air even _____ .
18. Different kinds of clouds can be classified into _____ .
19. The types of clouds have different features, or _____ .
20. When it snows, this back road is the _____ one in town.

1. _____
2. _____
3. _____
4. _____
5. _____
6. _____
7. _____
8. _____
9. _____
10. _____
11. _____
12. _____
13. _____
14. _____
15. _____
16. _____
17. _____
18. _____
19. _____
20. _____

Summing Up

If a word ends with a consonant and *y*, change the *y* to *i* when adding *-es*, *-ed*, *-er*, or *-est*.

Basic

1. sunnier
2. cloudier
3. windier
4. cities
5. heaviest
6. prettiest
7. studied
8. easier
9. noisier
10. families
11. ferries
12. crazier
13. funnier
14. earlier
15. copied
16. hobbies
17. angriest
18. emptied
19. worried
20. happiest

■ Challenge

21. iciest
22. hazier
23. breezier
24. categories
25. qualities

Review

1. hurried
2. stories
3. carried
4. pennies
5. babies

Proofreading Marks

¶ Indent
∧ Add something
ℓ Take out something
≡ Capitalize
/ Make a small letter

Expanding Vocabulary

Exact Words for *noise*   Which sentence below helps you hear the sound of a bell?

I heard the **noise** of the bell. I heard the **clang** of the bell.

Clang is an exact word that describes the sound of metal hitting metal. Exact words make your writing clearer.

Practice   Write the best word below to replace *noise* in each sentence. Use your Thesaurus.

blare   racket   roar   patter

1. Crows make a <u>noise</u> each morning in our back yard.
2. The <u>noise</u> of the kitten's paws scared the mouse away.
3. The <u>noise</u> of the lion was heard throughout the zoo.
4. We heard the <u>noise</u> of the trumpets in the band.

1. _____   3. _____

2. _____   4. _____

Proofreading

Nouns in Direct Address   Use a comma or commas to set off the name of a person who is directly spoken to, or addressed.

Jim, today will be cold.   You, Kate, need a sweater today.

Practice   Proofread this script for a radio weather report. Find four misspelled words and three missing commas. Use proofreading marks to correct the errors.

Example: Will it be ~~sunnyer~~ *sunnier* in the afternoon, Lin?

Al: Have you studyed tomorrow's forecast, Lin?

Lin: I think Al, that it will be cloudier and

windyer than it was today.

Al: Are you worred about heavy rain, Lin?

Lin: Al it may rain lightly earlier in the day

until the clouds are carryed out to sea.

Al: Thank you, Lin for your report.

Review: Spelling Spree

Adding Endings   Write the Basic or Review Word that combines each base word and ending.

Example: study + ed   *studied*

1. carry + ed
2. worry + ed
3. copy + ed
4. angry + est
5. funny + er
6. easy + er
7. windy + er
8. sunny + er
9. hurry + ed
10. empty + ed
11. happy + est
12. crazy + er
13. family + es
14. pretty + est
15. cloudy + er

Silly Titles   Write a Basic or Review Word to complete each book title. Remember that the first, last, and each important word in a title begins with a capital letter.

Example: ____ *About the Future* by Ima Worrywart   *Worried*

16. *Dimes, Nickels, and* ____ by Count U. R. Change
17. *Big* ____ *and Small Towns* by Sid E. Slicker
18. *Small Boats and* ____ by Shep O. Hoy
19. *Louder and* ____ by Willie B. Quiet
20. *Feeding* ____ *and Children* by Hoo Flung Chow
21. *Books and* ____ *About Fishing* by Rod N. Reel
22. *Woodworking and Other* ____ by Whit Ling
23. *I* ____ *for Tests While Sleeping* by Betty Failed
24. *The* ____ *Weight* by Meg A. Ton
25. *How to Wake Up* ____ *in the Morning* by Earl E. Bird

■ **Challenge Words**   Look at the Silly Titles activity. Write five book titles, using a Challenge Word in each title. Make up a funny author's name that goes with each book. Use capital letters correctly, and underline your titles.

 **Writing Application:** A Description   What kind of weather do you like the best? What kind of weather do you like the least? Write a description of either your favorite or your least favorite weather. Try to use five words from the list on page 158.

1. _____
2. _____
3. _____
4. _____
5. _____
6. _____
7. _____
8. _____
9. _____
10. _____
11. _____
12. _____
13. _____
14. _____
15. _____
16. _____
17. _____
18. _____
19. _____
20. _____
21. _____
22. _____
23. _____
24. _____
25. _____

25   Spelling Across the Curriculum

Science: *Weather*

Theme Vocabulary

lightning
thunder
hurricane
blizzard
frost
drought
monsoon
hail

Using Vocabulary   Write the Vocabulary Words to complete the paragraph. Use your Spelling Dictionary.

Do you have unusual weather where you live? Africa has periods of __(1)__ with no water. In Asia there are heavy __(2)__ rains in April. The tropics have a __(3)__ season with rain and strong winds. New England can be hit by a __(4)__ with heavy snow. Hard balls of __(5)__ fall in Colorado. Fruit growers in Florida must guard crops against an icy __(6)__. Rainstorms with loud __(7)__ and flashes of __(8)__ are common in New Mexico.

Understanding Vocabulary   Write the Vocabulary Word that matches each clue.

9. Crops need rain. They can't grow during one of these.
10. It is caused by a charge of electricity.
11. You would be snowed in by one of these.
12. It can be as small as peas or as large as baseballs.

1. _____

2. _____

3. _____

4. _____

5. _____

6. _____

7. _____

8. _____

9. _____

10. _____

11. _____

12. _____

FACT FILE

Dog days are hot days in July and August. The star Sirius, or Dog Star, appears in those months. Long ago, people thought that the heat from the star caused the hot weather.

Enrichment

👪 *Heat Wave*

Players: 2 **You need:** 25 cards with a Basic or Review Word on each one, a game board like the one shown, game markers

How to play: Players take turns drawing a card and reading it aloud. If the other player spells the word correctly, he or she moves the marker to the next block that has the same ending as the word. If the player spells the word incorrectly, the marker stays where it is. The first player to reach 100 degrees wins.

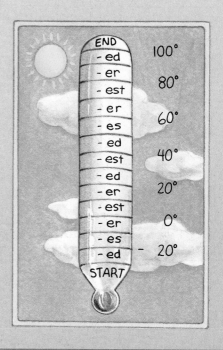

📖 *Writing*
Storm Clouds Brewing

Pretend that you are a weather forecaster. You are expecting very severe weather, such as a hurricane or a blizzard, in your area in the next few days. Write a weather report. Tell your audience what to expect. Try to use words from the lists in this unit. Be sure to proofread your paper.

A WEATHER CHART

Make a weather chart to show the weather changes for a school week. Divide a piece of paper into five sections labeled Monday, Tuesday, Wednesday, Thursday, and Friday. Make a key for your chart by drawing symbols that stand for different kinds of weather, such as a kite for a windy day. Record the weather each day by drawing one or more symbols in that day's section.

Theme: Flying

26 VCV Pattern

LOOK   at each word.

SAY   each word.

Basic Words   ■ Challenge

1. pilot	11. tiger	21. license
2. pupil	12. spider	22. radar
3. navy	13. tiny	23. waver
4. female	14. tuna	24. feature
5. silent	15. fever	25. diesel
6. human	16. frozen	
7. chosen	17. moment	
8. music	18. season	
9. paper	19. stolen	
10. reason	20. basic	

THINK   about the words.

Each word has two syllables and the vowel-consonant-vowel (VCV) pattern. Divide the word into syllables before the consonant. Look for patterns you have learned, and spell the word by syllables.

V | CV	V | CV
pi | lot	si | lent

- Look at the examples. Does the first syllable in each word have a long or a short vowel sound? Where would you divide each word in the list into syllables?

■ Challenge

WRITE   the words.

Practice **Write the twenty Basic Words.** Draw a line between the two syllables in each word.

■ **Now write the five Challenge Words.** Draw a line between the two syllables in each word.

CHECK   your spelling.

**huma[n]
huma[a]nity**

Spelling-Meaning Hint How can you remember how to spell the schwa sound in *human*? Think of the |ă| sound in the related word *humanity*.

Independent Practice

Spelling-Meaning Look at the Spelling-Meaning Hint.

1-2. Write *human* and *humanity*. Then underline the letter in *humanity* that helps you remember how to spell the schwa sound in *human*.

Word Analysis Complete the exercises with Basic Words.

3-4. Write the two words that have the |ē| sound spelled *ea*.

5-7. Write the word that has each base word.

  5. froze   **7.** chose
  6. stole

Making Inferences Write the Basic Word that fits each clue.
  8. This person flies planes.
  9. It is used to write on.
  10. It growls.
  11. It spins a web.
  12. It describes the *k* in *knit*.
  13. It lives in the sea.
  14. A band plays it.
  15. This person is in school.

V CV
pi lot

■ **Challenge Words** Write the Challenge Word that fits each meaning. Use your Spelling Dictionary.
  16. used to locate airplanes   **19.** to be uncertain
  17. legal permission   **20.** powered by an
  18. a special part or quality   engine that burns oil

1. _____
2. _____
3. _____
4. _____
5. _____
6. _____
7. _____
8. _____
9. _____
10. _____
11. _____
12. _____
13. _____
14. _____
15. _____
16. _____
17. _____
18. _____
19. _____
20. _____

Summing Up

When the first vowel sound in a VCV word is long, divide the word into syllables before the consonant. Look for patterns you have learned, and spell the word by syllables.

Basic

1. pilot
2. pupil
3. navy
4. female
5. silent
6. human
7. chosen
8. music
9. paper
10. reason
11. tiger
12. spider
13. tiny
14. tuna
15. fever
16. frozen
17. moment
18. season
19. stolen
20. basic

■ **Challenge**

21. license
22. radar
23. waver
24. feature
25. diesel

Review

1. bird
2. once
3. knew
4. straight
5. through

1. _____

_____

2. _____

_____

3. _____

4. _____

Expanding Vocabulary

Synonyms and Antonyms Many words have both synonyms and antonyms. Synonyms are words with similar meanings. Antonyms are words with opposite meanings.

	SYNONYM	ANTONYM
silent	quiet	noisy

Practice For each numbered word below, write one synonym from the box. Then write one antonym from the box. Use your Thesaurus.

frozen	boiling	begin	tiny
big	firm	end	soft

1. hard   **2.** start   **3.** cold   **4.** small

1. _____   _____

2. _____   _____

3. _____   _____

4. _____   _____

Dictionary

Parts of Speech A dictionary entry has a **part-of-speech label**, such as *n.* (noun), *v.* (verb), or *adj.* (adjective). The label tells how the word can be used in a sentence. Some words have more than one part-of-speech label.

part-of-speech label

pa·per |pā′ pər| *n., pl.* **papers 1.** A material made in thin sheets from pulp. **2.** A single sheet of paper. *v.* **papered, papering** To cover with wallpaper.

Practice Write *noun*, *verb*, or *adjective* to tell how each word below can be used. Use your Spelling Dictionary.

1. reason   **2.** welcome

Write *noun* or *verb* to show how *reason* is used.
3. I have a good <u>reason</u> for being late.
4. Jay tried to <u>reason</u> with Jenny to get her vote.

Review: Spelling Spree

Alphabet Puzzler   Write the Basic or Review Word that comes in the alphabet between each pair of words.

1. straggly, ____, strain
2. reach, ____, recent
3. stock, ____, stomach
4. timid, ____, tiptoe
5. tide, ____, tight
6. motor, ____, mustard
7. fell, ____, fence
8. jar, ____, matter
9. tulip, ____, tune
10. sniffle, ____, stand
11. panda, ____, parade
12. glad, ____, ink
13. barrel, ____, basket
14. forget, ____, fruit
15. poster, ____, race
16. nature, ____, neat
17. fern, ____, fewer
18. nest, ____, pale

Proofreading   **19-25.** Find and cross out seven misspelled Basic or Review Words in this ad. Then write each word correctly.

*A*irplane Rides ⬥ $30 for One Hour

Come fly throw the air like a brid. An experienced pilet, who has been choosen for her skill, will take you straight up into the wild blue yonder. High above the clouds, the world is silant and peaceful. The world below and all your problems will seem tiny. Once you have flown, you will catch the flying fever. Don't waste a momant. *Fly now!* The seson ends November 1.

■ **Challenge Words**   Write a question or a riddle for each Challenge Word. Then write the answers on the back of your paper. Trade questions with a classmate, and answer each other's questions.

Example: What do you have to apply for? *license*

Writing Application: An Interview   Pretend that you are interviewing a pilot. Write some questions you would like to ask. Then write answers that the pilot might give. Try to use five words from the list on page 164.

1. _____
2. _____
3. _____
4. _____
5. _____
6. _____
7. _____
8. _____
9. _____
10. _____
11. _____
12. _____
13. _____
14. _____
15. _____
16. _____
17. _____
18. _____
19. _____
20. _____
21. _____
22. _____
23. _____
24. _____
25. _____

26   Spelling Across the Curriculum

Careers: *Flying*

Theme Vocabulary

helicopter
runway
hangar
control tower
glider
parachute
aviation
terminal

Using Vocabulary   Write the Vocabulary Words to complete the paragraph. Use your Spelling Dictionary.

On Career Day we took a tour of an airport because we were studying __(1)__. We started in the __(2)__ where planes arrived and departed. Then we watched an air traffic controller in the __(3)__ tell a pilot which __(4)__ to use for takeoff. To see where planes are kept and repaired, we visited a __(5)__. A worker fixed the blades of a __(6)__, and a pilot packed a __(7)__ in case of an emergency. Later, I saw a __(8)__ land silently in a field.

Understanding Vocabulary   Write the Vocabulary Word that answers each question.

9. Which needs an engine: a <u>glider</u> or a <u>helicopter</u>?
10. Which is larger: a <u>hangar</u> or a <u>glider</u>?
11. Do you need a <u>parachute</u> or a <u>runway</u> to land a plane?
12. Do passengers wait in a <u>terminal</u> or in a <u>hangar</u>?

1. _____
2. _____
3. _____
4. _____
5. _____
6. _____
7. _____
8. _____
9. _____
10. _____
11. _____
12. _____

FACT FILE

The Concorde, a French airplane, travels faster than the speed of sound. It sends shock waves through the air that make an explosive sound called a sonic boom.

Enrichment

👥 *Tailspin*

Players: 2–4 **You need:** a game board like the one shown, with a plane for a spinner; a paper fastener; a list of the unit Basic Words
How to play: Fasten the plane to the game board with the paper fastener. Work as a group to write Basic Words in the spaces around the circle. Players take turns spinning the airplane. When the airplane stops on a word, the player must use the word correctly in a sentence. Players receive one point for using each word correctly. The first player with seven points wins.

AIRPLANE DESIGN

Look up pictures of early airplanes in an encyclopedia or other book about aviation. Draw a picture of one of the models. Below your drawing, write a brief description or history of the plane. Try to use words from the lists in this unit.

📖 *Writing*
Haiku

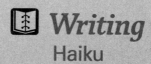

A haiku is a Japanese poem. It has three unrhymed lines. The first and third lines have five syllables. The second line has seven syllables. Write a haiku about how you think it feels to fly. Read this example.

> *High above the ground*
> *I am a fearless pilot.*
> *White clouds cradle me.*

Try to use words from the lists in this unit. Be sure to proofread your poem.

Theme: A Nature Walk

27 VCV Pattern

LOOK   at each word.

SAY   each word.

Basic Words   ■ Challenge

1. cabin	11. talent	21. pheasant
2. robin	12. modern	22. quiver
3. cover	13. limit	23. hazard
4. planet	14. cousin	24. vivid
5. visit	15. oven	25. jealous
6. finish	16. prison	
7. salad	17. punish	
8. seven	18. habit	
9. magic	19. never	
10. exact	20. busy	

THINK   about the words.

Here are more two-syllable words with the VCV pattern. Each word is divided into syllables after the consonant. Look for patterns you have learned. Spell each word by syllables.

VC | V	VC | V
cab | in	**plan | et**

- Do you hear a long or a short vowel sound in the first syllable of each word? Does the first syllable end with a vowel or a consonant sound? Where would you divide each word in the list into syllables?

WRITE   the words.

Practice   Write the twenty Basic Words. Draw a line between the two syllables in each word.

■ **Now write the five Challenge Words.** Draw a line between the two syllables in each word.

CHECK   your spelling.

■ Challenge

> *Spelling-Meaning Hint*   How can you remember to spell the |sh| sound in *magician* with a *c*? Think of the related word *magic*. **Think of this:** A *magician* is a person who performs *magic*.

**magic
magician**

Independent Practice

Spelling-Meaning   Look at the Spelling-Meaning Hint.

1-2. Write *magic* and *magician*. Underline the letter in *magic* that helps you spell the |sh| sound in *magician*.

Word Analysis   Complete the exercises with Basic Words.

3-6. Write the four words with the |z| sound spelled *s*.

7-10. Write four words by adding the missing syllables.

    7. tal | ____   **9.** lim | ____

    8. ____ | act   **10.** cov | ____

Classifying   Write the Basic Word that fits in each group.

11. five, six, ____
12. sparrow, jay, ____
13. hut, lodge, ____
14. sun, moon, ____
15. soup, sandwich, ____

VC V
rob in

■ **Challenge Words**   Write the Challenge Word that fits each meaning. Use your Spelling Dictionary.

16. brightly colored game bird
17. bright and strong
18. envious
19. to tremble
20. something that may cause injury or harm

1. _____
2. _____
3. _____
4. _____
5. _____
6. _____
7. _____
8. _____
9. _____
10. _____
11. _____
12. _____
13. _____
14. _____
15. _____
16. _____
17. _____
18. _____
19. _____
20. _____

Summing Up

When the first syllable of a VCV word has a short vowel sound followed by a consonant sound, divide the word into syllables after the consonant. Look for patterns you have learned, and spell the word by syllables.

Basic

1. cabin
2. robin
3. cover
4. planet
5. visit
6. finish
7. salad
8. seven
9. magic
10. exact
11. talent
12. modern
13. limit
14. cousin
15. oven
16. prison
17. punish
18. habit
19. never
20. busy

■ Challenge

21. pheasant
22. quiver
23. hazard
24. vivid
25. jealous

Review

1. travel
2. would
3. orange
4. ever
5. second

Proofreading Marks

¶ Indent
∧ Add something
ℓ Take out something
≡ Capitalize
/ Make a small letter

Expanding Vocabulary

Word Histories Many words have changed in meaning over time. Did you know that long ago you could buy things with your talents? Read the word history below.

> **Talent** comes from the Greek word *talanton*, which meant "a large sum of money." In ancient Greece, Rome, and the Middle East, a talent was also a coin.

Talent now means a special skill or ability. Like money, a talent is something that has value.

Practice **Look up each word below in your Spelling Dictionary, and read its word history. First, write what the word meant long ago. Then write what the word means now.**

1. polite   **2.** alley   **3.** cattle

1. _____

2. _____

3. _____

Proofreading

Quotations Use quotation marks before and after a speaker's exact words. Begin the first word with a capital letter. Put punctuation marks inside the last quotation marks.

Lou exclaimed, "These woods are beautiful!"

Practice **Proofread this conversation. Find four misspelled words, two missing quotation marks, and two letters that need capitalizing. Use proofreading marks to correct the errors.**

Example: "Have you ~~aver~~ *ever* slept in the woods?" asked Lou.

Pete said, "I am going to visit my cusin today."

"Is she the one who lives in a log caben? asked Lou.

"yes, I travle to see her every year, replied Pete.

"I have never seen those woods," sighed Lou.

Pete said, "maybe you woud like to come along."

Review: Spelling Spree

Silly Rhymes Write the Basic or Review Word that completes each sentence. Each answer rhymes with the underlined word.
1. It is <u>tragic</u> that the wizard forgot his ____ .
2. Elephants do not ____ say the word <u>never</u>.
3. Ralph <u>could</u> fly if he ____ only try.
4. We could not <u>unravel</u> the plans we made to ____ .
5. Do four and ____ make <u>eleven</u>?
6. Kim tried but could ____ lift the <u>lever</u>.

Familiar Phrases Write the Basic or Review Word that completes each phrase.
7. an apple and an ____
8. first, ____ , third
9. a log ____
10. a wren and a ____
11. break a bad ____
12. aunt and ____
13. a sweet ____ dressing
14. give the ____ change
15. the ____ line of a race
16. bake in the ____
17. behind the bars of a ____
18. as ____ as a bee
19. the ____ Earth
20. to drive at the speed ____
21. a special skill or ____
22. a new and ____ building
23. a short ____ with friends
24. to judge a book by its ____
25. reward the good and ____ the bad

■ **Challenge Words** Make a mini-thesaurus. Staple together five half sheets of paper. On each one, write a Challenge Word and a word that could replace it. Write a definition and a sample sentence for each word. Use your Spelling Dictionary and a class dictionary.

📖 ***Writing Application:* A Trail Guide** Imagine that you are writing a trail guide for a nature walk. Describe four or five sights to see on your trail, such as plants, flowers, or birds. You may want to give the trail a name. Try to use five words from the list on page 170.

1. _____
2. _____
3. _____
4. _____
5. _____
6. _____
7. _____
8. _____
9. _____
10. _____
11. _____
12. _____
13. _____
14. _____
15. _____
16. _____
17. _____
18. _____
19. _____
20. _____
21. _____
22. _____
23. _____
24. _____
25. _____

27   Spelling Across the Curriculum

Science: *A Nature Walk*

Theme Vocabulary

porcupine
spruce
maple
caterpillar
owl
chipmunk
rattlesnake
insect

Using Vocabulary   Write the Vocabulary Words to complete the paragraph. Use your Spelling Dictionary.

I thought my job as a nature guide would be easy. After all, I know the difference between a six-legged __(1)__ and a fuzzy __(2)__ . I can identify an __(3)__ by its hoot and a __(4)__ by its stripes. I can identify the needles of a __(5)__ tree and the leaves of a __(6)__ . But I did not expect that one child would try to pet the sharp quills of the __(7)__ , or that another child would try to go near a dangerous __(8)__ . This is not an easy job!

Understanding Vocabulary   Write the Vocabulary Word that matches each clue.

9. A fly is one of these.
10. This animal would be painful to pet.
11. A night hike would be a good way to see this bird.
12. This creature walks before it flies.

1. _____
2. _____
3. _____
4. _____
5. _____
6. _____
7. _____
8. _____
9. _____
10. _____
11. _____
12. _____

FACT FILE

Deciduous trees lose their leaves in the fall. Deciduous trees, such as maple trees, have broad leaves. Evergreen trees, such as spruce trees, keep their needle-shaped leaves.

Enrichment

👪 *Inch by Inch*

With a partner go on a 108-inch hike. Measure and cut a piece of string three yards long. Find a place outside that might seem like a forest to an ant. Lay out the string in a straight line or a curve. Follow the string, and make a complete record of the different kinds of plants, insects, and soil you find. Take samples of the plants and soil, and draw pictures of the insects and other creatures. Label your samples. Display your collection on a large chart or poster.

📖 *Writing*

As I See It

What does the world look like to an ant, a tree, or a rock? Choose something that you might see along a nature walk, and write a story from its point of view. What might a rock be afraid of? How might an ant feel about humans? Try to include words from the lists in this unit. Be sure to proofread your paper.

VCV CATERPILLARS

Make VCV caterpillars of three or more words. Cut out twenty circles from sheets of different colored paper. On one circle, write the first syllable of a spelling word. On another circle of the same color, write the last syllable of that word. Paste the circles in order on a large piece of paper. Draw or paste a head and legs on each caterpillar.

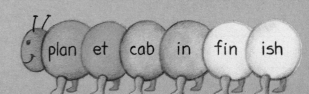

Theme: Medicine

28 Words with Suffixes

LOOK at each word.

SAY each word.

Basic Words   ■ Challenge

1. sickness   11. movement   21. ailment
2. illness   12. restless   22. appointment
3. treatment   13. darkness   23. resourceful
4. painful   14. useless   24. numbness
5. careless   15. kindness   25. cleanliness
6. fearful   16. hopeless
7. colorful   17. statement
8. endless   18. powerful
9. beautiful   19. friendliness
10. awful   20. peaceful

THINK about the words.

Each word is made up of a base word and a suffix. A **suffix** is a word part added to the end of a base word.

BASE WORD		SUFFIX		NEW WORD	MEANING
sick	+	ness	=	sick**ness**	quality of being sick
treat	+	ment	=	treat**ment**	act of treating
beauty	+	ful	=	beauti**ful**	full of beauty
care	+	less	=	care**less**	without care

• What four suffixes do you see in the list? How does the spelling of base words that end with *y* change when the suffix is added? Which word has the base word *awe*?

WRITE the words.

Practice   **Write the twenty Basic Words.** Underline the suffix in each word.

■ **Now write the five Challenge Words.** Underline the suffix in each word.

CHECK your spelling.

■ Challenge

> *Spelling-Meaning Hint* Can you see *pain* in *painful* and *painless*? Different suffixes can be added to the same base word to form new related words.

pain
pain**ful**
pain**less**

Independent Practice

Spelling-Meaning Look at the Spelling-Meaning Hint.
1-2. Write *painless*. Then write the Basic Word that is related to *painless* in spelling and meaning.

Word Analysis Complete the exercises with Basic Words.

3-4. Write the two words ending with *-ness* that are synonyms.

5-9. Write the word that has each underlined base word.

    5. <u>hope</u>ful
    6. <u>color</u>less
    7. <u>fear</u>less
    8. <u>use</u>ful
    9. <u>power</u>less

Word Clues Write the Basic Word that fits each clue.
10. synonym for *horrible*   **13.** synonym for *calm*
11. antonym for *ugly*   **14.** having no light
12. unable to sit still   **15.** never finishing

■ **Challenge Words** Write the Challenge Word that fits each clue. Use your Spelling Dictionary.
    16. an arrangement to meet
    17. free from dirt
    18. an illness
    19. clever and capable
    20. lacking the power to feel or move

Summing Up

A **suffix** is a word part added to the end of a base word. It adds meaning to the base word. When a suffix begins with a consonant, the spelling of the base word usually does not change unless the base word ends with *y*. Then the *y* is changed to *i* before the suffix is added.

1. _____
2. _____
3. _____
4. _____
5. _____
6. _____
7. _____
8. _____
9. _____
10. _____
11. _____
12. _____
13. _____
14. _____
15. _____
16. _____
17. _____
18. _____
19. _____
20. _____

Basic

1. sickness
2. illness
3. treatment
4. painful
5. careless
6. fearful
7. colorful
8. endless
9. beautiful
10. awful
11. movement
12. restless
13. darkness
14. useless
15. kindness
16. hopeless
17. statement
18. powerful
19. friendliness
20. peaceful

■ Challenge

21. ailment
22. appointment
23. resourceful
24. numbness
25. cleanliness

Review

1. hopeful
2. useful
3. careful
4. thankful
5. singer

Expanding Vocabulary

Color Words Which phrase better describes colorful autumn leaves of deep red and yellow?

> **red** and **yellow** leaves
> **scarlet** and **gold** leaves

Scarlet and *gold* are exact words that describe specific shades of deep red and yellow.

Practice **Write a word below to replace the underlined word or words in each sentence. Use your Thesaurus.**

scarlet   amber   turquoise
lavender   tangerine

1. The yellowish-brown cider looked refreshing.
2. The marching band wore red uniforms.
3. I bought a blue-green bracelet at the crafts fair.
4. Jacob used the orange crayon to add color to his picture.
5. Anika decided to paint her room purple.

1. _____   4. _____

2. _____   5. _____

3. _____

Dictionary

Suffixes Some words with suffixes are not listed as entry words. However, suffixes have separate entries. Look up the base word and the suffix, and combine the two meanings.

> **-less** A suffix that forms adjectives and means "not having" or "without": *harmless*.

Practice **Look up the base word and the suffix of each word below. Write a short definition of each word.**

1. firmness   **2.** flavorful   **3.** friendless

1. _____

2. _____

3. _____

Review: Spelling Spree

Suffix Match   Write Basic or Review Words by matching the base words and suffixes. Be careful of the word that ends with *y*!

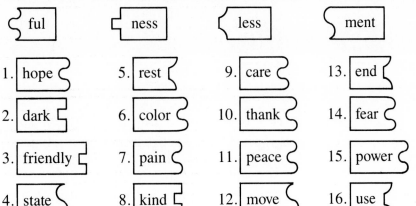

| ful | ness | less | ment |

1. hope
2. dark
3. friendly
4. state
5. rest
6. color
7. pain
8. kind
9. care
10. thank
11. peace
12. move
13. end
14. fear
15. power
16. use

Proofreading   17-25. Find and cross out nine misspelled Basic or Review Words in this conversation. Then write each word correctly.

DOCTOR: Aren't you the famous singor Johnny Jazz? What happened to your beutiful voice? You sound aweful!

PATIENT: I was carless with my health, and now I have a painful sore throat. Can you give me some powerful medicine to cure my sikness? I have to perform tonight.

DOCTOR: I am afraid it is hopeliss. The only usefull treetment for your ilness is to rest your voice.

■ **Challenge Words**   Write each Challenge Word on a piece of paper. Draw a picture around the words. Then cut the picture into ten puzzle pieces. Include the base word or suffix of one word on each piece. Trade puzzles with a classmate.

Writing Application: A Personal Story   Were you ever too sick to do something you wanted to do? Did you ever pretend to be sick? Write a paragraph about that time. Try to use five words from the list on page 176.

1. _____
2. _____
3. _____
4. _____
5. _____
6. _____
7. _____
8. _____
9. _____
10. _____
11. _____
12. _____
13. _____
14. _____
15. _____
16. _____
17. _____
18. _____
19. _____
20. _____
21. _____
22. _____
23. _____
24. _____
25. _____

28   Spelling Across the Curriculum

Health: *Medicine*

Theme Vocabulary

medicine
patient
infected
disease
surgery
clinic
wound
prescription

Using Vocabulary Write the Vocabulary Words to complete the paragraph. Use your Spelling Dictionary.

Dr. Davis runs the only __(1)__ for miles around, and every __(2)__ who comes in is important to her. Whether she is writing a __(3)__ for a child with a fever, cleaning a bleeding __(4)__ so it does not become __(5)__ , or treating someone with a serious __(6)__ such as cancer, she is always kind and gentle. She has even performed emergency __(7)__ on a cat! Dr. Davis knows that to be a good doctor you must do more than just give out __(8)__ .

Understanding Vocabulary Write *yes* if the underlined word or phrase is used correctly. Write *no* if it is not.

9. The <u>wound</u> on Paula's finger was not deep.
10. The doctor's <u>prescription</u> was that I had the flu.
11. The nurse put a bandage on my <u>disease</u>.
12. The doctor operated on the <u>patient</u>.

1. _____
2. _____
3. _____
4. _____
5. _____
6. _____
7. _____
8. _____
9. _____
10. _____
11. _____
12. _____

FACT FILE

Doctors promise to serve patients well when they take the Hippocratic oath. This oath is named after Hippocrates, a doctor in ancient Greece, called the father of modern medicine.

Enrichment

👥 *Suffix Squares*

Players: 2 or more, a caller **You need:** a pencil and paper for each player

How to play: Each player draws a card with nine squares and writes *ful*, *ness*, *less*, or *ment* in each square. Any suffix can be written in any square. The caller reads a list word. Each player writes the word in any square with that suffix. The first player to fill in all the squares on his or her card wins.

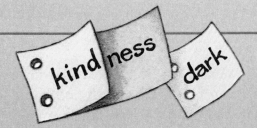

SUFFIX FLIP FUN

Punch two holes in the left side of a large index card. On the right side, write a suffix, such as *ness*. Then cut five index cards in half. Punch holes in the cards to line up with the holes in the large card. On the small cards, print base words that can be used with the suffix. Try to use words from the unit lists. Tie strings through the holes so you can flip the words back and forth.

📖 *Writing*
Medical Greats

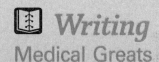

Read about someone famous in the field of medicine. You might choose one of the people listed below. Then write a brief report about the person. Try to use words from the lists in this unit. Be sure to proofread your paper.

Elizabeth Blackwell
Charlotte Friend
Joseph Lister
Florence Nightingale
Jonas Salk
Albert Schweitzer

Theme: Space Exploration

29 VCCV Pattern

LOOK at each word.

SAY each word.

Basic Words		■ Challenge
1. rocket	11. agree	21. descent
2. achieve	12. apron	22. vibrate
3. afraid	13. bucket	23. method
4. machine	14. pocket	24. reflect
5. secret	15. ticket	25. abrupt
6. gather	16. chicken	
7. other	17. degree	
8. package	18. bother	
9. declare	19. rather	
10. asleep	20. whether	

THINK about the words.

Each word has the VCCV pattern. The two consonants form a cluster, like the *fr* in *afraid*, or spell one sound, like the *ck* in *rocket*. Divide the word into syllables before or after the two consonants. Look for patterns you have learned. Spell the word by syllables.

V | CCV   VCC | V
a | f r a i d   **rock | et**

- Look at the example words. Does the first syllable of each word end with a vowel sound or a consonant sound? Where is each word divided into syllables?

WRITE the words.

Practice   Write the twenty Basic Words. Draw a line between the syllables. Use your Spelling Dictionary.

■ **Now write the five Challenge Words.** Draw a line between the syllables in each word.

CHECK your spelling.

■ Challenge

> *Spelling-Meaning Hint* Can you see *declare* in the word *declaration*? These words are related in spelling and meaning. **Think of this:** The countries will *declare* peace in the *declaration*.

declare
declaration

Independent Practice

Spelling-Meaning Look at the Spelling-Meaning Hint.
1-2. Write *declaration*. Then write the Basic Word that is related to *declaration* in spelling and meaning.

Word Analysis Complete the exercises with Basic Words.

3. Write the word that is a homophone for *weather*.

4-7. Write the four words that begin with the schwa sound spelled *a*.

8-9. Write the two words that rhyme with *locket*.

Synonyms Write the Basic Word that is a synonym for each word below.
10. somewhat
11. disturb
12. pail
13. bundle
14. hen
15. collect

■ **Challenge Words** Write the Challenge Word that fits each meaning. Use your Spelling Dictionary.
16. to give back an image of
17. a downward slope
18. taking place without warning
19. to move back and forth rapidly
20. a regular way of doing something

1. _____
2. _____
3. _____
4. _____
5. _____
6. _____
7. _____
8. _____
9. _____
10. _____
11. _____
12. _____
13. _____
14. _____
15. _____
16. _____
17. _____
18. _____
19. _____
20. _____

Summing Up

If the consonants in a VCCV word are different and form a cluster or spell one sound, divide the word before or after the two consonants. Look for patterns you have learned, and spell the word by syllables.

Basic

1. rocket
2. achieve
3. afraid
4. machine
5. secret
6. gather
7. other
8. package
9. declare
10. asleep
11. agree
12. apron
13. bucket
14. pocket
15. ticket
16. chicken
17. degree
18. bother
19. rather
20. whether

■ Challenge

21. descent
22. vibrate
23. method
24. reflect
25. abrupt

Review

1. nothing
2. between
3. teacher
4. helper
5. farmer

Proofreading Marks

¶ Indent
∧ Add something
ℓ Take out something
≡ Capitalize
/ Make a small letter

Expanding Vocabulary

Regional Differences   People who live in different parts of the United States call some things by different names. What do you call this item where you live?

bucket   pail

Practice   Which word in parentheses is used where you live? Write the word.

1. Brian and Cheryl played on the (seesaw, teeter-totter).
2. Our (basement, cellar) flooded during the storm.
3. Ms. Ramos fixed the leaking (tap, faucet, spigot).
4. Tim put (elastics, rubber bands) around the papers.

1. _____   3. _____

2. _____   4. _____

Proofreading

Friendly Letters   Be sure to use commas and capital letters correctly in friendly letters.

DAY AND YEAR: May 9, 1989   GREETINGS: Dear Sam,
CITY AND STATE: Bath, Maine   CLOSINGS: Your friend,

Practice   Proofread Michael's letter. Find four misspelled words, one letter that needs capitalizing, and two missing commas. Use proofreading marks to correct the errors.

Example: your ~~secert~~ *secret* friend,
              ≡

June 22, 1990

dear Lisa

Today our teecher took us to the Space Museum. We saw a real roket. Now there is nuthing I would rather do than travel in space! I would not be afrade.

Your brother
Michael

Review: Spelling Spree

Syllable Scramble Two of the three syllables in each item below form a Basic or Review Word. Write the words correctly.

Example: ing be noth   *nothing*

1. er et help
2. de er both
3. buck ma et
4. a gath sleep
5. cret se pock
6. fraid de a
7. clare et rock
8. er buck wheth
9. pock cret et
10. se clare de
11. er age gath
12. ma rock chine
13. chieve both a
14. age pack cret

Word Search Write the Basic or Review Word that is hidden in each sentence.

Example: I made both errors.   *bother*

15. It is hot here.
16. I see no thin goats.
17. I bet we enter there.
18. I bought each eraser.
19. You are far merrier today.
20. What is a pronoun?
21. He is a greedy man.
22. I need a plastic kettle.
23. There was no rat here.
24. The chick enjoys its food.
25. We made green beans.

Challenge Words Write a tongue twister for each Challenge Word. Make each tongue twister a complete sentence.

Example: **Did Daddy dine during the descent?**

Writing Application: Creative Writing Pretend you have landed on a distant planet. What is it like? Write a paragraph comparing and contrasting the place with Earth. Try to use five words from the list on page 182.

1. _____
2. _____
3. _____
4. _____
5. _____
6. _____
7. _____
8. _____
9. _____
10. _____
11. _____
12. _____
13. _____
14. _____
15. _____
16. _____
17. _____
18. _____
19. _____
20. _____
21. _____
22. _____
23. _____
24. _____
25. _____

29   Spelling Across the Curriculum

Science: *Space Exploration*

Theme Vocabulary

satellite
space shuttle
galaxy
astronaut
orbit
gravity
capsule
booster

Using Vocabulary   Write the Vocabulary Words to complete the paragraph. Use your Spelling Dictionary.

In 1962 John Glenn became the first American __(1)__ to go into __(2)__ around the earth. He viewed outer space from the small __(3)__ of his spacecraft. Now a vehicle called the __(4)__ goes back and forth between Earth and space. Its strong __(5)__ rockets thrust it away from the pull of Earth's __(6)__. It can carry an information-gathering __(7)__ into space. Someday this vehicle may take us across the Milky Way, our __(8)__.

Understanding Vocabulary   Write *yes* if the underlined word is used correctly. Write *no* if it is not.

9. The rocket used up a lot of gravity during takeoff.
10. The weather satellite circled Earth.
11. The space shuttle returned after a two-week flight.
12. The astronaut needed a booster to board the capsule.

1. _____
2. _____
3. _____
4. _____
5. _____
6. _____
7. _____
8. _____
9. _____
10. _____
11. _____
12. _____

FACT FILE

In 1961 President Kennedy started the Apollo program to try to put an astronaut on the moon by 1970. In 1969 Neil Armstrong became the first person to walk on the moon.

Enrichment

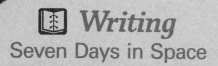 ## What's the Question?

Players: 2   **You need:** 25 word cards with one Basic or Review Word written on each card

How to play: The cards are placed face down in a pile. The first player draws a card and gives a clue for the spelling word on the card. The clue must be in the form of a statement. The second player responds by asking a question using the spelling word. He or she must also spell the word correctly to get a point.

Player 1: It goes up in space.

Player 2: What is a *rocket*? *r-o-c-k-e-t*

Players take turns drawing cards. The player with more points at the end of the game wins.

Writing
Seven Days in Space

Pretend that you are the youngest person ever to travel into space. You are spending a week on the space shuttle. Write a journal entry for each day. What kinds of things are you doing? What is it like to live on the shuttle? Try to use words from the lists in this unit. Be sure to proofread your paper.

PLANET MOBILE

Make a mobile of the solar system. Look up the size and location of each planet. Then draw the sun and the planets on colored paper, and cut them out. On each cutout, write the object's name and one sentence about it. Tape string to each cutout. Tie the sun and the planets in their correct order on a coat hanger.

30 Review: Units 25–29

| cities | prettiest | studied | families | easier |
| earlier | angriest | ferries | happiest | worried |

Remember: If a word ends with a consonant and **y**, change the **y** to **i** when adding **-es, -ed, -er,** or **-est.**

cloud ier

Write the word that fits each group.

1. study, studying, ____
2. pretty, prettier, ____
3. early, ____, earliest
4. easy, ____, easiest

5. worry, worrying, ____
6. angry, angrier, ____
7. happy, happier, ____

Write the word that completes each phrase.

8. towns and ____
9. parents and ____

10. sailboats and ____

1. _____
2. _____
3. _____
4. _____
5. _____
6. _____
7. _____
8. _____
9. _____
10. _____

| pupil | female | chosen | reason | paper |
| season | tiny | tiger | spider | frozen |

Remember: When the first vowel sound in a VCV word is long, divide the word into syllables before the consonant.

V CV
pi lot

Write a word by adding the missing syllable.

11. fro | ____
12. cho | ____
13. rea | ____

14. pu | ____
15. fe | ____

Write the word that matches each clue.

16. has eight legs
17. has stripes
18. used to write on

19. describes an ant
20. summer or winter

11. _____
12. _____
13. _____
14. _____
15. _____
16. _____
17. _____
18. _____
19. _____
20. _____

Half of the words from each unit are reviewed on these pages.
The rest are reviewed on pages 241–243.

Unit 27   VCV Pattern   pp. 168-173

cover	exact	robin	finish	cabin
oven	cousin	prison	busy	modern

Remember: When the first sylla-ble of a VCV word has a short vowel sound followed by a con-sonant sound, divide the word into syllables after the consonant.

Write a word by adding the missing syllable.

21. rob | ___   **23.** pris | ___   **25.** ___ | y

22. cous | ___   **24.** ___ | ern

Write the spelling word that you find in each word below.

26. refinish   **29.** cabinet

27. coverlet   **30.** ovenproof

28. exactly

21. _____

22. _____

23. _____

24. _____

25. _____

26. _____

27. _____

28. _____

29. _____

30. _____

Unit 28   Words with Suffixes   pp. 174-179

illness	beautiful	careless	treatment	awful
useless	friendliness	peaceful	powerful	movement

Remember:

beauty + **ful** = beaut**iful**

care + **less** = care**less**

Write the word that contains each base word below.

31. ill   **34.** move

32. treat   **35.** friendly

33. care

Write a word that is a synonym for each word.

36. quiet   **39.** worthless

37. lovely   **40.** terrible

38. mighty

31. _____

32. _____

33. _____

34. _____

35. _____

36. _____

37. _____

38. _____

39. _____

40. _____

30 Review

41. _____
42. _____
43. _____
44. _____
45. _____
46. _____
47. _____
48. _____
49. _____
50. _____

Unit 29   VCCV Pattern   pp. 180-185

declare	package	achieve	afraid	rocket
degree	chicken	bother	agree	whether

Remember: If the consonants in a VCCV word are different and form a cluster or spell one sound, divide the word before or after the two consonants.

v ccv
se cret

vcc v
rock et

Write the word that fits each meaning.
41. to share the same opinion   44. a step in a series
42. to give trouble to   45. if
43. a hen or a rooster   46. a bundle of things
Write the word that rhymes with each word below.
47. locket   49. believe
48. beware   50. braid

51. _____
52. _____
53. _____
54. _____
55. _____
56. _____
57. _____
58. _____
59. _____
60. _____

■ Challenge Words   Units 25-29   pp. 156-185

appointment	categories	breezier	feature	quiver
resourceful	license	pheasant	method	descent

Write the word that completes each phrase.
51. a special ____
52. to ____ with fear
53. a steep ____
54. to make an ____ with a dentist
55. the feathers of a ____
Write the word that can replace the underlined word or words.
56. a <u>way</u> of cooking chicken
57. a <u>clever</u> problem solver
58. organized into <u>groups</u>
59. <u>legal permission</u> to drive
60. a <u>windier</u> day than yesterday

Spelling-Meaning Strategy

30

Consonant Changes: The Sound of *c*

Words that end with *c* may have related words in which the *c* spells a different sound. Read these sentences.

music
musician

> The school band played some beautiful classical **music** during the concert in the high school auditorium. All of the young **musicians** played with great skill and feeling.

Think
- How are *music* and *musician* related in meaning?
- What sound does *c* spell in each word?

Here are more related words in which the letter *c* spells different sounds.

electric	mathematics
electrician	mathematician

Apply and Extend

Complete these activities on a separate piece of paper.

1. Look up the meaning of each word in the Word Box above in your Spelling Dictionary. Write four sentences, using each word in one sentence.

2. With a partner list as many words as you can that are related to *music*, *electric*, and *mathematics*. Then look on page 272 of your Spelling-Meaning Index. Add any other words that you find in these families to your list.

Summing Up   The |k| sound of *c* may change to |sh| when the suffix *-ian* is added. Thinking of a related word can help you remember that the |sh| sound is spelled *c*.

189

Persuasive Letter

Ben's class needed to raise money. Ben remembered the story Ernie and the Mile-Long Muffler *by Marjorie Lewis. The students in that story learned to knit and sold the things they made at a fair. Ben decided to write a persuasive letter to his neighbor. What did Ben want Mrs. Hendriks to do?*

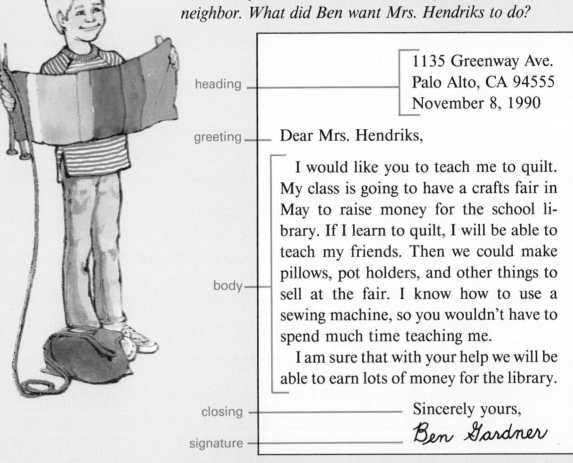

heading

1135 Greenway Ave.
Palo Alto, CA 94555
November 8, 1990

greeting

Dear Mrs. Hendriks,

body

   I would like you to teach me to quilt. My class is going to have a crafts fair in May to raise money for the school library. If I learn to quilt, I will be able to teach my friends. Then we could make pillows, pot holders, and other things to sell at the fair. I know how to use a sewing machine, so you wouldn't have to spend much time teaching me.

   I am sure that with your help we will be able to earn lots of money for the library.

closing

Sincerely yours,

signature

Ben Gardner

Think and Discuss

1. What did Ben want to **persuade** Mrs. Hendriks to do?
2. What **reasons** did Ben use to try to persuade her?
3. What is included in the **five parts** of a letter?

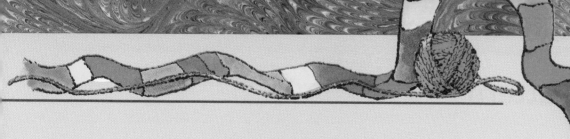

The Writing Process

Ben's letter on page 190 uses strong **reasons** that support his opinion and are important to his audience. He explains *why* he needs Mrs. Hendriks's help and how little time he will need from her. To write a persuasive letter, begin with a **topic sentence** that states your opinion. Use strong reasons that will make your audience agree with you.

Assignment: Write a Persuasive Letter

Step One: Prewriting

1. What would you like to persuade someone to do? Discuss your ideas. Choose one.
2. List strong reasons to support your opinion.

Step Two: Write a First Draft

1. Think about your purpose and your audience.
2. Do not worry about mistakes—just write!

Step Three: Revise

1. Did you state your opinion clearly in a topic sentence? Have you used strong, convincing reasons?
2. Use your Thesaurus to find exact words.
3. Read your letter to a classmate. Make other changes.

Step Four: Proofread

1. Did you include all five parts of a letter?
2. Did you capitalize and punctuate correctly?
3. Did you spell all words correctly? Copy any words that you misspelled into your Notebook for Writing.

Step Five: Publish

1. Copy your letter neatly.
2. Address and stamp an envelope. Mail your letter.

Composition Words

families
worried
human
basic
planet
talent
achieve
agree

Proofreading Marks

¶ Indent
∧ Add something
ℓ Take out something
≡ Capitalize
/ Make a small letter

Theme: Coast Guard

31 VCV Pattern

A. _____

_____

_____

_____

B. _____

_____

_____

_____

_____

_____

_____

_____

_____

_____

_____

_____

_____

_____

■ Challenge

_____

_____

_____

_____

LOOK at each word.

SAY each word.

Basic Words   ■ Challenge

1. ocean   11. exit   21. peril
2. police   12. polite   22. marine
3. depend   13. open   23. cadet
4. siren   14. figure   24. rival
5. defend   15. event   25. alert
6. today   16. belong
7. parent   17. award
8. become   18. palace
9. below   19. delay
10. relate   20. clever

THINK about the words.

Each two-syllable word has the VCV pattern. Some VCV words begin with the short vowel pattern. They are divided into syllables after the consonant. Other VCV words are divided before the consonant.

VC | V   V | CV

par | ent   **si | ren**

- Which Basic Words have first syllables with the short vowel pattern? Which Basic Words have first syllables that end with a vowel sound?

WRITE the words.

Practice **Write the Basic Words to answer the questions.**

A. Which **five** words are divided after the consonant?
B. Which **fifteen** words are divided before the consonant?

■ **Now write the five Challenge Words.** Draw lines between the syllables. Use your Spelling Dictionary.

CHECK your spelling.

> **Spelling-Meaning Hint** How can you remember how to spell the |sh| sound in *relation*? Think of the word *relate*. The *t* in *relate* is kept in *relation* even though the sound changes.

rela**t**e
rela**t**ion

Independent Practice

Spelling-Meaning Look at the Spelling-Meaning Hint.

1-2. Write *relate* and *relation*. Then underline the letter in *relate* that helps you spell the |sh| sound in *relation*.

Word Analysis Complete the exercises with Basic Words.

3. Write the word with the |sh| sound.

4-5. Write the two words that end with the |s| sound.

6-8. Write the three words with the first syllable *be*.

9-10. Write the two words that rhyme with *send*.

Classifying Write the Basic Word that belongs in each group.
11. yesterday, tomorrow, ____
12. symbol, number, ____
13. son, daughter, ____
14. bell, whistle, ____
15. medal, prize, ____

V CV   VC V
be low ex it

■ **Challenge Words** Write the Challenge Word that fits each meaning. Use your Spelling Dictionary.
16. quick to act
17. condition of being in danger
18. relating to the sea
19. someone who competes
20. student at a naval school

1. _____
2. _____
3. _____
4. _____
5. _____
6. _____
7. _____
8. _____
9. _____
10. _____
11. _____
12. _____
13. _____
14. _____
15. _____
16. _____
17. _____
18. _____
19. _____
20. _____

Summing Up

A two-syllable word with the VCV pattern can be divided into syllables before or after the consonant. Look for familiar patterns, and spell the word by syllables.

Basic

1. ocean
2. police
3. depend
4. siren
5. defend
6. today
7. parent
8. become
9. below
10. relate
11. exit
12. polite
13. open
14. figure
15. event
16. belong
17. award
18. palace
19. delay
20. clever

■ Challenge

21. peril
22. marine
23. cadet
24. rival
25. alert

Review

1. before
2. away
3. alive
4. begin
5. giraffe

Proofreading Marks

¶ Indent
∧ Add something
ℓ Take out something
≡ Capitalize
/ Make a small letter

Expanding Vocabulary

Exact Words for *relate* *Relate* means "to tell something." Other words meaning "to tell something" also express *how* the words are spoken. What does *complained* tell you?

"I am late," Ed **related.**   "I am late," Ed **complained.**

Practice   Write the word below that best fits each speaker. Use your Thesaurus.

exclaimed   questioned   agreed   suggested   groaned

1. "Do you want to sail beyond the harbor?" ____ Rita.
2. "I'm getting cold and wet," ____ Mark.
3. "Rita, watch out for that rock!" ____ Pat.
4. "Perhaps we should turn back," ____ Ping.
5. "Yes, I think you are right," ____ Rita.

1. _____   4. _____

2. _____   5. _____

3. _____

Proofreading

Book Titles   Remember to capitalize the first, last, and each important word in a book title. Underline the title.

My favorite book is <u>This Is the Story of the Sea.</u>

Practice   Proofread Yoko's book list. Find four misspelled words, one word that needs a capital letter, and a missing underline. Use proofreading marks to correct the errors.

Example: Does the book <u>On the high Seas</u> ~~belog~~ *belong* to you?

1. In the book <u>Sea Stories</u> a sailor is found aliv after being lost on the ochen for weeks.

2. The books <u>The World Below</u> and <u>Underwater</u> relat true stories of underwater exploration.

3. In <u>All Hands on deck</u> young sailors difend their ship and drive away pirates.

Review: Spelling Spree

Questions   Write a Basic or Review Word to answer each question.

1. What animal has a very long neck?
2. What do you do at the start of something?
3. How could you describe someone who is breathing?
4. What is the opposite of *after*?
5. What do you call someone who is smart?
6. Where does a king live?
7. What is another name for a shape?
8. What makes a loud warning noise?
9. Who keeps law and order in a city or a town?
10. Where do whales live?
11. What do you call someone who says *please*?

Syllable Addition   Write a Basic or Review Word by adding the underlined syllable of the first word to the underlined syllable of the second word.

12. <u>de</u>mand + sus<u>pend</u>
13. <u>to</u>morrow + birth<u>day</u>
14. be<u>tween</u> + <u>wel</u>come
15. re<u>move</u> + trans<u>late</u>
16. <u>o</u>dor + hap<u>pen</u>
17. e<u>rase</u> + pre<u>vent</u>
18. <u>a</u>mong + for<u>ward</u>
19. <u>de</u>part + of<u>fend</u>
20. <u>par</u>rot + <u>tal</u>ent
21. be<u>hind</u> + <u>fol</u>low
22. <u>ex</u>tra + <u>lim</u>it
23. de<u>light</u> + <u>re</u>lay
24. be<u>lieve</u> + a<u>long</u>
25. a<u>head</u> + sub<u>way</u>

■ **Challenge Words**   Look at the Questions activity. Write a question or a riddle for each Challenge Word. Then write the Challenge Word that answers the question.

Writing Application: A Story   Pretend that you are sailing on the ocean. Suddenly a storm hits and damages your boat. What can you do? Write a short story, telling how you survive until the Coast Guard finds you. Try to use five words from the list on page 194.

1. _____
2. _____
3. _____
4. _____
5. _____
6. _____
7. _____
8. _____
9. _____
10. _____
11. _____
12. _____
13. _____
14. _____
15. _____
16. _____
17. _____
18. _____
19. _____
20. _____
21. _____
22. _____
23. _____
24. _____
25. _____

31 Spelling Across the Curriculum

Careers: *Coast Guard*

Theme Vocabulary

rescue
fleet
patrol
borders
uniform
cutter
beacon
academy

Using Vocabulary Write a Vocabulary Word to complete the paragraph. Use your Spelling Dictionary.

Frank stood on the deck of the Coast Guard __(1)__ . He peered into the fog, searching for the lighthouse __(2)__ . His life jacket and his blue __(3)__ were wet from the ocean spray. Ahead, a __(4)__ of fishing boats had crashed against the rocky coast. Frank knew these coastal __(5)__ well. As a student at the __(6)__ , he had been on __(7)__ to guard these waters many times. He knew that the __(8)__ of these boats now would depend on his skill.

Understanding Vocabulary Write *yes* if the underlined word is used correctly. Write *no* if it is not.

9. A <u>beacon</u> guided the sailor through the fog.
10. There was one boat in the <u>fleet</u>.
11. One of the fishing boats was a <u>cutter</u>.
12. A Coast Guard member wears a <u>uniform</u> on duty.

1. _____
2. _____
3. _____
4. _____
5. _____
6. _____
7. _____
8. _____
9. _____
10. _____
11. _____
12. _____

FACT FILE

The Morse code is a system of dots, dashes, and spaces used to send messages over wires. SOS is a famous distress signal sent by ships and boats that are in trouble.

Enrichment

 **Match Game**

Players: 2 **You need:** 10 word cards with a Basic or Review Word on each; 10 cards with the meaning for one of the words on each card
How to play: Shuffle the word and meaning cards. Place the cards face down in four rows of five. Players take turns turning over two cards at a time, hoping to make a match between a word and its meaning. If the cards match, the player may keep the cards after using the word correctly in a sentence. If the cards do not match, they are turned face down again. The player with the most cards at the end wins.

MORSE CODE

Look up the Morse code in an encyclopedia or a resource book. Imagine that your boat is in trouble. Make up an SOS message to call for help. Write your message in Morse code on a large piece of paper. Underneath the code, write out the message. Display your work on the bulletin board. Try to use list words.

 **Writing**
Words to Live By

The motto of the Coast Guard is Always Ready. If you had to write a motto or saying that you live by, what would it be? Make up a motto and give examples of how you follow it. For example, suppose your motto is Depend on Me. You could describe some situations that show you can be depended upon. Try to use words from the lists in this unit. Be sure to proofread your paper.

32 VCCV and VCV Patterns

A. _____
_____
_____
_____
_____
_____

B. _____
_____
_____
_____
_____
_____
_____
_____
_____
_____
_____
_____

■ **Challenge**
_____
_____
_____
_____
_____

LOOK at each word.

SAY each word.

Basic Words   ■ Challenge

1. wagon	11. parade	21. frontier
2. capture	12. narrow	22. sheriff
3. silver	13. corner	23. prairie
4. reward	14. bacon	24. stampede
5. shelter	15. amaze	25. corral
6. divide	16. diner	
7. nature	17. dinner	
8. alone	18. eager	
9. office	19. minute	
10. famous	20. fancy	

THINK about the words.

Each two-syllable word has the VCCV or the VCV pattern. Divide each word into syllables. Look for patterns that you have learned, and spell each word by syllables.

VC | CV	VC | V	V | CV
din | ner	**wag | on**	**di | vide**

- Where is a VCCV word divided into syllables? Where do you divide a VCV word that has the short vowel pattern in the first syllable? Where do you divide a VCV word when the first syllable ends with a vowel sound?

WRITE the words.

Practice   Write the Basic Words to answer the questions.

A. Which **eight** words have the VCCV pattern?

B. Which **twelve** words have the VCV pattern?

■ **Now write the five Challenge Words.** Draw lines between the syllables. Use your Spelling Dictionary.

CHECK your spelling.

> **Spelling-Meaning Hint**   *Nature* and *natural* are related in spelling and meaning even though the two words have different vowel sounds. **Think of this:** *Nature* provides us with many important *natural* resources.

na|ture
na|tural

Independent Practice

Spelling-Meaning   Look at the Spelling-Meaning Hint.

1-2. Write *natural*. Then write the Basic Word that is related to *natural* in spelling and meaning.

Word Analysis   Complete the exercises with Basic Words.

3-4. Write *diner*. Then add a letter to write another word.

5-6. Write the two words that begin or end with the |ē| sound.

7-8. Write two words that begin with the |ə| sound spelled *a*.

Word Clues   Write the Basic Word that fits each clue.

9. part of an hour
10. opposite of *wide*
11. a math operation
12. very well known
13. where two roads meet
14. has four wheels
15. a metal used for jewelry

V CV
re ward

VC CV
sil ver

■ **Challenge Words**   Write the Challenge Word that fits each meaning. Use your Spelling Dictionary.

16. flat, open grassland
17. a pen for horses
18. the farthest point of settlement
19. a sudden rush of animals
20. a person in charge of enforcing the law

1. _____
2. _____
3. _____
4. _____
5. _____
6. _____
7. _____
8. _____
9. _____
10. _____
11. _____
12. _____
13. _____
14. _____
15. _____
16. _____
17. _____
18. _____
19. _____
20. _____

Summing Up

To help you spell a word with more than one syllable, divide the word into syllables. Look for patterns you have learned, and spell the word by syllables.

Basic

1. wagon
2. capture
3. silver
4. reward
5. shelter
6. divide
7. nature
8. alone
9. office
10. famous
11. parade
12. narrow
13. corner
14. bacon
15. amaze
16. diner
17. dinner
18. eager
19. minute
20. fancy

■ Challenge

21. frontier
22. sheriff
23. prairie
24. stampede
25. corral

Review

1. again
2. enough
3. market
4. pencil
5. balloon

1._____
2._____
3._____
4._____

Expanding Vocabulary

The Suffix -ous The suffix -ous means "full of" or "having." How does the spelling of *fame* change when -ous is added?

BASE WORD   SUFFIX   MEANING
fame   + ous   = fa**mous**   having fame

Practice Add -ous to the words below to write words that complete the sentences. Use your Spelling Dictionary.

marvel   nerve   joy
adventure   humor

1. The _____ puppy was not afraid of anything.
2. We had a peaceful and _____ holiday together.
3. Kay took some _____ pictures of the mountains.
4. We laughed at the _____ message on the chalkboard.
5. Jake was a bit scared and _____ when he gave his speech.

1._____   4._____
2._____   5._____
3._____

Dictionary

Homographs Homographs are words that are spelled the same but have different meanings and may be pronounced differently. They are listed in the dictionary as separate entry words. Each homograph is followed by a number.

> **min·ute**[1] |mĭn′ ĭt| n., pl. **minutes** A unit of time equal to sixty seconds.
> **mi·nute**[2] |mī noōt′| or |mī nyoōt′| adj. Very, very small; tiny: *The wind blew a minute speck of dirt into her eye.*

Practice Write *minute*[1] or *minute*[2] to tell how *minute* is used in each sentence. Use the dictionary entry above.

1. The jeweler found a <u>minute</u> crack in the stone.
2. The rules allow one <u>minute</u> for you to answer.
3. A <u>minute</u> crumb would be a feast for some insects.
4. The runner finished the race in exactly one <u>minute</u>.

Review: Spelling Spree

Code Breaker   Some Basic and Review Words are written in the code below. Figure out each word, and write it correctly.

Example: 15-16-4-4-7-6   *dinner*

CODE:	1	2	3	4	5	6	7	8	9	10	11	12	13	14	15	16	17	18	19
LETTER:	p	b	o	n	a	r	e	w	l	m	f	k	c	t	d	i	g	s	u

1. 2-5-9-9-3-3-4   **7.** 4-5-14-19-6-7   **13.** 1-5-6-5-15-7

2. 10-5-6-12-7-14   **8.** 5-17-5-16-4   **14.** 2-5-13-3-4

3. 10-16-4-19-14-7   **9.** 1-7-4-13-16-9   **15.** 6-7-8-5-6-15

4. 15-16-4-7-6   **10.** 4-5-6-6-3-8   **16.** 7-5-17-7-6

5. 13-3-6-4-7-6   **11.** 13-5-1-14-19-6-7   **17.** 5-9-3-4-7

6. 11-5-10-3-19-18   **12.** 3-11-11-16-13-7   **18.** 8-5-17-3-4

Proofreading   19-25. Find and cross out seven misspelled Basic or Review Words in this story part. Then write each word correctly.

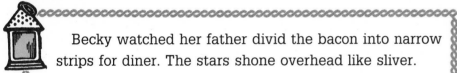

Becky watched her father divid the bacon into narrow strips for diner. The stars shone overhead like sliver.

"It may not be fansy, but it will be enuff," he smiled. His good spirits would always amaz Becky. They had been traveling for weeks, with only a covered wagon for sheltor, on their way to a new life in the West.

■ **Challenge Words**   Write each Challenge Word at the top of a half sheet of paper. Draw a picture that illustrates the meaning of each word. Staple your pages together to make a pictionary.

📖 *Writing Application:* A Persuasive Letter   Pretend you have taken a wagon train to the Wild West. Write a letter to friends back home, persuading them to move to the West. Try to use five words from the list on page 200.

1. _____
2. _____
3. _____
4. _____
5. _____
6. _____
7. _____
8. _____
9. _____
10. _____
11. _____
12. _____
13. _____
14. _____
15. _____
16. _____
17. _____
18. _____
19. _____
20. _____
21. _____
22. _____
23. _____
24. _____
25. _____

32 Spelling Across the Curriculum

Social Studies: *The Wild West*

stagecoach
rodeo
buffalo
homestead
settle
pioneer
ranch
cactus

Using Vocabulary Write the Vocabulary Words to complete the paragraph. Use your Spelling Dictionary.

Jake, a true __(1)__, had been one of the first people to __(2)__ in the small Texas town. When the government granted a __(3)__ to anyone willing to claim the land and build a home, Jake had come west. He cleared his land of prickly __(4)__ and roaming __(5)__. Now his cattle __(6)__ was thriving. Jake decided to give his cowhands time off to see the riding and roping at the __(7)__. Many were coming by __(8)__ to see the event.

Understanding Vocabulary Write a Vocabulary Word that fits each category.

9. Prickly Things
10. Things with Wheels
11. Government Gifts
12. Events for Cowhands

1. _____
2. _____
3. _____
4. _____
5. _____
6. _____
7. _____
8. _____
9. _____
10. _____
11. _____
12. _____

FACT FILE

In 1848 gold was discovered in California. The next year 75,000 people rushed there to find gold. Because this gold rush took place in 1849, these fortune seekers were called *forty-niners*.

Enrichment

🖼 *Pin the Tail on the Buffalo*

Players: 2 or more, a caller **You need:** a large picture of a buffalo for the bulletin board, 25 strips of paper for "tails," thumbtacks, a blindfold

How to play: The caller reads aloud a Basic or Review Word to one player. The player must write the word correctly on a tail. The player is then blindfolded and tries to pin the tail on the buffalo. If the word is written incorrectly, the player must pass. The player with the tail closest to its mark wins.

📖 Writing
Colorful Characters

Read about famous people who lived in the old West. Write a biographical sketch about one person. You could choose a famous outlaw such as Billy the Kid or a famous sharpshooter such as Annie Oakley. Try to use words from the lists in this unit. Be sure to proofread your paper.

WANTED!

Imagine that you are living in the Wild West. A famous outlaw is on the loose. Make a *Wanted* poster about this outlaw. Tell who the outlaw is and why the outlaw is wanted. Offer a reward for his or her capture. Try to use list words.

33 Three-Syllable Words

A. _____

_____

_____

_____

_____

_____

_____

_____

_____

B. _____

_____

_____

_____

_____

_____

_____

_____

_____

■ Challenge

_____

_____

_____

_____

_____

LOOK   at each word.

SAY   each word.

Basic Words   ■ Challenge

1. deliver   11. enemy   21. interview
2. department   12. animal   22. article
3. camera   13. another   23. journalist
4. yesterday   14. however   24. edition
5. tomorrow   15. banana   25. photograph
6. important   16. alphabet
7. together   17. hospital
8. victory   18. hamburger
9. remember   19. carpenter
10. library   20. several

THINK   about the words.

Each word has three syllables. Look for familiar spelling patterns in each syllable. One syllable in each word has more stress than the other two syllables. Pay close attention to the spelling of the unstressed syllables.

yes | ter | day |yĕs′ tər dā| **de | liv | er** |dĭ lĭv′ ər|

• Look at the examples. Which syllables are stressed? Which syllables are unstressed? Why should you pay close attention to the unstressed syllables in each word?

WRITE   the words.

Practice   Write the Basic Words to answer the questions. You may want to use your Spelling Dictionary.

A. Which **eleven** words have stressed first syllables?
B. Which **nine** words have stressed second syllables?

■ Now write the five Challenge Words. Underline the unstressed syllables. Use your Spelling Dictionary.

CHECK   your spelling.

Spelling-Meaning Hint How can you remember how to spell the |ə| sound in *victory*? Think of the |ôr| sounds in the related word *victorious*.

victo**ry**
victor**ious**

Independent Practice

Spelling-Meaning Look at the Spelling-Meaning Hint.
  1-2. Write *victorious*. Then write the Basic Word that is related in spelling and meaning to *victorious*.

Word Analysis Complete the exercises with Basic Words.

  3. Write the word that has the |ī| sound.

  4-7. Write the word that contains each word below.
    4. depart   **6.** day
    5. other   **7.** how

  8-10. Write the three words with the final |əl| sounds spelled with the *al* pattern.

Word Clues Write the Basic Word that fits each clue.
  11. synonym for *recall*
  12. A photographer uses one.
  13. opposite of *friend*
  14. the day after today
  15. a fruit with yellow skin

■ **Challenge Words** Write the Challenge Word that fits each meaning. Use your Spelling Dictionary.
  16. a short piece of writing
  17. a reporter or an editor
  18. a meeting of people face to face
  19. an image on film
  20. all copies of a book printed at one time

1. _____
2. _____
3. _____
4. _____
5. _____
6. _____
7. _____
8. _____
9. _____
10. _____
11. _____
12. _____
13. _____
14. _____
15. _____
16. _____
17. _____
18. _____
19. _____
20. _____

Summing Up

To spell a three-syllable word, divide the word into syllables. Look for familiar spelling patterns. Pay attention to the spelling of the unstressed syllables. Spell the word by syllables.

Basic

1. deliver
2. department
3. camera
4. yesterday
5. tomorrow
6. important
7. together
8. victory
9. remember
10. library
11. enemy
12. animal
13. another
14. however
15. banana
16. alphabet
17. hospital
18. hamburger
19. carpenter
20. several

■ Challenge

21. interview
22. article
23. journalist
24. edition
25. photograph

Review

1. grandmother
2. grandfather
3. October
4. November
5. unhappy

1. _____
2. _____
3. _____
4. _____
5. _____

Expanding Vocabulary

Words from Names   Some foods are named for the places where they were first made or for the people who first made them. Where did the word *hamburger* come from?

Hamburger is named after *Hamburg*, a large city in West Germany. Hamburgers were first made there.

Practice   **Write the food that matches each description.**

graham cracker   McIntosh apple
bologna   Swiss cheese
cantaloupe

1. a melon first grown in Cantalupo, Italy
2. a cheese first made in Switzerland
3. a fruit first grown by John McIntosh
4. a luncheon meat named for Bologna, Italy
5. a snack invented by Sylvester Graham

1. _____   4. _____
2. _____   5. _____
3. _____

Dictionary

Stressed Syllables   Some words with more than one syllable may have two accent marks in the dictionary pronunciation.

ham·bur·ger |hăm′ bûr′ gər|

The syllable shown in dark print with a heavy accent mark has **primary stress**. It is pronounced with the most stress. The syllable with a light accent mark has **secondary stress**. It is pronounced with less stress.

Practice   **Write each word in syllables. Then underline the syllable that has primary stress. Circle the syllable with secondary stress. Use your Spelling Dictionary.**

1. anything   4. library
2. alphabet   5. understand
3. afternoon

Review: Spelling Spree

Syllable Scramble   Rearrange the syllables in each item to form a Basic or Review Word. Write the words correctly. (One syllable in each item is extra.)

1. hap un ham py
2. grand er moth to
3. er an oth ful
4. car cam pen ter
5. my e mal en
6. pen por tant im
7. cam ar er a
8. sev de er liv
9. fa grand ther al
10. ger vem bur ham
11. a ba em nan
12. tal tant pi hos
13. bo vic y tor
14. day yes am ter
15. part mem ment de
16. mor row to lot

Proofreading   17-25. Find and cross out nine misspelled Basic or Review Words in this newspaper story. Then write each word correctly.

Librarian Solves Mystery

Did you know that some mystery stories in a libary aren't in books? Just ask Mrs. White, the librarian.

"Last Octobor two people from the anamal hospital came in togather. They checked out sevral alfabet books," said Mrs. White. "I rember thinking that was odd. It wasn't until Noveber, howevery, that I learned why they had checked out the books. They had been trying to teach a parrot to read!"

■ **Challenge Words**   Write five newspaper headlines, using a Challenge Word in each headline. Remember to capitalize the first, last, and each important word in your headlines.

Writing Application: A News Story   Write a news story about an event in your school or neighborhood. Be sure to tell *who, what, when, where, why,* and *how.* Try to use five words from the list on page 206.

1. _____
2. _____
3. _____
4. _____
5. _____
6. _____
7. _____
8. _____
9. _____
10. _____
11. _____
12. _____
13. _____
14. _____
15. _____
16. _____
17. _____
18. _____
19. _____
20. _____
21. _____
22. _____
23. _____
24. _____
25. _____

33 Spelling Across the Curriculum

Language Arts: *Newspapers*

Theme Vocabulary

newspaper
editor
press
headline
cartoon
caption
deadline
reporter

Using Vocabulary Write the Vocabulary Words to complete the paragraph. Use your Spelling Dictionary.

Many people work together to produce a story for a daily __(1)__ in time to meet the __(2)__. First, a __(3)__ gathers the news and writes the story. Next, the story goes to an __(4)__, who checks it for grammar. Another person gives the story a catchy __(5)__. For some stories, an artist might draw a __(6)__ with a funny __(7)__ under it. Then, before the paper goes to the printing __(8)__, someone decides on which page the story should appear.

Understanding Vocabulary Write a Vocabulary Word to match each clue.

9. If you meet it, you have done a job on time.
10. This person makes sure commas are used correctly.
11. This person questions people to get information.
12. It is usually set in big letters.

1. _____

2. _____

3. _____

4. _____

5. _____

6. _____

7. _____

8. _____

9. _____

10. _____

11. _____

12. _____

AP photo

FACT FILE

Most newspapers get some of their stories from a news service called the Associated Press, or AP. Reporters for the AP send their reports to newsrooms by computer.

Enrichment

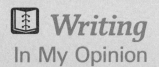 *Class Newspaper*

Make a class newspaper. You will need reporters to interview people and write articles about school events. Artists may draw pictures or create comic strips. Editors should check the grammar and spelling of the reporters' stories. Include advertisements, letters to the editor, or any other features that you think might interest your readers. Neatly print one copy of your paper for the bulletin board, or find out if your teacher can make classroom copies.

Writing
In My Opinion

In a newspaper editorial, the writer gives an opinion about a topic. Write an editorial about something that is important to you. Perhaps you would like to improve something in your neighborhood or at school. Try to use words from the lists in this unit. Be sure to proofread your paper.

WHAT'S NEWS?

A newspaper is made up of many sections. They are listed in the index on the front page. Cut up a newspaper, and make a poster showing the different sections and features. Label the sections, and describe what a reader will find in them.

Theme: The Middle Ages

34 Silent Consonants

A. _____

_____

_____

B. _____

_____

C. _____

_____

D. _____

_____

_____

E. _____

_____

_____

F. _____

_____

_____

G. _____

_____

■ **Challenge**

_____

_____

_____

_____

LOOK   at each word.

SAY   each word.

Basic Words   ■ Challenge

1. *knight*	11. *listen*	21. *reign*
2. *castle*	12. *calm*	22. *knoll*
3. *honor*	13. *knit*	23. *heir*
4. *kneel*	14. *often*	24. *debt*
5. *climb*	15. *palm*	25. *wrestle*
6. *wrinkle*	16. *thumb*	
7. *limb*	17. *wrist*	
8. *handsome*	18. *lamb*	
9. *answer*	19. *knob*	
10. *calf*	20. *honest*	

THINK   about the words.

Each word has a consonant that is not pronounced, or "silent."

kneel   clim**b**   cal**f**   **w**rinkle   **h**onest

• Look at the words on the list. Which letters are silent?

WRITE   the words.

Practice   **Write the Basic Words to answer the questions.**

A. Which **four** words have the |n| sound spelled *kn*?
B. Which **two** words begin with the |r| sound spelled *wr*?
C. Which **two** words begin with the |ŏ| sound spelled *ho*?
D. Which **four** words end with the |m| sound spelled *mb*?
E. Which **three** words have a silent *l*?
F. Which **three** words have a silent *t*?
G. Which **two** words have a silent *d* or *w*?

■ **Now write the five Challenge Words.** Underline the silent consonants. (One word has two silent consonants.)

CHECK   your spelling.

Spelling-Meaning Hint   How can you remember that *limb* ends with a *b*? Think of the related word *limber* in which the *b* is pronounced.

lim**b**
lim**b**er

Independent Practice

Spelling-Meaning   Look at the Spelling-Meaning Hint.
1-2. Write *limb* and *limber*. Underline the letter that is silent in one word and pronounced in the other.

Word Analysis   Complete the exercises with Basic Words.

3-6. Write the word that rhymes with each word below.
   3. glisten
   4. numb
   5. half
   6. soften

7-8. Write the two words with the final |əl| sounds spelled *le*.

9-10. Write *palm*. Then change one letter to write another word.

Analogies   Write the Basic Word that completes each analogy.
11. *Up* is to *down* as *stand* is to ____.
12. *Cat* is to *kitten* as *sheep* is to ____.
13. *Suitcase* is to *handle* as *door* is to ____.
14. *Thread* is to *sew* as *yarn* is to ____.
15. *Rough* is to *gentle* as *ugly* is to ____.

kneel

calm

■ **Challenge Words**   Write the Challenge Word that fits each meaning. Use your Spelling Dictionary.
16. a small hill
17. to rule over
18. to struggle with
19. something owed
20. a person who has the right to property when someone dies

1. _____
2. _____
3. _____
4. _____
5. _____
6. _____
7. _____
8. _____
9. _____
10. _____
11. _____
12. _____
13. _____
14. _____
15. _____
16. _____
17. _____
18. _____
19. _____
20. _____

Summing Up

Some words have silent consonants. The spellings of these words have to be remembered.

Basic

1. knight
2. castle
3. honor
4. kneel
5. climb
6. wrinkle
7. limb
8. handsome
9. answer
10. calf
11. listen
12. calm
13. knit
14. often
15. palm
16. thumb
17. wrist
18. lamb
19. knob
20. honest

■ **Challenge**

21. reign
22. knoll
23. heir
24. debt
25. wrestle

Review

1. talk
2. knife
3. wrong
4. knock
5. hour

Proofreading Marks

¶ Indent
∧ Add something
℮ Take out something
≡ Capitalize
/ Make a small letter

Expanding Vocabulary

Idioms If you are "all thumbs," are you made of thumbs?

I would undo the knot if I could, but I am **all thumbs.**

All thumbs means "having clumsy fingers." It is an **idiom,** an expression that has a special meaning. The meaning is different from the meanings of the separate words.

Practice **Write the letter of the correct meaning for each underlined idiom.**

1. I went out on a limb when I corrected the teacher.
   a. climbed a tree   **b.** took a risk   **c.** fell down
2. The greedy thief had an itchy palm.
   a. a desire for money   **b.** a rash   **c.** a large hand
3. I worked around the clock to finish the project.
   a. slowly   **b.** without stopping   **c.** next to a clock
4. Kate threw in the towel after she lost three times.
   a. cheered   **b.** put her towel away   **c.** gave up

1. _____   2. _____   3. _____   4. _____

Proofreading

Using *I* and *me* Use *I* as the subject of a sentence. Use *me* after action verbs and words such as *to* and *with*. If you use *I* or *me* with another noun or pronoun, name yourself last.

The **knight** and **I** met in the hall. He gave the ring to **me.**

Practice **Proofread the queen's note. Find four misspelled words and two incorrect pronouns. Use proofreading marks to correct the errors.**

Example: Who will ~~lisen~~ *listen* to the king and ~~I~~ *me*?

The king and me are looking for the most honist knight in the kingdom. Come tak with the king and I for one hour. Whoever can anser our questions the most truthfully will be given a feast in his honer.

Review: Spelling Spree

Words in Words   Write the Basic or Review Word that appears in each word below.

1. hourglass
2. wristwatch
3. thumbtack
4. listener
5. handsomest
6. kneeling
7. wronged
8. lambskin
9. limber
10. honesty
11. knitting
12. wrinkled
13. honorable
14. answered

Word Maze   **15-25.** Begin at the arrow and follow the Word Maze to find eleven Basic or Review Words. Write the words in order.

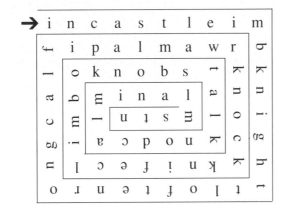

■ **Challenge Words**   How many Challenge Words can you use in one sentence? Write five sentences, using at least two Challenge Words in each one. Use each Challenge Word at least once. Example: The <u>heir</u> paid a <u>debt</u> to the queen during her <u>reign</u>.

📖 *Writing Application:* Creative Writing Pretend you have discovered a time machine that takes you back to the Middle Ages. Write the conversation you have with the first person you meet. What do you talk about? What questions do you ask each other? Try to use five words from the list on page 212.

1. _____
2. _____
3. _____
4. _____
5. _____
6. _____
7. _____
8. _____
9. _____
10. _____
11. _____
12. _____
13. _____
14. _____
15. _____
16. _____
17. _____
18. _____
19. _____
20. _____
21. _____
22. _____
23. _____
24. _____
25. _____

34 Spelling Across the Curriculum

Social Studies: *The Middle Ages*

Theme Vocabulary

lord
manor
coat of arms
tournament
squire
peasants
armor
joust

Using Vocabulary Write the Vocabulary Words to complete the paragraph. Use your Spelling Dictionary.

Edgar shifted his body inside the heavy __(1)__ . A crowd of poor __(2)__ lined the field. They had gathered to watch him compete in his first __(3)__ . He was nervous, but he knew he could __(4)__ better than any of the other knights. He had received excellent training since coming to serve as a young __(5)__ in the large __(6)__ of his wealthy __(7)__ and lady. Edgar looked at the __(8)__ on his shield. He must do it honor by winning.

Understanding Vocabulary Write *yes* if the under-lined word or phrase is used correctly. Write *no* if it is not.

9. The knight put on his <u>coat of arms</u> to keep warm.
10. Whenever the knight moved, his <u>armor</u> rattled.
11. The knight spoke in a calm <u>manor</u>.
12. The <u>peasants</u> farmed the lord's land.

1. _____
2. _____
3. _____
4. _____
5. _____
6. _____
7. _____
8. _____
9. _____
10. _____
11. _____
12. _____

FACT FILE

During the Middle Ages, knights followed a set of rules known as the code of chivalry. A knight had to love his homeland, fight against evil, and protect women.

Enrichment

👪 *Crown Jewels*

Players: 2, a caller **You need**: colored paper markers for "jewels"

How to play: Each player draws a crown with seven points. The caller reads a Basic or Review Word. The first player must spell it correctly and name the silent consonant. (Note: One word has *three* silent consonants!) If correct, he or she covers one of the points on his or her crown with a "jewel." Players take turns spelling words. The first player to cover all the points on his or her crown wins.

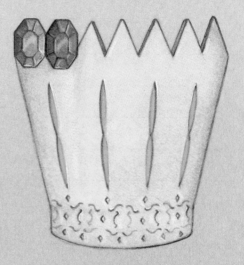

📖 *Writing*
That Was Then

What was it like to be a peasant or a knight in the Middle Ages? Write a research report about life in the Middle Ages. Use your library to find out what life was like for a lord or a lady of the manor, a knight, or a peasant. Try to use words from the lists in this unit. Be sure to proofread your paper.

COAT OF ARMS

Design a coat of arms for a knight. Draw the shape of a shield, and add a design. Include a motto, such as Always Calm in Battle. Try to use a unit list word. Then write a few sentences about the meaning of the symbols and colors in your design. What do they tell about the knight? Try to use list words.

35 Unusual Spellings

A. _____

_____

_____

_____

B. _____

C. _____

_____

_____

_____

_____

D. _____

_____

_____

_____

E. _____

_____

_____

F. _____

_____

_____

_____

_____

■ Challenge

_____

_____

_____

_____

_____

LOOK at each word.

SAY each word.

Basic Words ■ Challenge

1. health	11. guide	21. vaccine
2. blood	12. style	22. quarantine
3. type	13. wealth	23. guarantee
4. against	14. guilt	24. threaten
5. receive	15. says	25. rhyme
6. flood	16. guard	
7. month	17. wonder	
8. magazine	18. guest	
9. guess	19. gasoline	
10. women	20. either	

THINK about the words.

Each word has a sound with an unusual spelling pattern.

|ĕ| h**ea**lth, ag**ai**nst, **say**s |ē| rec**ei**ve, maga**z**i**n**e
|ĭ| w**o**men |ī| t**y**pe (*y*-consonant-*e*)
|ŭ| bl**oo**d, m**o**nth |g| **gu**ess

• Look at the examples. What unusual spellings do you see?

WRITE the words.

Practice   Write the Basic Words to answer the questions.

A. Which **four** words have an unusual spelling for |ĕ|?
B. Which **one** word has unusual spellings for |ĭ|?
C. Which **four** words have an unusual spelling for |ŭ|?
D. Which **four** words have an unusual spelling for |ē|?
E. Which **two** words have an unusual spelling for |ī|?
F. Which **five** words have an unusual spelling for |g|?

■ **Now write the five Challenge Words.** Underline unusual spellings for |ĕ|, |ē|, |ī|, and |g|.

CHECK your spelling.

> *Spelling-Meaning Hint* Can you see *heal* in *health*? These words are related in spelling and meaning, even though they have different vowel sounds. **Think of this:** When you *heal*, you regain your *health*.

hea|l
hea|lth

Independent Practice

Spelling-Meaning Look at the Spelling-Meaning Hint.
1-2. Write *heal* and the Basic Word that is related to *heal*.

Word Analysis Complete the exercises with Basic Words.

   3. Write the word that begins with the |ə| sound spelled *a*.

4-5. Write the two words that end with the |ər| sounds.

6-8. Write the word that rhymes with each word below.
   6. hard   **8.** chest
   7. ride

Definitions Write the Basic Word that fits each meaning.
   9. adult females
   10. four weeks
   11. fuel for cars
   12. a large amount of money
   13. a large flow of water
   14. liquid pumped by the heart
   15. something published weekly or monthly

y-consonant-e

■ **Challenge Words** Write the Challenge Word that completes each sentence. Use your Spelling Dictionary.
   16. Many diseases are curable and no longer ____ us.
   17. Jonas Salk developed a ____ to protect against polio.
   18. Sick people stay in ____ to keep germs from spreading.
   19. My mom read me a nursery ____ whenever I was sick.
   20. Eating properly cannot ____ good health, but it can help.

1. _____
2. _____
3. _____
4. _____
5. _____
6. _____
7. _____
8. _____
9. _____
10. _____
11. _____
12. _____
13. _____
14. _____
15. _____
16. _____
17. _____
18. _____
19. _____
20. _____

Summing Up

Some words have sounds with unusual spellings. The spellings of these words have to be remembered.

Basic

1. health
2. blood
3. type
4. against
5. receive
6. flood
7. month
8. magazine
9. guess
10. women
11. guide
12. style
13. wealth
14. guilt
15. says
16. guard
17. wonder
18. guest
19. gasoline
20. either

■ Challenge

21. vaccine
22. quarantine
23. guarantee
24. threaten
25. rhyme

Review

1. front
2. head
3. love
4. shoe
5. gym

Proofreading Marks

¶   Indent
∧   Add
      something
ℓ   Take out
      something
≡   Capitalize
/   Make a small
      letter

Expanding Vocabulary

Shortened Forms Many long words have shortened forms. Read these signs. How was *gasoline* shortened?

GASOLINE STATION	GAS STATION

Practice Write the short form of each underlined word.

gym   exam   phone   sub   math

1. The <u>telephone</u> rang two times before I answered it.
2. We have a history <u>examination</u> after every unit.
3. I wore my sneakers in the <u>gymnasium</u>.
4. The <u>submarine</u> moved slowly under the water.
5. Gloriann's favorite subject is <u>mathematics</u>.

1. _____   4. _____

2. _____   5. _____

3. _____

Proofreading

Contractions A **contraction** is formed by combining a verb and *not* or by combining a pronoun and a verb. Use an apostrophe to replace the letters that are dropped. (See page 250 in your Student's Handbook for more examples.)

I have not given blood before.   I will take your pulse.
I haven't given blood before.   I'll take your pulse.

Practice Proofread the instructions. Find four misspelled words and two missing apostrophes. Use proofreading marks to correct the errors.

Example: If you've come to give ~~blud~~ *blood*, go to the gym.

To give blood, see one of the woman at the frunt of the room. She'll record your blood tipe and make sure youre in good helth. Also, youll receive some forms to fill out.

Review: Spelling Spree

Hidden Words Write the Basic or Review Word that you find in each row of letters. Don't let the other words fool you!

Example: e i t h e a l t h e n *health*

1. r e g y m u n t h
2. s e e f r o n t y p
3. g e s g u a r d e
4. f i e i t h e r y l e
5. m a g a s a y s h o
6. w e a g u i d e i t
7. b a g a i n s t i n g
8. h a p r e c e i v e r
9. f l o d b l o o d e d

10. w o m o n t h e a f
11. g u e s h o e a d
12. f e w o n d e r e s t
13. w o n w o m e n d e r
14. g a s t y l e a n
15. s w e a l t h y p e
16. g i m a g a z i n e x t
17. f r u n t y p e n
18. b e g a s o l i n e a r

Find a Rhyme Write the Basic or Review Word that rhymes with each underlined word and makes sense in the sentence.

Example: The tour ____ will be giving us a <u>ride</u>. *guide*

19. Can you ____ who made this <u>mess</u>?
20. The man at the ____ of the table wants <u>bread</u>.
21. I would rather have good ____ than fame or <u>wealth</u>.
22. The <u>dove</u> is the symbol of ____ .
23. I admit my ____ . I let the flowers <u>wilt</u>.
24. We asked our ____ if she wanted to <u>rest</u>.
25. Please donate <u>blood</u> to help victims of the ____ .

■ **Challenge Words** Make a crossword puzzle, using all of the Challenge Words. Write clues, and draw your puzzle. Write your answers on the back. Trade puzzles with a classmate, and complete each other's puzzles.

Writing Application: A Personal Story The Red Cross helps people in need. How have you helped someone? Write a personal story describing what you did. Perhaps you helped a classmate in school or helped out at home. Try to use five words from the list on page 218.

1. _____
2. _____
3. _____
4. _____
5. _____
6. _____
7. _____
8. _____
9. _____
10. _____
11. _____
12. _____
13. _____
14. _____
15. _____
16. _____
17. _____
18. _____
19. _____
20. _____
21. _____
22. _____
23. _____
24. _____
25. _____

35   Spelling Across the Curriculum

Health: *The Red Cross*

Theme Vocabulary

nurse
volunteer
disaster
accident
donor
victims
supplies
assist

Using Vocabulary   Write the Vocabulary Words to complete the paragraph. Use your Spelling Dictionary.

Emma stood in the school gym. Workers were bringing in frightened __(1)__ of the earthquake, the city's worst natural __(2)__ ever. Emma had come to help out and __(3)__ her services. Nearby a registered __(4)__ in a white uniform was getting ready to __(5)__ a doctor with bandages and other __(6)__. Emma thought back to the time she had been in a car __(7)__ and had received blood from a blood __(8)__. Now it was her turn to help.

Understanding Vocabulary   Write *yes* if the underlined word is used correctly. Write *no* if it is not.

9. I plan to <u>volunteer</u> at the clinic to earn some money.
10. The <u>victims</u> of the flood needed food and shelter.
11. If you need blood, please sign up to be a <u>donor</u>.
12. No one could prevent the <u>accident</u>.

1. _____

2. _____

3. _____

4. _____

5. _____

6. _____

7. _____

8. _____

9. _____

10. _____

11. _____

12. _____

FACT FILE

In 1881 Clara Barton founded the American Red Cross to help wounded soldiers. Now the Red Cross also helps victims of floods and other disasters.

Enrichment

Spelling Tick-Tack-Toe

Players: 2, a caller **You need:** paper, two different colored pencils

How to play: Draw a tick-tack-toe board on a piece of paper. The caller reads a Basic or Review Word. The first player writes the word in any square, using a colored pencil. The caller then reads another word. The second player writes that word in any remaining square, using the other colored pencil. If a player misspells a word, the word is erased. The first player to write three correct words across, down, or diagonally wins.

PROJECT "POSTER"

Think of ways to volunteer in your community, such as picking up litter or sending cards to people in nursing homes. Draw a poster that will make your classmates want to volunteer. Illustrate the different ways to volunteer, and add captions. Try to use words from the unit lists.

Writing
News Flash!

Pretend that you are a radio announcer. A major natural disaster, such as a flood or a tornado, has just struck your town. Write a news bulletin about the disaster. Explain what the Red Cross is doing to help. Try to use words from the lists in this unit. Be sure to proofread your paper.

36 Review: Units 31–35

1. _____
2. _____
3. _____
4. _____
5. _____
6. _____
7. _____
8. _____
9. _____
10. _____

Unit 31   VCV Pattern   pp. 192-197

| depend | ocean | police | parent | today |
| palace | event | exit | belong | award |

Remember: VC | V   V | CV

par | ent   de | pend

V CV   be low   VC V   ex it

Write a spelling word by adding the missing syllable.

1. ____ | long   **3.** ____ | lice   **5.** pal | ____

2. ____ | vent   **4.** ____ | ward   **6.** ____ | pend

Write the word that completes each sentence.

7. Are we going on a field trip ____ or tomorrow?

8. In case of fire, walk quickly to the nearest ____.

9. I swim in the ____ almost every day during the summer.

10. Children will not be admitted to the show without a ____.

Unit 32   VCCV and VCV Patterns   pp. 198-203

11. _____
12. _____
13. _____
14. _____
15. _____
16. _____
17. _____
18. _____
19. _____
20. _____

| famous | reward | alone | wagon | divide |
| narrow | fancy | eager | parade | amaze |

Remember:

V CV   re ward

VC CV   sil ver

VC | CV   V | CV   VC | V

nar | row   di | vide   wag | on

Write a spelling word by adding the missing syllable.

11. ea | ____   **13.** ____ | rade   **15.** ____ | maze

12. fa | ____   **14.** ____ | ward   **16.** ____ | lone

Write the word that completes each analogy.

17. *Tall* is to *short* as *wide* is to ____.

18. *Runners* are to *sled* as *wheels* are to ____.

19. *Dull* is to *sharp* as *plain* is to ____.

20. *Add* is to *subtract* as *multiply* is to ____.

Half of the words from each unit are reviewed on these pages. The rest are reviewed on pages 244–246.

Unit 33   Three-Syllable Words   pp. 204-209

tomorrow	deliver	remember	department	yesterday
another	animal	several	hamburger	carpenter

Remember: To spell a three-syllable word, divide the word into syllables. Look for familiar patterns, and spell the word by syllables.

Write the word that fits each meaning.

21. the day before today   **24.** the day after today
22. a living creature   **25.** a second one
23. part of a company   **26.** to take to someone

Write the word that belongs in each group.

27. bun, ketchup, ____   **29.** plumber, mechanic, ____
28. few, some, ____   **30.** forget, think, ____

21. _____
22. _____
23. _____
24. _____
25. _____
26. _____
27. _____
28. _____
29. _____
30. _____

Unit 34   Silent Consonants   pp. 210-215

climb	honor	knight	handsome	castle
wrist	knob	listen	thumb	calm

Remember: Some words have silent consonants. The spellings of these words have to be remembered.

kneel
calm

Write the word that completes each phrase.

31. a ____ in shining armor   **34.** finger and ____
32. the stone walls of the ____   **35.** stop, look, and ____
33. truth, love, and ____   **36.** peaceful and ____

Write the word that fits each clue.

37. You turn it to open a door.   **40.** It describes someone
38. It's how you go up a ladder.   who is good-looking.
39. It joins your arm and hand.

31. _____
32. _____
33. _____
34. _____
35. _____
36. _____
37. _____
38. _____
39. _____
40. _____

36 Review

Unit 35   Unusual Spellings   pp. 216-221

| receive | against | flood | health | women |
| guide | wonder | says | style | gasoline |

Remember: Some words have sounds with unusual spellings. The spellings of these words have to be remembered.

y-consonant-e

Write the word that rhymes with each word below.

41. hide   **43.** blood

42. wealth

Write the word that completes each sentence.

44. A car runs on ___ .

45. Did you ___ a gift?

46. Many ___ have careers.

47. Don't lean ___ the door.

48. Simon ___ , "Sit down."

49. This suit is in ___ now.

50. I ___ what went wrong.

41. _____

42. _____

43. _____

44. _____

45. _____

46. _____

47. _____

48. _____

49. _____

50. _____

■ Challenge Words   Units 31-35   pp. 192-221

| quarantine | journalist | frontier | wrestle | reign |
| photograph | guarantee | stampede | marine | peril |

Write the word that belongs in each group.

51. fight, struggle, ___

52. danger, threat, ___

53. reporter, writer, ___

54. painting, drawing, ___

55. promise, vow, ___

Write the word that completes each sentence.

56. Dr. Pym put Jill in ___ so that we wouldn't get sick.

57. In the sea there are many kinds of ___ animals.

58. Cattle might ___ if they are frightened.

59. Queen Elizabeth I of England had a long ___ .

60. Life was often hard on the western ___ .

51. _____

52. _____

53. _____

54. _____

55. _____

56. _____

57. _____

58. _____

59. _____

60. _____

You have learned that some words in a word family often have the same spellings for different sounds. Read this paragraph.

> Casey needed time to **locate** her lost slippers. She finally found them in an odd **location.** They were in the wastebasket!

locate
location

Think

• What does *locate* mean? What does *location* mean? How are they related in meaning?

• What sound does the letter *t* spell in each word?

Here are more related words in which the spelling remains the same even though the sound of the *t* changes.

operate	decorate	punctuate
operation	decoration	punctuation

Apply and Extend

Complete these activities on a separate sheet of paper.

1. Look up the words in the Word Box above in the Spelling Dictionary. Write six sentences, using each word.

2. With a partner list as many words as you can that are related to *locate, operate, decorate,* and *punctuate.* Then look on page 272 of your Spelling-Meaning Index. Add any other words that you find in these families to your list.

Summing Up   Knowing that words are related may help you spell them. In many words the sound of a final *t* may change when the ending *-ion* is added, but the spelling stays the same.

Research Report

Adobes are buildings made of sun-dried bricks formed from a mixture of special soil, straw, and water. What kind of modern buildings were early Pueblo adobes like?

About two thousand years ago, the Pueblo Indians began building with adobe. If you visit the southwestern part of the United States today, you can still see very old Pueblo adobes, as well as new, modern ones.

The apartment-like buildings of the early Pueblos stood three to four stories high. Each level was built on top of the other in tiers, which were like giant steps. The flat roof of the ground floor made a front porch for the families living on the second floor, and so on up to the top.

The Pueblo adobes were simple but pleasant. The living spaces inside the apartments were small, and each family lived in one room. Narrow, T-shaped doors connected the rooms on each apartment level. The walls were painted with a fresh whitewash made from a chalk found in the desert. The whitewash gave the room a clean, fresh look and reflected firelight.

from "The Adobe Way"

Think and Discuss

1. Early Pueblo adobes were similar to what kind of modern building? Why?
2. What **facts** do you learn about adobes in the first paragraph?
3. What is the **topic sentence** of the last paragraph? What **supporting details** are given in the other sentences?

The Writing Process

The passage from "The Adobe Way" gives facts about adobes. When you write a research report, include only **facts**, not opinions. Each paragraph should be about one topic. Begin each paragraph with a **topic sentence** that states the main idea. Then give **supporting details**.

Assignment: Write a Research Report

Steps One and Two: Prewriting and Planning

1. Make a list of topics you would like to learn about. Discuss them with a classmate. Choose one.
2. Write questions you want to answer in your report.
3. Find facts that answer the questions. Take notes.
4. Organize your notes into an outline.

Step Three: Write a First Draft

1. Follow your outline as you write.
2. Think about your purpose and your audience.
3. Do not worry about mistakes—just write!

Step Four: Revise

1. Does each paragraph have a topic sentence and supporting details? Have you included only facts?
2. Use your Thesaurus to find exact words.
3. Read your report to a classmate. Make other changes.

Step Five: Proofread

1. Did you capitalize and punctuate correctly?
2. Did you spell all words correctly? Copy any words that you misspelled into your Notebook for Writing.

Step Six: Publish

1. Copy your report neatly, and add a title.
2. Add pictures that illustrate your topic. Share your report.

Composition Words

today
important
event
tomorrow
amaze
honest
famous
wonder

Proofreading Marks

¶ Indent
∧ Add something
ℓ Take out something
= Capitalize
/ Make a small letter

Student's Handbook

Extra Practice and Review

Cycle 1

Unit 1   Spelling |ă| and |ā| pp. 12-17

blade	gain	safe	drag	drain
plant	sale	shall	jail	glass

Remember: The |ă| sound is usually spelled **a** followed by a consonant sound. The |ā| sound is often spelled **a**-consonant-**e**, **ai**, or **ay**.

Write the word that rhymes with each word below.
1. flag   3. pass
2. ant   4. shade

Write the word that fits each clue.
5. It means the opposite of *lose*.
6. You can keep valuables in it.
7. It takes place at a store.
8. Its rooms are cells.
9. Water goes down it.
10. It often means *will*.

1. _____
2. _____
3. _____
4. _____
5. _____
6. _____
7. _____
8. _____
9. _____
10. _____

Unit 2   Spelling |ĕ| and |ē| pp. 18-23

free	feast	cream	fresh	peach
real	speed	dream	desk	east

Remember: The |ĕ| sound is usually spelled **e** followed by a consonant sound. The |ē| sound is often spelled **ea** or **ee**.

Write the word that belongs in each group.
11. milk, butter, ____
12. chair, table, ____
13. new, clean, ____
14. west, north, ____

Write the word that rhymes with each underlined word.
15. The <u>beast</u> ate at the ____.
16. Did I <u>scream</u> in my ____?
17. I tried to <u>reach</u> the ____.
18. Do the <u>deed</u> with ____!
19. Please ____ the <u>bee</u>.
20. Is that a ____ <u>seal</u>?

11. _____
12. _____
13. _____
14. _____
15. _____
16. _____
17. _____
18. _____
19. _____
20. _____

Cycle 1

Unit 3 Spelling |ĭ| and |ī| pp. 24-29

brick	lift	skill	pride	crime
sting	inch	wind	ripe	sigh

Remember: The |ĭ| sound is often spelled **i** followed by a consonant sound. The |ī| sound is often spelled i-consonant-**e**, **igh**, or **i**.

i-consonant-e

s t r i p e

Write the word that appears in each word below.
21. prideful   24. skillful
22. ripen   25. inching
23. sighed   26. lifted

Write the word that completes each phrase.
27. a bee ___   29. to commit a ___
28. the cold, blowing ___   30. a ___ wall

21. _____
22. _____
23. _____
24. _____
25. _____
26. _____
27. _____
28. _____
29. _____
30. _____

Unit 4 Spelling |ŏ| and |ō| pp. 30-35

globe	goal	spoke	snow	odd
chose	folk	shock	bowl	host

Remember: The |ŏ| sound is usually spelled **o** followed by a consonant sound. The |ō| sound is often spelled o-consonant-**e**, **oa**, **ow**, or **o**.

globe
coast ⊙ snow
gold

Write the word that means the same as each word below.
31. picked   34. aim
32. strange   35. said
33. surprise   36. people

Write the word that belongs in each group.
37. party, guests, ___   39. map, chart, ___
38. cup, plate, ___   40. rain, sleet, ___

31. _____
32. _____
33. _____
34. _____
35. _____
36. _____
37. _____
38. _____
39. _____
40. _____

Unit 5   Homophones   pp. 36-41

lead	peak	beet	creek	deer
led	peek	beat	creak	dear

ring

wring

Remember: **Homophones** are words that sound alike but have different meanings and spellings.

Write the word that fits each clue.
41. This metal is very heavy.
42. This plant is tasty.
43. A mountaintop has one.
44. An old door might do this.
45. This animal is very swift.
46. This person is much loved.

Write a word to replace the underlined word or words in each phrase below.
47. to <u>win against</u> another team
48. to be <u>guided</u> through a cave
49. a <u>quick look</u> at a baby
50. to wade in a <u>brook</u>

■ Challenge Words   Units 1-5   pp. 12–41

recognize	relay	vane	restaurant	advice
longitude	rigid	vain	activity	motion
accomplish	yeast	vein	champion	menu

Write the word that rhymes with the word in parentheses to complete each phrase.
51. ___ for bread (least)
52. a ___ attempt (pain)
53. a weather ___ (cane)
54. to ___ the news (delay)
55. a swift ___ (lotion)
56. ___ planks of wood (frigid)

Write the word that fits each clue.
57. may help you solve a problem
58. to succeed in doing something
59. to remember someone's face
60. something you do to keep busy
61. something that lists sandwiches
62. where waiters work
63. opposite of *latitude*
64. a blood vessel
65. the one who finished the race first

41. _____

42. _____

43. _____

44. _____

45. _____

46. _____

47. _____

48. _____

49. _____

50. _____

51. _____

52. _____

53. _____

54. _____

55. _____

56. _____

57. _____

58. _____

59. _____

60. _____

61. _____

62. _____

63. _____

64. _____

65. _____

Cycle 2

Unit 7 Spelling |ŭ|, |yo͞o|, and |o͞o| pp. 48-53

brush	few	true	crumb	juice
pump	sum	dull	blew	due

Remember:

|ŭ| → **u** followed by a consonant sound

|yo͞o| or |o͞o| → **u**-consonant-**e**,
        ew, ue, ui

Write the word that fits each meaning.
1. liquid from fruit   **3.** total   **5.** not interesting
2. sent a stream of air   **4.** owed   **6.** a small number

Write the word that completes each analogy.
   7. *Wrong* is to *right* as *false* is to ____.
   8. *Wood* is to *chip* as *bread* is to ____.
   9. *Water* is to *faucet* as *gasoline* is to ____.
   10. *Pen* is to *pencil* as *comb* is to ____.

1. _____
2. _____
3. _____
4. _____
5. _____
6. _____
7. _____
8. _____
9. _____
10. _____

Unit 8 Spelling |o͞o| and |o͝o| pp. 54-59

brook	wool	roof	put	full
stood	bush	fool	shoot	smooth

Remember: |o͞o| → **oo**

        |o͝o| → **oo** or **u** followed
                by a consonant sound

Write the word that rhymes with each word below.
11. push   **13.** boot   **15.** cook
12. wood   **14.** pool   **16.** proof

Write the word that fits each clue.
17. You can make mittens from it.
18. It could describe the feeling of silk.
19. It means the opposite of *empty*.
20. It can mean "to place."

11. _____
12. _____
13. _____
14. _____
15. _____
16. _____
17. _____
18. _____
19. _____
20. _____

Cycle 2

Unit 9   Spelling |ou| and |ô| pp. 60-65

bounce	shout	aloud	south	jaw
drawn	proud	scout	mount	gown

Remember: |ou| → **ou, ow**
           |ô| → **aw, au, a** before **l**

|ou||ou|
how**l**

Write the word that means the same as each word below.
21. dress   23. yell   25. climb
22. sketched   24. explore

Write the word that completes each sentence.
26. The weather grows warmer as you travel ____ .
27. Sarah felt ____ to be a member of the winning team.
28. Emilio had a funny thought, but he did not say it ____ .
29. The baby watched the ball ____ down the steps.
30. Charlie has a toothache in his lower ____ .

21. _____
22. _____
23. _____
24. _____
25. _____
26. _____
27. _____
28. _____
29. _____
30. _____

Unit 10   Spelling |îr|, |är|, and |âr| pp. 66-71

gear	spear	sharp	stare	hairy
year	scarf	starve	charge	stairs

Remember: |îr| → **ear, eer**
           |är| → **ar**
           |âr| → **are, air**

|är| |är| al a r m |är| |är|

Write the word by adding the missing letters.
31. ch __ __ ge   33. st __ __ __   35. sh __ __ p
32. sp __ __ __   34. st __ __ ve   36. y __ __ __

Write the word that belongs in each group.
37. supplies, equipment, ____
38. elevator, escalator, ____
39. belt, tie, ____
40. feathery, woolly, ____

31. _____
32. _____
33. _____
34. _____
35. _____
36. _____
37. _____
38. _____
39. _____
40. _____

Cycle 2

Unit 11   Spelling |ôr|, |ûr|, and |yo͞or| pp. 72-77

chore	firm	dirty	world	pure
worn	earn	curl	burn	shirt

Remember: |ôr| → **or, ore**

|ûr| → **ir, ur, ear, or**

|yo͞or| → **ure**

hor**se**
chore

Write the word that rhymes with the word in parentheses to complete each phrase.

41. to button a _____ (flirt)   **44.** a tiring _____ (store)

42. _____ from much use (born)   **45.** to _____ a living (learn)

43. a _____ white horse (cure)   **46.** _____ laundry (thirty)

Write the word that fits each clue.

47. where all humans live   **49.** solid or fixed in place

48. to set on fire   **50.** a ring of hair

■ Challenge Words   Units 7-11   pp. 48–77

earnest	cocoon	weary	attitude	marvel
startle	superb	doubt	foreign	soot
slumber	hurdle	prowl	tissue	gnaw

Write the word that is a synonym for each word below.

51. strange   **56.** frighten

52. magnificent   **57.** doze

53. tired   **58.** truthful

54. dirt   **59.** chew

55. distrust

Write a word to replace the underlined word or words in each phrase below.

60. to <u>move secretly</u> in the dark   **63.** wrapped in <u>thin paper</u>

61. a moth leaving its <u>shell</u>   **64.** to <u>jump over</u> a fence

62. to <u>gaze with wonder at</u>   **65.** a happy <u>state of mind</u>

41. _____

42. _____

43. _____

44. _____

45. _____

46. _____

47. _____

48. _____

49. _____

50. _____

51. _____

52. _____

53. _____

54. _____

55. _____

56. _____

57. _____

58. _____

59. _____

60. _____

61. _____

62. _____

63. _____

64. _____

65. _____

Unit 13   Compound Words   pp. 84-89

Cycle 3

railroad	airport	understand	ninety-nine	homesick
whenever	all right	everything	fireplace	afternoon

Remember: A compound word may be written as one word, as two words joined by a hyphen, or as two separate words.

Write the compound word that contains each underlined word.
1. <u>sick</u>ly   2. <u>noth</u>ing   3. re<u>place</u>   4. <u>stand</u>ing   5. <u>air</u>y

Write the compound word that fits each clue.
6. It is the last number before one hundred.
7. This time of day is neither morning nor night.
8. It means "good enough."
9. It has tracks that go all over the country.
10. It means "at whatever time."

1. _____
2. _____
3. _____
4. _____
5. _____
6. _____
7. _____
8. _____
9. _____
10. _____

Unit 14   Final |ər| pp. 90-95

enter	labor	ladder	suffer	weather
favor	bitter	shower	temper	proper

Remember: The final |ər| sounds are spelled **er, or,** or **ar** in two-syllable words.

Write the word that rhymes with each underlined word.
11. Nothing looked <u>sadder</u> than the old, broken ____ .
12. Please ____ through the door in the <u>center</u>.
13. Fish is the <u>flavor</u> that most kittens ____ .
14. If you were a <u>flower</u>, you would like a spring ____ .

Write the word by adding the missing syllable.
15. weath | ____   17. bit | ____   19. tem | ____
16. prop | ____   18. la | ____   20. suf | ____

11. _____
12. _____
13. _____
14. _____
15. _____
16. _____
17. _____
18. _____
19. _____
20. _____

Cycle 3

nickel	metal	total	middle	bottle
handle	title	uncle	simple	battle

Remember: The final |l| or |əl| sounds are often spelled **el, al,** or **le** in two-syllable words.

|əl|
nickel
total
eagle

Write the word that is a synonym for each word below.

21. center
22. easy
23. fight

24. name
25. complete

Write the word that belongs in each group.

26. wood, plastic, ____
27. strap, knob, ____
28. cousin, nephew, ____

29. can, jar, ____
30. penny, dime, ____

21. _____
22. _____
23. _____
24. _____
25. _____
26. _____
27. _____
28. _____
29. _____
30. _____

dancing	hiking	flipped	landed	dared
wasting	dimmed	tanning	traced	smelling

Remember: land + **ed**   = land**ed**
  dare − e + **ed** = dar**ed**
  tan + n + **ing** = ta**nning**

skip
ed

Write the word that rhymes with each word below.

31. cared
32. tripped
33. tasting

34. placed
35. prancing

Write the word that fits each clue.

36. the opposite of *brightened*
37. happening from the sun
38. sniffing an odor

39. climbing mountains
40. past tense of *land*

31. _____
32. _____
33. _____
34. _____
35. _____
36. _____
37. _____
38. _____
39. _____
40. _____

Cycle 3

Unit 17   Final |ē| pp. 108-113

ugly	lazy	marry	sorry	empty
duty	body	plenty	turkey	monkey

Remember: final |ē| → **y, ey**

Write the word that means the opposite of each word below.
41. glad   **44.** active
42. full   **45.** pretty
43. few
Write the word that completes each sentence.
46. The Pacific Ocean is the largest ____ of water.
47. The ____ leaped from tree to tree.
48. A doctor's ____ is to help the sick.
49. Uncle Lenny roasted a big ____ for Thanksgiving.
50. The princess agreed to ____ the prince.

■ Challenge Words   Units 13-17   pp. 84–113

motorcycle	anchor	lunar	breathing	landmark
postscript	cancel	mercy	scarred	solar
industrial	urged	fiery	decimal	envy

Write the word that fits each meaning.
51. fraction   **53.** damaged   **55.** to end   **57.** ablaze
52. sympathy   **54.** longing   **56.** inhaling   **58.** begged
Write the word that completes each analogy.
59. *Pedals* are to *bicycle* as *engine* is to ____.
60. *Tree* is to *roots* as *boat* is to ____.
61. *Book* is to *bookmark* as *land* is to ____.
62. *Pole* is to *polar* as *sun* is to ____.
63. *Star* is to *moon* as *stellar* is to ____.
64. *Dr.* is to *doctor* as *P.S.* is to ____.
65. *Finance* is to *financial* as *industry* is to ____.

41. _____
42. _____
43. _____
44. _____
45. _____
46. _____
47. _____
48. _____
49. _____
50. _____
51. _____
52. _____
53. _____
54. _____
55. _____
56. _____
57. _____
58. _____
59. _____
60. _____
61. _____
62. _____
63. _____
64. _____
65. _____

Cycle 4

Unit 19   Spelling |k|, |ng|, and |kw| pp. 120-125

shark	attack	risk	blank	public
drink	struck	junk	topic	crooked

Remember: |k| → **k, ck, c**
|ng| → **n** before **k**
|kw| → **qu**

Write the word that rhymes with the word in parentheses to complete each phrase.

1. a box full of ____ (chunk)   **4.** a cool ____ (think)
2. a ____ in the water (park)   **5.** a dangerous ____ (disk)
3. ____ out the batter (luck)   **6.** a ____ page (crank)

Write the word that fits each meaning.

7. subject   **9.** open to all people
8. not straight   **10.** to make a sudden, violent move against

Unit 20   Final |j| and |s| pp. 126-131

cottage	fence	chance	cage	village
cabbage	ridge	manage	dodge	marriage

Remember: |j| → **dge, ge** (one-syllable words)
|ij| → **age** (two-syllable words)
|s| → **ce**

strange
edge

Write the word by adding the missing letters.

11. ri _ _ _   **13.** fen _ _   **15.** chan _ _
12. man _ _ _   **14.** do _ _ _   **16.** vill _ _ _

Write the word that completes each analogy.

17. *Fruit* is to *apple* as *vegetable* is to ____.
18. *Carry* is to *carriage* as *marry* is to ____.
19. *Fish* is to *bowl* as *bird* is to ____.
20. *Big* is to *little* as *castle* is to ____.

1.
2.
3.
4.
5.
6.
7.
8.
9.
10.

11.
12.
13.
14.
15.
16.
17.
18.
19.
20.

Unit 21   Words with Prefixes   pp. 132-137

Cycle 4

> refill   discolor   untidy   rewind   redo
> reheat   distrust   unpaid   unpack   reread

Remember: A **prefix** is a word part added to the beginning of a base word to form a new word. **Un-**, **re-**, and **dis-** are prefixes.

Write the word that contains each underlined base word below.
21. <u>package</u>   **23.** <u>filled</u>   **25.** un<u>wind</u>
22. mi<u>strust</u>   **24.** <u>color</u>less   **26.** <u>doing</u>

Write the word that completes each sentence.
27. We will ____ the leftovers in the oven.
28. A room with an unmade bed always looks ____ .
29. Have you written a check for your ____ bill?
30. I liked the book so much that I am going to ____ it.

21. _____

22. _____

23. _____

24. _____

25. _____

26. _____

27. _____

28. _____

29. _____

30. _____

Unit 22   VCCV Pattern   pp. 138-143

> attend   number   support   person   offer
> helmet   tender   suppose   fellow   harvest

Remember: To find the syllables of a word with the VCCV pattern, divide the word between the consonants.

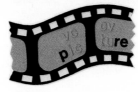

Write the word by adding the missing syllable.
31. ____ | son   **34.** ____ | pose
32. fel | ____   **35.** of | ____
33. ____ | port   **36.** har | ____

Write a word to replace the underlined word or words in each phrase below.
37. to <u>go to</u> a wedding   **39.** <u>gentle</u>, loving care
38. an even <u>numeral</u>   **40.** a football <u>head covering</u>

31. _____

32. _____

33. _____

34. _____

35. _____

36. _____

37. _____

38. _____

39. _____

40. _____

Cycle 4

Unit 23   VCCV Pattern   pp. 144-149

| bottom | hollow | member | current | plastic |
| pillow | master | thirty | lumber | engine |

Remember: To find the syllables of a word with the VCCV pattern, divide the word between the consonants.

VC   CV

can   yon

Write the word that rhymes with each word below.
41. faster   **44.** ember
42. number   **45.** elastic
43. dirty
Write the word that belongs in each group.
46. top, middle, ____   **49.** tires, steering wheel, ____
47. sheet, blanket, ____   **50.** empty, vacant, ____
48. wave, tide, ____

Challenge Words   Units 19-23   pp. 120–149

aquatic	fleece	filter	discontinue	peculiar
venture	vessel	rascal	fragrance	squid
unusual	candid	fringe	rearrange	eddy

Write the word that is a synonym for each word below.
51. reorganize   **53.** ship   **55.** smell   **57.** edge
52. scoundrel   **54.** risk   **56.** unposed   **58.** stop
Write the word that completes each sentence.
59. The ability to breathe underwater is ____ to fish.
60. An octopus has eight arms, but a ____ has ten!
61. Blue is an ____ color for a rose.
62. The ____ was caused by a change in the water's direction.
63. The swimmers practiced diving and other ____ skills.
64. Those fluffy white clouds remind me of a sheep's ____.
65. My sunglasses have a ____ that blocks out harmful rays.

41. _____
42. _____
43. _____
44. _____
45. _____
46. _____
47. _____
48. _____
49. _____
50. _____
51. _____
52. _____
53. _____
54. _____
55. _____
56. _____
57. _____
58. _____
59. _____
60. _____
61. _____
62. _____
63. _____
64. _____
65. _____

Unit 25   Changing Final *y* to *i*   pp. 156-161

Cycle 5

sunnier	noisier	cloudier	windier	heaviest
funnier	hobbies	crazier	copied	emptied

Remember: If a word ends with a consonant and **y**, change the **y** to **i** when adding **-es, -ed, -er,** or **-est**.

Write the word by adding the missing letters.

1. hobb _ _ _   3. wind _ _ _   5. craz _ _ _
2. cloud _ _ _   4. cop _ _ _   6. sunn _ _ _

Write the word that completes each analogy.

7. *Smallest* is to *largest* as *lightest* is to ____ .
8. *Softer* is to *quieter* as *louder* is to ____ .
9. *Added* is to *subtracted* as *filled* is to ____ .
10. *Silly* is to *sillier* as *funny* is to ____ .

Unit 26   VCV Pattern   pp. 162-167

navy	silent	human	music	pilot
tuna	stolen	basic	fever	moment

Remember: When the first vowel sound in a VCV word is long, divide the word into syllables before the consonant.

Write the word that belongs in each group.

11. cough, sore throat, ____   14. cod, salmon, ____
12. aqua, blue, ____   15. art, dance, ____
13. driver, conductor, ____

Write the word that fits each meaning.

16. taken without right   19. quiet
17. forming the main part   20. an instant
18. a person

1. _____

2. _____

3. _____

4. _____

5. _____

6. _____

7. _____

8. _____

9. _____

10. _____

11. _____

12. _____

13. _____

14. _____

15. _____

16. _____

17. _____

18. _____

19. _____

20. _____

Cycle 5

Unit 27   VCV Pattern   pp. 168-173

planet	visit	salad	magic	seven
talent	limit	never	habit	punish

Remember: When the first sylla-ble of a VCV word has a short vowel sound followed by a con-sonant sound, divide the word into syllables after the consonant.

Write the word by adding the missing syllable.

21. vis | _____   **23.** plan | _____   **25.** nev | _____

22. _____ | ic   **24.** _____ | ish

Write the word that fits each clue.

26. It is an action you repeat.   **29.** It comes after six.

27. You need it to be an artist.   **30.** It stops you.

28. It often includes lettuce.

21. _____

22. _____

23. _____

24. _____

25. _____

26. _____

27. _____

28. _____

29. _____

30. _____

Unit 28   Words with Suffixes   pp. 174-179

sickness	colorful	painful	fearful	endless
darkness	restless	kindness	statement	hopeless

Remember:

beauty + **ful** = beaut**iful**

hope + **less** = hope**less**

Write the word that means the opposite of each word below.

31. limited   **33.** cruelty   **35.** health

32. still   **34.** brightness   **36.** brave

Write the word that completes each sentence.

37. The speaker answered the question with a brief _____.

38. The _____ bouquet of flowers cheered me up.

39. Cool water can relieve a _____ burn.

40. With no chance of winning, the team felt _____.

31. _____

32. _____

33. _____

34. _____

35. _____

36. _____

37. _____

38. _____

39. _____

40. _____

Unit 29 VCCV Pattern pp. 180-185

Cycle 5

machine	secret	gather	other	asleep
bucket	apron	pocket	ticket	rather

Remember: If the consonants in a VCCV word are different and form a cluster or spell one sound, divide the word before or after the two consonants.

v ccv
se cret

vcc v
rock et

Write the word that completes each phrase.

41. on the ____ hand
42. a hole in your shirt ____
43. a ____ that needs oil
44. a free ____ to a game

Write the word that fits each clue.

45. to come together
46. something hidden
47. to a certain extent
48. worn for cooking
49. not awake
50. holds water

■ Challenge Words Units 25-29 pp. 156-185

ailment	abrupt	vivid	reflect	cleanliness
jealous	diesel	waver	hazard	qualities
vibrate	hazier	radar	iciest	numbness

Write the word that contains each word below.

51. clean 52. numb 53. ail

Write the word that fits each clue.

54. It uses radio waves to locate objects.
55. If you sway back and forth about a decision, you do this.

Write a word to replace each underlined word or phrase.

56. sudden changes in the weather
57. the most frozen, slippery road
58. piano strings that quiver
59. a less clear sky than yesterday
60. resentful of another's fortune
61. to mirror
62. clear, bright colors
63. a fire danger
64. oil-burning engines
65. positive features

41. _____
42. _____
43. _____
44. _____
45. _____
46. _____
47. _____
48. _____
49. _____
50. _____
51. _____
52. _____
53. _____
54. _____
55. _____
56. _____
57. _____
58. _____
59. _____
60. _____
61. _____
62. _____
63. _____
64. _____
65. _____

Cycle 6

Unit 31 VCV Pattern pp. 192-197

defend	become	below	relate	siren
polite	figure	delay	clever	open

1. _____

2. _____

3. _____

4. _____

5. _____

6. _____

7. _____

8. _____

9. _____

10. _____

Remember: VC | V   V | CV

fig | ure   si | ren

Write the word by adding the missing syllable.

1. ____ | fend   3. fig | ____   5. ____ | late

2. o | ____   4. ____ | come   6. si | ____

Write the word that completes each rhyme.

7. On the lake people <u>row</u>
   while the fish swim ____.

8. After farmers cut the <u>hay</u>,
   they gather it without ____.

9. Dogs that <u>bite</u>
   are not ____.

10. My teacher has <u>never</u>
    had students so ____!

Unit 32 VCCV and VCV Patterns pp. 198-203

silver	nature	office	capture	shelter
corner	dinner	minute	bacon	diner

11. _____

12. _____

13. _____

14. _____

15. _____

16. _____

17. _____

18. _____

19. _____

20. _____

Remember:

VC | CV   V | CV   VC | V

din | ner   ba | con   min | ute

Write the word that belongs in each group.

11. ham, pork, ____

12. breakfast, lunch, ____

13. cafeteria, restaurant, ____

14. second, hour, ____

15. copper, tin, ____

Write the word that fits each clue.

16. It is a synonym for *catch*.

17. It keeps you warm and dry.

18. The outdoors is part of it.

19. A circle never has one.

20. It is a place to work.

Unit 33   Three-Syllable Words   pp. 204-209

Cycle 6

camera	victory	library	important	together
banana	however	alphabet	hospital	enemy

Remember: To spell a three-syllable word, divide the word into syllables. Look for familiar patterns, and spell the word by syllables.

Write the word that contains each underlined syllable.
21. <u>vic</u>tim   **23.** <u>li</u>cense   **25.** some<u>how</u>
22. di<u>gi</u>tal   **24.** <u>al</u>bum   **26.** <u>por</u>tion

Write the word that completes each analogy.
27. *Painter* to is *paintbrush* as *photographer* is to ____ .
28. *Love* is to *hate* as *friend* is to ____ .
29. *Red* is to *tomato* as *yellow* is to ____ .
30. *Divided* is to *whole* as *apart* is to ____ .

21. _____
22. _____
23. _____
24. _____
25. _____
26. _____
27. _____
28. _____
29. _____
30. _____

Unit 34   Silent Consonants   pp. 210-215

kneel	limb	calf	wrinkle	answer
often	lamb	knit	honest	palm

Remember: Some words have silent consonants. The spellings of these words have to be remembered.

Write the word by adding the missing letter.
31. lim __   **33.** __ rinkle   **35.** ca __ f
32. __ nit   **34.** pa __ m   **36.** lam __

Write the word that completes each sentence.
37. Chandra raised her hand to ____ the question.
38. We trust Caleb because he is always ____ .
39. I wish Aunt Grace would visit us more ____ .
40. I had to ____ to get a closer look at the tiny flower.

31. _____
32. _____
33. _____
34. _____
35. _____
36. _____
37. _____
38. _____
39. _____
40. _____

Cycle 6

41. _____
42. _____
43. _____
44. _____
45. _____
46. _____
47. _____
48. _____
49. _____
50. _____
51. _____
52. _____
53. _____
54. _____
55. _____
56. _____
57. _____
58. _____
59. _____
60. _____
61. _____
62. _____
63. _____
64. _____
65. _____

Unit 35   Unusual Spellings   pp. 216-221

blood	guess	month	type	magazine
guest	guilt	guard	wealth	either

Remember: Some words have sounds with unusual spellings. The spellings of these words have to be remembered.

t y p e
y-consonant-e

Write the word that fits each clue.
41. rhymes with *neither*
42. someone who keeps watch
43. opposite of *host*
44. a bad feeling from doing something wrong

Write the word that belongs in each group.
45. fame, fortune, ____
46. heart, veins, ____
47. book, newspaper, ____
48. day, week, ____
49. write, print, ____
50. assume, suppose, ____

■ Challenge Words   Units 31-35   pp. 192–221

rhyme	vaccine	cadet	alert	interview
sheriff	prairie	rival	heir	threaten
edition	article	knoll	debt	corral

Write the word that completes each phrase.
51. a polio ____
52. an owed ____
53. ____ to the throne
54. horses in a ____
55. a ____ wearing a badge
56. a ____ in training to be an officer

Write the word that belongs in each group.
57. field, meadow, ____
58. conversation, meeting, ____
59. enemy, opponent, ____
60. copy, version, ____
61. endanger, bother, ____
62. awake, aware, ____
63. hill, rise, ____
64. poem, verse, ____
65. story, report, ____

Writer's Resources

Capitalization and Punctuation Guide

Abbreviations

Abbreviations are shortened forms of words. Most abbreviations begin with a capital letter and end with a period.

Titles

Mr. *(Mister)* Mr. Juan Albano   Sr. *(Senior)* John Helt, Sr.
Mrs. *(Mistress)* Mrs. Frances Wong   Jr. *(Junior)* John Helt, Jr.
Ms. Leslie Clark   Dr. *(Doctor)* Dr. Janice Dodd

Note: *Miss* is not an abbreviation and does not end with a period.

Words used in addresses

St. *(Street)*   Blvd. *(Boulevard)*
Rd. *(Road)*   Ave. *(Avenue)*

Days of the week

Sun. *(Sunday)*   Thurs. *(Thursday)*
Mon. *(Monday)*   Fri.   *(Friday)*
Tues. *(Tuesday)*   Sat.   *(Saturday)*
Wed. *(Wednesday)*

Months of the year

Jan. *(January)*   Apr. *(April)*   Oct. *(October)*
Feb. *(February)*   Aug. *(August)*   Nov. *(November)*
Mar. *(March)*   Sept. *(September)*   Dec. *(December)*

Note: *May, June,* and *July* are not abbreviated.

States

The United States Postal Service uses two capital letters and no period in each of its state abbreviations.

AL	*(Alabama)*	IN	*(Indiana)*	NE	*(Nebraska)*
AK	*(Alaska)*	IA	*(Iowa)*	NV	*(Nevada)*
AZ	*(Arizona)*	KS	*(Kansas)*	NH	*(New Hampshire)*
AR	*(Arkansas)*	KY	*(Kentucky)*	NJ	*(New Jersey)*
CA	*(California)*	LA	*(Louisiana)*	NM	*(New Mexico)*
CO	*(Colorado)*	ME	*(Maine)*	NY	*(New York)*
CT	*(Connecticut)*	MD	*(Maryland)*	NC	*(North Carolina)*
DE	*(Delaware)*	MA	*(Massachusetts)*	ND	*(North Dakota)*
FL	*(Florida)*	MI	*(Michigan)*	OH	*(Ohio)*
GA	*(Georgia)*	MN	*(Minnesota)*	OK	*(Oklahoma)*
HI	*(Hawaii)*	MS	*(Mississippi)*	OR	*(Oregon)*
ID	*(Idaho)*	MO	*(Missouri)*	PA	*(Pennsylvania)*
IL	*(Illinois)*	MT	*(Montana)*	RI	*(Rhode Island)*

(continued)

Abbreviations (continued)

States (continued)						
SC	(South Carolina)	UT	(Utah)	WV	(West Virginia)
SD	(South Dakota)	VT	(Vermont)	WI	(Wisconsin)
TN	(Tennessee)	VA	(Virginia)	WY	(Wyoming)
TX	(Texas)	WA	(Washington)		

Titles

Underlining	**Titles of books, newspapers, magazines, and TV series are underlined. The important words and the first and last words are capitalized.**
	Life on the Mississippi Newsweek Nova
Quotation marks	**Put *quotation marks (" ")* around the titles of short stories, articles, songs, poems, and book chapters.**
	"The Necklace" *(short story)*
	"Home on the Range" *(song)*

Quotations

Quotation marks	**A *direct quotation* tells a speaker's exact words. Use *quotation marks (" ")* to set off a direct quotation from the rest of the sentence.**
	"Please put away your books now," said Mr. Emory.
	Begin a quotation with a capital letter. When a quotation comes at the end of a sentence, use a comma to separate the quotation from the words that tell who is speaking. Put end marks inside the last quotation marks.
	The driver announced, "This is the Summer Street bus."
Writing a conversation	**Begin a new paragraph each time a new person begins speaking.**
	"Are your seats behind home plate or along the first-base line?" asked the voice on the phone.
	"I haven't bought any tickets yet," said Mr. Williams. "I was hoping that you would reserve three seats for me now."

Capitalization

Rules for capitalization

Capitalize the first word of every sentence.

What an unusual color the roses are!

Capitalize the pronoun _I_.

What should I do next?

Capitalize every important word in the names of particular people, pets, places, and things (proper nouns).

Rover   District of Columbia   Elm Street   Lincoln Memorial

Capitalize titles and initials that are parts of names.

Governor Bradford   Emily G. Hesse   Senator Smith

Capitalize family titles when they are used as names or as parts of names.

We visited Uncle Harry.   May we play now, Grandma?

Capitalize the names of months and days.

My birthday is on the last Monday in March.

Capitalize the names of groups.

Sutton Bicycle Club   National League

Capitalize the names of holidays.

Memorial Day   Fourth of July   Veterans Day

Capitalize the first and last words and all important words in the titles of books and newspapers.

From Earth to the Moon   The New York Times

Capitalize the first word in the greeting and the closing of a letter.

Dear Marcia,   Yours truly,

(continued)

Capitalization (continued)

Rules for capitalization (continued)	**In an outline, each Roman numeral and capital letter is followed by a period. Capitalize the first word of each main topic and subtopic.**

	I. Types of libraries
	  A. Large public library
	  B. Bookmobile

Punctuation

End marks	**There are three end marks. A *period (.)* ends a statement or a command. A *question mark (?)* follows a question. An *exclamation point (!)* follows an exclamation.**
	The scissors are on my desk. *(statement)*
	Look up the spelling of that word. *(command)*
	How is the word spelled? *(question)*
	This is your best poem so far! *(exclamation)*
Apostrophe	**To form the possessive of a singular noun, add an apostrophe and *s* ('s).**
	baby's Russ's grandmother's family's
	For a plural noun ending in *s*, add only an apostrophe (').
	sisters' families' Smiths' hound dogs'
	For a plural noun that does not end in *s*, add an apostrophe and *s* ('s).
	women's mice's children's
	Use an apostrophe in contractions in place of dropped letters.
	isn't *(is not)* it's *(it is)* can't *(cannot)* I'm *(I am)* won't *(will not)* you'll *(you will)* wasn't *(was not)* they've *(they have)* you're *(you are)*

Punctuation (continued)

Comma

A *comma (,)* tells the reader to pause between the words that it separates.

Use commas to separate items in a series. Put a comma after each item in the series except the last one.

Clyde asked if we had any apples, peaches, or grapes.

You can combine two short, related sentences to make one compound sentence. Use a comma and the connecting word *and, but,* or *or.*

Some students were at lunch, but others were studying.

Use commas to set off the words *yes, no,* and *well* when they are at the beginning of a sentence.

Well, it's just too cold out.   No, it isn't six yet.

Use a comma or commas to set off the names of people who are spoken to directly.

Jean, help me fix this tire.   How was your trip, Grandpa?

Use a comma to separate the month and the day from the year.

Our nation was born on July 4, 1776.

Use a comma between the names of a city and a state.

Chicago, Illinois   Miami, Florida

Use a comma after the greeting in a friendly letter.

Dear Deena,   Dear Uncle Rudolph,

Use a comma after the closing in a letter.

Your nephew,   Sincerely yours,

Friendly Letter

Use correct letter form, capitalization, and punctuation when you write a friendly letter. Remember that a friendly letter has five parts.

- The **heading** gives your complete address and the date.
- The **greeting** usually includes the word *Dear* and the name of the person to whom you are writing.
- The **body** is the main part of the letter. It includes all the information that you want to tell your reader.
- The **closing** says "good-by." Use closings such as *Your friend* or *Love*.
- The **signature** is your name. Sign your first name below the closing.

Study this model.

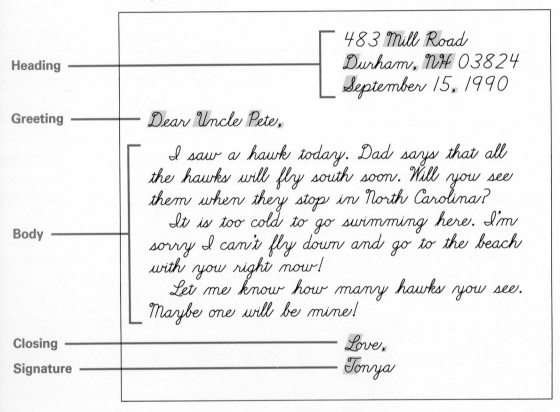

Heading

483 Mill Road
Durham, NH 03824
September 15, 1990

Greeting

Dear Uncle Pete,

Body

I saw a hawk today. Dad says that all the hawks will fly south soon. Will you see them when they stop in North Carolina?

It is too cold to go swimming here. I'm sorry I can't fly down and go to the beach with you right now!

Let me know how many hawks you see. Maybe one will be mine!

Closing

Love,

Signature

Tonya

How to Use This Thesaurus

Use this Thesaurus to make your writing more exact and more interesting. Suppose you write this sentence:

July 4 is an *important* date in history.

You decide that you want to replace the word *important* with another, more exact word. Turn to your Thesaurus Index to help you find words to use in place of *important*.

Using the Thesaurus Index The Thesaurus Index lists all the words in the Thesaurus in alphabetical order. Follow these steps to use the Thesaurus Index:

1. Look up your word in the Thesaurus Index under the letter it begins with. For example, look up *important* under *I*.
2. Note the main entry word in blue print. Look up the main entry word in the Thesaurus.

main entry word → important *adj.*

Suppose you already have the word *major* in mind to replace *important*. In the Thesaurus Index you will find

major important *adj.*

The slanted print shows you that you will find the word *major* under the main entry word *important* in the Thesaurus.

The Thesaurus Index also lists antonyms, or opposites, of words. They are shown like this:

unimportant important *adj.*

The black print shows you that *unimportant* is the opposite of the main entry word *important*.

Using the Thesaurus Entry The main entry words in the Thesaurus are listed in alphabetical order. Study this entry for the main entry word *important*.

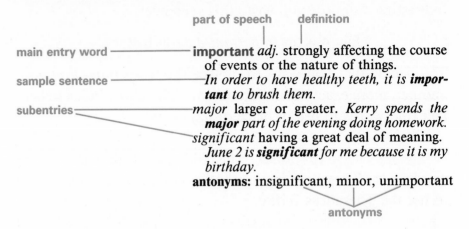

Notice that the entry gives two subentries, or words that you can use in place of *important*: *major* and *significant*. To help you choose one, the Thesaurus gives you

1. a meaning for each subentry, and
2. a sample sentence to show you how to use each word.

Now you can choose the more exact word for your sentence.

July 4 is a *significant* date in history.

Practice **Look up each word below in the Thesaurus Index. Write the main entry word for each word.**
1. funny   2. messy   3. keen   4. lovely   5. silence

Use the Thesaurus to choose a more exact word to replace each underlined word. Rewrite each sentence, using the new word.
6. My father drove the tractor over the rough field.
7. Cam's clothes were dirty after he planted the seeds.
8. Kate tried to break the hard, cold soil with her hoe.
9. My father's instructions were easy to follow.
10. Everyone on the farm helped to gather the crops.

Thesaurus Index

A

ability skill *n.*
accomplish do *v.*
accurate true *adj.*
achieve do *v.*
acid sharp *adj.*
acrid sharp *adj.*
actual true *adj.*
acute sharp *adj.*
admire dislike *v.*
adore dislike *v.*
adult grown *adj.*
after before *adv.*
agree *v.*
agree relate *v.*
ailment sickness *n.*
alarm fright *n.*
allow let *v.*
alone lonely *adj.*
always *adv.*
amaze surprise *v.*
amber yellow *adj.*
amusing funny *adj.*
animosity kindness *n.*
answer question *n.*
antique modern *adj.*
anxious upset *adj.*
appalling awful *adj.*
approve agree *v.*
aptitude skill *n.*
assemble gather *v.*
astound surprise *v.*
at the end last *adv.*
attractive pretty *adj.*
authentic true *adj.*
award *n.*
awful *adj.*

B

barbed sharp *adj.*
bare empty *adj.*
beautiful pretty *adj.*
before *adv.*

begin start *v.*
behold look *v.*
bellow shout *v.*
big small *adj.*
bite burn *v.*
biting sharp *adj.*
bitter sharp *adj.*
blank empty *adj.*
blare noise *n.*
board wood *n.*
boiling cold *adj.*
bounce jump *v.*
bound jump *v.*
break *v.*
bright dark *adj.*
bright sharp *adj.*
bumpy rough *adj.*
burn *v.*
burning cold *adj.*

C

calm upset *adj.*
capture throw *v.*
care for dislike *v.*
careful careless *adj.*
careful safe *adj.*
careless *adj.*
careless safe *adj.*
carry out do *v.*
cast throw *v.*
catch throw *v.*
cause reason *n.*
cautious careless *adj.*
challenging easy *adj.*
charity kindness *n.*
charming pretty *adj.*
chartreuse green *adj.*
cheer shout *v.*
chief main *adj.*
childish grown *adj.*
chilly cold *adj.*
clang noise *n.*
clean dirty *adj.*
clear dark *adj.*
close start *v.*

cloudy dark *adj.*
clever sharp *adj.*
coarse rough *adj.*
coil wind *v.*
cold *adj.*
collect gather *v.*
comical funny *adj.*
commence start *v.*
common strange *adj.*
complain relate *v.*
comply agree *v.*
conceal show *v.*
conclude start *v.*
consent agree *v.*
consent let *v.*
constant true *adj.*
contemplate look *v.*
contemporary modern
    adj.
continually always *adv.*
cool cold *adj.*
correct true *adj.*
counterfeit true *adj.*
countless many *adj.*
count on depend *v.*
cover *n.*
crack break *v.*
cruel sharp *adj.*
curl wind *v.*
current modern *adj.*
curve wind *v.*

D

danger *n.*
dangerous safe *adj.*
dark *adj.*
dash run *v.*
dawdle run *v.*
delay wait *v.*
demonstrate show *v.*
deny agree *v.*
depart wait *v.*
depend *v.*
dependable true *adj.*
deplorable awful *adj.*

deserve earn *v.*
despise dislike *v.*
detest dislike *v.*
difficult easy *adj.*
dim dark *adj.*
dirty *adj.*
discover learn *v.*
disease sickness *n.*
disgusting awful *adj.*
disheveled dirty *adj.*
dislike *v.*
disloyal true *adj.*
disperse gather *v.*
display show *v.*
disregard look *v.*
distrust depend *v.*
do *v.*
doubt depend *v.*
drag pull *v.*
dreadful awful *adj.*

E

earlier before *adv.*
earn *v.*
easy *adj.*
easygoing upset *adj.*
edged sharp *adj.*
effortless easy *adj.*
embark start *v.*
empty *adj.*
end start *v.*
endlessly always *adv.*
endure live *v.*
erroneous true *adj.*
errorless true *adj.*
escape wait *v.*
estimate guess *v.*
eternally always *adv.*
event *n.*
exact true *adj.*
examination question *n.*
excellent awful *adj.*
exclaim relate *v.*
exit wait *v.*
experience event *n.*
explanation reason *n.*
exposed safe *adj.*

exposure cover *n.*
exquisite awful *adj.*
eye look *v.*

F

factual true *adj.*
faculty skill *n.*
faithless true *adj.*
false true *adj.*
familiar strange *adj.*
famished hungry *adj.*
fancy dislike *v.*
fast quick *adj.*
fear fright *n.*
fearful awful *adj.*
fever sickness *n.*
few many *adj.*
filthy dirty *adj.*
finally last *adv.*
find out learn *v.*
fine awful *adj.*
finish start *v.*
firm hard *adj.*
first last *adv.*
fitness sickness *n.*
forever always *adv.*
foul dirty *adj.*
friendless lonely *adj.*
friendliness kindness *n.*
fright *n.*
frightful awful *adj.*
frozen cold *adj.*
full empty *adj.*
full hungry *adj.*
funny *adj.*

G

gain earn *v.*
gape look *v.*
gather *v.*
gawk look *v.*
gaze look *v.*
generosity kindness *n.*
ghastly awful *adj.*
glance look *v.*
glower look *v.*

gold yellow *adj.*
grab throw *v.*
great small *adj.*
green *adj.*
grimy dirty *adj.*
groan relate *v.*
grounds reason *n.*
group gather *v.*
grown *adj.*
grubby dirty *adj.*
guess *v.*
guide show *v.*

H

handsome pretty *adj.*
harbor cover *n.*
hard *adj.*
hard easy *adj.*
hard sharp *adj.*
harvest gather *v.*
hasty quick *adj.*
hate dislike *v.*
hatred kindness *n.*
hazard danger *n.*
health sickness *n.*
heartiness sickness *n.*
helpfulness kindness *n.*
hide show *v.*
hinder let *v.*
homely pretty *adj.*
homesick lonely *adj.*
honed sharp *adj.*
honest true *adj.*
honorable true *adj.*
horrendous awful *adj.*
horrible awful *adj.*
hostility kindness *n.*
hot cold *adj.*
howl shout *v.*
huge small *adj.*
humorous funny *adj.*
hungry *adj.*
hurl throw *v.*
hush noise *n.*
hushed silent *adj.*

I

ignore look *v.*
illness sickness *n.*
immaculate dirty *adj.*
immature grown *adj.*
important adj.
incident event *n.*
incorrect true *adj.*
infer guess *v.*
inquiry question *n.*
insecure safe *adj.*
insignificant important *adj.*
instant minute *n.*
intelligent sharp *adj.*
interrogation question *n.*

J

jiffy minute *n.*
jump *v.*

K

keen sharp *adj.*
kindling wood *n.*
kindness n.
knifelike sharp *adj.*

L

large small *adj.*
last *adv.*
later before *adv.*
laughable funny *adj.*
lavender purple *adj.*
leap jump *v.*
learn *v.*
leave wait *v.*
lemon yellow *adj.*
let *v.*
light dark *adj.*
like dislike *v.*
linger wait *v.*
little small *adj.*

live *v.*
loathe dislike *v.*
lonely adj.
look *v.*
lose earn *v.*
loud silent *adj.*
love dislike *v.*
lovely pretty *adj.*
lowly main *adj.*
lumber wood *n.*

M

main *adj.*
major important *adj.*
many *adj.*
master learn *v.*
mature grown *adj.*
meager many *adj.*
medal award *n.*
melody music *n.*
menace danger *n.*
mend break *v.*
merit earn *v.*
messy dirty *adj.*
mindful careless *adj.*
miniature small *adj.*
minor important *adj.*
minute *n.*
minute small *adj.*
miss look *v.*
modern *adj.*
moment minute *n.*
muddy dirty *adj.*
murky dark *adj.*
murmur shout *v.*
music *n.*

N

nasty awful *adj.*
nasty dirty *adj.*
neat dirty *adj.*
negligent careless *adj.*
nervous upset *adj.*
nice awful *adj.*
nip burn *v.*
noise *n.*

noisy silent *adj.*
notice look *v.*
numerous many *adj.*

O

obnoxious awful *adj.*
observe look *v.*
occasion event *n.*
odd strange *adj.*
official true *adj.*
old modern *adj.*
old-fashioned modern *adj.*
old-time modern *adj.*
olive green *adj.*
once before *adv.*
openness cover *n.*
orange *adj.*
ordinary strange *adj.*
original true *adj.*
outdated modern *adj.*
overfed hungry *adj.*
overlook look *v.*

P

packed empty *adj.*
pass throw *v.*
past modern *adj.*
patch break *v.*
patter noise *n.*
peculiar strange *adj.*
peek look *v.*
peep look *v.*
perform do *v.*
peril danger *n.*
permit let *v.*
persist live *v.*
phony true *adj.*
piercing sharp *adj.*
pitch throw *v.*
plain pretty *adj.*
pleasing awful *adj.*
point minute *n.*
pointed sharp *adj.*
polished rough *adj.*

precise true *adj.*
present modern *adj.*
presume guess *v.*
pretty *adj.*
prevent let *v.*
previously before *adv.*
primary main *adj.*
principal main *adj.*
prize award *n.*
protected safe *adj.*
protection cover *n.*
pull *v.*
pungent sharp *adj.*
purple *adj.*
push pull *v.*

Q

question *n.*
question relate *v.*
quick *adj.*
quick sharp *adj.*
quiet noise *n.*
quiet silent *adj.*
quiz question *n.*

R

race run *v.*
racket noise *n.*
rapid quick *adj.*
rash careless *adj.*
ravenous hungry *adj.*
real true *adj.*
reason *n.*
reckless careless *adj.*
red *adj.*
reek smell *v.*
refuge cover *n.*
refuse agree *v.*
regard look *v.*
relate *v.*
relaxed upset *adj.*
rely depend *v.*
remain wait *v.*
repair break *v.*
reply question *n.*

repulsive awful *adj.*
response question *n.*
reveal show *v.*
revolting awful *adj.*
reward award *n.*
ripe grown *adj.*
risk danger *n.*
roar noise *n.*
rotten awful *adj.*
rough *adj.*
rough sharp *adj.*
run *v.*
rush run *v.*

S

safe *adj.*
safety danger *n.*
scan look *v.*
scant many *adj.*
scarlet red *adj.*
scatter gather *v.*
scorching cold *adj.*
scream shout *v.*
secure safe *adj.*
security danger *n.*
seize throw *v.*
serious funny *adj.*
several many *adj.*
shabby dirty *adj.*
shady dark *adj.*
sharp *adj.*
shatter break *v.*
shelter cover *n.*
shock surprise *v.*
shocking awful *adj.*
shoot throw *v.*
shout *v.*
shove pull *v.*
show *v.*
shrewd sharp *adj.*
sickness *n.*
sigh shout *v.*
significant important *adj.*
silence noise *n.*
silent *adj.*
simple easy *adj.*

skill *n.*
sloppy dirty *adj.*
slow quick *adj.*
small *adj.*
smart burn *v.*
smart sharp *adj.*
smell *v.*
smooth rough *adj.*
soft hard *adj.*
soiled dirty *adj.*
solemn funny *adj.*
solid hard *adj.*
solitary lonely *adj.*
song music *n.*
speedy quick *adj.*
spiked sharp *adj.*
spiral wind *v.*
splendid awful *adj.*
spongy hard *adj.*
spot look *v.*
spotless dirty *adj.*
spread gather *v.*
spring jump *v.*
squalid dirty *adj.*
stabbing sharp *adj.*
stained dirty *adj.*
stare look *v.*
start *v.*
starving hungry *adj.*
stay wait *v.*
steady true *adj.*
still silent *adj.*
sting burn *v.*
stinging sharp *adj.*
stink smell *v.*
stop let *v.*
straighten wind *v.*
strange *adj.*
stroll run *v.*
study learn *v.*
study look *v.*
stuffed empty *adj.*
suggest relate *v.*
sunny dark *adj.*
superb awful *adj.*
suppose guess *v.*
surprise *v.*
survey look *v.*

survive live *v.*

T

talent skill *n.*
tangerine orange *adj.*
tart sharp *adj.*
terror fright *n.*
thoughtless careless *adj.*
throw *v.*
tidy dirty *adj.*
timber wood *n.*
tiny small *adj.*
torrid cold *adj.*
toss throw *v.*
tough hard *adj.*
tow pull *v.*
trophy award *n.*
troubled upset *adj.*
true adj.
trust depend *v.*
trustworthy true *adj.*
tune music *n.*
turquoise green *adj.*
twist wind *v.*

U

ugly pretty *adj.*
unattractive pretty *adj.*
uncomplicated easy *adj.*
uncurl wind *v.*
uneven rough *adj.*
unhurried quick *adj.*
unimportant important *adj.*
unimportant main *adj.*
unsoiled dirty *adj.*
untidy dirty *adj.*
untrue true *adj.*
untwist wind *v.*
unusual strange *adj.*
upset *adj.*
up-to-date modern *adj.*

V

vacant empty *adj.*
view look *v.*
vile awful *adj.*

W

wait *v.*
walk run *v.*
warm cold *adj.*
watch look *v.*
weather live *v.*
weird strange *adj.*
well-being sickness *n.*
whisper shout *v.*
win earn *v.*
wind v.
wonderful awful *adj.*
wood *n.*
worried upset *adj.*

Y

yell shout *v.*
yellow *adj.*
yielding hard *adj.*
young grown *adj.*
youthful grown *adj.*

Thesaurus

A

agree *v.* to express one's willingness or approval. *My parents agreed to get a dog for my brother and me.*

approve to say officially that something is correct or should be done. *The principal approved the plan for the field trip.*

comply to follow a request or a rule. *Please comply with the rules when you visit the museum.*

consent to say yes. *Did Judy consent to the plan?*

antonyms: deny, refuse

always *adv.* for as long as one can imagine. *Tina and Laurie will always be best friends.*

continually for a long time without a break or a pause. *My little sister continually bothers me when I am doing my homework.*

endlessly constantly, incessantly. *The highway seemed to stretch forward endlessly.*

eternally in a manner that seems to last forever. *I will be eternally grateful to the firefighters who saved my dog.*

forever for all time. *The character Peter Pan wanted to be young forever.*

award *n.* something given for outstanding performance or quality. *Jon received an award for perfect attendance.*

medal a small, flat, often circular piece of metal with a design, often awarded to honor a person, an action, an accomplishment, or an event. *The officer won a medal for bravery.*

prize something offered or won in a competition. *Ed won a prize for the best story.*

reward something that is offered, given, or received in return for a worthy act, service, or accomplishment. *Sue received a reward for returning the lost wallet.*

trophy a prize given or received as a symbol of victory or achievement. *The team won a trophy for winning the championship.*

Word Bank

awful *adj.* very bad; horrible.

appalling	*horrible*
deplorable	*nasty*
disgusting	*obnoxious*
dreadful	*repulsive*
fearful	*revolting*
frightful	*rotten*
ghastly	*shocking*
horrendous	*vile*

antonyms: excellent, exquisite, fine, nice, pleasing, splendid, superb, wonderful

B

before *adv.* in the past. *He was excited about his trip because he had not been to Texas before.*

earlier coming or happening before the usual or expected time. *Since the game ended earlier than usual, we had time to spare.*

once at a time in the past. *Once we lived in a big city, but now we live in the country.*

previously taking place in the past. *Previously she wore her hair long, but now it is short.*

antonyms: after *adv.,* later *adv.*

break *v.* to separate into pieces as the result of force or strain. *A branch broke under the weight of the snow.*

crack to come apart with a sudden sharp sound. *Dale hit the ball hard enough to crack the bat.*

shatter to come apart suddenly into many pieces. *The delicate cup shattered against the floor.*

antonyms: mend, patch *v.,* repair *v.*

burn *v.* to feel or cause to feel a burning sensation. *The fire's heat made my face **burn.***

bite to cause to sting. *The icy water **bit** my cheeks when I splashed it on my face.*

nip to sting or chill. *The cold wind **nipped** my nose and ears.*

smart to cause to feel a stinging pain. *I clapped so hard that my hands **smarted.***

sting to feel or cause to feel a sharp, burning pain. *After a few minutes in the smoky room, my eyes began to **sting.***

C

careless *adj.* not taking the necessary care. *I made a **careless** mistake on my math test.*

negligent not acting with proper care or concern. *The **negligent** boy left his jacket out in the rain.*

rash too hasty; reckless. *Wanda regretted her **rash** statement about David.*

reckless not careful or cautious. *The **reckless** driver sped through the red light.*

thoughtless not thinking; careless. *It was **thoughtless** of Jenny to forget her bus fare.*

antonyms: careful, cautious, mindful

cold *adj.* having or being at a lower temperature than normal. *The water in the lake is **cold** in early spring.*

chilly cold enough to cause or feel unpleasant coldness. *My light clothes did not protect me from the damp, **chilly** air.*

cool somewhat cold. *We were relieved to find a **cool**, shady place to rest after our long hike.*

frozen uncomfortably cold. *After a day of skating, my feet were **frozen.***

antonyms: boiling *adj.*, burning *adj.*, hot, scorching *adj.*, torrid, warm

cover *n.* a shelter or protection. *When it began to rain, we ran to find **cover.***

harbor a shelter; refuge. *The large rock served as a **harbor** for rattlesnakes.*

protection something that guards against harm, attack, or injury. *Special glasses provide **protection** for the workers' eyes.*

refuge a place of protection. *Hunting is not allowed in the wildlife **refuge.***

shelter something that protects or covers. *The hikers found **shelter** for the night.*

antonyms: exposure, openness

D

danger *n.* the chance of harm or destruction. *The sailor knew the **dangers** of sailing at night.*

hazard something that may cause injury or harm. *Fire fighters face many **hazards.***

menace a threat or danger. *The damaged electrical lines were a **menace** to public safety.*

peril the condition of being in danger. *We had put our lives in **peril** by going out in the blizzard.*

risk the possibility of suffering harm or loss. *You will have to cross that broken bridge at your own **risk.***

antonyms: safety, security

dark *adj.* without light or with very little light. *We used a flashlight to find our way through the **dark** house.*

cloudy not clear. *The science teacher held up a glass of **cloudy** liquid.*

dim somewhat dark. *I could barely see the stack of boxes in the **dim** basement.*

murky very dark or gloomy. *The river water was so **murky** that we could not see the rocky bottom.*

shady blocked off from the light. *Our porch is **shady** and cool because a large tree shelters it from the sun.*

antonyms: bright, clear, light, sunny

depend *v.* to have trust. *Mrs. Li knew that she could **depend** on Al to feed the dog while she was gone.*

count on to rely on for help or support. *We can **count on** the fifth grade to help us with the book fair.*

rely to have confidence. *You can **rely** on us to be on time for the play.*

trust to have or put confidence in. *Sumi **trusted** her best friend to keep her secret.*

antonyms: distrust *v.*, doubt *v.*

dirty, dirtier, dirtiest

dirty *adj.* full of or covered with dirt.

1. somewhat dirty:

disheveled   sloppy
messy   untidy
shabby

2. quite dirty:

grimy   soiled
grubby   stained
muddy

3. extremely dirty:

filthy   nasty
foul   squalid

antonyms: 1. neat, tidy **2.** clean, unsoiled **3.** immaculate, spotless

dislike *v.* to have a feeling of not liking. *I **dislike** scary movies.*

despise to regard with great dislike. *The spy **despised** the enemy agents.*

detest to dislike very much. *Rich **detests** liver and onions.*

hate to feel strong dislike for. *I **hate** to shop.*

loathe to feel great dislike for. *Katherine **loathes** being called Kate.*

antonyms: admire, adore, care for, fancy *v.*, like, love *v.*

do *v.* to carry out an act or action. *Nate **does** his homework right after school.*

accomplish to perform a task. *We can **accomplish** the job in an hour.*

achieve to succeed in doing or accomplishing. *Emily **achieved** good grades this year.*

carry out to put into practice. *My dog **carried out** my command to sit.*

perform to carry out; do. *Mrs. Hudson **performed** the science experiment in class.*

E

earn *v.* to gain by working or by supplying service. *Lisa **earns** her allowance.*

deserve to be worthy of or have a right to. *Alex **deserves** credit for his hard work.*

gain to get or obtain by effort. *Jill has **gained** the respect of her classmates.*

merit to be worthy of. *This problem **merits** our close attention.*

win to get by hard work. *George **won** the right to hold the flag in the parade.*

antonym: lose

easy *adj.* needing very little effort or thought. *I finished the book quickly because it was **easy** to read.*

effortless easily done. *The excellent players made winning the game look **effortless**.*

simple not complicated. *The game is so **simple** that a young child can play it.*

uncomplicated not hard to understand or deal with. *A cat's life is **uncomplicated**.*

antonyms: challenging, difficult, hard

empty *adj.* containing nothing. *Please put the papers in the **empty** box on the porch.*

bare without the usual furniture or supplies. *The shelves of the refrigerator were **bare** when we returned from vacation.*

blank free of marks or decoration. *The teacher told each student to get out a **blank** piece of paper.*

vacant not occupied or rented. *Our steps echoed as we walked through the **vacant** rooms of the new house.*

antonyms: full, packed *adj.*, stuffed *adj.*

event *n.* something that happens. *Ronald's wedding was a happy **event**.*

experience a happening that one has lived through. *My trip was a good **experience**.*

incident a brief or unimportant happening. *There was a funny **incident** at school.*

occasion a very important event. *Grandma's birthday was a great **occasion**.*

F

fright *n.* sudden, strong fear. *A sudden movement in the bushes gave us a **fright**.*

alarm sudden fear caused by a feeling that danger is near. *The chance of a flood always causes **alarm** in my town.*

fear a feeling caused by a sense of danger. *Toni has a **fear** of high places.*

terror very great fear. *The monsters in the movie made the children in the theater scream in **terror**.*

funny *adj.* causing amusement or laughter. *The joke was so **funny** that we could not stop laughing.*

amusing pleasantly entertaining. *The playful kittens were **amusing**.*

comical producing laughter; silly. *A clown is supposed to be **comical**.*

humorous being funny. *Kim told a **humorous** story about camping with her family.*

laughable causing laughter. *Putting my shirt on backwards was a **laughable** mistake.*

antonyms: serious, solemn

G

gather *v.* to bring or come together into one place. *I **gathered** all the books to take back to the library.*

assemble to bring together to make a group. *Bev **assembled** the broken pieces.*

collect to bring or come together in a group. *Tad **collects** baseball cards.*

group to arrange or gather in a group. *Our teacher always **groups** us in alphabetical order.*

harvest to gather a crop. *Farmers **harvest** wheat at this time of year.*

antonyms: disperse, scatter, spread *v.*

green *adj.* having the color of growing grass. *The plant's **green** leaves turned brown in the hot weather.*

chartreuse light yellowish green. *Cora's **chartreuse** scarf looks almost yellow in this light.*

olive dull yellowish green. *Ted's **olive** jacket blended in with the leaves on the trees and bushes.*

turquoise light bluish green. *White sea gulls dove into the **turquoise** ocean water.*

grown *adj.* having reached an adult age; mature. *When I am **grown,** I want to work in a clinic or hospital.*

adult fully developed and mature. ***Adult** turtles do not stay with their young.*

mature fully grown or developed. *Dad wanted a **mature** dog rather than a puppy.*

ripe fully grown and developed. *Those apples will be bright red when they are **ripe**.*

antonyms: childish, immature, young, youthful

guess *v.* to form an opinion without enough information to be sure of it. *I correctly **guessed** the answer to the math problem.*

estimate to guess about; calculate roughly. *Can you **estimate** the distance to Dallas?*

infer to conclude from evidence. *We **inferred** from the dark house that no one was home.*

presume to suppose to be true. *If you are watching TV, I **presume** that you have already done your homework.*

suppose to be inclined to think; assume. *I **suppose** that Sylvia will be late as usual.*

H

hard *adj.* not bending or yielding when pushed. *The child skinned his knee on the **hard** cement steps.*

firm not giving way when pressed or pushed; solid. *The fresh melon was **firm** to the touch.*

solid strong and firm. *This toy furniture is so **solid** that you could sit on it.*

tough strong and not likely to break or tear. *Football helmets are made out of **tough** plastic.*

antonyms: soft, spongy, yielding

hungry *adj.* wanting food. *Ellen was **hungry** and tired after her walk.*

famished extremely hungry. *We missed lunch and were **famished** by the time we arrived.*

ravenous greedily eager for food. *The **ravenous** puppy gobbled down the bowl of food.*

starving suffering or dying from lack of food. *The stray kitten was **starving** and weak.*

antonyms: full, overfed

I

important *adj.* strongly affecting the course of events or the nature of things. *In order to have healthy teeth, it is **important** to brush them.*

major larger or greater. *Kerry spends the **major** part of the evening doing homework.*

significant having a great deal of meaning. *June 2 is **significant** for me because it is my birthday.*

antonyms: insignificant, minor, unimportant

J

jump *v.* to rise up and move through the air by using the legs. *How high can you **jump**?*

bounce to come back or up after hitting a surface. *I **bounced** on the trampoline.*

bound to leap upward and forward. *The dog **bounded** after the frightened rabbit.*

leap to jump quickly or suddenly. *Vera **leaped** up to catch the ball.*

spring to move upward in one quick motion. *The diver **sprang** off of the high diving board.*

K

kindness *n.* the quality or condition of being helpful or considerate; generosity. *Grandpa is known for his **kindness** to animals.*

charity good will or love toward others. *Keith's volunteer work in the hospital is an act of **charity**.*

friendliness the quality of showing or encouraging friendship. *Our host's **friendliness** made us feel right at home.*

generosity willingness to give or share. *Letting others use your favorite toys shows great **generosity**.*

helpfulness usefulness, assistance. *My parents appreciated Roy's **helpfulness**.*

antonyms: animosity, hatred, hostility

L

last *adv.* after all the others. *Add the ice **last** so that it does not melt.*

at the end at the conclusion. *Karen delivered a good speech, but she stumbled **at the end**.*

finally after a long while. *After we had waited two hours, the train **finally** arrived.*

antonym: first *adv.*

learn *v.* to get knowledge of or skill in through study or instruction. *I finally **learned** my times tables.*

discover to find out. *Rick **discovered** that the strange rock was a mineral.*

find out to get information about. *Did you **find out** what time our train leaves?*

master to become skilled in. *Chris **mastered** skating in just three lessons.*

study to try to learn. *I will **study** my spelling words before the test on Friday.*

let *v.* to give permission to. *Ron took the leash off his dog and **let** her run free.*

allow to let do or happen. *Please **allow** me to go to Jenny's party.*

consent to agree to let do. *My parents finally **consented** to my request.*

permit to give permission or the opportunity to. *The state law **permits** sixteen-year-olds to drive cars.*

antonyms: hinder, prevent, stop *v.*

live *v.* to be alive; exist. *Insects can **live** in almost every part of the world.*

endure to continue to exist; last. *Many trees can **endure** for hundreds of years.*

persist to continue to happen or exist. *Jay's bad mood **persisted** for several days.*

survive to stay alive or in existence. *The lost child **survived** by eating nuts and berries.*

weather to pass through safely. *The rabbits **weathered** the harsh winter by burrowing deep in the snow.*

lonely *adj.* sad at being alone. *Phil was **lonely** when his best friend moved away.*

alone without anyone or anything else. *Grandmother enjoys living **alone** in the apartment above ours.*

friendless without friends. *The **friendless** boy ate lunch by himself.*

homesick unhappy and longing for home and family. *I was **homesick** during the first week of camp.*

solitary being or living alone. *A lighthouse keeper lives a **solitary** life.*

Word Bank

look *v.* to use the eyes to see.

behold		
contemplate		
eye		
gape		
gawk		
gaze	peek	stare
glance	peep	study
glower	regard	survey
notice	scan	view
observe	spot	watch

antonyms: disregard, ignore, miss, overlook

M

main *adj.* most important or primary. *The **main** street in our town is called Main Street!*

chief most important. *Wheat is the **chief** product of the state.*

primary first in importance, degree, or quality. *Mr. Chang's **primary** goal is to learn English.*

principal first in rank or importance. *Safety is my **principal** concern.*

antonyms: lowly *adj.,* unimportant

many *adj.* adding up to a great number. ***Many** people bought tickets to the show.*

countless too many to count. ***Countless** fans were disappointed by the canceled game.*

numerous made up of a large number. *Colds and other illnesses are more **numerous** in the winter.*

several more than two but not many. *Kathy walks **several** blocks to school.*

antonyms: few *adj.,* meager, scant

minute *n.* a short time. *Dinner will be ready in a **minute.***

instant a very brief period of time. *She recognized me in an **instant.***

jiffy a moment; no time at all. *I will be ready to go in a **jiffy.***

moment a very short period of time. *A **moment** later, the doorbell rang.*

point an instant in time. *At that **point**, the bell rang.*

modern *adj.* of or relating to the present or recent past. ***Modern** transportation is fast and clean.*

contemporary living or occurring during the present time. *We heard the recordings of some **contemporary** musicians.*

current belonging to the present time. *We read about **current** events in the newspaper.*

present being or happening now. *At the **present** time, there is no cure for that disease.*

up-to-date showing or using the latest improvements or style. *Sonia's clothes are always **up-to-date.***

antonyms: antique, old, old-fashioned, old-time, outdated, past *adj.*

music *n.* vocal or instrumental sounds that have rhythm, melody, and harmony. *Beautiful **music** filled the auditorium.*

melody a pleasing series of musical tones. *That **melody** sounds familiar to me.*

song a usually short musical piece that is meant to be sung. *The class learned a **song** about civil rights.*

tune a melody, especially one that is simple and easy to remember. *Can you remember the name of this **tune**?*

N

noise *n.* a loud or unpleasant sound. *We closed the windows to block out the **noise.***

blare a loud, harsh noise, as of a horn. *The **blare** of the car's horn made Eric jump.*

(continued)

noise (continued)

clang a loud, ringing, metallic sound. *I listened to the **clang** of the lighthouse bell.*

patter quick, light sounds. *I love to hear the **patter** of rain on the roof.*

racket a loud, unpleasant noise. *The hens in the barnyard make a **racket** whenever they see a dog or a cat.*

roar a loud, deep noise or cry, as that made by a lion. *The **roar** of the jet engines was so loud that we could not hear the captain's words.*

antonyms: hush *n.*, quiet *n.*, silence *n.*

O

orange *adj.* reddish yellow. *Alice placed a large, **orange** pumpkin on the front porch.*

tangerine deep reddish orange. *Dick used a **tangerine** crayon to color in the sunset.*

P

pretty *adj.* pleasing, attractive, or appealing to the eye or ear. *Betty thought that the dress was **pretty**, but Jane did not like it.*

attractive appealing or charming. *The color green looks **attractive** on a redhead.*

beautiful being very pleasing to the senses or the mind. *The audience fell silent as **beautiful** music filled the hall.*

charming very pleasing; delightful. *The **charming** hostess made us feel at home.*

handsome pleasing in appearance; good-looking. *The two ice skaters made a **handsome** couple.*

lovely having pleasant qualities. *The clear sky and warm breeze made it a **lovely** night.*

antonyms: homely, plain *adj.*, ugly, unattractive

pull *v.* to apply force to in order to draw someone or something in the direction of the force. *I **pulled** the door toward me as hard as I could.*

drag to draw along the ground by force. *Jim **dragged** the trash barrel across the lawn.*

tow to draw along behind with a chain or a rope. *With a strong rope, the big boat **towed** our canoe into the harbor.*

antonyms: push, shove

purple *adj.* having the color between red and blue. *The **purple** grape juice stained the tablecloth.*

lavender pale purple. *Greg picked a bunch of **lavender** and white flowers to take to the hospital.*

Q

question *n.* something that is asked. *I do not know the answer to that **question**.*

examination a set of questions designed to test knowledge. *Ed has to take an **examination** to become a lawyer.*

inquiry a request for information. *The governor responded to Ms. Pitt's **inquiry** about safety regulations.*

interrogation the act of questioning closely. *During the **interrogation**, the thief confessed to the crime.*

quiz a short test. *Ms. Smith gave us a surprise math **quiz**.*

antonyms: answer *n.*, reply *n.*, response

quick *adj.* very fast; rapid. *With a **quick** leap, the basketball player caught the ball.*

fast moving, acting, or done quickly. ***Fast** cars should stay in the left lane.*

hasty acting or done fast. *Glenn made a **hasty** sketch of the building.*

rapid marked by speed. *The river became more **rapid** as we floated downstream.*

speedy moving quickly; swift. *Joe is a **speedy** runner and wins almost every race.*

antonyms: slow, unhurried

R

reason *n.* an explanation for an act or belief. *The **reason** we took no pictures is that I forgot my camera!*

cause someone or something that makes something happen. *Was lightning the **cause** of the fire?*

explanation something that reveals why something else is so. *There is an **explanation** for why iron is heavier than wood.*

grounds the reason for a belief, action, or thought. *What **grounds** do you have for being angry?*

red *adj.* having the color of blood or of a ruby. *All cars must stop for a **red** traffic light.*

scarlet bright red. *Rick wore a **scarlet** scarf so that he could be seen in the woods.*

relate *v.* to tell or narrate. *Yoko **related** the tale of the hidden treasure.*

agree to express one's willingness or approval; consent. *I **agreed** that the movie was scary.*

complain to express unhappiness or discontent. *Lee always **complains** about having too much homework.*

exclaim to cry out or speak suddenly. *"Surprise!" **exclaimed** the guests.*

groan to make a deep sound that expresses pain, grief, or annoyance. *The class **groaned** when Mr. Price announced the test.*

question to ask questions of. *The police **questioned** us about the accident.*

suggest to offer for consideration. *Hal **suggested** having a car wash to earn money.*

rough *adj.* full of bumps and ridges. *The carpenter sanded the **rough** wood until it was smooth.*

bumpy covered with lumps. *Riding on the **bumpy** road made us bounce in our seats.*

coarse not polished or fine. *Sandpaper has a **coarse** surface.*

uneven not level, smooth, or straight. *Because the floor was **uneven,** the bookcase would not sit straight.*

antonyms: smooth *adj.*, polished *adj.*

run *v.* to move quickly on foot. *Please do not **run** in the halls.*

dash to move with sudden speed. *We **dashed** out the door when the alarm sounded.*

race to rush at top speed. *Leon **raced** to catch the bus.*

rush to hurry. *I had to **rush** to get to school on time this morning.*

antonyms: dawdle, stroll *v.*, walk *v.*

S

safe *adj.* free from danger, risk, or harm. *This old bridge is not **safe.***

careful taking the necessary caution. *My mother is a **careful** driver.*

protected covered or guarded from harm. *Wild animals are **protected** in this park.*

secure safe against danger or risk of loss. *The shed is a **secure** place to keep your bicycle.*

antonyms: careless, dangerous, exposed, insecure

Shades of Meaning

sharp *adj.*

1. having a thin edge that cuts or a fine point that pierces:

barbed	knifelike
edged	pointed
honed	spiked
keen	

2. harsh; severe:

acute	rough
cruel	stabbing
hard	stinging
piercing	

3. acting strongly on the senses:

acid	bitter
acrid	pungent
biting	tart

4. alert in noticing or thinking:

bright	quick
clever	shrewd
intelligent	smart

shout *v.* to cry out or say loudly. *Sally **shouted** a good-by as her bus left the station.*

bellow to give a load roar. *The army officer **bellowed** his commands in a deep voice.*

(continued)

shout (continued)

cheer to shout in happiness, approval, encouragement, or enthusiasm. *People cheered as the astronauts in the parade passed by.*

howl to cry or scream, as in pain. *Jordan howled when he caught his hand in the door.*

scream to make a long, loud, piercing cry. *Joe screamed when Sid jumped out of the bushes.*

yell to cry out loudly. *Jenny yelled at her puppy when it wandered into the busy street.*

antonyms: murmur *v.*, sigh *v.*, whisper *v.*

show *v.* to cause or allow to be seen. *Mother showed us pictures of her grandparents.*

demonstrate to show with the help of examples or explanation. *Ana demonstrated how to make paper.*

display to put on view; exhibit. *Ms. Wong displayed our work on the bulletin board.*

guide to show the way to; direct. *Mr. Rodriguez will guide us through the museum exhibits.*

reveal to make known. *This map reveals where the treasure is hidden.*

antonyms: conceal, hide *v.*

sickness *n.* the condition of being sick. *Brett missed the school play because of sickness.*

ailment an illness or disease. *The doctor talked with Uncle Edgar about his ailment.*

disease a condition that keeps the body from functioning normally. *This disease affects the heart and lungs.*

fever a body temperature that is higher than normal. *Mr. Sims used an ice pack to bring down his fever.*

illness a sickness or disease. *Many people have caught the same illness this winter.*

antonyms: fitness, health, heartiness, wellbeing

silent *adj.* making or having no sound; quiet. *The students were absolutely silent during the fire drill.*

hushed becoming quiet or still. *The librarian spoke to us in a hushed voice.*

quiet marked by little or no noise. *We could scarcely hear the quiet breathing of the sleeping baby.*

still without noise; silent. *The class remained still while the principal was speaking.*

antonyms: loud, noisy

skill *n.* the ability to do something well. *Eduardo has skill in carpentry.*

ability the quality of being able to do something. *I wish I had the ability to take good photographs.*

aptitude a natural ability or talent. *Hilda seems to have an aptitude for math.*

faculty an ability for doing something. *This story shows Tony's faculty for creative writing.*

talent a natural ability to do something well. *Pat's musical talent was apparent at the concert.*

small *adj.* little in size, amount, or extent. *I would like a small piece of meat, please.*

little small in size or quantity. *These little chairs must be for very young children.*

miniature much smaller than the usual size. *The dollhouse even had a miniature stove in the kitchen.*

minute very, very small; tiny. *You need a magnifying glass to read that minute print.*

tiny extremely small. *Grandma made tiny clothes for each of our dolls.*

antonyms: big, great, huge, large

smell *v.* to give off an odor. *The air smells like burning leaves.*

reek to give off an unpleasant odor. *Our tent reeked of campfire smoke.*

stink to give off a strong, bad smell. *Old garbage in the kitchen made the whole house stink.*

start *v.* to begin to move, go, or act. *The racers started to run at the sound of the whistle.*

begin to start to do. *Mrs. Stone began to read as soon as the class was quiet.*

commence to perform the first part of an action. *The concert will commence at noon.*

embark to set out on an activity or task. *Fred **embarked** on a new project right after he completed his model train.*
antonyms: close *v.*, conclude, end *v.*, finish *v.*

strange *adj.* not known before; unfamiliar. *We turned down a **strange** street and realized that we were lost.*
odd not ordinary or usual. *I read a story about an **odd** animal that had three humps!*
peculiar hard to understand or explain. *The cat's **peculiar** behavior was a mystery.*
unusual rare or different from what might be expected. *Her **unusual** name was hard to say.*
weird strange, odd, or unusual. *A **weird** noise in the empty house frightened the children.*
antonyms: common, familiar, ordinary

surprise *v.* to cause to feel astonishment. *Rico **surprised** his grandfather with a birthday party.*
amaze to fill with surprise or wonder. *The magician's tricks **amazed** the young children.*
astound to strike with sudden wonder. *The team's victory **astounded** the fans.*
shock to surprise or upset greatly. *The news of the fire **shocked** us all.*

T

throw *v.* to send through the air with a fast motion of the arm. *Matt **threw** a rock into the pond.*
cast to throw or fling. *Dora **cast** the net over the side of the boat.*
hurl to throw with great force. *The prisoner **hurled** himself over the fence and escaped into the woods.*
pass to hand or throw to another person. *Tina quickly **passed** the basketball to her teammate.*
pitch to throw or toss, as in baseball or horseshoes. *Tim **pitched** six strikes in a row.*

shoot to throw toward a target. *Kate **shot** the ball toward the basket.*
toss to throw with a quick, easy movement. *Chuck **tossed** his hat into the closet.*
antonyms: capture, catch, grab, seize

Shades of Meaning

true *adj.*

1. being in agreement with fact or reality:

accurate	*exact*
correct	*factual*
errorless	*precise*

2. faithful and loyal:

constant	*honorable*
dependable	*steady*
honest	*trustworthy*

3. properly so called; genuine:

actual	*original*
authentic	*real*
official	

antonyms: **1.** erroneous, false, incorrect **2.** disloyal, faithless, untrue **3.** counterfeit, phony

U

upset *adj.* sad or unsettled. *I was **upset** when I heard the bad news.*
anxious unsettled about something that is uncertain. *The **anxious** riders were not quite sure where they were going.*
nervous shaken and jittery because of fear or challenge. *Dean was very **nervous** when he gave a speech in front of the class.*
troubled upset and worried. *Becky was **troubled** by her brother's bad mood.*

(continued)

upset (continued)

worried uneasy. *Janet was **worried** about getting lost in the big city.*

antonyms: calm *adj.*, easygoing, relaxed *adj.*

W

wait *v.* to do nothing or stay in a place until something expected happens. *Please **wait** here until I return.*

delay to slow, stop, or prevent for a time. *We **delayed** our departure.*

linger to stay in a place longer than usual. *The children **lingered** on the playground after school.*

remain to stay in the same place. *We **remained** in our seats after the bell rang.*

stay to remain in one place or condition. ***Stay** indoors when the temperature is below zero.*

antonyms: depart, escape *v.*, exit *v.*, leave

wind *v.* to wrap or be wrapped around something. *This road **winds** around the mountainside.*

coil to wind into a ring or a series of rings. *Please **coil** the garden hose after you finish watering the flowers.*

curl to twist into or form ringlets. *Long ago, women used rags to **curl** their hair.*

curve to move in or take the shape of a curve. *The path **curves** gently along the seashore.*

spiral to make a curve that gradually widens as it winds around. *A staircase **spiraled** up to the top of the tower.*

twist to wind together to form a single strand. *A spinning wheel **twists** wool into yarn.*

antonyms: straighten, uncurl, untwist

wood *n.* the hard material beneath the bark of trees and shrubs that makes up the trunk and branches. *The saw made a deep cut in the hard **wood**.*

board a piece of sawed lumber that has more length and width than thickness. *Wanda used a **board** to make a shelf in her room.*

kindling dry sticks of wood used for building a fire. *Please collect some **kindling** for the campfire.*

lumber timber that is sawed into boards and planks. *The hardware store delivered a truckload of **lumber** to our house.*

timber wood for building. *The pioneers used **timber** to build their houses.*

Y

yellow *adj.* having the color of ripe lemons or dandelions. ***Yellow** sunflowers dotted the field.*

amber brownish yellow. *The cat in the painting had large **amber** eyes.*

gold having a deep yellow color. *Wheat turns **gold** when it is ripe.*

lemon having a bright yellow color named for the fruit. *The **lemon** walls seemed to fill the room with sunshine.*

Spelling-Meaning Index

This Spelling-Meaning Index contains pairs of words related in spelling and in meaning. The letters in dark print in these words show that the spelling stays the same even though the sound may change. This Index also includes other words in the same family as the related word pairs. The words in each part of this Index are in alphabetical order.

Consonant Changes

Word pairs are listed under the heading for the kind of consonant change that fits the word pairs.

Consonant Changes: Silent to Sounded

Sometimes you can remember how to spell a word with a silent consonant by thinking of a related word in which the letter is pronounced.

bomb-bombard
bombarded, bombarder, bombardier, bombarding, bombardment, bombards, bombed, bomber, bombing, bombs

column-columnist
columnar, columned, columnists, columns

crumb-crumble
crumbled, crumbles, crumbliness, crumbling, crumbly, crumbs, crumby

fasten-fast
fastened, fastener, fastening, fastens, faster, fastest, fastness, unfasten

hasten-haste
hastened, hastening, hastens, hastily, hastiness, hasty

heir-inherit
disinherit, heirdom, heiress, heirless, heirs, heirship, hereditary, heredity, heritage, inheritable, inheritance, inherited, inheriting, inheritor, inherits

limb-limber
limbered, limbering, limberly, limberness, limbers, limbs

moisten-moist
moistened, moistener, moistening, moistens, moister, moistest, moistly, moistness, moisture, moisturize, moisturizer

muscle-muscular
muscled, muscles, muscling, muscularity, muscularly, musculature

receipt-reception
receipts, receivable, receive, receiver, receptacle, receptionist, receptions, receptive, receptor, recipient

sign-signal
signaled, signaler, signaling, signals, signature, signed, signer, signet, signifiable, significance, significant, significantly, signification, signifier, signify, signing, signs, unsigned

soften-soft
softened, softener, softening, softens, softer, softest, softly, softness

(continued)

Consonant Changes (continued)

Consonant Changes: The Sound of *c*

The |k| sound of *c* may change to |s| or |sh| in some words. Thinking of a related word can help you remember that the sound is spelled *c*.

electric-electrician
    electrical, electrically,
    electricians, electricity,
    electrifiable, electrification,
    electrifier, electrify, electrocute,
    electrocution, electrode,
    electron, electronic
magic-magician
    magical, magically, magicians
mathematics-mathematician
    math, mathematic,
    mathematical, mathematically,
    mathematicians,
    nonmathematical
music-musician
    musical, musicale, musically,
    musicianly, musicians,
    musicianship, musicologist,
    musicology, unmusical
practical-practice
    impracticable, impracticably,
    impractical, impracticality,
    impracticalness, impractically,
    practicable, practicably,
    practicality, practically,
    practicalness, practiced,
    practicer, practices, practicing,
    practicum, practitioner,
    unpracticed

Consonant Changes: The Sound of *t*

The sound of a final *t* may change when an ending or suffix is added. Thinking of a related word can help you remember that the sound is spelled *t*.

create-creature
    created, creates, creating,
    creation, creational, creative,
    creatively, creativeness,
    creativity, creator, creaturely,
    creatures, noncreative, re-create
decorate-decoration
    decor, decorated, decorates,
    decorating, decorations,
    decorative, decoratively,
    decorativeness, decorator,
    decorous, decorously,
    decorousness, decorum,
    indecorously, indecorum,
    redecorate, redecoration,
    undecorated
depart-departure
    departed, departing, departs,
    departures, undeparted
fact-factual
    factitious, factitiously,
    factitiousness, factor, facts,
    factually, nonfactual
habit-habitual
    habits, habitualize, habitually,
    habitualness, habituate,
    habituation
invent-invention
    invented, inventing, inventions,
    inventive, inventively,
    inventiveness, inventor, invents
locate-location
    dislocate, dislocated,
    dislocation, local, locatable,
    located, locater, locates,
    locating, locational, locations,
    locus, nonlocal, relocate,
    relocation
moist-moisture
    moisten, moistener, moister,
    moistest, moistly, moistness,
    moisturize, moisturizer
object-objection
    objected, objecting,
    objectionability, objectionable,
    objectionably, objector, objects
operate-operation
    cooperate, cooperation,
    cooperative, cooperatively,
    cooperativeness, inoperability,

Consonant Changes (continued)

inoperable, inoperably,
operability, operable, operably,
operated, operates, operating,
operational, operationally,
operations, operative,
operatively, operator,
nonoperating, nonoperative

punctuate-punctuation

punctual, punctuality,
punctuated, punctuates,
punctuating, punctuator

regulate-regulation

deregulate, deregulation,
irregular, irregularity,
irregularly, regular, regularity,
regularization, regularize,
regularizer, regularly, regulated,
regulates, regulating,
regulations, regulative,
regulator, regulatory,
unregulated

relate-relation

relatable, related, relatedness,
relater, relates, relating,
relational, relations,
relationship, relative, relatively,
relativeness, relativism,
relativity, unrelated,
unrelatedness

Vowel Changes

Word pairs are listed under the
heading for the kind of vowel
change that fits the word pairs.

Vowel Changes: Long to Short Vowel Sound

Words that are related in meaning
are often related in spelling, even
though one word has a long vowel
sound and the other word has a
short vowel sound.

breathe-breath

breathable, breathed, breather,
breathes, breathily, breathiness,
breathing, breathless,
breathlessly, breathlessness,
breaths, breathtaking, breathy

cave-cavity

caved, cavern, cavernous,
cavernously, caves, caving,
cavities

clean-cleanse

cleanable, cleaned, cleaner,
cleanest, cleaning, cleanliness,
cleanly, cleanness, cleans,
cleansed, cleanser, cleanses,
cleansing, unclean,
uncleanable, uncleanliness,
uncleanly

compete-competition

competed, competes,
competing, competitions,
competitive, competitively,
competitiveness, competitor,
noncompeting, noncompetitive,
noncompetitively,
noncompetitiveness

crime-criminal

crimes, criminality,
criminalize, criminally,
criminals, criminologist,
criminology, decriminalization,
decriminalize, incriminate,
incrimination, incriminatory,
recriminate, recrimination,
recriminatory

cycle-bicycle

bicycled, bicycles, bicycling,
bicyclist, cycled, cycler, cycles,
cycling, cyclist, tricycle,
unicycle, unicyclist

deal-dealt

dealer, dealership, dealing,
deals

dream-dreamt

dreamed, dreamer, dreamily,
dreaminess, dreaming,
dreamless, dreamlike, dreams,
dreamy

heal-health

healable, healed, healer,
healing, heals, healthful,
healthfully, healthfulness,
healthily, healthiness, healthy,

(continued)

Vowel Changes (continued)

unhealthful, unhealthily, unhealthiness, unhealthy

mean-meant
meaning, meaningful, meaningfully, meaningfulness, meaningless, meaninglessly, meaninglessness, means, unmeaning, unmeant

minus-minimum
minimal, minimalism, minimalization, minimally, minimize, minimizer, minor, minimums, minuscule

nation-national
denationalize, international, internationalism, internationalist, internationalize, internationally, nationalism, nationalist, nationalistic, nationality, nationalization, nationalize, nationalizer, nationally, nationals, nationhood, nationwide, native, natively, nativeness

nature-natural
denaturalization, denaturalize, denature, naturalism, naturalist, naturalistic, naturalistically, naturalization, naturalize, naturally, naturalness, natures, supernatural, unnatural, unnaturally, unnaturalness

page-paginate
paged, pages, paginated, paginates, paginating, pagination, paging

pale-pallid
paled, paleness, paler, pales, palest, paling, pallidly, pallidness, pallor

please-pleasant
displease, displeasing, displeasure, plea, plead, pleasantly, pleasantness, pleasantry, pleased, pleases, pleasing, pleasingly,
pleasingness, pleasurable, pleasurableness, pleasurably, pleasure, pleasureless, unpleasant, unpleasantly, unpleasantness

sole-solitary
solely, soliloquy, solitarily, solitariness, solitude, solo, soloist

steal-stealth
stealer, stealing, steals, stealthily, stealthiness, stealthy

wise-wisdom
wisely, wiser, wisest, unwise, unwisely

Vowel Changes: Schwa to Long Vowel Sound

You can remember how to spell the schwa sound in some words by thinking of a related word with a long vowel sound spelled the same way.

ability-able
abilities, abler, ablest, ably, disability, disable, disabled, inability, unable

admiration-admire
admirable, admirableness, admirably, admired, admirer, admires, admiring, admiringly

composition-compose
component, composed, composedly, composedness, composer, composes, composing, composite, compositional, compositor, compost, composure, decomposable, decompose, decomposition, discompose, discomposure, recompose, recomposition

definition-define
definability, definable, definably, defined, definer, defines, defining, definite, definitely, definiteness, definitional, definitions,

Vowel Changes (continued)

definitive, definitively, definitiveness, definitude, indefinable, indefinableness, indefinably, indefinite, indefinitely, indefiniteness

proposition-propose
proposal, proposed, proposer, proposes, proposing, propositional, propositionally, propositions

relative-relate
related, relatedness, relater, relates, relating, relation, relational, relationally, relations, relationship, relative, relatively, relativeness, relatives, relativism, relativist, relativistic, relativity, unrelated, unrelatedness

supposition-suppose
supposed, supposedly, supposes, supposing, suppositional, suppositionally, suppositions

Vowel Changes: Schwa to Short Vowel Sound

You can remember how to spell the schwa sound in some words by thinking of a related word with a short vowel sound spelled the same way.

democratic-democracy
democracies, democrat, democratically, democratization, democratize, undemocratic, undemocratically

final-finality
finale, finalist, finalities, finalization, finalize, finally, finals

formal-formality
form, formalism, formalist, formalistic, formalities, formalization, formalize, formally, format, formula, informal, informality, informally, nonformal, reform, transform, unformed

general-generality
generalist, generalities, generalization, generalize, generally, generalness, generic, generically, genre

history-historical
historian, historic, historically, historicalness, histories, historiographer, historiographic, historiographical, historiographically, historiography, prehistoric, prehistorical, prehistorically, prehistory

human-humanity
humane, humanely, humaneness, humanism, humanist, humanistic, humanistically, humanitarian, humanitarianism, humanities, humanization, humanize, humanizer, humankind, humanlike, humanly, humanness, humanoid, humans, inhuman, inhumane, inhumanely, inhumanity, inhumanly, inhumanness

individual-individuality
individualism, individualist, individualistic, individualistically, individualities, individualization, individualize, individually, individuals

legal-legality
illegal, illegality, illegally, legalese, legalism, legalist, legalistic, legalistically, legalities, legalization, legalize, legally

(continued)

Vowel Changes (continued)

local-locality
  locale, localism, localities,
  localization, localize, locally,
  locate, locus, nonlocal,
  relocate, relocation
major-majority
  majoritarian, majoritarianism,
  majorities
medal-medallion
  medalist, medallions, medals
mental-mentality
  demented, mentalities,
  mentally
metal-metallic
  metallically, metallographer,
  metallographic, metallography,
  metalloid, metalloidal,
  metallurgic, metallurgical,
  metallurgically, metallurgist,
  metallurgy, metals, nonmetal,
  nonmetallic
method-methodical
  methodic, methodically,
  methodicalness, methodize,
  methodizer, methodology,
  methods, unmethodical,
  unmethodically
mortal-mortality
  immortal, immortality,
  immortalize, immortally,
  immortals, mortalities,
  mortally, mortals, nonmortal
normal-normality
  abnormal, abnormality,
  abnormally, norm, normalcy,
  normalization, normalize,
  normalizer, normally,
  normative, subnormal,
  supernormal
perfect-perfection
  imperfect, imperfection,
  imperfectly, imperfectness,
  perfected, perfecter,
  perfectibility, perfectible,
  perfecting, perfectionism,
  perfectionist, perfections,
  perfectly, perfectness, perfects

personal-personality
  depersonalize, impersonal,
  impersonally, impersonalize,
  impersonate, impersonation,
  impersonator, interpersonal,
  intrapersonal, person, persona,
  personable, personalism,
  personalities, personalization,
  personalize, personally,
  personification, personifier,
  personify, personnel
poem-poetic
  poems, poet, poetical,
  poetically, poetics, poetize,
  poetizer, poetry, nonpoetic,
  unpoetic, unpoetical
regular-regularity
  irregular, irregularity,
  irregularly, regularities,
  regularization, regularize,
  regularly, regulate, regulation,
  regulative, regulatory,
  unregulated
reside-resident
  nonresident, nonresidential,
  resided, residence, residency,
  residential, residentially,
  resider, resides, residing
similar-similarity
  dissimilar, dissimilarity,
  dissimilarly, similarities,
  similarly, simile, similitude
total-totality
  totaled, totaling, totalitarian,
  totalitarianism, totalities,
  totalization, totalize, totalizer,
  totally, totals
victory-victorious
  victor, victories, victoriously,
  victoriousness

Spelling Dictionary

Spelling Table

This Spelling Table shows many of the letter combinations that spell the same sounds in different words. Use this table for help in looking up words that you do not know how to spell.

Sounds	Spellings	Sample Words
|ă|	a, au	bat, have, laugh
|ā|	a, ai, ay, ea	made, later, rain, play, great
|âr|	air, ar, are, eir, ere	fair, scarce, care, their, where
|ä|	a, al	father, calm
|är|	ar, ear	art, heart
|b|	b, bb	bus, rabbit
|ch|	ch, tch, tu	chin, match, culture
|d|	d, dd	dark, sudden
|ĕ|	a, ai, ay, e, ea, ie	any, said, says, went, head, friend
|ē|	e, ea, ee, ei, ey, i, ie, y	these, we, beast, fleet, receive, honey, ski, chief, bumpy, magazine
|f|	f, ff, gh	funny, off, enough
|g|	g, gg, gu	get, egg, guide
|h|	h, wh	hat, who
|hw|	wh	when
|ĭ|	a, e, ee, i, ia, u, ui, y	cottage, before, been, mix, give, carriage, busy, build, gym
|ī|	ei, i, ie, igh, y	height, time, mind, pie, fight, try, type
|îr|	ear, eer, eir, ier	near, deer, weird, pier
|j|	dge, g, ge, j	judge, gem, range, jet
|k|	c, ch, ck, k	picnic, school, tick, key
|kw|	qu	quick
|l|	l, ll	last, all
|m|	m, mb, mm, mn	mop, bomb, summer, column
|n|	gn, kn, n, nn	sign, knee, no, inn
|ng|	n, ng	think, ring
|ŏ|	a, ho, o	was, honor, pond
|ō|	o, oa, ough, ow	most, hope, float, though, row
|ô|	a, al, au, aw, o, ough	wall, talk, haunt, lawn, soft, brought
|ôr|	oar, oor, or, ore, our	roar, door, storm, store, court
|oi|	oi, oy	join, toy
|ou|	ou, ough, ow	loud, bough, now
|oͦo|	oo, ou, u	good, could, put
|ōo|	ew, o, oe, oo, ou, u, ue, ui	flew, do, lose, shoe, spoon, you, truth, blue, juice
|p|	p, pp	paint, happen
|r|	r, rh, rr, wr	rub, rhyme, borrow, write
|s|	c, ce, ps, s, sc, ss	city, fence, psychology, same, scent, lesson
|sh|	ce, ch, ci, s, sh, ss, ti	ocean, machine, special, sure, sheep, mission, nation
|t|	ed, t, tt	stopped, talk, little
|th|	th	they, other
|th|	th	thin, teeth
|ŭ|	o, oe, oo, ou, u	front, come, does, flood, tough, sun
|yōo|	eau, ew, iew, u, ue	use, beauty, few, view, fuel, cue
|ûr|	ear, er, ir, or, ur	learn, herd, girl, word, turn
|v|	f, v	of, very
|w|	o, w	one, way
|y|	i, y	million, yes
|z|	s, z, zz	rise, zoo, fizz
|zh|	ge, s	garage, usual
|ə|	a, ai, e, eo, i, o, ou, u	about, captain, silent, surgeon, pencil, lemon, famous, circus

How to Use a Dictionary

Finding an Entry Word

Guide Words

The word you want to find in a dictionary is listed in alphabetical order. To find it quickly, turn to the part of the dictionary that has words with the same first letter. Use the guide words at the top of each page. Guide words name the first and last entries on the page.

Base Words

To find a word ending in **-ed** or **-ing,** you usually must look up its base word. To find **cooked** or **cooking,** for example, look up the base word **cook.**

Homographs

Homographs have separate, numbered entries. For example, **minute** meaning "sixty seconds" is listed as **minute**[1]. **Minute** meaning "very, very small" is listed as **minute**[2].

Reading an Entry

Read the dictionary entry below. Note the purpose of each part.

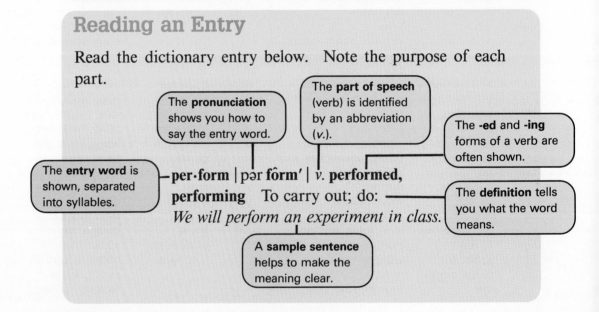

The **pronunciation** shows you how to say the entry word.

The **part of speech** (verb) is identified by an abbreviation (*v.*).

The **-ed** and **-ing** forms of a verb are often shown.

The **entry word** is shown, separated into syllables.

per·form | pər fôrm′ | *v.* performed, performing To carry out; do: *We will perform an experiment in class.*

The **definition** tells you what the word means.

A **sample sentence** helps to make the meaning clear.

Spelling Dictionary

A

a·ble |ā′ bəl| *adj.* **abler, ablest** Having what is necessary to do something: *I will be able to see you tomorrow.*

-able A suffix that forms adjectives and means: **1.** Capable of; able to: *refillable.* **2.** Worthy of; deserving: *lovable.*

a·brupt |ə brŭpt′| *adj.* Taking place without warning: *I made an abrupt turn.*

a·cad·e·my |ə kăd′ ə mē| *n., pl.* **academies** A school where a special field of study is taught: *I went to a police academy.*

ac·ci·dent |ăk′ sĭ dənt| *n., pl.* **accidents** An unexpected and undesirable event: *An accident held up traffic for miles.*

ac·com·plish |ə kŏm′ plĭsh| *v.* **accomplished, accomplishing** To carry out or achieve: *We accomplished the job quickly.*

ache |āk| *v.* **ached, aching** To feel a dull, steady pain: *I ache all over. n., pl.* **aches** A steady pain: *I have an ache in my back.*

a·chieve |ə chēv′| *v.* **achieved, achieving** To succeed in doing or accomplishing.

ac·tiv·i·ty |ăk tĭv′ ĭ tē| *n., pl.* **activities** **1.** Energetic movement or action: *The store was a scene of great activity.* **2.** Something done for fun: *Stamp collecting is my favorite activity.*

ad·mi·ra·tion |ăd′ mə rā′ shən| *n.* Great pleasure and delight.

ad·mire |ăd mīr′| *v.* **admired, admiring** To regard with great pleasure and delight.

ad·ven·tur·ous |əd vĕn′ chər əs| *adj.* Willing to risk danger in order to have exciting adventures.

ad·vice |əd vīs′| *n.* An idea or suggestion about how to solve a problem: *My father gave me some advice on how to pitch.*

a·fraid |ə frād′| *adj.* Filled with fear; scared.

af·ter·noon |ăf′ tər noon′| *n., pl.* **afternoons** The part of the day from noon until sunset.

a·gain |ə gĕn′| *adv.* Once more: *If you don't win, try again.*

Pronunciation Key

ă	pat	ŏ	pot	û	fur
ā	pay	ō	go	*th*	the
â	care	ô	paw, for	th	thin
ä	father	oi	oil	hw	which
ĕ	pet	oo	book	zh	usual
ē	be	ōō	boot	ə	ago, item
ĭ	pit	yōō	cute		pencil, atom
ī	ice	ou	out		circus
î	near	ŭ	cut	ər	butter

Abbreviation Key

n.	noun	*prep.*	preposition
v.	verb	*interj.*	interjection
adj.	adjective	*sing.*	singular
adv.	adverb	*pl.*	plural
pron.	pronoun	*p.*	past
conj.	conjunction	*p. part.*	past participle

a·gainst |ə gĕnst′| *prep.* In or into contact with: *I leaned against a tree to rest.*

a·gree |ə grē′| *v.* **agreed, agreeing** To have or share the same opinion; concur: *I agree with you that it's too hot to work.*

aid |ād| *v.* **aided, aiding** To give help to; assist: *Glasses aid my sight. A map aids us in finding our way. n., pl.* **aids** **1.** Help or assistance given. **2.** Someone or something that helps or is helpful.

ail·ment |āl′ mənt| *n., pl.* **ailments** An illness or disease.

air |âr| *n., pl.* **airs** The colorless, odorless, tasteless mixture of gases that surrounds the earth. The two main gases in air are nitrogen and oxygen.

air·port |âr′ pôrt′| *n., pl.* **airports** A place with marked, open spaces where aircraft can take off and land.

-al A suffix that forms adjectives and means "having to do with": *coastal.*

a·larm |ə lärm′| *n., pl.* **alarms** A bell, light, or other signal that warns people of possible danger. *v.* **alarmed, alarming** To fill with sudden fear; frighten.

a•lert |ə lûrt'| *adj.* Quick to notice or act: *The alert child caught the falling dish.*

a•live |ə līv'| *adj.* Having life; living: *My grandfather is dead, but my grandmother is still alive.*

al•ley |ăl' ē| *n., pl.* **alleys** A narrow street or passageway between buildings.

History • alley

Alley comes from the Old French word *alée,* meaning "a walk."

al•li•ga•tor |ăl' ĭ gā' tər| *n., pl.* **alligators** A large reptile with sharp teeth and long, powerful jaws.

al•low |ə lou'| *v.* **allowed, allowing** To let do or happen; permit: *No ball playing is allowed! Please allow me to finish.*

all right |ôl rīt| *adj. and adv.* Satisfactory but not excellent; good enough: *These peaches are all right, but they could be fresher.*

a•lone |ə lōn'| *adj.* Without anyone or anything else: *The person next door is alone all day. adv.* Without help.

a•loud |ə loud'| *adv.* Not in a whisper or to oneself; out loud: *I read the story aloud.*

al•pha•bet |ăl' fə bĕt'| *n., pl.* **alphabets** The letters used to represent the different sounds in a language, arranged in a set order.

al•read•y |ôl rĕd' ē| *adv.* By this time: *I ran to the station, but the bus had already left.*

a•lu•mi•num |ə lōō' mə nəm| *n.* A lightweight, silver-white metal that is one of the elements. It is used to make pots and pans, tools, airplanes, parts of buildings, and many other things.

al•ways |ôl' wāz| or |ôl' wĭz| *adv.* **1.** At all times; every single time: *I always leave at six o'clock.* **2.** For as long as one can imagine; forever: *They will always be friends.*

a•maze |ə māz'| *v.* **amazed, amazing** To fill with surprise or wonder; astonish: *The idea of water carving a deep canyon out of solid rock amazes me.*

an•chor |ăng' kər| *n., pl.* **anchors** A heavy metal device that is attached to a ship by a cable. An anchor is dropped overboard and keeps the ship in place by its weight or by catching on the sea bottom.

an•gry |ăng' grē| *adj.* **angrier, angriest** Feeling or showing strong displeasure with someone or something: *You say you aren't angry, but your face looks angry.*

an•i•mal |ăn' ə məl| *n., pl.* **animals** A living being that is not a plant. Unlike plants, most animals move from place to place, have sense organs, and eat food rather than make it. Human beings, horses, fish, and ants are all animals.

an•oth•er |ə nŭ*th*' ər| *adj.* Being a second or an additional one: *I'd love another helping.*

an•swer |ăn' sər| *v.* **answered, answering** To say, write, or do something in reply or in reply to.

an•y |ĕn' ē| *adj.* **1.** One or some, no matter which, out of three or more: *Take any books you want.* **2.** Every: *Any student in my class can come to the party.*

an•y•bod•y |ĕn' ē bŏd' ē| *pron.* Any person at all; anyone.

an•y•place |ĕn' ē plās'| *adv.* To, in, or at any place; anywhere: *Move the chair anyplace you like.*

an•y•thing |ĕn' ē thĭng'| *pron.* Any thing whatever: *Is there anything left in the box?*

ap•ple |ăp' əl| *n., pl.* **apples** A firm, rounded, often red-skinned fruit that can be eaten.

ap•point•ment |ə point' mənt| *n., pl.* **appointments** An arrangement to meet at a particular time or place.

ap•proach |ə prōch'| *v.* **approached, approaching** To come toward; to come near or nearer: *The car approached the garage.*

a•pron |ā' prən| *n., pl.* **aprons** A garment worn over the front of the body to protect the clothes.

a•quat•ic |ə kwăt' ĭk| *adj.* Of, living in, or growing in water: *The water lily is an aquatic plant.*

ar•mor |är' mər| *n.* A heavy covering, especially of metal, worn to protect the body in battle.

ar·my |är′ mē| *n., pl.* **armies** A large body of men and women organized and trained for land warfare.

ar·row |ăr′ ō| *n., pl.* **arrows** A straight, thin shaft that is shot from a bow. An arrow has a pointed head at one end and feathers at the other.

ar·ti·cle |är′ tĭ kəl| *n., pl.* **articles** A short piece of writing that forms an independent part of a newspaper, magazine, or book: *Write an article about your hobbies.*

a·sleep |ə slēp′| *adj.* Not awake; sleeping.

as·sist |ə sĭst′| *v.* **assisted, assisting** To give help; aid.

as·tro·naut |ăs′ trə nôt′| *n., pl.* **astronauts** A person trained to travel in a spacecraft.

ath·lete |ath′ lēt′| *n., pl.* **athletes** A person who is trained in or is good at physical exercises, games, or sports.

ath·let·ic |ăth lĕt′ ĭk| *adj.* **1.** Of or for athletics or athletes. **2.** Good at sports.

at·tack |ə tăk′| *v.* **attacked, attacking** To make a sudden violent move against; assault. *n., pl.* **attacks** The act of attacking.

at·tend |ə tĕnd′| *v.* **attended, attending** To be present at: *Everyone attended the party.*

at·ti·tude |ăt′ ĭ tōōd′| or |ăt′ ĭ tyōōd′| *n., pl.* **attitudes** A state of mind; point of view: *Take a positive attitude toward studying.*

Au·gus·ta |ô gŭs′ tə| The capital of Maine.

Aus·tin |ô′ stən| The capital of Texas.

av·er·age |ăv′ ər ĭj| *adj.* Typical, usual, or ordinary: *The average two-year-old loves teddy bears.*

a·vi·a·tion |ā′ vē ā′ shən| *n.* The operation of aircraft. *Airplane pilots receive special training in aviation.*

a·wake |ə wāk′| *v.* **awoke** *or* **awaked, awaked** *or* **awoken, awaking** To wake up: *The alarm clock awoke me at seven. I always awake at dawn. adj.* Not asleep.

a·ward |ə wôrd′| *n., pl.* **awards** Something given for outstanding performance or quality.

a·ware·ness |ə wâr′ nĭs| *n.* **1.** Knowledge of something: *to have an awareness of the news.* **2.** Alertness; watchfulness.

ă	pat	ŏ	pot	û	fur
ā	pay	ō	go	*th*	the
â	care	ô	paw, for	th	thin
ä	father	oi	oil	hw	which
ĕ	pet	ōō	book	zh	usual
ē	be	ōō	boot	ə	ago, item
ĭ	pit	yōō	cute		pencil, atom
ī	ice	ou	out		circus
î	near	ŭ	cut	ər	butter

a·way |ə wā′| *adv.* At or to a distance: *The lake is two miles away.*

aw·ful |ô′ fəl| *adj.* Very bad; terrible; horrible: *That movie was awful.*

B

ba·by |bā′ bē| *n., pl.* **babies** A very young child; infant.

back·ground |băk′ ground′| *n., pl.* **backgrounds** The part of a picture, scene, or view that appears far away.

back·pack |băk′ păk′| *n., pl.* **backpacks** A bag worn on the back to carry camping supplies. It is sometimes mounted on a light metal frame.

ba·con |bā′ kən| *n.* Salted and smoked meat from the back and sides of a pig.

bal·ance |băl′ əns| *n., pl.* **balances** A steady or stable position: *I lost my balance on ice skates and fell.*

bal·loon |bə lōōn′| *n., pl.* **balloons** A large bag filled with hot air or some other gas that is lighter than normal air; hot-air balloon.

ba·nan·a |bə năn′ ə| *n., pl.* **bananas** A curved fruit with sweet, soft flesh and yellow or reddish skin that peels off easily. Bananas grow in bunches on large tropical plants.

bank |băngk| *n., pl.* **banks** A place of business where money is kept and loans are made.

ban·quet |băng′ kwĭt| *n., pl.* **banquets** A large elaborate meal; a feast.

bar·be·cue |bär′ bĭ kyōō′| *v.* **barbecued, barbecuing** To cook over a grill, pit, or fireplace.

bar·ber |bär′ bər| *n., pl.* **barbers** A person whose work is cutting hair and shaving or trimming beards.

bar·na·cle |bär′ nə kəl| *n., pl.* **barnacles** A small, hard-shelled sea animal that attaches itself to the bottoms of ships and to underwater rocks.

bar·ra·cu·da |băr′ ə ko͞o′ də| *n., pl.* **barracudas** A sea fish with a long, narrow body and very sharp teeth, found mostly in tropical waters.

base·ball |bās′ bôl′| *n., pl.* **baseballs** A game played with a bat and ball by two teams of nine players each. Baseball is played on a field with four bases laid out in a diamond pattern. A run is scored when a player is able to touch all the bases while his or her team is at bat.

ba·sic |bā′ sĭk| *adj.* Forming the base or main part of something: *The ability to read is basic to an education.*

bas·set |băs′ ĭt| *n.* Also **basset hound.** A dog with a long, heavily built body, short legs, and long, drooping ears.

ba·tik |bə tēk′| or |băt′ ĭk| *n.* A method of dyeing a design on cloth by putting wax over the areas not meant to be dyed.

bat·tle |băt′ l| *n., pl.* **battles** A fight between two armed forces, usually in a war.

bea·con |bē′ kən| *n., pl.* **beacons** A light or fire used as a warning or guide.

beard |bîrd| *n., pl.* **beards** The hair on the chin and cheeks of a man.

beat |bēt| *v.* **beat, beaten** or **beat, beating** To win against: *We beat their team.*
◆ *These sound alike* **beat, beet.**

beau·ti·ful |byo͞o′ tə fəl| *adj.* Being very pleasing to the senses or mind: *Beautiful music filled the air.*

beau·ty |byo͞o′ tē| *n., pl.* **beauties** A quality that pleases the sense or the mind: *We were charmed by the beauty of the singer's voice. There is great beauty in the poetry.*

be·come |bĭ kŭm′| *v.* **became** |bĭ kām′|, **become, becoming** To grow or come to be: *The children became restless.*

beet |bēt| *n., pl.* **beets** A leafy plant with a thick, round, dark-red root eaten as a vegetable.
◆ *These sound alike* **beet, beat.**

be·fore |bĭ fôr′| *adv.* In the past: *I've heard that before. prep.* Ahead of; earlier than: *The dog got home before me.*

beg·gar |bĕg′ ər| *n., pl.* **beggars** A person who begs for a living.

be·gin |bĭ gĭn′| *v.* **began** |bĭ găn′|, **begun** |bĭ gŭn′|, **beginning** To start to do: *I began taking piano lessons last year.*

bel·low |bĕl′ ō| *v.* **bellowed, bellowing** To shout in a deep, loud voice.

be·long |bĭ lông′| *v.* **belonged, belonging** To have a proper place.

be·low |bĭ lō′| *adv.* In or to a lower place or position: *Look at the valley below.*

be·tween |bĭ twēn′| *prep.* In the position separating: *A few trees stand between the house and the road.*

bird |bûrd| *n., pl.* **birds** A warm-blooded animal that lays eggs and that has wings and a body covered with feathers.

birth·day |bûrth′ dā′| *n., pl.* **birthdays** The day of a person's birth.

bit·ter |bĭt′ ər| *adj.* **bitterer, bitterest** Sharp and unpleasant: *The fruit is bitter. We nearly froze in the bitter cold.*

blade |blād| *n., pl.* **blades** **1.** The flat, sharp-edged part of a cutting instrument, such as a knife, saw, razor, or sword. **2.** A wide, flat part, as of an oar, fan, or propeller. **3.** A thin, narrow leaf of grass. **4.** The metal runner of an ice skate.

blank |blăngk| *adj.* **blanker, blankest** **1.** Free of marks or decoration: *Give me a blank piece of paper.* **2.** Having empty spaces to be filled in: *Fill in this blank form.*

blank·et |blăng′ kĭt| *n., pl.* **blankets** A covering for beds, used to keep a sleeper warm.

blew |blōo| v. Past tense of **blow**: *A gust of wind blew the door shut.*

blind |blīnd| adj. **blinder, blindest** Unable to see; sightless.

bliz·zard |blĭz′ ərd| n., pl. **blizzards** A very long, heavy snowstorm with strong winds.

block |blŏk| n., pl. **blocks** A solid piece of a material, such as wood or stone, that has one or more flat sides.

blood |blŭd| n. The fluid circulated by the heart through the arteries, veins, and capillaries of persons and animals.

blue |blōo| n., pl. **blues** The color of a clear sky. adj. **bluer, bluest 1.** Of the color blue. **2.** Sad and gloomy.

board |bôrd| n., pl. **boards 1.** A piece of sawed lumber that has more length and width than thickness; plank. **2.** A flat piece of hard material that has a special use: *Here's a notice for your bulletin board.*
♦ *These sound alike* **board, bored.**

bod·y |bŏd′ ē| n., pl. **bodies 1.** The whole physical structure of a living person or animal. **2.** A separate mass of matter: *The Pacific Ocean is a vast body of water.*

book·let |bŏŏk′ lĭt| n., pl. **booklets** A small book or pamphlet.

boost·er |bōō′ stər| n., pl. **boosters** A device used to help launch a vehicle such as a spacecraft.

bor·der |bôr′ dər| n., pl. **borders** The line where an area, as a country, ends and another area begins.

bore |bôr| v. **bored, boring** To cause to feel that one has had enough, as by seeming dull or uninteresting: *The movie bored us.*
♦ *These sound alike* **bored, board.**

bor·row |bŏr′ ō| v. **borrowed, borrowing** To get from someone else with the understanding that what is gotten will be returned or replaced: *The book I borrowed from the library is due today.*

both·er |bŏth′ ər| v. **bothered, bothering 1.** To disturb or irritate: *That constant little noise bothers me.* **2.** To concern, worry, or trouble: *High places bother me.*

bot·tle |bŏt′ l| n., pl. **bottles** A container, usually made of glass or plastic, with a narrow neck and mouth and no handle.

ă	pat	ŏ	pot	û	fur
ā	pay	ō	go	*th*	the
â	care	ô	paw, for	th	thin
ä	father	oi	oil	hw	which
ĕ	pet	ōō	book	zh	usual
ē	be	ōō	boot	ə	ago, item
ĭ	pit	yōō	cute		pencil, atom
ī	ice	ou	out		circus
î	near	ŭ	cut	ər	butter

bot·tom |bŏt′ əm| n., pl. **bottoms** The lowest part of something.

bounce |bouns| v. **bounced, bouncing** To come back or up after hitting a surface. n., pl. **bounces** A sudden spring or leap.

bowl |bōl| n., pl. **bowls** A round, hollow container or dish.

break |brāk| v. **broke** |brōk|, **broken, breaking** To separate into two or more pieces as the result of force or strain; crack or split: *The rock broke the window. We pulled until the rope broke.*

break·fast |brĕk′ fəst| n., pl. **breakfasts** The first meal of the day. v. **breakfasted, breakfasting** To eat breakfast.

breath |brĕth| n., pl. **breaths** The air taken into the lungs and forced out when a person breathes.

breathe ||brēth| v. **breathed, breathing** To inhale and exhale: *All mammals breathe air. Quiet! Don't even breathe.*

breez·y |brē′ zē| adj. **breezier, breeziest.** Exposed to breezes; windy. adv. **breezily**

brick |brĭk| n., pl. **bricks** An oblong block of clay, baked by the sun or in an oven until hard. Bricks are used for building and paving.

bridge |brĭj| n., pl. **bridges** A structure built over a river, railroad, or other obstacle so that people or vehicles can cross from one side to the other.

bri·dle |brīd′ l| n., pl. **bridles** The straps, bit, and reins that are placed over a horse's head and used to control the animal. v. **bridled, bridling** To put a bridle on: *I saddled and bridled my favorite horse.*

bril·liant |brĭl′ yənt| adj. Very vivid in color: *The lilies in the field were a brilliant yellow.*

broke |brōk| *v.* Past tense of **break**: *When I fell I broke my wristwatch.*

bronze |brŏnz| *n.* **1.** A yellowish brown metal that is a mixture of copper and tin and sometimes other elements. Bronze is used for statues, bells, machine parts, and other things. **2.** A yellowish brown color.

brook |brŏok| *n., pl.* **brooks** A small, natural stream.

brush |brŭsh| *n., pl.* **brushes** A device for scrubbing, grooming the hair, or applying liquids. A brush is made of bristles, hairs, or wire fastened to a hard back or a short handle.

buck•et |bŭk′ ĭt| *n., pl.* **buckets** A round, open container with a curved handle, used for carrying things such as water, coal, and sand; pail.

buf•fa•lo |bŭf′ ə lō′| *n., pl.* **buffaloes** *or* **buffalos** *or* **buffalo** A large animal of western North America that has a shaggy, dark-brown mane and short, curved horns; the bison.

build |bĭld| *v.* **built, building** To make or form by putting together materials or parts; construct: *Engineers build bridges.*

built |bĭlt| *v.* Past tense and past participle of **build**: *We built a birdhouse for a wren.*

bul•le•tin |bŏol′ ĭ tn| *n., pl.* **bulletins** A short announcement on a matter of public interest, as in a newspaper or on radio.

burn |bûrn| *v.* **burned** *or* **burnt, burning** To undergo or cause to undergo damage, destruction, or injury by fire or heat; scorch.

bur•ro |bûr′ ō| *n., pl.* **burros** A small donkey, usually used for riding or carrying loads.

bush |bŏosh| *n., pl.* **bushes** An often low woody plant with many branches; shrub.

bush•y |bŏosh′ ē| *adj.* **bushier, bushiest** Thick and shaggy.

bus•y |bĭz′ ē| *adj.* **busier, busiest** Engaged in work or activity: *I am busy studying.*

C

cab•bage |kăb′ ĭj| *n., pl.* **cabbages** A plant with a rounded head of tightly overlapping leaves. It is eaten as a vegetable.

cab•in |kăb′ ĭn| *n., pl.* **cabins** A small, simply built house; a cottage or hut.

cac•tus |kăk′ təs| *n., pl.* **cacti** |kăk′ tī| *or* **cactuses** One of many kinds of plants that have thick, often spiny stems without leaves and that grow in hot, dry places.

ca•det |kə dĕt′| *n., pl.* **cadets** A student at a military or naval school who is training to be an officer.

cage |kāj| *n., pl.* **cages** An enclosure that has openings covered with wire mesh or bars and is used for confining birds or animals.

cal•ci•um |kăl′ sē əm| *n.* A silvery, moderately hard metallic chemical element that is found in substances such as milk, bone, and shells.

calf |kăf| *n., pl.* **calves** |kăvz| The young of cattle; a young cow or bull.

calm |käm| *adj.* **calmer, calmest** Peaceful; quiet: *A calm summer night.* *v.* **calmed, calming** To become or make calm: *I calmed down after the argument.*

cam•er•a |kăm′ ər ə| *n., pl.* **cameras** A device for taking photographs or motion pictures. Most cameras consist of a box that has a lens through which an image is recorded on film.

camp•site |kămp′ sīt′| *n., pl.* **campsites** An area used for camping.

can•cel |kăn′ səl| *v.* **canceled, canceling** **1.** To give up; call off: *I canceled my dentist appointment.* **2.** To invalidate or end: *cancel a magazine subscription.*

can•did |kăn′ dĭd| *adj.* Not posed or rehearsed: *a candid photograph.*

can•dle |kăn′ dl| *n., pl.* **candles** A solid stick of wax or tallow with a wick inside that is lit and burned to give light.

can•teen |kăn tēn′| *n., pl.* **canteens** A container for carrying liquid, as drinking water.

can•yon |kăn′ yən| *n., pl.* **canyons** A deep valley with steep walls on both sides that was formed by running water; gorge.

cap•sule |kăp′ səl| *n., pl.* **capsules** A compartment in a spacecraft, especially one that carries the crew.

cap•tain |kăp′ tən| *n., pl.* **captains** The person in command of a ship.

cap·tion |kăp′ shən| *n., pl.* **captions** A title or explanation that goes with an illustration or photograph.

cap·ture |kăp′ chər| *v.* **captured, capturing** To seize and hold, as by force or skill; catch: *The play captured my imagination.*

care |kâr| *v.* **cared, caring** To be concerned or interested: *Who cares what happens?*

care·ful |kâr′ fəl| *adj.* Done or made with attention, effort, or caution: *The doctor gave the patient a careful examination.*

care·less |kâr′ lĭs| *adj.* Done or made without attention, effort, or caution: *Careless work merits a low grade.*

car·pen·ter |kär′ pən tər| *n., pl.* **carpenters** A person who builds or repairs wooden objects and structures.

car·pet |kär′ pĭt| *n., pl.* **carpets** A heavy woven fabric used as a covering for a floor.

car·riage |kăr′ ĭj| *n., pl.* **carriages** A vehicle that has wheels and is used for carrying passengers.

car·ry |kăr′ ē| *v.* **carried, carrying** To take from one place to another: *Please carry my groceries into the house.*

car·toon |kär tōōn′| *n., pl.* **cartoons** A sketch or drawing, often with a caption, that is meant to be funny.

cas·tle |kăs′ əl| *n., pl.* **castles** A large fort or building with high, thick walls, towers, and other defenses against attack.

cat·e·go·ry |kăt′ ə gôr′ ē| *n., pl.* **categories** A division or group within a system; class: *The strings are one category of musical instruments.*

cat·er·pil·lar |kăt′ ər pĭl′ ər| *n., pl.* **caterpillars** The wormlike larva of a moth or butterfly that has just hatched from its egg. A caterpillar has a long body that is often covered with hair or bristles.

cat·tle |kăt′ l| *pl. n.* Large, heavy animals, as cows, bulls, or oxen, that have hoofs, grow horns, and are raised for milk, meat, or hides.

History • cattle

Cattle comes from the Old French word *catel,* meaning "wealth or property."

ă	pat	ŏ	pot	û	fur
ā	pay	ō	go	*th*	the
â	care	ô	paw, for	th	thin
ä	father	oi	oil	hw	which
ĕ	pet	ōō	book	zh	usual
ē	be	ōō	boot	ə	ago, item
ĭ	pit	yōō	cute		pencil, atom
ī	ice	ou	out		circus
î	near	ŭ	cut	ər	butter

cause |kôz| *n., pl.* **causes 1.** Someone or something that makes something happen: *What was the cause of the fire?* **2.** An ideal or goal that many people believe in and support: *World peace is a cause we should all work for.* *v.* **caused, causing** To be the cause of; bring about.

cav·ern |kăv′ ərn| *n., pl.* **caverns** A very large cave. Many caverns have unusual formations of rock.

cel·lar |sĕl′ ər| *n., pl.* **cellars** A room or rooms under a building where things are stored.

cent |sĕnt| *n., pl.* **cents** A coin used in the United States and Canada. One hundred cents equals one dollar.

cen·ter |sĕn′ tər| *n., pl.* **centers** A point that is the same distance from every other point of a circle or a sphere.

ce·re·al |sîr′ ē əl| *n., pl.* **cereals** A food made from the seeds of such plants as wheat, oats, or corn.

chair |châr| *n., pl.* **chairs** A piece of furniture that is built for sitting on. A chair has a seat, a back, and usually four legs.

chal·lenge |chăl′ ənj| *n., pl.* **challenges 1.** A call to take part in a contest or fight to see who is better, faster, or stronger: *The Red Team will meet the challenge of the Blue Team.* **2.** Something that requires all of a person's efforts and skills: *That job will be a challenge.*

cham·pi·on |chăm′ pē ən| *n., pl.* **champions** The winner of a game or contest, accepted as the best of all.

chance |chăns| *n., pl.* **chances** The possibility or probability that something will happen: *We have a good chance of winning the game.*

change |chānj| *n., pl.* **changes 1.** The act or result of making or becoming different. **2.** The money returned when the amount given in paying for something is more than what is owed. **3.** Coins. *v.* **changed, changing** To make or become different.

chap·ter |chăp′ tər| *n., pl.* **chapters** A main division of a book. A chapter may have a number or a title or both.

charge |chärj| *v.* **charged, charging** To ask as payment; set a price: *How much will you charge me for repairing my bike? n., pl.* **charges** An amount asked as payment; cost: *There is no charge for this service.*

charm |chärm| *n., pl.* **charms** The power or ability to please or delight; appeal: *the charm of the peaceful countryside.*

cheap |chēp| *adj.* **cheaper, cheapest** Low in price; inexpensive: *Tomatoes are cheap in August.*

check |chĕk| *n., pl.* **checks 1.** Something that restrains or controls. **2.** Examination to be sure that something is as it should be. **3.** A mark made to show that something has been noted. **4.** A restaurant bill. *v.* **checked, checking** To test, examine, or compare to find out if something is correct or in good condition: *Check your answers after doing the arithmetic.*

cheer |chîr| *v.* **cheered, cheering** To shout in happiness, approval, encouragement, or enthusiasm: *The audience cheered and clapped. n., pl.* **cheers 1.** A shout of happiness, approval, encouragement, or enthusiasm. **2.** Good spirits; happiness.

cheer·ful |chîr′ fəl| *adj.* In good spirits; happy.

cheer·less |chîr′ lĭs| *adj.* Lacking cheer; gloomy and depressing.

cheer·y |chîr′ ē| *adj.* **cheerier, cheeriest** Bright and cheerful.

cheese·bur·ger |chēz′ bûr′ gər| *n., pl.* **cheeseburgers** A hamburger topped with melted cheese.

chef |shĕf| *n., pl.* **chefs** A cook, especially the chief cook of a restaurant.

chew |chōō| *v.* **chewed, chewing** To bite and grind with the teeth. *n., pl.* **chews** The act of chewing.

chick·en |chĭk′ ən| *n., pl.* **chickens** The common domestic fowl; hen or rooster.

chief |chēf| *adj.* Highest in rank: *My cousin was appointed chief engineer of the project.*

chip·munk |chĭp′ mŭngk′| *n., pl.* **chipmunks** An animal that resembles a squirrel but is smaller and has a striped back.

chore |chôr| *n., pl.* **chores** A small job, usually done on a regular schedule.

chose |chōz| *v.* Past tense of **choose.** Picked: *Each captain chose ten players for their team.*

cho·sen |chō′ zən| *v.* Past participle of **choose:** *We have chosen you to be class president.*

cir·cle |sûr′ kəl| *n., pl.* **circles** A curved line made up of points that are all at the same distance from an inside point called the center.

cit·y |sĭt′ ē| *n., pl.* **cities** A place where many people live close to one another. Cities are larger than towns and are usually centers of business activity.

clam |klăm| *n., pl.* **clams** A shellfish that has a shell with two parts hinged together. Clams burrow into sand where they live. The soft body of the clam can be eaten.

clamp |klămp| *n., pl.* **clamps** A device for gripping or fastening two things together.

clay |klā| *n., pl.* **clays** A firm kind of earth made up of small particles. Clay is soft when wet and can be shaped. After heating, clay hardens. It is used to make bricks and pottery.

clean |klēn| *adj.* **cleaner, cleanest** Free from dirt, stains, or clutter: *Put on a clean shirt.*

clean·li·ness |klĕn′ lē nĭs| *n.* Condition of being free from dirt: *the cleanliness of the house.*

clean·ly |klĕn′ lē| *adj.* **cleanlier, cleanliest** Habitually and carefully neat and clean: *A cat is a very cleanly animal.* |klēn′ lē| *adv.* In a clean manner: *The fruit had been severed cleanly by a knife.*

clev·er |klĕv′ ər| *adj.* **cleverer, cleverest** Having or showing a quick mind; smart: *I tried to be as clever as I could and think what to do before it was too late.*

climb |klīm| *v.* **climbed, climbing** To go in various directions, such as up, down, or over, often by use of the hands and feet: *I climbed up the ladder.*

clin·ic |klĭn′ ĭk| *n., pl.* **clinics** A place that gives medical treatment to patients who do not have to stay in a hospital.

clock |klŏk| *n., pl.* **clocks** An instrument for measuring and indicating time, often having a numbered dial with moving hands.
◊ *Idiom* **around the clock** Nonstop; night and day.

cloud·y |klou′ dē| *adj.* **cloudier, cloudiest** Full of or covered with clouds: *The sky was cloudy, so I took my umbrella.*

clown |kloun| *n., pl.* **clowns** A performer, often in a circus, who does funny tricks.

coal |kōl| *n., pl.* **coals** A black natural solid substance that is formed from partly decayed plant matter, consists mainly of carbon, and is widely used as a fuel.

coarse |kôrs| *adj.* **coarser, coarsest** Not smooth; rough.
♦ *These sound alike* **coarse, course.**

coast |kōst| *n., pl.* **coasts** The land next to or near the sea; seashore.

coast·al |kō′ stəl| *adj.* On, along, or near a coast: *We swam in coastal water.*

coast·line |kōst′ līn′| *n., pl.* **coastlines** The shape or outline of a seacoast.

coat of arms |kōt ŭv ärmz| *n., pl.* **coats of arms** A design, as on a shield, that serves as the emblem of a nation or group.

cob·ble·stone |kŏb′ əl stōn′| *n., pl.* **cobblestones** A round stone formerly used for paving streets.

ă	pat	ŏ	pot	û	fur
ā	pay	ō	go	*th*	the
â	care	ô	paw, for	th	thin
ä	father	oi	oil	hw	which
ĕ	pet	o͞o	book	zh	usual
ē	be	o͞o	boot	ə	ago, item
ĭ	pit	yo͞o	cute		pencil, atom
ī	ice	ou	out		circus
î	near	ŭ	cut	ər	butter

co·coon |kə ko͞on′| *n., pl.* **cocoons** The silky covering spun by a caterpillar to protect itself until it turns into a fully developed moth or butterfly.

cold |kōld| *adj.* **colder, coldest** Feeling a lack of warmth; chilly.

col·lage |kə läzh′| *n., pl.* **collages** A picture made by pasting various materials or objects on a surface.

col·lar |kŏl′ ər| *n., pl.* **collars** The part of a garment that fits around the neck.

col·lie |kŏl′ ē| *n., pl.* **collies** A large dog with long hair and a narrow snout, often used to herd sheep.

col·or·ful |kŭl′ ər fəl| *adj.* Full of color, especially having several vivid colors: *Many butterflies have colorful wings.*

colt |kōlt| *n., pl.* **colts** A young horse, especially a male.

Co·lum·bi·a |kə lŭm′ bē ə| The capital of South Carolina.

comb |kōm| *n., pl.* **combs** A strip of hard material that has teeth and is used to arrange the hair. *v.* **combed, combing** To smooth or arrange with a comb.

com·mon |kŏm′ ən| *adj.* **commoner, commonest** Often seen; ordinary: *Windy weather is common in March.*

com·mute |kə myo͞ot′| *v.* **commuted, commuting** To travel regularly between home and work or school.

com·pass |kŭm′ pəs| *n., pl.* **compasses** An instrument with a magnetic needle that is used to show directions. The needle always points to the north.

com·pose |kəm pōz′| *v.* **composed, composing** To make or create by putting parts or elements together: *An artist composes a picture by arranging forms and colors.*

com·po·si·tion |kŏm pə zĭsh′ ən| *n., pl.*
compositions A work that has been composed, especially a musical work.

con·ti·nent |kŏn′ tə nənt| *n., pl.* **continents** One of the main land masses of the earth, including Africa, Antarctica, Asia, Australia, Europe, North America, and South America.

con·trol tow·er |kən trōl′ tou′ ər| *n., pl.* **control towers** A tower at an airport from which the takeoffs and landings are controlled by radio and radar.

cook |kŏ͝ok| *v.* **cooked, cooking** To prepare food for eating by using heat.

cop·per |kŏp′ ər| *n.* A   reddish-brown metal that is an excellent conductor of heat and electricity. Copper is a chemical element. *adj.* Made of or containing copper.

cop·y |kŏp′ ē| *v.* **copied, copying** To make something that is exactly like an original.

cor·al |kôr′ əl| *n., pl.* **corals** A hard, stony substance formed by the skeletons of tiny sea animals massed together in great numbers. It is often white, pink, or reddish.

cor·ner |kôr′ nər| *n., pl.* **corners** The place where two lines, walls, or streets meet.

cor·ral |kə răl′| *n., pl.* **corrals** A fenced-in area or pen for cattle or horses.

cot·tage |kŏt′ ĭj| *n., pl.* **cottages** A small house in the country.

couch |kouch| *n., pl.* **couches** A sofa.

coun·try |kŭn′ trē| *n., pl.* **countries** An area of land; region: *The country near our house is full of forests.*

cou·ple |kŭp′ əl| *n., pl.* **couples 1.** Two things of the same kind that are connected or considered together; pair: *I wrote a couple of letters.* **2.** Two persons who are closely associated, especially a man and woman who are married.

course |kôrs| *n., pl.* **courses 1.** A series of studies that leads to a degree: *The student finished the four-year course in high school.* **2.** A place where a race is held or a sport is played: *a golf course.*
♦ *These sound alike* **course, coarse.**

cous·in |kŭz′ ən| *n., pl.* **cousins** A child of one's aunt or uncle.

cov·er |kŭv′ ər| *n., pl.* **covers** Something that is put over or on something else.

cra·zy |krā′ zē| *adj.* **crazier, craziest** Not sensible: *It's crazy to drive too fast.*

creak |krēk| *v.* **creaked, creaking** To make or move with a squeaking sound: *The rusty gate creaked. n., pl.* **creaks** A creaking sound.
♦ *These sound alike* **creak, creek.**

creak·i·ness |krē′ kē nĭs| *n.* Squeakiness.

creak·y |krē′ kē| *adj.* **creakier, creakiest** Giving off a creak or creaks.

cream |krēm| *n., pl.* **creams** The yellowish fatty part of milk. Cream can be separated from milk and is used in cooking. It is also used to make butter.

creek |krēk| or |krĭk| *n., pl.* **creeks** A small stream of water, often one that flows into a river.
♦ *These sound alike* **creek, creak.**

crime |krīm| *n., pl.* **crimes** Unlawful activity in general: *The police fight crime.*

crim·i·nal |krĭm′ ə nəl| *n., pl.* **criminals** A person who has committed or been convicted of a crime.

crook·ed |krŏ͝ok′ ĭd| *adj.* Not straight.

crow |krō| *n., pl.* **crows** A large black bird with a harsh, hoarse call.

cru·el·ty |kro͞o′ əl tē| *n., pl.* **cruelties** Lack of kindness.

crumb |krŭm| *n., pl.* **crumbs** A tiny piece of food, especially of bread or cake.

crum·ble |krŭm′ bəl| *v.* **crumbled, crumbling** To break or fall into small pieces or crumbs: *The lump of dirt crumbled into dust.*

cup·board |kŭb′ ərd| *n., pl.* **cupboards** A cabinet, usually with shelves, for storing food or dishes.

cure |kyŏor| *v.* **cured, curing** To bring back to good health; heal.

curl |kûrl| *v.* **curled, curling** To twist into or form ringlets. *n., pl.* **curls** A ring of hair.

cur•rent |kûr′ ənt| *n., pl.* **currents** A mass of liquid or gas that is in motion: *We paddled the canoe into the current of the river.*

curve |kûrv| *n., pl.* **curves** A line or surface that keeps bending smoothly without sharp angles.

cut•ter |kŭt′ ər| *n., pl.* **cutters** A small, lightly armed boat used by the Coast Guard.

D

dair•y |dâr′ ē| *n., pl.* **dairies** A farm that produces milk.

dam•age |dăm′ ĭj| *n., pl.* **damages** Harm or injury that causes loss or makes something less valuable. *v.* **damaged, damaging** To harm or injure.

dance |dăns| *v.* **danced, dancing** To move with rhythmic steps and motions, usually in time to music.

dan•ger |dān′ jər| *n., pl.* **dangers** The chance of harm or destruction; peril: *The settlers faced danger with courage.*

dare |dâr| *v.* **dared, daring** To be brave or bold enough: *The explorer dared to sail alone across the ocean.*

dark |därk| *adj.* **darker, darkest** Without light or with very little light; shaded.

dark•ness |därk′ nĭs| *n.* Absence of light; partial or total blackness: *the darkness before dawn.*

dark•room |därk′ rŏŏm′| or |därk′ rŏŏm′| *n., pl.* **darkrooms** A room in which photographic materials are processed, either in total darkness or under light to which they are not sensitive.

daugh•ter |dô′ tər| *n., pl.* **daughters** A female offspring or child.

dawn |dôn| *n., pl.* **dawns** The time each morning when the sun comes up.

dead•line |dĕd′ līn′| *n., pl.* **deadlines** A set time by which something must be done.

ă	pat	ŏ	pot	û	fur
ā	pay	ō	go	*th*	the
â	care	ô	paw, for	th	thin
ä	father	oi	oil	hw	which
ĕ	pet	ŏŏ	book	zh	usual
ē	be	ŏŏ	boot	ə	ago, item
ĭ	pit	yŏŏ	cute		pencil, atom
ī	ice	ou	out		circus
î	near	ŭ	cut	ər	butter

dear |dîr| *adj.* **dearer, dearest** Much loved; precious: *You are my dear friend.*
♦ *These sound alike* **dear, deer.**

debt |dĕt| *n., pl.* **debts** Something that is owed to another: *I always pay my debts.*

dec•i•mal |dĕs′ ə məl| *n., pl.* **decimals** A fraction in which the denominator is 10 or a multiple of 10: *The decimal .1 = 1/10, and the decimal .12 = 12/100. adj.* Of or based on 10.

deck |dĕk| *n., pl.* **decks** One of the floors dividing a ship into different levels.

de•clare |dĭ klâr′| *v.* **declared, declaring** To say with emphasis or certainty.

dec•la•ra•tion |dĕk′ lə rā′ shən| *n., pl.* **declarations** The act of declaring.

dec•o•rate |dĕk′ ə rāt′| *v.* **decorated, decorating** To furnish with something attractive or beautiful; adorn: *We decorated the room with flowers.*

dec•o•ra•tion |dĕk′ ə rā′ shən| *n., pl.* **decorations** An ornament; something that decorates.

deer |dîr| *n., pl.* **deer** Any of several animals that have hoofs and chew the cud. The males usually have antlers.
♦ *These sound alike* **deer, dear.**

de•fend |dĭ fĕnd′| *v.* **defended, defending** To protect from attack, harm, danger, or challenge.

de•fine |dĭ fīn′| *v.* **defined, defining** To explain the meaning of: *Dictionaries define words.*

def•i•ni•tion |dĕf′ ə nĭsh′ ən| *n., pl.* **definitions** A statement of the meaning of a word or phrase.

de•gree |dĭ grē′| *n., pl.* **degrees** A step or stage in a series or process: *My shyness decreased by degrees.*

de•lay |dĭ lā′| *n., pl.* **delays** The act of delaying or condition of being delayed: *Do your homework without delay.* *v.* **delayed, delaying** To put off; postpone: *We delayed dinner an hour.*

de•liv•er |dĭ lĭv′ ər| *v.* **delivered, delivering** To take and turn over to the proper person or at the proper destination: *The mail carrier delivers packages.*

de•part•ment |dĭ pärt′ mənt| *n., pl.* **departments** A separate division of an organization, as a government or business.

de•pend |dĭ pĕnd′| *v.* **depended, depending** To be determined by something else: *Success depends on hard work.*

de•pos•it |dĭ pŏz′ ĭt| *v.* **deposited, depositing** To put money into a bank account.

de•scent |dĭ sĕnt′| *n., pl.* **descents** A downward slope.

des•ert |dĕz′ ərt| *n., pl.* **deserts** A dry area, usually covered with sand, in which few plants or animals live.

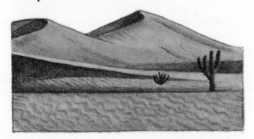

desk |dĕsk| *n., pl.* **desks** A piece of furniture with a top for use in reading or writing, often in a classroom.

de•vel•op |dĭ vĕl′ əp| *v.* **developed, developing** To treat a film with chemicals so that a picture can be seen.

di•a•ry |dī′ ə rē| *n., pl.* **diaries** A daily written record of a person's thoughts, activities, opinions, and experiences.

die•sel |dē′ zəl| *n.* Something powered by a diesel engine, especially a locomotive. *adj.* Powered by or intended for a diesel engine; oil-burning.

dim |dĭm| *adj.* **dimmer, dimmest 1.** Somewhat dark. **2.** Giving off little light: *a dim lamp.* **3.** Not clearly seen: *a dim shape.* *v.* **dimmed, dimming** To make or become dim.

din•er |dī′ nər| *n., pl.* **diners** A railroad car in which meals are served or a restaurant that looks like one.

din•ner |dĭn′ ər| *n., pl.* **dinners** The main meal of the day.

dirt•y |dûr′ tē| *adj.* **dirtier, dirtiest** Full of or covered with dirt; not clean.

dis- A prefix that means: **1.** Not; opposite: *dishonest.* **2.** Not having; lack of: *discomfort.*

dis•as•ter |dĭ zăs′ tər| *n., pl.* **disasters** Something, such as a flood, that causes great destruction.

dis•col•or |dĭs kŭl′ ər| *v.* **discolored, discoloring** To spoil the color of; stain.

dis•con•tin•ue |dĭs′ kən tĭn′ yōō| *v.* **discontinued, discontinuing** To bring or come to an end; stop.

dis•ease |dĭ zēz′| *n., pl.* **diseases** A condition that keeps the body from functioning normally; illness.

dis•like |dĭs līk′| *v.* **disliked, disliking** To have a feeling of not liking: *I dislike beans.*

dis•or•der |dĭs ôr′ dər| *n., pl.* **disorders** Lack of order; confusion.

dis•please |dĭs plēz′| *v.* **displeased, displeasing** To make dissatisfied.

dis•trust |dĭs trŭst′| *n.* Lack of trust; suspicion.

dis•turb |dĭ stûrb′| *v.* **disturbed, disturbing 1.** To trouble or worry: *Your noisy play disturbs me.* **2.** To break in on; interrupt: *The fire sirens disturbed our sleep.*

di•vide |dĭ vīd′| *v.* **divided, dividing 1.** To separate into two or more parts or groups. **2.** To determine how many times one number contains another: *The teacher told me to divide 20 by 2.*

doc•tor |dŏk′ tər| *n., pl.* **doctors** A physician, dentist, or veterinarian trained in and licensed to practice a healing art.

dodge |dŏj| *v.* **dodged, dodging** To move quickly aside: *The cat dodged the dog.*

dol•lar |dŏl′ ər| *n., pl.* **dollars** A unit of money equal to 100 cents that is used in the United States and Canada.

dol•phin |dŏl′ fĭn| *n., pl.* **dolphins** A sea animal that is related to the whales but is smaller and has a snout that looks like a beak. It can be trained by human beings.

done |dŭn| *v.* Past participle of **do**: *Have you done your homework?*

do•nor |dō′ nər| *n., pl.* **donors** A person who gives, donates, or contributes.

dou•ble |dŭb′ əl| *adj.* Twice as much in size, strength, number, or amount.

doubt |dout| *v.* **doubted, doubting** To be uncertain or unsure about; distrust: *I doubt my ability to win the contest.*

drag |drăg| *v.* **dragged, dragging** To draw along the ground or haul by force; to pull.

drag•on |drăg′ ən| *n., pl.* **dragons** An imaginary fire-breathing monster that is usually pictured as a giant lizard or reptile with wings and claws.

drain |drān| *n., pl.* **drains** A pipe or channel by which liquid is drained off: *The water was stopped up in the drain.*

drawn |drôn| *v.* Past participle of **draw**: *The artist has drawn a wonderful picture of my brother.*

dream |drēm| *n., pl.* **dreams** A series of pictures, thoughts, or emotions occurring during sleep.

drill |drĭl| *n., pl.* **drills** A tool used to make holes in solid materials.

drink |drĭngk| *n., pl.* **drinks** A kind of liquid for drinking; beverage. *v.* **drank** |drăngk|, **drunk** |drŭngk|, **drinking** To swallow liquid.

drop |drŏp| *v.* **dropped, dropping** 1. To fall or let fall in drops. 2. To fall or let fall: *I dropped a dish.*

drop•let |drŏp′ lĭt| *n., pl.* **droplets** A small drop.

drought |drout| *n., pl.* **droughts** A period of little or no rain.

due |dōō| or |dyōō| *adj.* Owed or owing as a right or debt: *Please pay the amount that is still due.*

dull |dŭl| *adj.* **duller, dullest** 1. Not interesting; boring: *This story is dull.*

dun•geon |dŭn′ jən| *n., pl.* **dungeons** A dark underground prison.

du•ty |dōō′ tē| or |dyōō′ tē| *n., pl.* **duties** 1. Something that a person ought to do: *We feel it is our duty to help the poor.* 2. Action that a person's occupation or position requires: *The candidate can perform the duties of a senator.*

ă	pat	ŏ	pot	û	fur
ā	pay	ō	go	*th*	the
â	care	ô	paw, for	th	thin
ä	father	oi	oil	hw	which
ĕ	pet	ōō	book	zh	usual
ē	be	ōō	boot	ə	ago, item
ĭ	pit	yōō	cute		pencil, atom
ī	ice	ou	out		circus
î	near	ŭ	cut	ər	butter

E

ea•ger |ē′ gər| *adj.* **eagerer, eagerest** Full of strong desire; impatient: *We're ready and eager to get started.*

ea•gle |ē′ gəl| *n., pl.* **eagles** A large bird with a hooked bill, broad strong wings, and sharp eyesight. Eagles soar high in the air.

ear•ly |ûr′ lē| *adv.* **earlier, earliest** At or near the beginning: *We always get up early in the morning.*

earn |ûrn| *v.* **earned, earning** 1. To gain by working or by supplying service: *Computer programmers earn good salaries.* 2. To deserve as a result of effort or behavior: *They earned good grades by working hard.* ♦ *These sound alike* **earn, urn.**

ear•nest |ûr′ nĭst| *adj.* Not playful or trifling; sincere: *Make an earnest apology for your mistake.*

eas•i•ly |ē′ zə lē| *adv.* Without difficulty or stress.

east |ēst| *n.* The direction in which the sun is seen rising in the morning. *adj.* 1. Of, in, or toward the east: *We camped on the east side of the lake.* 2. Coming from the east: *An east wind blew all day. adv.* Toward the east: *We drove east.*

eas•y |ē′ zē| *adj.* **easier, easiest** Needing very little effort or thought; not hard: *The homework was easy.*

ed•dy |ĕd′ ē| *n., pl.* **eddies** A current, as of a liquid or gas, that moves contrary to the direction of a main current, especially in a circular motion.

edge |ĕj| *n., pl.* **edges** 1. The line or point where an object or area ends; rim; border.

e·di·tion |ĭ dĭsh′ ən| *n., pl.* **editions** The entire number of copies of a book, magazine, or newspaper printed at one time: *the morning edition of a newspaper.*

ed·i·tor |ĕd′ ĭ tər| *n., pl.* **editors** A person who prepares material for publication by correcting, revising, or marking directions for a printer.

eel |ēl| *n., pl.* **eels** A long, slippery, snake-like fish.

ei·ther |ē′ thər| or |ī′ thər| *pron.* One or the other of two: *They went a mile before either spoke.*

e·lec·tric |ĭ lĕk′ trĭk| *adj.* **1.** Of, relating to, or produced by electricity: *An electric current runs through the wiring of a house.* **2.** Exceptionally tense; charged with emotion: *an atmosphere electric with suspicion.*

e·lec·tri·cian |ĭ lĕk trĭsh′ ən| *n., pl.* **electricians** A person whose work is installing, repairing, or operating electric equipment.

e·lec·tric·i·ty |ĭ lĕk trĭs′ ĭ tē| or |ē′ lĕk trĭs′ ĭ tē| *n.* Power that is transmitted by electrical means; electric power.

elf |ĕlf| *n., pl.* **elves** A tiny, often mischievous, imaginary creature with magical powers.

em·broi·der·y |ĕm broi′ də rē| *n., pl.* **embroideries** A decorated fabric or design made with a needle and thread.

emp·ty |ĕmp′ tē| *adj.* Containing nothing: *You can fill the empty bottle with orange juice.* *v.* **emptied, emptying** To make or become empty.

en·chant |ĕn chănt′| *v.* **enchanted, enchanting** To put under a magic spell; bewitch.

end·less |ĕnd′ lĭs| *adj.* Having or seeming to have no end or limit; infinite: *endless stretches of sandy beaches.*

en·e·my |ĕn′ ə mē| *n., pl.* **enemies** A person, animal, or group that hates or wishes harm to another; foe.

en·er·gy |ĕn′ ər jē| *n., pl.* **energies** Strength and vigor in action: *Good food helps give us energy.*

en·gine |ĕn′ jən| *n., pl.* **engines** A machine that uses energy, as that produced by oil or steam, to make something run or move; motor.

en·joy |ĕn joi′| *v.* **enjoyed, enjoying** To receive pleasure from: *We enjoy living in the country.*

e·nor·mous |ĭ nôr′ məs| *adj.* Extremely large; huge.

e·nough |ĭ nŭf′| *adj.* Being as much or as many as needed to meet a requirement; adequate: *There is enough food for everybody.*

en·ter |ĕn′ tər| *v.* **entered, entering** To come or to go in or into: *The ship entered the harbor.*

en·vi·ous |ĕn′ vē əs| *adj.* Having a bad feeling toward a competitor: *I was envious of Jake's gold medal in swimming.*

en·vy |ĕn′ vē| *n., pl.* **envies** A feeling of discontent at the advantages or success enjoyed by another together with a strong desire to have them for oneself; jealousy: *I was filled with envy when I saw their new car.*

e·qua·tor |ĭ kwā′ tər| *n., pl.* **equators** An imaginary line around the middle of the earth at an equal distance from the North and South Poles. The equator divides the earth into the Northern Hemisphere and the Southern Hemisphere.

-er A suffix that forms nouns and means: **1.** Something or someone who does: *baker.* **2.** Someone who is: *foreigner.* **3.** A person who was born in or lives in a place: *islander.*

es·cape |ĭ skāp′| *v.* **escaped, escaping** To get free: *The prisoners escaped by climbing the wall.*

-et A suffix that forms nouns and means "small": *jacket.*

e·vent |ĭ vĕnt′| *n., pl.* **events** Something that happens; occurrence: *The town newspaper reports events such as accidents, marriages, and births.*

ev·er |ĕv′ ər| *adv.* At any time: *Have you ever caught a fish?*

eve·ry·thing |ĕv′ rē thĭng′| *pron.* All things: *Everything in the store is for sale.*

eve·ry·where |ĕv′ rē hwâr′| *adv.* In every place; in all places: *I looked everywhere for my lost keys.*

ex·act |ĭg zăkt'| *adj.* Accurate in every detail: *It cost me about five dollars—the exact amount was $5.03.*

ex·am·ine |ĭg zăm' ĭn| *v.* **examined, examining** To look at carefully: *The detective examined the tracks to see if they matched the suspect's boot soles.*

ex·cel·lence |ĕk' sə lens| *n.* The condition or quality of being excellent or of high quality; superiority.

ex·er·cise |ĕk' sər sīz'| *n., pl.* **exercises** Physical activity for the good of the body: *We try to get some exercise every day.*

ex·it |ĕg' zĭt| or |ĕk' sĭt| *n., pl.* **exits** A way out.

ex·pert |ĕk' spûrt'| *n., pl.* **experts** A person who has great knowledge or skill in a special area: *My teacher is an expert on American history.* |ĕk' spûrt'| or |ĭk spŭrt'| *adj.* Having or displaying special knowledge or skill in a field.

ex·plore |ĭk splôr'| *v.* **explored, exploring** To go into or travel through an unknown or unfamiliar place for the purpose of discovery: *The Spanish explored the New World.*

F

face |fās| *n., pl.* **faces** The front part of the head from the forehead to the chin.

faint |fānt| *v.* **fainted, fainting** To lose consciousness for a short time.

false |fôls| *adj.* **falser, falsest 1.** Not true, real, honest, or correct: *a false statement.* **2.** Lacking loyalty: *They turned out to be false friends.*

fam·i·ly |făm' ə lē| *n., pl.* **families** A group consisting of parents and their children.

fa·mous |fā' məs| *adj.* Very well known.

fan·cy |făn' sē| *adj.* **fancier, fanciest** Not plain or simple; elaborate.

farm·er |fär' mər| *n., pl.* **farmers** A person who owns or operates a piece of land on which crops or animals are raised.

fast |făst| *adj.* **faster, fastest** Firmly fixed, attached, or fastened: *Keep a fast grip on the rope.*

ă	pat	ŏ	pot	û	fur
ā	pay	ō	go	*th*	the
â	care	ô	paw, for	th	thin
ä	father	oi	oil	hw	which
ĕ	pet	o͞o	book	zh	usual
ē	be	o͞o	boot	ə	ago, item
ĭ	pit	yo͞o	cute		pencil, atom
ī	ice	ou	out		circus
î	near	ŭ	cut	ər	butter

fas·ten |făs' ən| *v.* **fastened, fastening** To attach firmly; secure: *We fastened our skis to a rack on the roof of the car.*

fa·vor |fā' vər| *n., pl.* **favors** A kind or helpful act. *v.* **favored, favoring** To show preference for.

fear·ful |fîr' fəl| *adj.* Feeling afraid: *I was fearful of losing my way in the forest.*

feast |fēst| *n., pl.* **feasts** A fancy meal; banquet: *We prepared a feast for the wedding.*

feath·er |fĕ*th*' ər| *n., pl.* **feathers** One of the light horny structures forming the outer covering of a bird.

fea·ture |fē' chər| *n., pl.* **features** The part or quality that is most noticeable.

fel·low |fĕl' ō| *n., pl.* **fellows** A man or boy.

fe·male |fē' māl'| *adj.* Of or belonging to the sex that can give birth to young or produce eggs. *n., pl.* **females** A female person or animal.

fence |fĕns| *n., pl.* **fences** A structure set up to prevent entry into an area or to mark it off.

fer·ry |fĕr' ē| *n., pl.* **ferries** A boat or boat service used to carry people, cars, or goods across water.

fe·ver |fē' vər| *n., pl.* **fevers** A body temperature that is higher than normal.

few |fyo͞o| *adj.* **fewer, fewest** Amounting to a small number: *The bag held a few apples.* *n.* *(used with a plural verb)* A small number: *Most of the kids went home, but a few stayed to help clean up.* *pron.* *(used with a plural verb)* A small number of persons or things: *Few passed the test.*

field |fēld| *n., pl.* **fields** An area of land where a crop is grown, a natural product is obtained, or a special activity is done:

fier•y |fīr′ ē| *adj.* **fierier, fieriest** Of or glowing like fire: *The fiery sunset lit up the western sky.*

fif•ty |fĭf′ tē| *n., pl.* **fifties** The number, written 50, that is equal to the product of 10 x 5. *adj.* Being equal to ten times five.

fig•ure |fĭg′ yər| *n., pl.* **figures** **1.** A written symbol that stands for a number. **2.** A shape or form: *A tall figure stood in the doorway.*

fil•ly |fĭl′ ē| *n., pl.* **fillies** A young female horse.

film |fĭlm| *n., pl.* **films** A thin strip of material coated with a chemical that changes when light strikes it. Film is used in taking photographs.

fil•ter |fĭl′ tər| *n., pl.* **filters** A sheet of material that changes the colors of light passing through it by blocking certain light waves and letting others pass through.

fi•nal |fī′ nəl| *adj.* **1.** Coming at the end: *We took a final spelling test at the end of the school year.* **2.** Not to be reconsidered; decisive: *The judge's decision is final.*

fi•nal•i•ty |fī năl′ ĭ tē| *n., pl.* **finalities** The quality of being final; decisiveness: *The nurse spoke loudly and with finality.*

fi•nan•cial |fī năn′ shəl| *or* |fī năn′ shəl| *adj.* Of or having to do with the management or use of money: *The store was a financial failure and soon closed.*

fin•ish |fĭn′ ĭsh| *n., pl.* **finishes** The conclusion of; end: *The finish of the race was exciting.*

fire•place |fīr′ plās′| *n., pl.* **fireplaces** A structure for holding a fire for heating or cooking. An indoor fireplace is an opening in the wall of a room with a chimney leading up from it.

firm |fûrm| *adj.* **firmer, firmest** Not giving way when pressed or pushed; solid; hard: *The firm ground of the track was ideal for running.*

first |fûrst| *n., pl.* **firsts** **1.** The number in a series that matches the number one. **2.** A person or thing that is first: *Would the first in line come here? adj.* Coming before all others: *the first house on the block.*

fit•ness |fĭt′ nĭs| *n.* The state or quality of being physically sound; healthy: *Jogging is a good way to maintain fitness.*

fix |fĭks| *v.* **fixed, fixing** **1.** To place or fasten firmly: *We fixed the lightning rod to the chimney.* **2.** To set right; mend: *I fixed the broken radio.*

flash |flăsh| *n., pl.* **flashes** A short, sudden burst of light: *We were startled by the flash of lightning.*

fla•vor |flā′ vər| *n., pl.* **flavors** The quality that causes something to have a certain taste.

fleece |flēs| *n., pl.* **fleeces** The wool forming the coat of an animal, especially a sheep.

fleet |flēt| *n., pl.* **fleets** A number of boats, ships, or vehicles that form a group: *The company owns a fleet of cars for its sales force to use.*

flight |flīt| *n., pl.* **flights** The act or process of flying: *The bird's flight was almost too swift to see.*

flip |flĭp| *v.* **flipped, flipping** To move or turn by tossing in the air: *Let's flip a coin to decide who goes first.*

flip•per |flĭp′ ər| *n., pl.* **flippers** A wide, flat rubber shoe worn for swimming and skin diving.

flood |flŭd| *n., pl.* **floods** A large flow of water over dry land.

folk |fōk| *n., pl.* **folk** or **folks** The people who make up a nation or tribe.

fol·low |fŏl′ ō| *v.* **followed, following** To go or come after: *The cat followed me home.*

fool |fool| *n., pl.* **fools** A person who lacks judgment or good sense.

for·eign |fôr′ ĭn| *adj.* **1.** Of or from another country: *I tried to learn a foreign language.* **2.** Strange.

for·ev·er |fər ĕv′ ər| *adv.* For all time; always: *I'll be your friend forever.*

for·get |fər gĕt′| *v.* **forgot** |fər gŏt′|, **forgotten** or **forgot, forgetting** To be unable to bring to mind; fail to remember: *I forgot my friend's new address.*

for·mal |fôr′ məl| *adj.* Following the usual forms, customs, or rules: *I received a formal wedding invitation.*

for·mal·i·ty |fôr măl′ ĭ tē| *n., pl.* **formalities** Rigorous observance of accepted rules or forms.

fra·grance |frā′ grəns| *n., pl.* **fragrances** A sweet or pleasant scent or odor.

free |frē| *v.* **freed, freeing** To set at liberty: *We opened the cage and freed the bird.*

fresh |frĕsh| *adj.* **fresher, freshest 1.** Just made, grown, or gathered: *We ate warm, fresh bread with our salad.* **2.** Rested, revived: *I feel fresh as a daisy.*

fresh·ness |frĕsh′ nĭs| *n.* Quality of being fresh.

friend |frĕnd| *n., pl.* **friends** A person one knows, likes, and enjoys being with.

friend·li·ness |frĕnd′ lē nĭs| *n.* The quality of showing or encouraging friendship.

friend·ly |frĕnd′ lē| *adj.* **friendlier, friendliest** Of or suitable to friend or friends: *friendly cooperation; a friendly letter.*

fright |frīt| *n., pl.* **frights** Sudden, strong fear; terror.

fringe |frĭnj| *n., pl.* **fringes** A border or edge of hanging threads or strips. Fringes are used on curtains and bedspreads.

front |frŭnt| *n., pl.* **fronts** The forward part or surface of a thing or place: *The front of a shirt has buttons.*

fron·tier |frŭn tîr′| *n., pl.* **frontiers** A remote area that marks the farthest point of settlement: *The American frontier gradually moved westward.*

ă	pat	ŏ	pot	û	fur
ā	pay	ō	go	*th*	the
â	care	ô	paw, for	th	thin
ä	father	oi	oil	hw	which
ĕ	pet	oo	book	zh	usual
ē	be	oo	boot	ə	ago, item
ĭ	pit	yoo	cute		pencil, atom
ī	ice	ou	out		circus
î	near	ŭ	cut	ər	butter

frost |frôst| *n., pl.* **frosts** A covering of small ice particles formed from frozen water vapor: *Our windows were covered with frost.*

frost·y |frô′ stē| or |frŏs′ tē| *adj.* **frostier, frostiest** Of or producing frost: *It will be frosty tonight.*

frown |froun| *n., pl.* **frowns** The act of wrinkling the forehead when puzzled, unhappy, or thinking.

fro·zen |frō′ zən| *v.* Past participle of **freeze:** *There are some frozen berries in the freezer.*

fruit |froot| *n., pl.* **fruit** or **fruits** A seed-bearing plant part that is fleshy or juicy, eaten as fruit. Apples, oranges, grapes, strawberries, and bananas are fruits.

fry |frī| *v.* **fried, frying** To cook over direct heat in hot oil or fat: *Fry the chicken lightly in butter.*

-ful A suffix that forms adjectives and means: **1.** Having; having the qualities of: *beautiful.* **2.** Able to; apt to: *forgetful.* **3.** An amount that fills: *cupful.*

full |fool| *adj.* **fuller, fullest** Holding as much as possible; filled: *Water trickled down the side of the full bucket.*

fun·ny |fŭn′ ē| *adj.* **funnier, funniest** Causing amusement or laughter; humorous.

G

gain |gān| *v.* **gained, gaining 1.** To get or obtain by effort: *We gained experience by working in a number of jobs.* **2.** To develop gradually; pick up: *The movement gained strength.*

gal·ax·y |găl′ ək sē| *n., pl.* **galaxies** A very large group of stars. Our sun and its planets are in a single galaxy called the Milky Way.

gal·ley |găl′ ē| *n., pl.* **galleys** The kitchen of a ship.

game |gām| *n.* Wild birds hunted for food or sport: *The thick underbrush hid the game from the hunter.*

gar·bage |gär′ bĭj| *n.* Food and trash to be thrown away, as from a kitchen.

gar·den |gär′ dn| *n., pl.* **gardens** A piece of land where flowers, vegetables, or fruit are grown.

gas·o·line |găs′ ə lēn′| or |găs′ ə lēn′| *n.* A liquid made from petroleum. Gasoline burns easily and is used as a fuel to make engines run.

gath·er |găth′ ər| *v.* **gathered, gathering** To bring or come together into one place, collect: *I gathered the papers together.*

gear |gîr| *n., pl.* **gears 1.** A wheel with teeth that fit into the teeth of another wheel. **2.** Equipment, such as tools or clothing, used for a particular activity: *I packed our fishing gear.*

gen·u·ine |jĕn′ yōō ĭn| *adj.* Not false; real; true.

gi·raffe |jĭ răf′| *n., pl.* **giraffes** A tall African animal with short horns, a very long neck and legs, and a tan coat with brown blotches.

glad |glăd| *adj.* **gladder, gladdest** Pleased; happy.

glance |glăns| *v.* **glanced, glancing** To look quickly: *I glanced at my watch.* *n., pl.* **glances** A quick look.

glass |glăs| *n., pl.* **glasses** A hard, usually clear substance that breaks easily. Glass is used for making windowpanes.

glid·er |glī′ dər| *n., pl.* **gliders** An aircraft without an engine that glides on currents of air.

globe |glōb| *n., pl.* **globes 1.** Something shaped like a ball; sphere. **2.** A map of the earth or heavens that is shaped like a globe. **3.** The earth.

gloss |glôs| *n., pl.* **glosses** A bright shine on a smooth surface: *The old spoons were polished to give them a beautiful gloss.*

glove |glŭv| *n., pl.* **gloves** A covering for the hand that has a separate section for each finger.

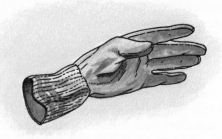

glue |glōō| *n., pl.* **glues** A thick, sticky substance that is used to stick things together. *v.* **glued, gluing** To stick with or as if with glue.

gnaw |nô| *v.* **gnawed, gnawing** To chew or bite on: *The mouse gnawed the cheese.*

goal |gōl| *n., pl.* **goals** Something wanted or worked for; purpose; aim: *My goal in life is to help other people.*

gold |gōld| *n.* A soft, yellow metallic chemical element used in making coins and jewelry.

gorge |gôrj| *n., pl.* **gorges** A deep, narrow passage, as between mountains.

gown |goun| *n., pl.* **gowns** A woman's dress, especially a formal one.

grace·ful |grās′ fəl| *adj.* Showing grace or beauty in movement: *The deer is a graceful animal.*

grand·fa·ther |grănd′ fä′ thər| *n., pl.* **grandfathers** The father of one's father or mother.

grand·moth·er |grănd′ mŭth′ ər| *n., pl.* **grandmothers** The mother of one's father or mother.

grate |grāt| *v.* **grated, grating** To break into fragments or shreds by rubbing against a rough surface: *I grated a little nutmeg on the top of the custard.*

grav·i·ty |grăv′ ĭ tē| *n., pl.* **gravities** The natural force that causes smaller objects to move toward the center of the earth. A ball that is tossed in the air falls back to the ground because of the pull of gravity.

gray |grā| *n., pl.* **grays** A color made by mixing black and white.

greed |grēd| *n.* A selfish desire for more than what one needs or deserves.

grey·hound |grā′ hound′| *n., pl.* **greyhounds** A slender dog with long legs, a smooth coat, and a narrow head. Greyhounds can run very fast.

grind |grīnd| *v.* **ground** |ground|, **grinding** To rub, pound, or crush something into powder or very small pieces: *Our grocery store has a machine that grinds coffee beans.*

group |grōōp| *n., pl.* **groups** A number of persons or things gathered or located together: *A group of people are waiting for the bus.*

grown |grōn| *adj.* Having reached an adult age; mature. *v.* Past participle of **grow.**

guar·an·tee |găr′ ən tē′| *n., pl.* **guarantees** A way of making sure of a certain outcome or result: *Buying a ticket ahead of time is a guarantee of a good seat at the show. v.* **guaranteed, guaranteeing** To make certain.

guard |gärd| *n., pl.* **guards** A person or group that keeps watch or protects: *The palace guards stood in line at attention.*

guess |gĕs| *v.* **guessed, guessing** To form an opinion without enough information to be sure of it; estimate: *I'd guess there were 6,000 people at the concert. n., pl.* **guesses** An opinion or estimate arrived at by guessing: *If you're not sure of the answer, at least make a guess.*

guest |gĕst| *n., pl.* **guests** A person who is at another person's home for a visit or a meal; visitor: *Our parents cooked a special meal for their dinner guests.*

guide |gīd| *n., pl.* **guides** Someone or something that shows the way, directs, leads, or teaches: *Our guide led us safely out of the woods.*

guilt |gĭlt| *n.* A feeling of responsibility or deep shame for having done something bad or illegal: *I felt guilt for having quarreled with my friend.*

gym |jĭm| *n., pl.* **gyms** A room or building with equipment for physical exercises and training and for indoor sports; a gymnasium.

ă	pat	ŏ	pot	û	fur
ā	pay	ō	go	*th*	the
â	care	ô	paw, for	th	thin
ä	father	oi	oil	hw	which
ĕ	pet	ōō	book	zh	usual
ē	be	ōō	boot	ə	ago, item
ĭ	pit	yōō	cute		pencil, atom
ī	ice	ou	out		circus
î	near	ŭ	cut	ər	butter

H

hab·it |hăb′ ĭt| *n., pl.* **habits** An activity or action done so often that one does it without thinking: *I have a habit of getting up early every morning.*

hail |hāl| *n.* Small round pieces of frozen rain that fall to the earth, often during thunderstorms.

hair·y |hâr′ ē| *adj.* **hairier, hairiest** Having much hair or covered with hair: *Gorillas are hairy animals.*

hall |hôl| *n., pl.* **halls** A passageway or corridor in a house, hotel, or other building. ◆ *These sound alike* **hall, haul.**

ham·bur·ger |hăm′ bûr′ gər| *n., pl.* **hamburgers** A patty of ground beef, fried or broiled and usually served in a roll or bun.

ham·mer |hăm′ ər| *n., pl.* **hammers** A hand tool with a metal head and a long handle, used especially for driving nails.

hand·ker·chief |hăng′ kər chĭf| *n., pl.* **handkerchiefs** A small square of cloth used to wipe the nose or face.

han·dle |hăn′ dl| *n., pl.* **handles** The part of a tool, door, or container that is made to be held or pulled with the hand.

hand·saw |hănd′ sô′| *n., pl.* **handsaws** A saw used with one hand for cutting hard material.

hand·some |hăn′ səm| *adj.* **handsomer, handsomest** Pleasing in appearance; good-looking.

hang |hăng| *v.* **hung** *or* **hanged, hanging** To fasten or be attached at the upper end only: *Hang the clothes on the line.*

han·gar |hăng′ ər| *n., pl.* **hangars** A building in which aircraft are kept and repaired.

hap·pen |hăp′ ən| *v.* **happened, happening** To take place; occur: *Tell me everything that happened today.*

hap·py |hăp′ ē| *adj.* **happier, happiest** Showing or feeling pleasure or joy: *I'm happy that we're all home safe.*

har·bor |här′ bər| *n., pl.* **harbors** A sheltered place along a coast where ships can safely anchor or dock; port.

hard |härd| *adj., adv.* **harder, hardest 1.** Not bending or yielding when pushed; firm. **2.** Difficult to solve or understand: *There were some hard questions on the test.*

har·vest |här′ vĭst| *v.* **harvested, harvesting** To gather a crop: *We harvested the corn.*

haste |hāst| *n.* Speed in moving or acting: *We ate with great haste to get to school on time.*

has·ten |hā′ sən| *v.* **hastened, hastening** To move or act swiftly; hurry: *I hastened home to tell my family the good news.*

haul |hôl| *v.* **hauled, hauling** To pull, drag, or carry; tug: *We hauled the sled up the hill.*
 ◆ *These sound alike* **haul, hall.**

haz·ard |hăz′ ərd| *n., pl.* **hazards** Something that may cause injury or harm; a danger: *Piles of oily rags are a fire hazard.*

haz·y |hā′ zē| *adj.* **hazier, haziest** Marked by or covered with fine dust, smoke, or water vapor in the air: *It was a humid day with a hazy sun.*

head |hĕd| *n., pl.* **heads** *or* **head 1.** The top part of the body, containing the brain, eyes, ears, nose, mouth, and jaws. **2.** The uppermost part of something; top: *Place the label at the head of each column.*

head·line |hĕd′ līn′| *n., pl.* **headlines** A group of words that is printed in large type over a newspaper article. Headlines tell what the articles are about.

heal |hēl| *v.* **healed, healing** To make or become healthy and sound.
 ◆ *These sound alike* **heal, heel.**

health |hĕlth| *n.* Freedom from disease or injury: *We wish you a speedy return to health.*

heart |härt| *n., pl.* **hearts** The hollow, muscular organ that pumps blood throughout the body.

hearth |härth| *n., pl.* **hearths** The floor of a fireplace and the area in front of it, usually made of stone or brick.

heav·y |hĕv′ ē| *adj.* **heavier, heaviest** Weighing a lot; not light.

heel |hēl| *n, pl.* **heels** The rounded rear portion of the human foot, under and behind the ankle.
 ◆ *These sound alike* **heel, heal.**

heir |âr| *n., pl.* **heirs** A person who receives or has the right to receive the property or title of another when the other person dies.

hel·i·cop·ter |hĕl′ ĭ kŏp′ tər| *n., pl.* **helicopters** An aircraft without wings that is kept in the air by horizontal propellers that rotate above the craft.

hel·lo |hĕ lō′| *or* |hə lō′| *interj.* An expression that is used as a greeting or to attract attention.

hel·met |hĕl′ mĭt| *n., pl.* **helmets** A head covering made of a hard material such as metal. A helmet is worn to protect the head, as in some sports.

help |hĕlp| *v.* **helped, helping** To give assistance or support to; aid: *She helped him with the farming. n., pl.* **helps** The act or an example of helping: *We appreciate your help.*

help·er |hĕlp′ ər| *n., pl.* **helpers** Someone who helps or assists.

hike |hīk| *v.* **hiked, hiking** To go on a long walk for pleasure or exercise. *n., pl.* **hikes** A long walk.

hint |hĭnt| *n., pl.* **hints** A piece of useful information; clue: *Here are some hints to help you solve the riddle.*

hoarse |hôrs| *adj.* **hoarser, hoarsest** Low, rough, or harsh in sound: *The cry of the crow is hoarse.*
 ◆ *These sound alike* **hoarse, horse.**

hob·by |hŏb′ ē| *n., pl.* **hobbies** An activity done for pleasure in one's spare time: *Building airplane models is my favorite hobby.*

hock·ey |hŏk′ ē| *n.* A game played by two teams who try to drive a puck or ball through a goal with curved sticks. Hockey is played on ice with a puck or on a field with a ball.

hol·low |hŏl′ ō| *adj.* **hollower, hollowest** Having a space or opening inside: *The squirrel hid in a hollow log.*

home·sick |hōm′ sĭk′| *adj.* Unhappy and longing for home and family.

home·stead |hōm′ stĕd′| *n., pl.* **homesteads** A piece of land that is given by the government to a settler who claims it and builds a home on it.

hon·est |ŏn′ ĭst| *adj.* Not lying, stealing, or cheating.

hon·ey |hŭn′ ē| *n., pl.* **honeys** A sweet, thick, syrupy substance made by bees from the nectar of flowers and used as food.

hon·or |ŏn′ ər| *n., pl.* **honors** **1.** Special respect or high regard: *We display the flag to show honor to the United States.* **2.** High moral standards.

hook |hŏŏk| *n., pl.* **hooks** A curved or bent object, often of metal, that is used to catch, hold, fasten, or pull something: *I put a hook on my fishing line.*

hope·ful |hōp′ fəl| *adj.* Feeling or showing hope.

hope·less |hōp′ lĭs| *adj.* Having no hope: *The lost hikers felt hopeless.*

horse |hôrs| *n., pl.* **horses** A large hoofed animal that has a long mane and tail. Horses are used for riding, pulling vehicles, and carrying loads.

♦ *These sound alike* **horse, hoarse.**

hos·pi·tal |hŏs′ pĭ təl| *n., pl.* **hospitals** A medical institution that treats sick and injured people.

host |hōst| *n., pl.* **hosts** A person or group that receives or entertains guests.

ă	pat	ŏ	pot	û	fur
ā	pay	ō	go	*th*	the
â	care	ô	paw, for	th	thin
ä	father	oi	oil	hw	which
ĕ	pet	ōō	book	zh	usual
ē	be	ōō	boot	ə	ago, item
ĭ	pit	yōō	cute		pencil, atom
ī	ice	ou	out		circus
î	near	ŭ	cut	ər	butter

hour |our| *n., pl.* **hours** A unit of time that is equal to sixty minutes: *There are twenty-four hours in a day.*

how·ev·er |hou ĕv′ ər| *conj.* In spite of that; yet; nevertheless: *It was growing very dark; however, we were not worried.*

howl |houl| *n., pl.* **howls** A long, wailing cry, such as the one made by a dog, wolf, or coyote.

huge |hyōōj| *adj.* **huger, hugest** Very big; enormous.

hull |hŭl| *n., pl.* **hulls** The body or frame of a ship or boat, including only its sides and bottom.

hu·man |hyōō′ mən| *adj.* Of or characteristic of people: *Many people can't afford basic human comforts, like food, shelter, and clothing.* *n., pl.* **humans** A person.

hu·man·i·ty |hyōō mǎn′ ĭ tē| *n.* The human race; people.

hu·mor·ous |hyōō′ mər əs| *adj.* Funny, amusing, or comical.

hun·gry |hŭng′ grē| *adj.* **hungrier, hungriest** Wanting food.

hur·dle |hûr′ dl| *n., pl.* **hurdles** A barrier, usually consisting of a horizontal bar held in place by two upright supports. Hurdles are used in certain track and field events. *v.* **hurdled, hurdling** To jump over: *The horse hurdled the fence with ease.*

hur·ri·cane |hûr′ ĭ kān′| *n., pl.* **hurricanes** A very powerful storm with extremely strong winds over 75 miles per hour and heavy rains.

hur·ry |hûr′ ē| *v.* **hurried, hurrying** To act or move quickly: *Don't hurry through your work.*

hurt |hûrt| *v.* **hurt, hurting** To cause pain or injury to: *I fell and hurt my wrist.*

husk•y |hŭs′ kē| *n., pl.* **huskies** A dog with a thick, furry coat. Huskies are used for pulling sleds in the far north.

I

ic•y |ī′ sē| *adj.,* **icier, iciest** Covered with ice; frozen: *I slid on the icy sidewalk.*

i•den•ti•fy |ī děn′ tə fī| *v.* **identified, identifying** To acknowledge as being a certain person or thing: *We could not identify the person in the old snapshot.*

ill•ness |ĭl′ nĭs| *n., pl.* **illnesses** A sickness or disease: *Pneumonia is a serious illness.*

i•mag•i•nar•y |ĭ măj′ ə něr′ ē| *adj.* Existing only in the imagination; not real: *Ghosts are imaginary creatures.*

im•por•tant |ĭm pôr′ tnt| *adj.* Strongly affecting the course of events or the nature of things; significant: *This is an important message about safety.*

inch |ĭnch| *n., pl.* **inches** A unit of length equal to 1/12 of a foot.

in•dus•tri•al |ĭn dŭs′ trē əl| *adj.* Of or having to do with industry: *Steel and gasoline are industrial products.*

in•ex•pen•sive |ĭn′ ĭk spěn′ sĭv| *adj.* Not expensive; low-priced; cheap.

in•fect |ĭn fěkt′| *v.* **infected, infecting** To cause to come in contact with germs or bacteria that cause disease.

in•fect•ed |ĭn fěkt′ əd| *adj.* Being contaminated with germs or bacteria.

in•flex•i•ble |ĭn flěk′ sə bəl| *adj.* Not bending; stiff: *The leather belt was so old and dry that it had become inflexible.*

in•sect |ĭn′ sěkt′| *n., pl.* **insects** Any of a large group of animals that have six legs, a body with three main divisions, and usually wings. Flies, bees, grasshoppers, butterflies, and moths are insects.

in•side |ĭn′ sīd′| or |ĭn sīd′| *n., pl.* **insides** The inner part, side, or surface; interior: *The inside of the house looked better than the outside.*

in•spect |ĭn spěkt′| *v.* **inspected, inspecting** To look over carefully; examine: *Supervisors inspected the rivets to be sure the jet would be safe to fly.*

in•ter•view |ĭn′ tər vyo͞o′| *n., pl.* **interviews 1.** A meeting of people face to face: *The principal asked the new student to report for an interview.* **2.** A conversation between a reporter and a person during which the reporter asks for facts, information, or statements.

i•ron |ī′ ərn| *n., pl.* **irons** A hard, gray metal that can be magnetized. It is used to make steel. Iron is used in making many tools and machines.

is•land |ī′ lənd| *n., pl.* **islands** A piece of land that is encircled by water.

its |ĭts| *adj.* Relating or belonging to it: *Everything was in its place.*
♦ *These sound alike* **its, it's.**

it's |ĭts| Contraction of "it is" or "it has": *It's a very good book.*
♦ *These sound alike* **it's, its.**

i•vy |ī′ vē| *n., pl.* **ivies** A climbing vine with evergreen leaves and black berries that grows on houses and walls.

J

jack•et |jăk′ ĭt| *n., pl.* **jackets** A short coat.

jail |jāl| *n., pl.* **jails** A place for keeping persons who are serving sentences for crimes.

jaw |jô| *n., pl.* **jaws** One of a pair of structures that hold the teeth and form the framework and shape of the mouth. The jaws are made of bone and cartilage.

jeal•ous |jěl′ əs| *adj.* Having a bad feeling toward another person who is a competitor; envious: *I was jealous of my friend's new skates.*

joke |jōk| *v.* **joked, joking** To say or do something as a joke: *I was only joking when I said that.*

jour•nal•ist |jûr′ nə lĭst| *n., pl.* **journalists** A person who gathers and reports news, especially a reporter or editor.

joust |joust| *v.* **jousted, jousting** To take part in a combat with lances between two knights on horses.

joy•ous |joi′ əs| *adj.* Feeling, showing, or causing great happiness or delight.

judge |jŭj| *n., pl.* **judges** A public official who listens to and makes decisions about cases in a court of law.

juice |jōōs| *n., pl.* **juices** A liquid contained in meats or in the fruit, stem, or roots of plants: *Orange juice is rich in vitamins.*

juic•y |jōō′ sē| *adj.* **juicier, juiciest** Full of juice.

June |jōōn| *n.* The sixth month of the year. June has 30 days.

jun•gle |jŭng′ gəl| *n., pl.* **jungles** A heavy growth of tropical trees and plants or land that is covered with such growth.

junk |jŭngk| *n.* Materials, such as rags or machine parts, that are thrown away but can be used again in some way.

K

kept |kĕpt| *v.* Past tense and past participle of **keep.** Held and not given away: *Neva kept her money in the bank for five years.*

kin•dle |kĭn′ dl| *v.* **kindled, kindling** To start a fire: *Kindle a fire with these matches, please.*

kin•dling |kĭnd′ lĭng| *n.* Material such as dry sticks of wood used for building a fire.

kind•ness |kīnd′ nĭs| *n., pl.* **kindnesses** The quality or condition of being helpful, considerate, or gentle; generosity: *The teacher's kindness made her popular.*

knead |nēd| *v.* **kneaded, kneading** To mix and work a substance, as by folding, rolling, or pressing it: *We helped to knead the bread dough.*

kneel |nēl| *v.* **knelt** |nĕlt| *or* **kneeled, kneeling** To rest or get down on a bent knee or knees: *We knelt around the campfire.*

knew |nōō| *or* |nyōō| *v.* Past tense of know: *I knew you when you were a baby.*

knife |nīf| *n., pl.* **knives** |nīvz| A device made of a sharp blade attached to a handle. A knife is used for cutting or carving.

knight |nīt| *n., pl.* **knights** A soldier in the Middle Ages who served and pledged loyalty to a king or lord. In return, the knight was given the right to hold land.

ă	pat	ŏ	pot	û	fur
ā	pay	ō	go	*th*	the
â	care	ô	paw, for	th	thin
ä	father	oi	oil	hw	which
ĕ	pet	ōō	book	zh	usual
ē	be	ōō	boot	ə	ago, item
ĭ	pit	yōō	cute		pencil, atom
ī	ice	ou	out		circus
î	near	ŭ	cut	ər	butter

knit |nĭt| *v.* **knit** *or* **knitted, knitting** To make a fabric or garment by interlocking yarn or thread in connected loops with special needles: *I am knitting a sweater.*

knob |nŏb| *n., pl.* **knobs** A rounded dial or handle, as for operating a television or stereo or for opening a drawer or door.

knock |nŏk| *v.* **knocked, knocking** To make a loud noise by hitting a hard surface; rap: *I knocked and knocked, but nobody came to the door.*

knoll |nōl| *n., pl.* **knolls** A small, rounded hill.

know |nō| *v.* **knew** |nōō| *or* |nyōō|, **known, knowing** To understand or have the facts about: *Do you know what causes thunder?*

L

la•bor |lā′ bər| *n., pl.* **labors** Hard work: *It took months of labor to dig the tunnel.*

lab•o•ra•tor•y |lăb′ rə tôr′ ē| *n., pl.* **laboratories** A room or building with special equipment for doing scientific tests and experiments.

lad•der |lăd′ ər| *n., pl.* **ladders** A device for climbing, made of two long side pieces joined by short rods or bars that serve as steps.

la·goon |lə goon'| *n., pl.* **lagoons** A shallow body of water along a coast or shore.

lamb |lăm| *n., pl.* **lambs** A young sheep.

land |lănd| *v.* **landed, landing** To come or bring to shore: *The boat landed at the dock.*

land·mark |lănd' märk| *n., pl.* **landmarks** A familiar or easily seen object or building that marks or identifies a place: *The Golden Gate Bridge is a landmark of San Francisco.*

lan·tern |lăn' tərn| *n., pl.* **lanterns** A portable container for holding a light, with sides that let the light shine through.

large |lärj| *adj.,* **larger, largest** Bigger than average in size or amount: *The zoo has large animals such as elephants.*

las·so |lăs' ō| *or* |lăs soo'| *n., pl.* **lassos** *or* **lassoes** A long rope with a noose at one end that is used to catch horses or cattle.

last |lăst| *adj.* Coming, being, or placed after all others; final: *We won the last game of the season.*

latch |lăch| *n., pl.* **latches** A movable bar that is used to hold a door, gate, or window closed.

lat·i·tude |lăt' ĭ tood'| *or* |lăt' ĭ tyood| *n., pl.* **latitudes** Distance north or south of the equator measured in degrees.

launch |lônch| *v.* **launched, launching** To set afloat: *The new ship was launched.*

lawn |lôn| *n., pl.* **lawns** A piece of ground, as near a house or in a park, planted with grass.

la·zy |lā' zē| *adj.,* **lazier, laziest** Not willing to work or be active: *Lazy students usually receive poor grades.*

lead[1] |lēd| *v.* **led** |lĕd|, **leading** 1. To show or direct along the way, as by going with or ahead of: *The ranger will lead us to the top of the mountain.* 2. To be or go at the head of: *The color guard will lead the parade.*

lead[2] |lĕd| *n., pl.* **leads** 1. A soft, heavy, gray metal that is easy to bend, melt, and shape. Lead is a chemical element. 2. A thin piece of graphite used as the writing substance in pencils.
♦ *These sound alike* **lead[2], led.**

learn |lûrn| *v.* **learned** *or* **learnt, learning** To get knowledge of or skill in through study or instruction: *The third-graders are learning Spanish.*

learn·er |lûr' nər| *n., pl.* **learners** One who learns.

least |lēst| *adj.* Smallest in degree or size: *Don't let the least criticism upset you.* *adv.* In the smallest or lowest degree: *I like tennis best and baseball least.* *n.* The smallest amount or degree: *The least you can do is offer to help.*

led |lĕd| *v.* Past tense and past participle of **lead[1]**: *The captain led us to victory.*
♦ *These sound alike* **led, lead[2].**

left[1] |lĕft| *n.* The side from which a person begins to read a line of English: *The number 9 is on the left of a clock's face.*

left[2] |lĕft| *v.* Past tense of **leave.**

lens |lĕnz| *n., pl.* **lenses** A combination of two or more lenses used to form or magnify an image, as in a camera or telescope.

-less A suffix that forms adjectives and means "not having" or "without": *harmless.*

les·son |lĕs' ən| *n., pl.* **lessons** Something to be learned or taught.

-let A suffix that forms nouns and means "small": *droplet.*

li·brar·y |lī' brĕr' ē| *n., pl.* **libraries** A place where books, magazines, records, and reference materials are kept for reading or borrowing.

li·cense |lī' səns| *n., pl.* **licenses** Legal permission to do or own something.

lift |lĭft| *v.* **lifted, lifting** To raise from a lower to a higher position or condition: *The suitcase is too heavy to lift.*

light·ning |līt' nĭng| *n.* The flash of light in the sky when electricity passes between clouds.

limb |lĭm| *n., pl.* **limbs** 1. A paired and jointed animal part, such as a leg, arm, wing, or flipper. 2. One of the larger branches of a tree.
◇ *Idiom* **out on a limb** In a dangerous or risky position.

lim·ber |lĭm' bər| *adj.* Moving easily; agile: *a limber athlete.*

lim·it |lĭm' ĭt| *n., pl.* **limits** A point beyond which someone or something cannot go: *The speed limit is 55 miles per hour.*

lis·ten |lĭs' ən| *v.* **listened, listening** To try to hear something: *If you listen, you can hear the ocean.*

lit·tle |lĭt' l| *adj.* **littler** *or* **less, littlest** *or* **least** Small in size or quantity: *Dolls look like little people. We have little food to waste.*

live¹ |lĭv| *v.* **lived, living** To be alive; exist: *Fish cannot live long out of water.*

live² |līv| *adj.* **1.** Having life; living: *The zoo has live animals.* **2.** Carrying an electric current: *Don't touch that live wire.*

lo·cate |lō' kāt'| *v.* **located, locating** To find by searching.

lo·ca·tion |lō' kā' shən| *n., pl.* **locations** A place where something is located; position: *We finally found the location of the airport.*

lock·et |lŏk' ĭt| *n., pl.* **lockets** A small ornamental case for a picture or other keepsake. A locket is often worn on a chain around the neck.

lodge |lŏj| *n., pl.* **lodges** A cottage or cabin, especially one used as a temporary place to stay.

lone·ly |lōn' lē| *adj.,* **lonelier, loneliest** Sad at being alone: *The lonely child had no friends.*

lon·gi·tude |lŏn' jĭ tōōd'| or |lŏn' jĭ tyōōd'| *n., pl.* **longitudes** Distance measured in degrees east or west of the meridian at Greenwich, a city in southeastern England.

lord |lôrd| *n., pl.* **lords 1.** A man of noble rank in Great Britain. **2.** An owner of an estate.

lose |lōōz| *v.* **lost** |lôst|, **losing** To fail to win or gain.

loud |loud| *adj.* **louder, loudest** Having a high volume of sound; noisy: *We heard a loud crash.*

love |lŭv| *n., pl.* **loves** Strong affection and warm feelings for another.

luck |lŭk| *n.* The chance happening of good or bad events; fortune: *Good luck seemed to favor the other team, and we lost the game.*

lum·ber |lŭm' bər| *n.* Timber sawed into boards and planks. *v.* To cut down and prepare timber for market.

ă	pat	ŏ	pot	û	fur
ā	pay	ō	go	*th*	the
â	care	ô	paw, for	th	thin
ä	father	oi	oil	hw	which
ě	pet	ōō	book	zh	usual
ē	be	ōō	boot	ə	ago, item
ĭ	pit	yōō	cute		pencil, atom
ī	ice	ou	out		circus
î	near	ŭ	cut	ər	butter

lu·nar |lōō' nər| *adj* Of, on, or having to do with the moon: *The spacecraft made a perfect lunar landing.*

lunch |lŭnch| *n., pl.* **lunches** A meal eaten at midday. *v.* **lunched, lunching**

M

ma·chine |mə shēn'| *n., pl.* **machines** A combination of mechanical parts that operate together to perform a certain task: *Vacuum cleaners are useful machines.*

Mad·i·son |măd' ĭ sən| The capital of Wisconsin.

mag·a·zine |măg' ə zēn'| or |măg' ə zēn'| *n., pl.* **magazines** A publication that is issued regularly, as every week or month.

History • magazine

Magazine comes from an Arabic word meaning "storehouse." A magazine is a "storehouse" of information.

mag·ic |măj' ĭk| *n.* The pretended art of controlling natural forces by using charms or spells.

ma·gi·cian |mə jĭsh' ən| *n., pl.* **magicians** A person who uses magic; wizard.

make-be·lieve |māk' bĭ lēv'| *n.* A playful pretending: *Elves live only in the world of make-believe. adj.* Pretended; imaginary.

man·age |măn' ĭj| *v.* **managed, managing** To have control over; direct: *Who will manage the business while you are away?*

man·or |măn' ər| *n., pl.* **manors** A lord's estate in the Middle Ages.

map |măp| *n., pl.* **maps** A drawing or chart of all or part of the earth's surface that shows features such as rivers and mountains.

ma·ple |mā′ pəl| *n., pl.* **maples** A tree that has leaves with deep notches, seeds that grow in pairs and look like wings, and hard wood. One kind of maple has sap that is boiled to produce syrup and sugar.

mare |mâr| *n., pl.* **mares** A female horse or a related animal, such as a zebra.

ma·rine |mə rēn′| *adj.* Of, relating to, or living in the sea: *We studied marine plants and animals.*

mar·ket |mär′ kĭt| *n., pl.* **markets** A public place where people buy and sell goods: *We took our fruits and vegetables to market.*

ma·roon |mə rōōn′| *v.* **marooned, marooning** To be abandoned on a deserted shore or island with little hope of escaping or of being rescued.

mar·riage |măr′ ĭj| *n., pl.* **marriages** The condition of living together as husband and wife.

mar·ry |măr′ ē| *v.* **married, marrying** To take as husband or wife: *He married my sister.*

mar·vel |mär′ vəl| *v.* **marveled, marveling** To be filled with surprise, astonishment, or wonder: *We marveled at the beauty of the mountain scenery.*

mar·vel·ous |mär′ və ləs| *adj.* Of the highest or best kind or quality.

mask |măsk| *n., pl.* **masks** A covering worn over the face to protect: *The mask kept water out of the swimmer's eyes.*

mast |măst| *n., pl.* **masts** A tall upright pole that supports the sails and rigging of a ship or boat.

mas·ter |măs′ tər| *n., pl.* **masters** A person who has power, control, or authority over another: *The dog ran to its master.*

math·e·ma·ti·cian |măth′ ə mə tĭsh′ ən| *n., pl.* **mathematicians** A person who specializes in mathematics.

math·e·mat·ics |măth′ ə măt′ ĭks| *n.* (*used with a singular verb*) The study of numbers, shapes, and measurements.

mean·while |mēn′ hwīl′| *adv.* During the time between; meantime.

meas·ure |mĕzh′ ər| *v.* **measured, measuring** To find the size, amount, capacity, or degree of: *We measured the room twice.*

meat |mēt| *n., pl.* **meats** The flesh of an animal eaten as food.
♦ *These sound alike* **meat, meet.**

med·al |mĕd′ l| *n., pl.* **medals** A small, flat, often circular piece of metal with a design. A medal may be awarded to honor a person, an action, an accomplishment, or an event.

me·dal·lion |mə dăl′ yən| *n., pl.* **medallions** A large medal.

med·i·cine |mĕd′ ĭ sĭn| *n., pl.* **medicines** A substance used to treat a disease or relieve pain.

med·ley |mĕd′ lē| *n., pl.* **medleys** A piece of music made up of different songs or melodies.

meet |mēt| *v.* **met** |mĕt|, **meeting** To come face to face; encounter: *The two friends shook hands when they met.*
♦ *These sound alike* **meet, meat.**

mel·low |mĕl′ ō| *adj.* **mellower, mellowest** Soft and sweet to the taste; fully ripened: *We ate the juicy, mellow peaches.*

mem·ber |mĕm′ bər| *n., pl.* **members** A person or thing belonging to a group or organization: *The lion is a member of the cat family. My club has six members.*

-ment A suffix that forms nouns and means: **1.** Action; process: *government.* **2.** Condition: *amazement.*

men·u |mĕn′ yōō| *n., pl.* **menus** A list of foods and drinks available for a meal.

mer·cu·ry |mûr′ kyə rē| *n.* A silvery-white metal that is a liquid at room temperature. Mercury is one of the chemical elements. It is used in thermometers.

mer•cy |mûr′ sē| *n., pl.* **mercies** Kindness that goes beyond what can be expected.

met•al |mĕt′ l| *n., pl.* **metals** A substance, such as copper, iron, silver, or gold, that is usually shiny and hard, conducts heat and electricity, and can be hammered or cast into a desired shape. *adj.* Made of a metal or metals.

me•tal•lic |mə tăl′ ĭk| *adj.* Of or like metal.

meth•od |mĕth′ əd| *n., pl.* **methods** A regular or deliberate way of doing something.

mid•dle |mĭd′ l| *n., pl.* **middles** A point or part that is the same distance from each side or end; center: *A deer stood in the middle of the road.*

mince |mĭns| *v.* **minced, mincing** To cut or chop into very small pieces.

mind |mīnd| *n., pl.* **minds** The part of a human being that thinks, feels, understands, remembers, and reasons: *The mathematician has a brilliant mind. v.* **minded, minding** To object to or to dislike: *Would you mind if I sat down?*

min•ute¹ |mĭn′ ĭt| *n., pl.* **minutes** A unit of time equal to sixty seconds.

mi•nute² |mī nōot′| or |mī nyōot′| *adj.* Very, very small; tiny: *The wind blew a minute speck of dirt into her eye.*

mir•ror |mĭr′ ər| *n., pl.* **mirrors** A surface, as of glass, that reflects the image of an object placed in front of it.

mis•take |mĭ stāk′| *n., pl.* **mistakes** Something that is thought up, done, or figured out in an incorrect way: *I made a mistake in arithmetic.*

mix |mĭks| *v.* **mixed, mixing** To blend or combine into a single mass or substance: *Mix the flour, water, and eggs together.*

mod•el |mŏd′ l| *n., pl.* **models 1.** A small copy: *I built a model of a sailboat.* **2.** A person or thing that is a good example: *The farm is a model of efficient management.*

mod•ern |mŏd′ ərn| *adj.* Advanced, as in style; up-to-date: *My parents work in a modern office building.*

mo•ment |mō′ mənt| *n., pl.* **moments** A very short period of time; instant: *Wait a moment while I wash my hands.*

ă	pat	ŏ	pot	û	fur
ā	pay	ō	go	*th*	the
â	care	ô	paw, for	th	thin
ä	father	oi	oil	hw	which
ĕ	pet	ŏŏ	book	zh	usual
ē	be	ōō	boot	ə	ago, item
ĭ	pit	yōō	cute		pencil, atom
ī	ice	ou	out		circus
î	near	ŭ	cut	ər	butter

mon•ey |mŭn′ ē| *n.* Coins and bills issued by a government for use in buying or paying for goods and services; currency.

mon•key |mŭng′ kē| *n., pl.* **monkeys** Any of a group of animals that have long arms and legs, and hands and feet that are adapted for climbing and grasping objects. Monkeys, and especially the smaller ones, have long tails.

mon•soon |mŏn sōon′| *n., pl.* **monsoons** A wind in southern Asia that changes direction with the seasons. The monsoon brings on the rainy season.

month |mŭnth| *n., pl.* **months** One of the 12 periods that make up a year.

most |mōst| *adj.* Greatest, as in number, size, extent, or degree: *The player with the most skill won the game.*

mo•tion |mō′ shən| *n., pl.* **motions** The act or process of moving; movement or gesture.

motion picture *n., pl.* **motion pictures** A series of pictures projected on a screen so quickly that the objects in the pictures seem to move as they would in life; movie.

mo•tor |mō′ tər| *n., pl.* **motors** A device that provides the power to make something move or run; engine: *An electric motor drives the fan.*

mo•tor•cy•cle |mō′ tər sī′ kəl| *n., pl.* **motorcycles** A vehicle with two wheels that is driven by an engine.

mount |mount| *v.* **mounted, mounting** To go up; climb: *We mounted the stairs.*

move |mōov| *v.* **moved, moving 1.** To change or cause to change position: *Don't move while I take your picture.* **2.** To change the place where one lives or works: *My grandparents moved to Florida.*

move•ment |mōōv′ mənt| *n.*, *pl.* **movements** The act or process of moving: *Jay grabbed the ball in a quick movement.*

mov•ie |mōō′ vē| *n.*, *pl.* **movies** A motion picture.

muf•fin |mŭf′ ĭn| *n.*, *pl.* **muffins** A small, cup-shaped bread.

mu•sic |myōō′ zĭk| *n.* **1.** The art of combining tones or sounds in a pleasing or meaningful way. **2.** Vocal or instrumental sounds that have rhythm, melody, and harmony.

mu•si•cian |myōō zĭsh′ ən| *n.*, *pl.* **musicians** A person who is skilled in music, especially as a professional composer or performer.

mus•tang |mŭs′ tăng′| *n.*, *pl.* **mustangs** A small wild horse of the plains of western North America.

N

nar•rate |năr′ āt′| *v.* **narrated, narrating** To tell the story of in speech or writing.

nar•row |năr′ ō| *adj.* **narrower, narrowest** Small or slender in width: *The road was long and narrow.*

na•tion•wide |nā′ shən wīd′| *adj.* Throughout a whole nation.

nat•u•ral |năch′ ər əl| *adj.* Found in or produced by nature; not artificial or man-made.

na•ture |nā′ chər| *n.*, *pl.* **natures** The world of living things and the outdoors; wildlife and natural scenery: *We camped beside a lake to enjoy the beauties of nature.*

na•vy |nā′ vē| *n.*, *pl.* **navies** A dark blue color.

near |nîr| *adv.* To, at, or within a short distance or time: *The deer ran off as we came near. adj.* **nearer, nearest** Close in distance or time: *I'll see you in the near future. prep.* Close to: *Stay near me when we explore the cave. v.* **neared, nearing** To draw near; approach: *The ship neared the port.*

need |nēd| *n.*, *pl.* **needs** A lack of something required or desirable: *Their crops are in need of water. v.* **needed, needing** **1.** To have to: *I need to return the book today.* **2.** To have need of; require: *This toaster needs repair.*

neigh•bor |nā′ bər| *n.*, *pl.* **neighbors** A person who lives next door to or near another.

nerv•ous |nûr′ vəs| *adj.* Tense, anxious, or fearful.

-ness A suffix that forms nouns and means "condition" or "quality": *kindness.*

nev•er |nĕv′ ər| *adv.* At no time; not ever: *I have never been here before.*

news•cast |nōōz′ kăst′| or |nyōōz′ kăst′| *n.*, *pl.* **newscasts** A broadcast of news on radio or television.

news•pa•per |nōōz′ pā′ pər| or |nyōōz′ pā′ pər| *n.*, *pl.* **newspapers** A printed paper that is usually issued every day and contains news, articles, and advertisements.

nice |nīs| *adj.* **nicer, nicest** Pleasing; agreeable: *It was a nice party. You look nice in your new outfit.*

nick•el |nĭk′ əl| *n.*, *pl.* **nickels** A United States or Canadian coin worth five cents.

nine•ty-nine |nīn′ tē nīn′| *n.* A number, written 99 in Arabic numerals, that is equal to the sum of 98 + 1. It is the positive integer that comes after 98.

nois•y |noi′ zē| *adj.* **noisier, noisiest** Making a lot of sound; not quiet: *The audience was restless and noisy.*

noth•ing |nŭth′ ĭng| *pron.* Not anything: *I have nothing to say.*

No•vem•ber |nō vĕm′ bər| *n.* The eleventh month of the year. November has 30 days.

numb |nŭm| *adj.* **number, numbest** Deprived of the power to feel or move normally: *toes numb with cold.*

num·ber |nŭm′ bər| *n., pl.* **numbers** A numeral given to something to identify it: *What is your house number?*

numb·ness |nŭm′ nĭs| *n.* The condition of lacking the power to feel or move.

nurse |nûrs| *n., pl.* **nurses** A person who cares for or is trained to care for sick people.

O

ă	pat	ŏ	pot	û	fur
ā	pay	ō	go	*th*	the
â	care	ô	paw, for	th	thin
ä	father	oi	oil	hw	which
ĕ	pet	o͞o	book	zh	usual
ē	be	o͞o	boot	ə	ago, item
ĭ	pit	yo͞o	cute		pencil, atom
ī	ice	ou	out		circus
î	near	ŭ	cut	ər	butter

oar |ôr| *n., pl.* **oars** A long pole with a blade at one end that is used to row or steer a boat; a paddle.
♦ *These sound alike oar, ore.*

o·cean |ō′ shən| *n., pl.* **oceans** The great mass of salt water that covers about 72 percent of the earth's surface.

Oc·to·ber |ŏk tō′ bər| *n.* The tenth month of the year. The month of October has 31 days.

oc·to·pus |ŏk′ tə pəs| *n., pl.* **octopuses** A sea animal that has a large head, a soft, rounded body, and eight long arms. The undersides of the arms have sucking disks used for grasping and holding.

odd |ŏd| *adj.* **odder, oddest 1.** Not ordinary or usual; peculiar; strange: *The car is making an odd noise.* **2.** Being the only one left of a set or pair: *I found an odd mitten in the drawer.*

of·fer |ô′ fər| *v.* **offered, offering** To put forward to be accepted or refused: *They offered us some soup.*

of·fice |ô′ fĭs| *n., pl.* **offices** A place, as a room or series of rooms, in which the work of a business is carried on.

of·ten |ô′ fən| *adv.* Many times, frequently: *I often read before going to sleep.*

O·lym·pi·a |ō lĭm′ pē ə| The capital of the state of Washington.

once |wŭns| *adv.* One time only: *We feed our dog once a day.*

o·pen |ō′ pən| *adj.* Not shut, closed, fastened, or sealed: *An open book lay on the desk. The door is open.*

op·er·ate |ŏp′ ə rāt′| *v.* **operated, operating** To work or run: *This machine operates well.*

op·er·a·tion |ŏp′ ə rā′ shən| *n., pl.* **operations** The act, process, or way of operating: *We are learning the operation of a computer.*

-or A suffix that forms nouns and means "something or someone who does": *operator.*

or·ange |ôr′ ĭnj| *n., pl.* **oranges** A round, juicy fruit with a reddish-yellow rind. Oranges grow in warm regions on evergreen trees that have fragrant white flowers.

or·bit |ôr′ bĭt| *n., pl.* **orbits** The path of a heavenly body or manmade satellite as it circles around another body. The earth is in orbit around the sun: *The spacecraft went into orbit.*

ore |ôr| *n., pl.* **ores** A mineral from which a metal, such as gold, can be mined.
♦ *These sound alike ore, oar.*

or·gan |ôr′ gən| *n., pl.* **organs** A musical instrument with one or more keyboards that control the flow of air to pipes. The pipes sound tones when supplied with air.

oth·er |ŭth′ ər| *adj.* Different: *Call me some other time.*

our·selves |our sĕlvz′| *pron.* Our own selves: *Let's keep our plans to ourselves.*

-ous A suffix that forms adjectives and means "full of" or "having": *famous.*

out·side |out sīd′| *n., pl.* **outsides** An outer surface, side, or part; exterior: *I wrote my friend's name on the outside of the envelope.*

ov·en |ŭv′ ən| *n., pl.* **ovens** An enclosed chamber, as in a stove, used for baking, heating, or drying.

owl |oul| *n., pl.* **owls** Any of several birds of prey that usually fly at night and that have a large head, a short, hooked bill, and a flat, disklike face.

oy·ster |oi′ stər| *n., pl.* **oysters** A sea animal that lives in shallow waters and has an edible soft body with a shell made up of two hinged parts. Some kinds produce pearls inside their shells.

P

pack·age |păk′ ĭj| *n., pl.* **packages** A bundle of things packed together; parcel.

pack·et |păk′ ĭt| *n., pl.* **packets** A small package or bundle, as of mail.

pad·dle |păd′ l| *n., pl.* **paddles** A short oar with a flat blade at one or both ends, used to move and steer a small boat or canoe.

page |pāj| *n., pl.* **pages** One side of a printed or written sheet of paper, as in a book.

pain |pān| *n., pl.* **pains** Physical suffering caused by injury or sickness.

pain·ful |pān′ fəl| *adj.* **1.** Causing or full of pain; hurtful: *a painful injury.* **2.** Causing suffering or anxiety; distressing: *a painful decision.*

pain·less |pān′ lĭs| *adj.* Without pain.

paint |pānt| *n., pl.* **paints** A mixture of solid coloring matter and a liquid put onto surfaces to protect or decorate them.

pal·ace |păl′ ĭs| *n., pl.* **palaces** A ruler's official residence.

palm |päm| *n., pl.* **palms** The inner surface of the hand between the wrist and the fingers.

◇ *Idiom* **an itchy palm** A greedy desire for money.

pa·per |pā′ pər| *n., pl.* **papers** **1.** A material made in thin sheets from pulp. **2.** A single sheet of paper. *v.* **papered, papering** To cover with wallpaper.

par·a·chute |păr′ ə shoōt′| *n., pl.* **parachutes** A folding device shaped like an umbrella that is used to slow the fall of persons or objects from the sky.

pa·rade |pə rād′| *n., pl.* **parades** A festive public event in which people or vehicles pass by spectators: *Fourth of July parade.*

par·ent |păr′ ənt| *n., pl.* **parents** A father or mother.

par·ka |pär′ kə| *n., pl.* **parkas** A warm jacket with a hood.

pass·book |păs′ boŏk′| or |päs′ boŏk′| *n., pl.* **passbooks** A bankbook in which deposits and withdrawals are recorded.

past |păst| *adj.* Expressing a time gone by: *a past event. n., pl.* **pasts** A time before the present: *happy memories of the past.*

pas·ture |păs′ chər| *n., pl.* **pastures** Ground where animals graze.

pa·tient |pā′ shənt| *n., pl.* **patients** A person who is receiving medical treatment.

pa·trol |pə trōl′| *n., pl.* **patrols** The act of moving about an area in order to watch or guard.

peace |pēs| *n.* The absence of war or other hostilities.

◆ *These sound alike* **peace, piece.**

peace·ful |pēs′ fəl| *adj.* **1.** Not likely to go to war or to fight: *We live in a peaceful nation.* **2.** Marked by peace and calmness.

peach |pēch| *n., pl.* **peaches** A sweet, round, juicy fruit with fuzzy yellow or pink skin and a pit with a hard shell.

peak |pēk| *n., pl.* **peaks** The top of a mountain.

◆ *These sound alike* **peak, peek.**

peas·ant |pĕz′ ənt| *n., pl.* **peasants** A small farmer or farm laborer in Europe.

pe·cu·liar |pĭ kyoōl′ yər| *adj.* **1.** Not usual. **2.** Belonging to a particular person or place: *music peculiar to Asia.*

peek |pēk| *v.* **peeked, peeking** To glance or look quickly or secretly.

◆ *These sound alike* **peek, peak.**

pen·cil |pĕn′ səl| *n., pl.* **pencils** A thin stick of black or colored material used for writing or drawing.

pen·ny |pĕn' ē| *n., pl.* **pennies** A coin used in the United States and Canada; cent. One hundred pennies equal one dollar.

per·fect |pûr' fĭkt| *adj.* Having no flaws, mistakes, or defects: *My drawing is a perfect copy of yours.*

per·fec·tion |pər fĕc' shən| *n.* The quality or condition of being perfect.

per·form |pər fôrm'| *v.* **performed, performing** To carry out; do: *We will perform an experiment in class.*

per·il |pĕr' əl| *n., pl.* **perils 1.** The condition of being in danger: *The diver's life is in peril.* **2.** Something dangerous.

per·son |pûr' sən| *n., pl.* **persons** A human being; individual: *Any person who wants to can come.*

pheas·ant |fĕz' ənt| *n., pl.* **pheasants** A large, brightly colored game bird with a long tail: *Pheasants often were hunted for their beautiful feathers.*

phone |fōn| *v.* **phoned, phoning** To telephone.

pho·to·graph |fō' tə grăf'| *n., pl.* **photographs** An image formed on film by a camera and developed by chemicals to produce a print.

pic·nic |pĭk' nĭk'| *n., pl.* **picnics** A party in which those taking part carry their food with them and then eat it outdoors. *adj:* *We have a new picnic basket.*

pic·ture |pĭk' chər| *n., pl.* **pictures** A painting, drawing, or photograph.

piece |pēs| *n., pl.* **pieces** Something considered as a part of a larger quantity or group; a portion: *a piece of wood.*
♦ *These sound alike* **piece, peace.**

pig·let |pĭg' lĭt| *n., pl.* **piglets** A small, young pig.

pil·low |pĭl' ō| *n., pl.* **pillows** A case filled with soft material and used to cushion a person's head during rest or sleep.

pi·lot |pī' lət| *n., pl.* **pilots** A person who operates an aircraft in flight.

pi·o·neer |pī' ə nîr'| *n., pl.* **pioneers** A person who is first to settle in a region.

place |plās| *v.* **placed, placing** To put in a particular place or order: *I placed cups and saucers on the table. n., pl.* **places** An area or region: *We visited many places.*

ă	pat	ŏ	pot	û	fur
ā	pay	ō	go	*th*	the
â	care	ô	paw, for	th	thin
ä	father	oi	oil	hw	which
ĕ	pet	oͦo	book	zh	usual
ē	be	o͞o	boot	ə	ago, item
ĭ	pit	yo͞o	cute		pencil, atom
ī	ice	ou	out		circus
î	near	ŭ	cut	ər	butter

plan·et |plăn' ĭt| *n., pl.* **planets** A heavenly body that moves in an orbit around a star, such as the sun.

plank |plăngk| *n., pl.* **planks** A long board.

plant |plănt| *n., pl.* **plants** A living thing, as a flower, tree, fern, or mushroom, that is not an animal, that cannot usually move from place to place, but can usually make its own food. *v.* **planted, planting** To put in the ground or in soil to grow.

plas·tic |plăs' tĭk| *n., pl.* **plastics** Any of a large number of materials that are made from chemicals. Plastic can be formed into films, molded into objects, or made into fibers.

pleas·ant |plĕz' ənt| *adj.* **pleasanter, pleasantest** Pleasing; agreeable; delightful: *A pleasant aroma came from the bakery.*

please |plēz| *v.* **pleased, pleasing** To give (someone or something) pleasure or satisfaction.

pleas·ing |plē' zĭng| *adj.* Giving pleasure; agreeable: *Her smile was pleasing.*

pleas·ure |plĕzh' ər| *n., pl.* **pleasures** A feeling of happiness or enjoyment; delight: *She smiled with pleasure.*

plen·ty |plĕn' tē| *n.* A full supply or amount: *Children need plenty of exercise. adj.* More than enough; not few.

pli·ers |plī' ərz| *pl. n.* A tool consisting of a pair of pivoted jaws and a pair of handles, used for holding, bending, or cutting wire.

poach |pōch| *v.* **poached, poaching** To cook in gently boiling liquid.

pock·et |pŏk' ĭt| *n., pl.* **pockets** A small pouch, open at the side or top, that is sewn into or onto a garment for carrying small items.

po•lice |pə lēs′| *pl. n.* The members of a police department. The police keep order, see that laws are obeyed, and try to solve crimes.

pol•ish |pŏl′ ĭsh| *v.* **polished, polishing** To make smooth and shiny, especially by rubbing: *We polish the marble floor regularly. n., pl.* **polishes** A smooth and shiny surface; gloss: *We admired the polish on the new car.*

po•lite |pə līt′| *adj.* **politer, politest** Having or showing good manners; courteous.

History • polite

Polite comes from the Latin word *polītus,* meaning "polished."

pon•cho |pŏn′ chō| *n., pl.* **ponchos 1.** A cloak like a blanket with a hole in the center for the head. **2.** A waterproof poncho worn as a raincoat.

poo•dle |pood′ l| *n., pl.* **poodles** A dog with thick, curly hair.

por•cu•pine |pôr′ kyə pīn′| *n., pl.* **porcupines** An animal whose back and sides are covered with long, sharp quills.

History • porcupine

Porcupine comes from an Old French phrase that meant "spiny pig."

port |pôrt| *n., pl.* **ports** A place along a body of water where ships can dock or anchor.

por•trait |pôr′ trĭt′| *n., pl.* **portraits** A picture of someone's face or sometimes of the whole person.

pose |pōz| *n., pl.* **poses** A position taken, especially for a portrait.

post•script |pōst′ skrĭpt′| *n., pl.* **postscripts** A message added at the end of a letter after the writer's signature.

pot•ter•y |pŏt′ ə rē| *n.* Objects, such as pots, vases, or dishes, that are shaped from moist clay and hardened by heat in a kiln or oven.

pounce |pouns| *v.* **pounced, pouncing** To seize by or as if by swooping: *The kitten pounced on the ball. n., pl.* **pounces** The act of seizing with a swoop.

pound¹ |pound| *n., pl.* **pounds** A unit of weight and mass equal to 16 ounces.

pound² |pound| *n., pl.* **pounds** An enclosed place for keeping stray animals.

pow•er•ful |pou′ ər fəl| *adj.* Having power, authority, or influence; mighty: *The United States of America is a powerful nation.*

prai•rie |prâr′ ē| *n., pl.* **prairies** A wide area of flat or rolling land with tall grass and few trees.

pray |prā| *v.* **prayed, praying** To hope very much.

pre•scrip•tion |prĭ skrĭp′ shən| *n., pl.* **prescriptions** A written instruction from a doctor indicating the medicine or treatment a patient is to receive.

press |prĕs| *n., pl.* **presses** A printing press that prints letters, words, and designs by pressing sheets of paper onto an inked surface.

pret•ty |prĭt′ ē| *adj.* **prettier, prettiest** Pleasing, attractive, or appealing to the eye or ear.

pride |prīd| *n.* Pleasure or satisfaction in accomplishments or possessions: *My parents take pride in their children.*

prince |prĭns| *n., pl.* **princes** The son of a king or queen.

prin•cess |prĭn′ sĭs| or |prĭn′ sĕs′| *n., pl.* **princesses** The daughter of a king or queen.

pris•on |prĭz′ ən| *n., pl.* **prisons** A place where persons convicted of crimes are confined.

prop•er |prŏp′ ər| *adj.* Right for a purpose or occasion; appropriate: *I don't have the proper tools for mending the roof.*

proud |proud| *adj.* **prouder, proudest** Feeling pleased and satisfied over something one owns, makes, does, or is a part of.

prove |proov| *v.* **proved, proved** *or* **proven, proving** To show to be true by or as if by producing evidence or using convincing arguments: *The police could not prove that the person was guilty.*

prowl |proul| *v.* **prowled, prowling** To move about secretly and quietly as if looking for prey: *The cat prowled in the alley.*

pub·lic |pŭb′ lĭk| *adj.* Supported by, used by, or open to all people; not private: *I used a public telephone to make the call.*

pull |pŏŏl| *v.* **pulled, pulling** To apply force to in order to draw someone or something in the direction of the force; tug at: *A team of horses pulled the wagon.*

pump |pŭmp| *n., pl.* **pumps** A device used to move a liquid or gas from one place or container to another: *I filled the balloons with a small air pump.*

punc·tu·ate |pŭngk′ chŏŏ āt′| *v.* **punctuated, punctuating** To mark written or printed material with punctuation.

punc·tu·a·tion |pŭngk′ chŏŏ ā′ shən| *n.* Marks, such as periods, commas, and semicolons, that are used to make the meaning of written or printed material clear.

pun·ish |pŭn′ ĭsh| *v.* **punished, punishing** To cause to suffer for a crime, fault, or misbehavior.

pu·pil |pyŏŏ′ pəl| *n., pl.* **pupils** A young person who is being taught in a school or by a private teacher.

pure |pyŏŏr| *adj.* **purer, purest** Not mixed with anything else: *a cup of pure silver.*

pur·ple |pûr′ pəl| *n., pl.* **purples** A color between blue and red. *adj.* Of the color purple.

push |pŏŏsh| *v.* **pushed, pushing** To press against so as to move away: *I pushed the rock, but it wouldn't budge.*

put |pŏŏt| *v.* **put, putting** To cause to be in a particular position or condition: *Put the bowl on the table. Put the papers in order.*

Q

qual·i·ty |kwŏl′ ĭ tē| *n., pl.* **qualities** A property or feature that makes someone or something what it is: *I used vinegar in the dressing because of its sour quality.*

quar·an·tine |kwôr′ ən tēn′| *n., pl.* **quarantines** The prevention or tight control of the movement of people, animals, plants

ă	pat	ŏ	pot	û	fur
ā	pay	ō	go	*th*	the
â	care	ô	paw, for	th	thin
ä	father	oi	oil	hw	which
ĕ	pet	ŏŏ	book	zh	usual
ē	be	ōō	boot	ə	ago, item
ĭ	pit	yŏŏ	cute		pencil, atom
ī	ice	ou	out		circus
î	near	ŭ	cut	ər	butter

or goods out of a place or region to keep pests or disease from spreading.

quar·ter |kwôr′ tər| *n., pl.* **quarters** One fourth of a year; three months: *Sales were up in the second quarter.*

ques·tion |kwĕs′ chən| *n., pl.* **questions** Something that is asked: *I don't understand your question.*

quick |kwĭk| *adj.* **quicker, quickest** Very fast; rapid: *I turned on the light with a quick motion of my hand.*

quilt |kwĭlt| *v.* **quilted, quilting** To stitch together two layers of fabric with an inner padding of cotton, wool, down, or feathers.

quiv·er |kwĭv′ ər| *v.* **quivered, quivering** To shake with a slight vibrating motion; tremble: *My voice quivered with fear. n., pl.* **quivers** The act or motion of quivering.

R

race |rās| *v.* **raced, racing** **1.** To try to beat in a contest of speed. **2.** To rush at top speed: *I raced home when I heard the news.*

ra·dar |rā′ där′| *n.* A device for finding the location and measuring the speed of distant objects, such as airplanes.

ra·di·o |rā′ dē ō| *n., pl.* **radios** The equipment used to send or receive signals transmitted by radio.

raft |răft| *n., pl.* **rafts** A floating platform made of material such as logs or rubber.

rail·road |rāl′ rōd′| *n., pl.* **railroads** A system of transportation consisting of a railroad and the equipment and property, such as stations, land, and trains, that are needed for its operation.

ranch |rănch| *n., pl.* **ranches** A large farm where cattle, sheep, or horses are raised.

rap·ids |răp′ ĭdz| *pl. n.* A place in a river where the water flows very fast.

ras·cal |răs′ kəl| *n., pl.* **rascals 1.** A person who misbehaves in a playful way. **2.** A scoundrel.

rath·er |răth′ ər| *adv.* **1.** To a certain extent; somewhat: *I'm feeling rather sleepy.* **2.** More willingly: *I'd rather read.*

rat·tle·snake |răt′ l snāk′| *n., pl.* **rattlesnakes** A poisonous American snake that has dry, horny rings at the end of its tail. When the snake shakes its tail, the rings make a rattling sound.

re- A prefix that means: **1.** Again: *replay.* **2.** Back; backward: *recall.*

reach |rēch| *v.* **reached, reaching 1.** To go as far as; arrive at: *We managed to reach the house before it rained.* **2.** To stretch out; extend: *Nerves reach to every part of the body.* **3.** To touch or try to touch by extending a part of the body, as the hand: *I reached for a cup. n., pl.* **reaches 1.** An act of reaching. **2.** The distance or extent of reaching: *The grapes were within reach.*

read·y |rĕd′ ē| *adj.* **readier, readiest** Prepared for action or use: *Are you getting ready for school?*

re·al |rē′ əl| or |rēl| *adj.* **1.** Not artificial; genuine: *A real cat was sitting next to a picture of one.* **2.** Actual, not made up: *This is a story about real people.*

re·ar·range |rē′ ə rānj′| *v.* **rearranged, rearranging** To arrange in a different way or order; reorganize.

rea·son |rē′ zən| *n., pl.* **reasons** An explanation for an act or belief: *These are my reasons for being late. v.* **reasoned, reason-**

ing To use the ability to think clearly and sensibly.

re·build |rē bĭld′| *v.* **rebuilt** |rē bĭlt′|, **rebuilding** To build again; reconstruct.

re·call |rĭ kôl′| *v.* **recalled, recalling** To bring back to mind; remember: *I can't recall their telephone number.*

re·ceive |rĭ sēv′| *v.* **received, receiving** To take or acquire something given, offered, or sent: *I receive an allowance every week.*

rec·og·nize |rĕk′ əg nīz′| *v.* **recognized, recognizing** To know and remember from past experience: *I recognized my old friend right away.*

re·count |rĭ kount′| *v.* **recounted, recounting** To tell in detail; narrate.

re·dec·o·rate |rē dĕk′ ə rāt′| *v.* **redecorated, redecorating** *tr. v.* To change the decor of, as by painting. *intr. v.* To change the decor of a room, building, etc.

re·do |rē dōō′| *v.* **redid** |rē dĭd′|, **redoing** To do again.

reef |rēf| *n., pl.* **reefs** A strip or ridge of rock, sand, or coral that rises to or close to the surface of a body of water.

re·fill |rē fĭl′| *v.* **refilled, refilling** To fill again: *I used all the ice cubes and forgot to refill the tray. n., pl.* **refills** A replacement for something that has been used up.

re·flect |rĭ flĕkt′| *v.* **reflected, reflecting** To give back an image of, as a mirror does.

re·fresh |rĭ frĕsh′| *v.* **refreshed, refreshing** To make fresh again with food or rest.

re·fresh·ment |rĭ frĕsh′ mənt| *n., pl.* **refreshments** A light meal or snack.

re·heat |rē hēt′| *v.* **reheated, reheating** To heat again.

reign |rān| *n., pl.* **reigns** The power or rule of a monarch. *v.* **reigned, reigning** To rule as a monarch.
 ◆ *These sound alike* **reign, rein.**

rein |rān| *n., pl.* **reins** A long, narrow, leather strap attached to the bit of a bridle and held by the rider or driver to control an animal.
 ◆ *These sound alike* **rein, reign.**

re·late |rĭ lāt′| *v.* **related, relating 1.** To tell or narrate: *I related the story of our trip.* **2.** To have a relationship or connection to: *Family members are related.*

re·la·tion |rĭ lā′ shən| *n., pl.* **relations** A connection or association between two or more things.

rel·a·tive |rĕl′ ə tĭv| *n., pl.* **relatives** A person related to another by family.

re·lay |rē′ lā′| or |rĭ lā′| *v.* **relayed, relaying** To pass or send along: *The principal relayed the message to the teacher.*

re·make |rē māk′| *v.* **remade** |rē mād′|, **remaking** To make anew; reconstruct.

re·mem·ber |rĭ mĕm′ bər| *v.* **remembered, remembering 1.** To bring back to the mind; think of again; recall: *I could not remember how to stop the machine.* **2.** To keep carefully in one's memory: *Remember that we have to leave early tonight.*

re·paint |rē pānt′| *v.* **repainted, repainting** To paint again.

re·port·er |rĭ pôr′ tər| *n., pl.* **reporters** A person who gathers and reports news for a newspaper or magazine or for a radio or television station.

re·read |rē rēd′| *v.* **reread** |rē rĕd′|, **rereading** To read again.

res·cue |rĕs′ kyōo| *v.* **rescued, rescuing** To save from danger or harm: *Lifeguards learn how to rescue swimmers.* *n., pl.* **rescues** An act of rescuing or saving.

re·source·ful |rĭ sôrs′ fəl| or |rĭ sōrs′ fəl| *adj.* Clever and imaginative, especially in finding ways to deal with a difficult situation.

res·tau·rant |rĕs′ tər ənt| *n., pl.* **restaurants** A place where meals are served to the public.

rest·less |rĕst′ lĭs| *adj.* Unable to rest, relax, or be still: *The baby is restless.*

re·ward |rĭ wôrd′| *n., pl.* **rewards** Something that is offered, given, or received in return for a worthy act, service, or accomplishment.

re·wind |rē wīnd′| *v.* **rewound** |rē wound′|, **rewinding** To wind again.

re·write |rē rīt′| *v.* **rewrote** |rē rōt′|, **rewritten** |rē rĭt′ n|, **rewriting** To write again, especially in a different or improved form.

rhyme |rīm| *n., pl.* **rhymes** A poem that has the same or similar sounds at the ends of lines.

ă	pat	ŏ	pot	û	fur
ā	pay	ō	go	*th*	the
â	care	ô	paw, for	th	thin
ä	father	oi	oil	hw	which
ĕ	pet	ōō	book	zh	usual
ē	be	ōō	boot	ə	ago, item
ĭ	pit	yōo	cute		pencil, atom
ī	ice	ou	out		circus
î	near	ŭ	cut	ər	butter

ridge |rĭj| *n., pl.* **ridges** A long, narrow peak or crest of something: *the ridge of a roof.*

rig·ging |rĭg′ ĭng| *n.* The system of ropes, chains, and tackle used to support and control the masts, sails, and yards of a sailing vessel.

rig·id |rĭj′ ĭd| *adj.* Not bending; stiff; inflexible: *When you salute, keep your arm rigid.*

ring¹ |rĭng| *n., pl.* **rings** A circular band that is worn on a finger or is used to encircle or hold something.
   ♦ *These sound alike* **ring, wring.**

ring² |rĭng| *n., pl.* **rings** The clear piercing sound made by a bell.
   ♦ *These sound alike* **ring, wring.**

rink |rĭngk| *n., pl.* **rinks** An area with a smooth surface for skating.

ripe |rīp| *adj.* **riper, ripest** Fully grown and developed: *We ate ripe peaches and berries for dessert.*

risk |rĭsk| *n., pl.* **risks** The possibility of suffering harm or loss.

ri·val |rī′ vəl| *n., pl.* **rivals** Someone who tries to do as well as or better than another; competitor.

rob·in |rŏb′ ĭn| *n., pl.* **robins** A North American songbird with a rust-red breast and a dark gray back.

rock·et |rŏk′ ĭt| *n., pl.* **rockets** A device that is driven through the air by an explosive or by rapidly burning liquid or solid fuel. A rocket is tube-shaped, with one end open. Gases from the explosive or fuel escape from the open end. Large rockets carry space capsules into space. *v.* **rocketed, rocketing** To travel very fast in or as if in a rocket: *The train rocketed by.*

ro·de·o |rō′ dē ō′| or |rō dā′ ō| *n., pl.* **rodeos** A show in which cowboys and cowgirls display their skill in riding horses and steers and compete in events such as roping cattle.

roof |rōof| or |rŏŏf| *n., pl.* **roofs** The outside top covering of a building.

route |rōot| or |rout| *n., pl.* **routes** A road or course of travel between two places.

rou·tine |rōō tēn′| *n., pl.* **routines** A series of regular or usual activities; standard procedure: *a daily routine.*

rub |rŭb| *v.* **rubbed, rubbing** To put or spread on by rubbing: *Rub some stain on the boards. n., pl.* **rubs** An act of rubbing.

run·way |rŭn′ wā′| *n., pl.* **runways** A strip of level ground, usually paved, on which aircraft take off and land.

S

Sac·ra·men·to |săk′ rə měn′ tō| The capital of California.

sad·dle |săd′ l| *n., pl.* **saddles** A seat for a rider, as of a horse or bicycle. *v.* **saddled, saddling** To put a saddle on.

sad·ly |săd′ lē| *adv.* Sorrowfully; with regret: *She spoke sadly about her loss.*

safe |sāf| *adj.* **safer, safest 1.** Secure or free from danger, risk, or harm. **2.** Providing protection: *Let's put the silver in a safe place.* **3.** Showing caution; careful: *His sister is a safe driver. n., pl.* **safes** A metal container in which valuable things are kept for protection.

safe·ly |sāf′ lē| *adv.* Without harm.

safe·ty |sāf′ tē| *n., pl.* **safeties** Being safe; freedom from danger, accident, injury, or threat of harm.

sail·or |sā′ lər| *n., pl.* **sailors** A person who sails, especially as a member of a ship's crew.

Saint Ber·nard |sānt bər närd′| *n., pl.* **Saint Bernards** A large, strong dog that was originally used to rescue lost travelers in the mountains of Switzerland.

sal·ad |săl′ əd| *n., pl.* **salads** A cold dish of raw vegetables or fruit, often served with a dressing.

sale |sāl| *n., pl.* **sales 1.** The act of selling. **2.** A sale of goods at reduced prices.

salt·y |sôl′ tē| *adj.* **saltier, saltiest** Of, containing, tasting of, or full of salt.

sat·el·lite |săt′ l īt′| *n., pl.* **satellites** An object launched by a rocket in order to orbit and perhaps study a heavenly body.

sauce |sôs| *n., pl.* **sauces** A liquid dressing or relish served with food.

sav·ing |sā′ vĭng| *n., pl.* **savings** Money saved.

say |sā| *v.* **said** |sĕd|, **saying, says** |sĕz| To utter aloud; speak: *I said hello.*

scar |skär| *v.* **scarred, scarring** To mark with or form a scar from a healed wound.

scarce |skârs| *adj.* **scarcer, scarcest 1.** Not enough to meet a demand: *Food is scarce in some countries.* **2.** Not often found; rare: *Scarce supplies of coal.*

scare |skâr| *v.* **scared, scaring 1.** To frighten or become frightened. **2.** To frighten or drive away. *n., pl.* **scares** A sense of fear.

scarf |skärf| *n., pl.* **scarfs** *or* **scarves** |skärvz| A piece of cloth that is worn around the neck or head.

school |skōol| *n., pl.* **schools** A place for teaching and learning. *adj.: a school bus.*

schoo·ner |skōō′ nər| *n., pl.* **schooners** A ship with two or more masts and sails that are set lengthwise.

score |skôr| *n., pl.* **scores** The number of points made by each participant in a game, contest, or test.

scout |skout| *v.* **scouted, scouting** To observe or explore carefully for information.

scraw·ny |skrô′ nē| *adj.* **scrawnier, scrawniest** Thin and bony; skinny.

scraw·ni·ness |skrô′ nē nĭs| *n.* Condition of being scrawny.

scream |skrēm| *v.* **screamed, screaming** To make a long, loud, piercing cry.

screw·driv·er |skrōō′ drī′ vər| *n.,* *pl.* **screwdrivers** A tool that is used to turn screws.

scu·ba |skōō′ bə| *n.* One or more tanks of compressed air, worn on the back by divers for breathing underwater.

scu·ba di·ver |skōō′ bə dī′ vər| *n.,* *pl.* **scuba divers** One who uses scuba gear in underwater swimming.

sea·coast |sē′ kōst′| *n., pl.* **seacoasts** Land along the sea.

search |sûrch| *v.* **searched, searching** **1.** To look thoroughly and carefully: *We searched for fossils in the rocks.* **2.** To look over or go through carefully to find something. *n., pl.* **searches** An act or example of searching.

sea·son |sē′ zən| *n., pl.* **seasons** **1.** One of the four equal natural divisions of the year. The seasons are spring, summer, autumn, and winter. **2.** A period of the year marked by a certain activity or event: *Winter in New England is the skiing season.*

seat belt |sēt bĕlt| *n., pl.* **seat belts** A safety strap or harness that is designed to hold a person securely in a seat, as in a car or airplane.

sec·ond |sĕk′ ənd| *n., pl.* **seconds** The number in a series that matches the number two.

se·cret |sē′ krĭt| *adj.* Hidden from general knowledge or view.

seek |sēk| *v.* **sought** |sôt|, **seeking** To try to find; search.

seem |sēm| *v.* **seemed, seeming** To give the impression of being; appear to be: *You seem worried.*

sel·dom |sĕl′ dəm| *adv.* Not often; rarely.

set·tle |sĕt′ l| *v.* **settled, settling** To make a home or place to live in: *Pioneers settled the West.*

sev·en |sĕv′ ən| *n., pl.* **sevens** The number, written 7, that is equal to the sum of 6 + 1. *adj.* Being one more than six.

sev·er·al |sĕv′ ər əl| *adj.* More than two but not many: *We live several miles away.* *n.* More than two people or things.

ă	pat	ŏ	pot	û	fur
ā	pay	ō	go	*th*	the
â	care	ô	paw, for	th	thin
ä	father	oi	oil	hw	which
ĕ	pet	ōō	book	zh	usual
ē	be	ōō	boot	ə	ago, item
ĭ	pit	yōō	cute		pencil, atom
ī	ice	ou	out		circus
î	near	ŭ	cut	ər	butter

shall |shăl| *helping v., past tense* **should** Used to show: **1.** Something that will take place or exist in the future: *We shall arrive tomorrow.* **2.** The will to do something or make something happen: *I shall not cry.*

shape |shāp| *n., pl.* **shapes** **1.** The outer form of an object; outline: *We drew circles, triangles, and other shapes.* **2.** Proper physical condition or mechanical order: *Athletes must stay in shape.*

shark |shärk| *n., pl.* **sharks** A large, fierce ocean fish that has a big mouth and sharp teeth.

sharp |shärp| *adj.* **sharper, sharpest** **1.** Having a thin edge that cuts or a fine point that pierces. **2.** Not rounded or blunt; pointed. *adv.* Exactly; precisely: *It's three o'clock sharp.*

shel·ter |shĕl′ tər| *n., pl.* **shelters** Something that protects or covers.

sher·iff |shĕr′ ĭf| *n., pl.* **sheriffs** A county official who is in charge of enforcing the law.

shine |shīn| *v.* **shone** |shōn|, **shining** To give off light or reflect light; glow.

ship·wreck |shĭp′ rĕk′| *n., pl.* **shipwrecks** A wrecked ship.

shirt |shûrt| *n., pl.* **shirts** A garment for the upper part of the body. A shirt usually has a collar, sleeves, and an opening in the front.

shock |shŏk| *n., pl.* **shocks** **1.** A mental or emotional upset caused by something that happens suddenly; a bad surprise. **2.** The feeling caused by the passage of an electric current through the body.

shoe |shōō| *n., pl.* **shoes** An outer covering for the foot. A typical shoe has a stiff sole and heel and a flexible upper part.

shook |shŏŏk| *v.* Past tense of **shake**: *The puppy shook with fear.*

shoot |shōōt| *v.* **shot** |shŏt|, **shooting** To send or be sent forth with great force or speed: *They shot a rocket into outer space.*

shout |shout| *v.* **shouted, shouting** To cry out or say loudly; yell. *n., pl.* **shouts** A loud cry or yell.

show·er |shou′ ər| *n., pl.* **showers** A brief fall of rain.

shown |shōn| *v.* A past participle of **show**: *We have shown our pictures to the travel club.*

shut |shŭt| *v.* **shut, shutting** To move into a closed position: *Shut the door.*

shut·ter |shŭt′ ər| *n., pl.* **shutters** A movable cover over a camera lens that opens for an instant to let in light.

sick·ness |sĭk′ nĭs| *n., pl.* **sicknesses** The condition of being sick or without health; illness.

sift |sĭft| *v.* **sifted, sifting** To remove lumps or large chunks from by shaking or pushing through a sieve.

sigh |sī| *v.* **sighed, sighing** To let out a long, deep breath because of fatigue, sorrow, or relief. *n., pl.* **sighs** The act or sound of sighing.

sight |sīt| *n., pl.* **sights** The ability to see; vision.

si·lent |sī′ lənt| *adj.* **1.** Making or having no sound; quiet. **2.** Not pronounced or sounded: *The "k" in "knife" is silent.*

sil·ver |sĭl′ vər| *n.* A soft shiny white metal that is one of the chemical elements. Silver is used to make coins, jewelry, and table utensils.

sim·mer |sĭm′ ər| *v.* **simmered, simmering** To cook below or just at the boiling point: *The soup simmered on the stove.*

sim·ple |sĭm′ pəl| *adj.* **simpler, simplest** Not complicated; easy: *simple directions.*

since |sĭns| *adv.* Before now; ago: *I've long since forgotten.*

sing·er |sĭng′ ər| *n., pl.* **singers** Someone who performs songs, especially someone who has had special training.

sink |sĭngk| *n., pl.* **sinks** A basin with a drain and faucets for turning on and off a water supply.

si·ren |sī′ rən| *n., pl.* **sirens** A device that makes a loud whistling or wailing sound as a signal or warning.

skate |skāt| *n., pl.* **skates** A boot, shoe, or metal frame having a metal blade used for gliding on ice. *v.* **skated, skating** To move along on skates.

ski |skē| *v.* **skied, skiing** To move along over snow on skis.

skill |skĭl| *n., pl.* **skills** The ability to do something well.

skip |skĭp| *v.* **skipped, skipping** To jump lightly over: *I like to skip rope.*

sled |slĕd| *v.* **sledded, sledding** To ride on a sled.

sleigh |slā| *n., pl.* **sleighs** A vehicle on runners that is usually pulled by a horse over ice or snow.

slow |slō| *adj.* **slower, slowest** Not moving or able to move quickly; proceeding at a low speed: *a slow car.*

slow·ly |slō′ lē| *adv.* Proceeding at a low speed: *I drove slowly down the street.*

slum·ber |slŭm′ bər| *v.* **slumbered, slumbering** To sleep; doze. *n., pl.* **slumbers** Sleep.

small |smôl| *adj.* **smaller, smallest** Little in size, amount, or extent.

smell |smĕl| *v.* **smelled** *or* **smelt, smelling** To detect the odor of by using sense organs in the nose; to sniff: *I smell smoke.*

smile |smīl| *n., pl.* **smiles** A pleased or happy expression on the face formed by curving the corners of the mouth upward.

smoke |smōk| *n.* The mixture of gases and particles of carbon that rises from burning material.

smooth |smōōth| *adj.* **smoother, smoothest** Having a surface that is not rough or uneven.

snap |snăp| *v.* **snapped, snapping** To make or cause to make a sharp cracking sound.

snow |snō| *n., pl.* **snows** Soft white crystals of ice that form from water vapor in the upper air and fall to earth.

snow•mo•bile |snō' mō bēl'| *n., pl.* **snow-mobiles** A vehicle like a sled with a motor, used for traveling over snow.

soap |sōp| *n., pl.* **soaps** A substance that is usually made from fat and lye and is used for washing. *v.* **soaped, soaping** To treat, rub, or cover with soap.

sock |sŏk| *n., pl.* **socks** A short, knitted or woven covering for the foot that reaches above the ankle and ends below the knee.

soft |sôft| *adj.* **softer, softest** Not hard or firm.

sof•ten |sô' fən| *v.* **softened, softening** To make or become soft or softer.

so•lar |sō' lər| *adj.* Of or relating to the sun.

some•times |sŭm' tīmz'| *adv.* Now and then: *I see them sometimes but not often.*

soot |soŏt| *n.* A fine, black powder produced when something, such as wood or coal, burns.

sor•ry |sŏr' ē| *adj.* **sorrier, sorriest** Feeling sorrow, sympathy, pity, or regret: *I'm sorry I'm late.*

sound |sound| *n., pl.* **sounds** A kind of vibration that travels through a substance, such as air, and can be heard.

soup |soōp| *n., pl.* **soups** A liquid food prepared from meat, fish, or vegetable broth, often with various solid ingredients added.

south |south| *adv.* Toward the direction to the left of a person who faces the sunset: *We drove south to the camp. adj.* Of, in, or toward the south: *The south side.*

south•ern |sŭth' ərn| *adj.* Of, in, or toward the south: *We drove through the southern states.*

space shut•tle |spās shŭt' l| *n., pl.* **space shuttles** A space vehicle designed to carry astronauts back and forth between the earth and an orbiting space station.

span•iel |spăn' yəl| *n., pl.* **spaniels** A dog of small or medium size with drooping ears, short legs, and a silky wavy coat.

ă	pat	ŏ	pot	û	fur
ā	pay	ō	go	*th*	the
â	care	ô	paw, for	th	thin
ä	father	oi	oil	hw	which
ĕ	pet	oo	book	zh	usual
ē	be	oo	boot	ə	ago, item
ĭ	pit	yoo	cute		pencil, atom
ī	ice	ou	out		circus
î	near	ŭ	cut	ər	butter

spare |spâr| *v.* **spared, sparing** To show mercy or consideration to: *I tried to spare your feelings by not telling you about the problem. adj.* **sparer, sparest** Beyond what is needed; extra: *Do you have any spare change?*

speak |spēk| *v.* **spoke** |spōk|, **spoken, speaking** To utter words; talk.

spear |spîr| *n., pl.* **spears** A weapon with a long shaft and a sharply pointed head.

spe•cial |spesh' əl| *adj.* Different from what is common or usual; exceptional: *Birthdays are special occasions.*

speck•led |spĕk' əld| *adj.* Dotted or covered with small spots, especially a natural marking.

speed |spēd| *n., pl.* **speeds** The condition of moving or acting rapidly; quickness: *You work with amazing speed.*

spent |spĕnt| *v.* Past tense and past participle of **spend**: *I saved my allowance, but Jolen spent hers.*

spic•y |spī' sē| *adj.* **spicier, spiciest** Flavored with a spice or spices.

spi•der |spī' dər| *n., pl.* **spiders** An animal with eight legs and a body divided into two parts that spins webs to catch insects.

spoke |spōk| *v.* Past tense of **speak.** Said: *We spoke to her by phone.*

sponge |spŭnj| *n., pl.* **sponges** A water animal that has a soft skeleton with many small holes that absorb water.

spoon |spoōn| *n., pl.* **spoons** A utensil with a shallow bowl at the end of its handle. Spoons are used in measuring, serving, or eating food.

spruce |sproōs| *n., pl.* **spruces** An evergreen tree with short needles and soft wood.

square |skwâr| *n., pl.* **squares** A rectangle having four equal sides.

squid |skwĭd| *n., pl.* **squids** *or* **squid** A sea animal that is related to the octopus and has a long body and ten arms.

squire |skwīr| *n., pl.* **squires** A young man of noble birth who served a knight.

squir·rel |skwûr′ əl| *n., pl.* **squirrels** Any of several animals with gray, reddish-brown, or black fur and a bushy tail. Squirrels climb trees.

stage |stāj| *n., pl.* **stages** The raised platform in a theater on which entertainers perform.

stage·coach |stāj′ kōch′| *n., pl.* **stage-coaches** A coach with four wheels that is drawn by horses. Stagecoaches were once used to carry mail, baggage, and passengers.

stair |stâr| *n., pl.* **stairs** **1. stairs** A series or flight of steps; staircase. **2.** One of a flight of steps.

stam·pede |stăm pēd′| *n., pl.* **stampedes** A sudden rush of startled animals, such as cattle. *v.* **stampeded, stampeding** To take or cause to take part in a stampede.

star |stär| *n., pl.* **stars** A heavenly body that appears as a very bright point in the sky at night.

stare |stâr| *v.* **stared, staring** To look with a steady, often wide-eyed gaze. *n., pl.* **stares** A staring gaze.

start |stärt| *v.* **started, starting** To begin to move, go, or act.

star·tle |stär′ tl| *v.* **startled, startling** **1.** To cause to make a sudden movement, as of surprise: *A thud on the roof startled us.* **2.** To fill with sudden alarm.

starve |stärv| *v.* **starved, starving** **1.** To suffer or die from lack of food. **2.** To suffer or cause to suffer from a lack of something necessary: *The plants are starving for water.*

state·ment |stāt′ mənt| *n., pl.* **statements** Something expressed in words; a declaration.

steak |stāk| *n., pl.* **steaks** A slice of meat, as beef or fish, that is usually broiled or fried.

steal |stēl| *v.* **stole** |stōl|, **stolen, stealing** **1.** To take without right or permission: *Someone stole my bicycle.* **2.** To move very quietly: *A big cat stole through the garden.*

◆ *These sound alike* **steal, steel.**

stealth |stĕlth| *n.* The act of moving in a quiet, secret way so as to avoid notice.

steel |stēl| *n.* **1.** A metal made from iron and carbon.

◆ *These sound alike* **steel, steal.**

stee·ple |stē′ pəl| *n., pl.* **steeples** A tall tower that rises from the roof of a building, especially one on a church or courthouse.

steer |stîr| *v.* **steered, steering** To direct the course of: *The pilot steered the ship to the dock.*

stel·lar |stĕl′ ər| *adj.* Of or consisting of a star or stars.

sten·cil |stĕn′ səl| *v.* **stenciled** *or* **stencilled, stenciling** *or* **stencilling** To apply ink or paint to a sheet of material, such as paper, out of which letters or designs have been cut. When ink is applied, the patterns appear on the surface beneath.

stern |stûrn| *n., pl.* **sterns** The rear part of a ship or boat.

still |stĭl| *adj.* **stiller, stillest** Without motion; calm: *The air was still before the storm.*

sting |stĭng| *v.* **stung** |stŭng|, **stinging** **1.** To prick or wound with a small, sharp point: *A bee stung me on the foot.* **2.** To feel or cause to feel a sharp, burning pain: *My ears stung with the cold.* *n., pl.* **stings** The act of stinging.

stir·rup |stûr′ əp| *n., pl.* **stirrups** A ring or loop hanging by a strap from a saddle to support a rider's foot.

stock |stŏk| *n., pl.* **stocks** **1.** A supply for future use: *The farmer had a stock of grain for winter.* **2.** Animals, such as cows, sheep, or pigs, that are raised on a farm or ranch; livestock. *v.* **stocked, stocking** To provide with, keep, or lay in a supply of: *We stocked the cupboard with food. adj.* Kept regularly on hand for sale.

sto•len |stō′ lən| *v.* Past participle of **steal:** *My lunch was stolen.*

stom•ach |stŭm′ ək| *n., pl.* **stomachs** The large muscular pouch into which food passes when it leaves the mouth and esophagus and in which digestion takes place.

ston•y |stō′ nē| *adj.* **stonier, stoniest** Of, full of, or covered with stones.

stood |stŏŏd| *v.* Past tense and past participle of **stand:** *I stood on a footstool.*

stool |stŏŏl| *n., pl.* **stools** A seat without arms or a back.

storm |stôrm| *n., pl.* **storms** A strong wind with rain, hail, sleet, or snow. *v.* **stormed, storming** To blow with a strong wind and rain, hail, sleet, or snow.

sto•ry |stôr′ ē| *n., pl.* **stories** A tale made up to entertain people: *I just read an adventure story.*

straight |strāt| *adj.* **straighter, straightest** Not curving, curling, or bending: *I have straight hair.*

strange |strānj| *adj.* **stranger, strangest** Not ordinary; unusual.

strength•en |strĕngk′ thən| *v.* **strengthened, strengthening** To make or become strong.

stretch |strĕch| *v.* **stretched, stretching** To flex the muscles: *It feels good to stretch after a long drive.*

strip |strĭp| *v.* **stripped, stripping** To remove the covering from.

stripe |strīp| *n., pl.* **stripes** A long, narrow band of color or material that is different from its background.

striped |strīpt| *adj.* Having long, narrow lines of different colors.

strive |strīv| *v.* **strove** |strōv|, **striven** |strĭv′ ən|, *or* **strived, striving 1.** To exert much effort or energy; to reach a goal: *We must strive to improve working condi-*

ă	pat	ŏ	pot	û	fur
ā	pay	ō	go	*th*	the
â	care	ô	paw, for	th	thin
ä	father	oi	oil	hw	which
ĕ	pet	ŏŏ	book	zh	usual
ē	be	ŏŏ	boot	ə	ago, item
ĭ	pit	yŏŏ	cute		pencil, atom
ī	ice	ou	out		circus
î	near	ŭ	cut	ər	butter

tions. **2.** To struggle; contend: *The pioneers had to strive against great odds.*

struck |strŭk| *v.* Past tense and past participle of **strike:** *The batter struck the ball.*

stud•y |stŭd′ ē| *v.* **studied, studying** To try to learn: *We study Spanish.*

style |stīl| *n., pl.* **styles** A way of dressing or acting that is fashionable: *My clothes are out of style.*

sub•merge |səb mûrj′| *v.* **submerged, submerging** To cover with water: *Huge waves submerged the pier.*

sud•den |sŭd′ n| *adj.* Happening or arriving without warning: *We were caught in a sudden snowstorm.*

suf•fer |sŭf′ ər| *v.* **suffered, suffering** To feel pain or distress: *The dog was suffering in the hot weather.*

sug•ar |shŏŏg′ ər| *n., pl.* **sugars** A sweet substance gotten mainly from sugar beets or sugar cane. Sugar sweetens food.

sug•ges•tion |səg jĕs′ chən| *n., pl.* **suggestions** Something offered for consideration: *At the train conductor's suggestion we moved to a seat that had a better view.*

suit |sŏŏt| *n., pl.* **suits** A set of clothes to be used together: *We put on our gym suits.*

sum |sŭm| *n., pl.* **sums** **1.** The result of the operation of addition: *The sum of 2 + 2 is 4.* **2.** The whole amount: *The sum of my knowledge is very small.*

sum•mer |sŭm′ ər| *n., pl.* **summers** The hottest season of the year, between spring and autumn.

sun•ny |sŭn′ ē| *adj.* **sunnier, sunniest** Full of sunshine: *Let's hope for a sunny day.*

su•perb |sŏŏ pûrb′| *adj.* Being the very best; excellent; magnificent: *Your grades are superb.*

sup·ply |sə plī′| *n., pl.* **supplies** Necessary materials kept and used or given out when needed: *After three months, the explorers' supplies ran out.*

sup·port |sə pôrt′| *v.* **supported, supporting** To keep from falling; hold in position: *Two steel towers support the bridge.*

sup·pose |sə pōz′| *v.* **supposed, supposing** To be inclined to think; assume: *I suppose you're right.*

sup·po·si·tion |sŭp′ ə zĭsh′ ən| *n., pl.* **suppositions** The mental process of supposing; guesswork: *The idea that the cat broke the vase is pure supposition.*

sur·ger·y |sûr′ jə rē| *n.* A branch of medicine in which injury and disease are treated by cutting into and removing or repairing parts of the body.

sur·vive |sər vīv′| *v.* **survived, surviving** To stay alive or in existence.

sweet |swēt| *adj.* **sweeter, sweetest 1.** Having a pleasing taste like that of sugar. **2.** Not sour: *This milk is still sweet.*

swift |swĭft| *adj.* **swifter, swiftest** Moving or able to move very fast.

T

tal·ent |tăl′ ənt| *n., pl.* **talents** A natural ability to do something well: *If you give up music, you'll waste your talent.*

talk |tôk| *v.* **talked, talking** To say words.

tan |tăn| *v.* **tanned, tanning** To make or become brown from the sun.

tank |tăngk| *n., pl.* **tanks** A large container for holding compressed air, worn on the back by divers for breathing underwater.

tap |tăp| *v.* **tapped, tapping** To strike gently with a light blow: *I tapped my friend on the shoulder.*

teach·er |tē′ chər| *n., pl.* **teachers** A person who gives instructions or provides knowledge, usually in a school.

tear[1] |târ| *v.* **tore** |tôr| or |tōr|, **torn** |tôrn| or |tōrn|, **tearing** To pull or divide into pieces; split; rip.

tear[2] |tîr| *n., pl.* **tears** A drop of the clear liquid secreted by glands of the eyes.

tem·per |tĕm′ pər| *n., pl.* **tempers** A person's usual state of mind or emotions; disposition.

ten·der |tĕn′ dər| *adj.* **tenderer, tenderest 1.** Fragile. **2.** Not tough. **3.** Painful; sore. **4.** Gentle; loving.

tent |tĕnt| *n., pl.* **tents** A portable shelter, as of canvas, usually supported by poles.

ter·mi·nal |tûr′ mə nəl| *n., pl.* **terminals** A station at the end of a railway, bus line, or air line.

ter·ri·er |tĕr′ ē ər| *n., pl.* **terriers** A small, active dog that was once used for hunting small animals in their burrows.

thank·ful |thăngk′ fəl| *adj.* Showing or feeling gratitude; grateful.

thatch |thăch| *v.* **thatched, thatching** To cover with plant material, such as straw or reeds: *a thatched roof.*

their |thâr| *pron.* Relating or belonging to them: *They put their boots in the closet.*
   ◆ *These sound alike* **their, there, they're.**

there |thâr| *adv.* At or in that place: *Set the package there on the table.*
   ◆ *These sound alike* **there, their, they're.**

they're |thâr| Contraction of "they are."
   ◆ *These sound alike* **they're, their, there.**

third |thûrd| *n., pl.* **thirds 1.** The number in a series that matches the number three. **2.** One of three equal parts, written 1/3. *adj.* Coming after the second.

thir·teen |thûr′ tēn′| *n., pl.* **thirteens** The number, written 13, that is equal to the sum of 12 + 1. *adj.* Being one more than twelve.

thir·ty |thûr′ tē| *n., pl.* **thirties** The number, written 30, that is equal to the product of 10 × 3. *adj.* Being equal to ten times three.

thor•ough•bred |thûr′ ō brĕd′| or |thûr′ ə brĕd′| or |thŭr′ brĕd′| *n.* An animal bred of pure or pedigreed stock.

threat•en |thrĕt′ n| *v.* **threatened, threatening** To be a threat to; endanger: *Landslides threatened the village.*

three |thrē| *n., pl.* **threes** The number, written 3, that is equal to the sum of 2 + 1. *adj.* Being one more than two.

threw |thrōō| *v.* Past tense of **throw.**
◆ *These sound alike* **threw, through.**

through |thrōō| *prep.* In one side and out the other side of: *We walked through the park.*
◆ *These sound alike* **through, threw.**

thumb |thŭm| *n., pl.* **thumbs** A short, thick first finger of the human hand.
◇ *Idiom* **all thumbs** Clumsy; awkward.

thun•der |thŭn′ dər| *n.* The deep, rumbling noise that goes with or comes after a flash of lightning.

tick•et |tĭk′ ĭt| *n., pl.* **tickets** A paper slip or card that gives a person the right to a service, such as a bus ride or entrance to a theater.

ti•ger |tī gər| *n., pl.* **tigers** A large animal of Asia that belongs to the cat family. A tiger has light brown fur with black stripes.

tight |tīt| *adj.* **tighter, tightest** Not letting water or air pass through: *We were warm that night in our tight little cabin.*

tin |tĭn| *n., pl.* **tins** A soft, shiny metal that hardly rusts at all and is used to coat other metals. Tin is a chemical element.

ti•ny |tī′ nē| *adj.* **tinier, tiniest** Extremely small.

tire |tīr| *v.* **tired, tiring** To make or become weak from work or effort; weary: *The long walk tired me.*

tis•sue |tĭsh′ ōō| *n., pl.* **tissues 1.** Often **tissue paper** Light, thin paper used for wrapping. **2.** A piece of soft, absorbent paper used as a handkerchief.

ti•tle |tīt′ l| *n., pl.* **titles 1.** An identifying name given to a book, painting, song, or other work. **2.** A word or name given to a person to show his or her rank, office, or occupation. Some titles are *Mr., Ms., Dr., Senator,* and *Judge.*

ă	pat	ŏ	pot	û	fur
ā	pay	ō	go	*th*	the
â	care	ô	paw, for	th	thin
ä	father	oi	oil	hw	which
ĕ	pet	ōō	book	zh	usual
ē	be	ōō	boot	ə	ago, item
ĭ	pit	yōō	cute		pencil, atom
ī	ice	ou	out		circus
î	near	ŭ	cut	ər	butter

to•bog•gan |tə bŏg′ ən| *n., pl.* **toboggans** A long, narrow sled without runners. A toboggan curves upward at the front.

to•day |tə dā′| *adv.* During or on the present day. *n.* The present day, time, or age: *Are the athletes of today better than those of the past?*

to•geth•er |tə gĕth′ ər| *adv.* In or into a single group or place; with each other; not apart: *Many people were crowded together. We went to school together.*

to•mor•row |tə môr′ ō| *n.* The day after today.

tool |tōōl| *n., pl.* **tools** A device, such as a hammer or an axe, that is especially made or shaped to help a person do work. *v.* **tooled, tooling** To shape or decorate with tools.

tooth |tōōth| *n., pl.* **teeth** |tēth| One of a set of hard, bony parts in the mouth that are used to chew and bite.

To•pe•ka |tə pē′ kə| The capital of Kansas.

top•ic |tŏp′ ĭk| *n., pl.* **topics** A subject treated in a speech, conversation, or piece of writing: *Always support the main topic of your paragraph with details.*

to•tal |tōt′ l| *adj.* Absolute; complete: *Our play was a total success.*

to•tal•i•ty |tō tăl′ ĭ tē| *n., pl.* **totalities** A total amount; a sum.

tour•na•ment |tûr′ nə mənt| *n., pl.* **tournaments** A medieval contest between jousting knights.

tow•el |tou′ əl| *n., pl.* **towels** A piece of cloth or paper used for wiping or drying something that is wet.
◇ *Idiom* **throw in the towel** To admit defeat.

trace |trās| *v.* **traced, tracing 1.** To follow the track, course, or trail of: *The post office tried to trace the lost letter.* **2.** To copy by following lines seen through a sheet of transparent paper.

track |trăk| *n., pl.* **tracks** A rail or set of rails for vehicles such as trains to run on.

trav•el |trăv′ əl| *v.* **traveled, traveling** To go from one place to another; journey: *The whole family traveled around the world.*

treat•ment |trēt′ mənt| *n., pl.* **treatments** The use of something to relieve or cure a disease.

trem•ble |trĕm′ bəl| *v.* **trembled, trembling** To shake or shiver: *A slight breeze made the leaves on the tree tremble.*

Tren•ton |trĕn′ tən| The capital of New Jersey.

tri•fle |trī′ fəl| *n., pl.* **trifles 1.** Something unimportant or worthless. **2.** A small amount.

trou•ble |trŭb′ əl| *n., pl.* **troubles** A difficult, dangerous, or upsetting situation: *The damaged ship was in trouble.*

true |trōō| *adj.* **truer, truest** Being in agreement with fact or reality; accurate.

trunk |trŭngk| *n., pl.* **trunks 1.** The often tall, thick, woody main stem of a tree. **2.** The covered compartment of an automobile, used for storage.

truth |trōōth| *n., pl.* **truths 1.** The quality or condition of being true or accurate: *There was truth in what she said.* **2.** Something that is true: *I told him the truth.*

tube |tōōb| or |tyōōb| *n., pl.* **tubes** A flexible container from which substances such as toothpaste can be squeezed out.

tu•na |tōō′ nə| or |tyōō′ nə| *n., pl.* **tuna** or **tunas** An often large ocean fish caught in great numbers for food. Some tuna can be as long as 14 feet and can weigh 1,600 pounds.

tune |tōōn| or |tyōōn| *n., pl.* **tunes** A melody, especially one that is simple and easy to remember.

tur•key |tûr′ kē| *n., pl.* **turkeys** A large North American bird that is raised for food.

twice |twīs| *adv.* Two times: *He saw the movie twice.*

type |tīp| *n., pl.* **types** A group, kind, or class sharing common traits or characteristics: *What type of sailboat is that? v.* **typed, typing** To write with a typewriter.

U

ug•ly |ŭg′ lē| *adj.* **uglier, ugliest** Not pleasing to look at: *I think the hat is ugly.*

un- A prefix that means: **1.** Not: *unable; unbecoming.* **2.** Lack of: *unemployment.* **3.** To do the opposite of: *unlock.*

un•cle |ŭng′ kəl| *n., pl.* **uncles** The brother of one's mother or father.

un•clear |ŭn klîr′| *adj.* Not clear.

un•der•stand |ŭn′ dər stănd′| *v.* **understood** |ŭn dər stŏŏd′|, **understanding 1.** To get the meaning of: *Do you understand my question?* **2.** To be familiar with; know well: *I wish I could understand Spanish.*

un•der•wa•ter |ŭn′ dər wô′ tər| *adj.* Located, living, done, or used under the surface of the water: *The company drilled for underwater oil. adv.* Under the surface of the water: *to swim underwater.*

un•do |ŭn dōō′| *v.* **undid** |ŭn dĭd′|, **undoing** To do away with or reverse the result or effect of: *They wished they could undo their mistake.*

un•e•ven |ŭn ē′ vən| *adj.* **unevener, unevenest** Not level, smooth, or straight: *The surface of coral is uneven.*

un•fair |ŭn fâr′| *adj.* **unfairer, unfairest** Not fair or just: *an unfair punishment.*

un•fa•mil•iar |ŭn′ fə mĭl′ yər| *adj.* Not known; strange: *We saw an unfamiliar face at the door.*

un•hap•py |ŭn hăp′ ē| *adj.* **unhappier, unhappiest** Not happy; sad.

u•ni•form |yōō′ nə fôrm′| *n., pl.* **uniforms** Clothing that identifies those who wear it as members of a certain group, such as a police force.

un•kind |ŭn kīnd′| *adj.* **unkinder, unkindest** Harsh or cruel.

un•learn |ŭn lûrn′| *v.* **unlearned, unlearning** To learn not to do or respond to something learned previously: *Sometimes we must unlearn a bad habit.*

un·load |ŭn lōd′| *v.* **unloaded, unloading** To remove a load from: *We unloaded the truck.*

un·luck·y |ŭn lŭk′ ē| *adj.* **unluckier, unluckiest** Having or bringing bad luck.

un·pack |ŭn păk′| *v.* **unpacked, unpacking** To remove the contents of a container or vehicle, such as a suitcase or car: *I unpacked the old trunk.*

un·paid |ŭn pād′| *adj.* Not yet paid: *an unpaid bill.*

un·safe |ŭn sāf′| *adj.* Not safe; dangerous.

un·sure |ŭn shoŏr′| *adj.* Not sure; uncertain.

un·ti·dy |ŭn tī′ dē| *adj.* **untidier, untidiest** Not tidy or neat; sloppy; messy: *Jeff cleaned up his untidy room.*

un·til |ŭn tĭl′| *prep.* Up to the time of: *They studied until dinner.*

un·u·su·al |ŭn yoō′ zhoō əl| *adj.* Not usual, common, or ordinary: *It's unusual for me not to eat; I must be sick.*

urge |ûrj| *v.* **urged, urging** To try to convince; plead with: *My parents urged me to study harder.*

urn |ûrn| *n., pl.* **urns** A metal container with a spigot used for making and serving tea or coffee.
♦ *These sound alike* **urn, earn.**

use·ful |yoōs′ fəl| *adj.* Being of use or service; helpful: *Our map of Chicago was useful when we visited there.*

use·less |yoōs′ lĭs| *adj.* Being of no use or service; worthless: *We threw out the broken radio because it was useless.*

V

vac·cine |văk sēn′| *n., pl.* **vaccines** A preparation of weak or dead germs that are injected into a person or animal as a protection against the disease caused by those germs: *The children were given a vaccine against polio.*

vain |vān| *adj.* **vainer, vainest** Having no success: *Firefighters made a vain attempt to save the burning building.*
♦ *These sound alike* **vain, vane, vein.**

ă	pat	ŏ	pot	û	fur
ā	pay	ō	go	*th*	the
â	care	ô	paw, for	th	thin
ä	father	oi	oil	hw	which
ĕ	pet	oō	book	zh	usual
ē	be	oō	boot	ə	ago, item
ĭ	pit	yoō	cute		pencil, atom
ī	ice	ou	out		circus
î	near	ŭ	cut	ər	butter

val·ley |văl′ ē| *n., pl.* **valleys** A long, narrow area of low land between mountains or hills, often with a river running along the bottom.

vane |vān| *n., pl.* **vanes** A thin, flat piece of wood or metal, often having the shape of an arrow or a rooster, that turns on a vertical pivot to show the direction of the wind. Vanes are often placed on top of buildings.
♦ *These sound alike* **vane, vain, vein.**

va·nil·la |və nĭl′ ə| *n.* A flavoring made from the seed pods of a tropical plant: *The recipe called for a teaspoon of vanilla.*

vein |vān| *n.* **1.** A blood vessel through which blood returns to the heart. **2.** A long, regularly shaped deposit of mineral in rock: *a vein of gold ore.*
♦ *These sound alike* **vein, vain, vane.**

ven·ture |vĕn′ chər| *n., pl.* **ventures** A task or activity that is risky or dangerous: *Our first venture to the moon was a great success.* *v.* **ventured, venturing** To travel, undertake a project, etc., despite danger: *We ventured into the swirling waters.*

ves·sel |vĕs′ əl| *n., pl.* **vessels** A ship or large boat.

vi•brate |vī′ brāt′| *v.* **vibrated, vibrating** To move or cause to move back and forth rapidly: *Plucking a guitar string causes it to vibrate and produce a sound.*

vic•tim |vĭk′ tĭm| *n., pl.* **victims** A person or animal that is harmed, killed, or made to suffer.

vic•to•ri•ous |vĭk tôr′ ē əs| *adj.* Having won a victory.

vic•to•ry |vĭk′ tə rē| *n., pl.* **victories** The defeat of an opponent or enemy; success.

vil•lage |vĭl′ ij| *n., pl.* **villages** A group of houses that make up a community smaller than a town.

vis•it |vĭz′ ĭt| *n., pl.* **visits** A short stay or call: *I paid a visit to my former teacher.*

viv•id |vĭv′ ĭd| *adj.* Bright and strong; brilliant: *The coat was a vivid blue.*

vol•un•teer |vŏl′ ən tîr′| *v.* **volunteered, volunteering** To give or offer, usually without being asked: *I volunteered to lead the younger children on an overnight hike.*

W

wag•on |wăg′ ən| *n., pl.* **wagons** A four-wheeled vehicle for carrying loads or passengers.

wait |wāt| *v.* **waited, waiting** To do nothing or stay in a place until something expected happens: *Wait for me here.*
♦ *These sound alike* **wait, weight.**

walk |wôk| *v.* **walked, walking** To move or cause to move on foot at an easy, steady pace. *n., pl.* **walks 1.** An act of walking: *We took a walk on the beach.* **2.** A place, such as a path, that is set apart or designed for walking.

ware |wâr| *n.* **1.** Manufactured articles or goods of the same general kind, such as glassware or hardware. **2. wares.** Goods for sale: *At the fair all the merchants displayed their wares.*
♦ *These sound alike* **ware, wear.**

waste |wāst| *v.* **wasted, wasting** To spend or use foolishly or needlessly: *Don't waste the whole day watching television.*

wa•ter•proof |wô′ tər prōof′| *adj.* Capable of keeping water from coming through: *Raincoats should be made of waterproof material.*

wave•let |wāv′ lĭt| *n., pl.* **wavelets** A small wave or ripple.

wa•ver |wā′ vər| *v.* **wavered, wavering** To be uncertain; falter: *I never wavered in my choice.*

wealth |wĕlth| *n.* A great amount of money or valuable possessions.

wear |wâr| *v.* **wore** |wôr|, **worn, wearing** To have on the body: *All the students wear school uniforms.*
♦ *These sound alike* **wear, ware.**

wea•ry |wîr′ ē| *adj.* **wearier, weariest** Needing rest; tired: *The weary children went straight to bed.*

weath•er |wĕth′ ər| *n.* The condition or activity of the atmosphere with respect to whether it is hot or cold, sunny or cloudy, windy or calm, or wet or dry.
♦ *These sound alike* **weather, whether.**

weave |wēv| *v.* **wove** |wōv| *or* **weaved, woven** |wō′ vən|, **weaving** To make something, such as cloth or a basket, by passing something, such as threads or twigs, over and under one another. Weaving is often done on a loom.

week |wēk| *n., pl.* **weeks** A period of seven days: *We'll be there in a week.*
♦ *These sound alike* **week, weak.**

weight |wāt| *n., pl.* **weights** The measure of how heavy something is: *The weight of the box is 100 pounds.*
♦ *These sound alike* **weight, wait.**

weird |wîrd| *adj.* **weirder, weirdest** Strange, odd, or unusual: *Purple trousers, an orange shirt, and a pointed hat make a weird outfit.*

wel•come |wĕl′ kəm| *v.* **welcomed, welcoming** To greet with pleasure, hospitality, or special ceremony: *We stood to welcome our guests. n., pl.* **welcomes** The act of welcoming. *adj.* Greeted, received, or accepted with pleasure: *You are always a welcome visitor.*

west |wĕst| *n.* The direction in which the sun is seen setting in the evening. *adj.* Of, in, or toward the west: *We camped on the west side of the large lake. adv.* Toward the west: *We drove west.*

whale |hwāl| *n., pl.* **whales** An often very large sea animal that looks like a fish but is a mammal that breathes air.

ă	pat	ŏ	pot	û	fur
ā	pay	ō	go	*th*	the
â	care	ô	paw, for	th	thin
ä	father	oi	oil	hw	which
ĕ	pet	oo	book	zh	usual
ē	be	oo	boot	ə	ago, item
ĭ	pit	yoo	cute		pencil, atom
ī	ice	ou	out		circus
î	near	ŭ	cut	ər	butter

when·ev·er |hwĕn ĕv′ ər| *adv.* At whatever time: *Come whenever possible.* *conj.* At whatever time that: *We can start whenever you're ready.*

wheth·er |hwĕ*th*′ ər| *conj.* If: *Ask whether the museum is open.*
♦ *These sound alike* **whether, weather.**

whirl·pool |hwûrl′ pōol′| *n., pl.* **whirlpools** A current of water that rotates very rapidly.

whit·tle |hwĭt′ l| *v.* **whittled, whittling** To cut small bits or shavings from wood with a knife.

wick·ed |wĭk′ ĭd| *adj.* **wickeder, wickedest** Bad, evil, or mean.

wind¹ |wĭnd| *n., pl.* **winds** Air that is in motion.

wind² |wīnd| *v.* **wound** |wound|, **winding** To tighten the spring of: *I forgot to wind my watch.*

wind·y |wĭn′ dē| *adj.* **windier, windiest** Having much wind.

with·draw |wĭth drô′| *v.* **withdrew** |wĭth drōo′|, **withdrawn, withdrawing** To take back or away; remove: *I withdrew money from the bank.*

wiz·ard |wĭz′ ərd| *n., pl.* **wizards** A man thought to have magical powers; magician.

wom·an |wŏom′ ən| *n., pl.* **women** |wĭm′ ĭn| A fully grown female human being.

won·der |wŭn′ dər| *v.* **wondered, wondering** To be curious about; want to know: *I wonder what went wrong.*

wood |wŏod| *n., pl.* **woods** The hard material beneath the bark of trees and shrubs that makes up the trunk and branches. Wood is used as fuel and for building.

wood·y |wŏod′ ē| *adj.* **woodier, woodiest** Consisting of or containing wood.

wool |wŏol| *n., pl.* **wools** 1. The soft, thick, curly or wavy hair of animals such as sheep. 2. Yarn, cloth, or clothing made of wool.

wool·en |wŏol′ ən| *adj.* Made of wool.

wool·ly |wŏol′ ē| *adj.* **woollier, woolliest** Made of or covered with wool or a material like wool.

work |wûrk| *n., pl.* **works** 1. The physical or mental effort that is required to do something; labor: *Cleaning the house is hard work.* 2. An activity by which a person earns money; job: *Our neighbor is looking for work as a teacher.* *v.* **worked, working** 1. To put or cause to put out effort to do or make something: *We work hard to get good grades. The teacher works the sixth graders hard.* 2. To have a job: *My parents work in a hospital.*

work·out |wûrk′ out′| *n.* A period of exercise, especially in athletics: *Mark had a good workout in the gym.*

world |wûrld| *n., pl.* **worlds** The earth: *The world is round.*

worm |wûrm| *n., pl.* **worms** Any of several kinds of animals that have soft bodies and no backbone. Worms have no legs and move by crawling. *v.* **wormed, worming** To move by or as if by crawling: *We wormed our way through the crowd.*

worn |wôrn| *v.* Past participle of **wear.** *adj.* Very tired; exhausted.

wor·ry |wûr′ ē| *v.* **worried, worrying** To feel or cause to feel uneasy: *Your bad cough worries me.*

would |wŏŏd| *helping v.* Past tense of **will.** Used to show or express something that is likely: *They would be here if they had left on time.*

wound |wōōnd| *n., pl.* **wounds** An injury in which body tissue is cut or broken.

wrap |răp| *v.* **wrapped, wrapping** To wind or fold as a covering: *I wrapped a shawl around my shoulders.*

wrench |rĕnch| *n., pl.* **wrenches** A tool that has jaws for gripping nuts, bolts, or pieces of pipe so that they can be turned.

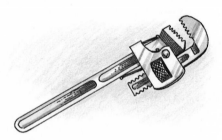

wres•tle |rĕs′ əl| *v.* **wrestled, wrestling** To struggle with and try to force or throw an opponent to the ground.

wring |rĭng| *v.* **wrung** |rŭng|, **wringing 1.** To twist or squeeze so as to force out liquid: *Wring out the wet clothes.* **2.** To force out by or as if by twisting or squeezing: *Wring the water from the towel.*
♦ *These sound alike* **wring, ring.**

wrin•kle |rĭng′ kəl| *n., pl.* **wrinkles** A small fold or crease.

wrist |rĭst| *n., pl.* **wrists** The joint between the hand and the arm.

wrong |rông| *adj.* Not correct or true: *You gave the wrong answer.*

wrote |rōt| *v.* Past tense of **write:** *He wrote a letter with his new pen.*

Y

-y A suffix that forms adjectives and means: **1.** Like a: *bushy.* **2.** Full of: *juicy.*

year |yîr| *n., pl.* **years 1.** The period of time in which the earth makes one complete trip around the sun. **2.** A period of 365 days, or 366 days in a leap year, divided into 52 weeks or 12 months, beginning January 1 and ending December 31. **3.** A period of 12 months: *We plan to return a year from now.*

yeast |yēst| *n., pl.* **yeasts** A substance that is used to make bread dough rise. Yeast consists of tiny one-celled plants that grow quickly.

yell |yĕl| *v.* **yelled, yelling** To shout or cry out loudly, as in anger, fear, or warning.

yel•low |yĕl′ ō| *n., pl.* **yellows** The color of ripe lemons or of dandelions.

yes•ter•day |yĕs′ tər dā| *n.* The day before today: *Yesterday was windy.*

Z

zinc |zĭngk| *n.* A shiny bluish-white metal, used as a coating for iron and in electric batteries. Zinc is one of the chemical elements.

Content Index

Spelling Across the Curriculum

art, 136, 142
careers, 166, 196
health, 52, 106, 178, 220
home economics, 22
industrial arts, 28
language arts, 112, 208
math, 100
recreation, 16, 58, 70, 94, 148
science, 40, 64, 76, 124, 160, 172, 184
social studies, 34, 88, 130, 202, 214

Spelling and Meaning

consonant changes, 49, 81, 121, 169, 189, 193, 211, 225
vowel changes, 25, 45, 61, 91, 97, 103, 117, 139, 145, 153, 163, 181, 199, 205, 217
word forms, 13, 19, 31, 37, 55, 67, 73, 85, 91, 109, 127, 133, 157, 175, 181

Thinking Skills

analogies, **19**, 44, 79, 97, 109, 114, 145, 151, 211, 222, 232, 237–238, 241, 245
analyzing. *See* A, B pages in each Basic Unit. *See also* 15, 21, 27, 29, 42–43, 45, 57, 63, 69, 75, 78, 80–81, 93, 111, 117, 141, 146, 153, 183, 189, 201, 207, 213, 219, 225, 233, 235, 238–239, 241–242, 244, 245
classifying, 25, 67, 78, 80, 115, 127, 152, 169, 186, 193, 223–224, 229–230, 233, 236, 240–241, 244, 246
comparing, 75, 82–**83**

contrasting, 75, 82–**83**
creative thinking, 17, 23, 29, 33, 35, 51, 53, 59, 65, 69, 71, 77, 89, 101, 107, 111, 123, 125, 131, 137, 147, 159, 167, 173, 183, 185, 197, 203, 207, 213, 215, 221
critical thinking, 16, 22, 28, 34, 40, 52, 58, 64, 70, 76, 88, 94, 100, 106, 112, 124, 130, 136, 142, 148, 160, 166, 172, 178, 184, 196, 202, 208, 214, 220
distinguishing between facts and opinions, 226–**227**
making generalizations. *See* A page in each Basic Unit.
making inferences, 17, 31, 42–44, 47, 49, 51, 55, 59, 61, 69, 78, 80, 91, 93, 103, 109, 111, 114, 116, 118, 121, 129, 143, 150, 152, 154, 163, 175, 185–186, 195, 199, 205, 223, 226, 229, 231–232, 234–236, 242, 243, 244, 246
persuasion, 123, 190–**191**, 201, 209
predicting outcomes, 118
problem solving, 17
sequencing, 20, 29, 143, 147, 165

Vocabulary

See also Spelling and Meaning.
antonyms, 42, 49, **74**, 78, 121, 152, 157, **164**, 175, 199, 205, 229, 231–232, 236–237, 242, 246
base words, 31, 33, 56, 104–105, 133, 135, 137, 151, 163, 177, 179, 187, 205, 230, 235, 239, 243

blending word parts, **86**
color words, **176**
compound words, 77, **84**–87, 89, 114, 235
content area vocabulary, 16, 22, 28, 34, 40, 52, 58, 64, 70, 76, 88, 94, 100, 106, 112, 124, 130, 136, 142, 148, 160, 166, 172, 178, 184, 196, 202, 208, 214, 220
context clues, **20**
definitions, 13, 15, 19, 25, 27, 31, 33, 37, 42–44, 49, 55, 73, 78–79, 85, 91, 97, 101, 103–104, 109, 115–116, 121, 127–129, 139–140, 145, 150–151, 163, 169, 175, 181, 185, 188, 193, 197, 199, 205, 211, 217, 219, 223, 229, 231–239, 241, 243
easily confused words, **68**
exact words, 32, 50, 62, 110, 158, 176, 194
homographs, 26, **200**
homophones, **36**–39, 41, 49, 73, 181
idioms, **212**
multimeaning words, 104, 128, 140
prefixes, **132**–135, 137, 151
regional differences, **182**
rhyming words, 13, 25, 42, 51, 55, 61, 65, 73, 79, 87, 97, 103, 115–116, 121, 145, 150, 171, 181, 188, 193, 211, 217, 219, 224, 229, 231–232, 234–236, 238, 240, 244, 246
shortened forms, **218**
suffixes, 56, 92, 98, 122, 134, **174**–177, 200
synonyms, 14, 27, 49, 61, **73**, 103, 109, 121, 133, **164**, 175, 181, 187, 205, 230, 233–234, 236, 240,

Writing

Credits

Series design and cover design by Ligature, Inc.
Front cover and title page photograph: © ELIZA
McFADDEN.

Illustrations

Meg Kelleher Aubrey: 17,23,24,27,29,30,33,35,
36,39,41,48,51,52,53,54,57,59,60,63,65,
66,69,71,72,75,77,89,101,107,113,125,131,
137,149,155,161,173,179,197,203,215,221.
Holly Berry: 125,131,161,167,215.
John Butler: 12,15,17,18,21,23.
Lorinda Cauley: 71.
Mai Vo Dinh: 154.
Lois Ehlert: 13,(42),19,(42),25,(43),31,(43),37,
(44),49,(78),55,(78),61,(79),67,(79),73,(80),85,
(114),91,(114),97,(115),103,(115),109,(116),
121,(150),127,(150),133,(151),139,(151),145,(152),
157,(186),163,(186),169,(187),175,(187),181,
(188),193,(222),199,(222),205,(223),211,(223),
217,(224).
John Ellis: 29,53,77,89,95,113,131,137,143,149,
210.
Harriet Fishman: 296,304,314,326.
Ruth Flanigan: 282,294,308,325.
Diane Dawson Hearn: 59,101.
Carol Inouye: 290,293,312,318.
Tom Leonard: 156,159,161,162,165,167,
168,171,173,174,177,179,180,183,185,192,
195,197,201,203,204,207,209,210,213,219,
221.
Fred Lynch: 95,143.
Martucci Studios: 13,19,25,31,37,49,55,61,67,
73,85,91,97,103,109,121,127,133,139,145,
157,163,169,175,181,193,199,205,211,217.
Cheryl Kirk Noll: 288,301,316,320.
Bernadette Pons: 59,65,77,84,87,89,90,93,95,
96,99,101,102,105,107,108,111,113,120,123,
126,129,132,135,138,144,147,179,203,209,
215.
Dee de Rosa: 190,191.
Robin Spowart: 125.
Ashley Wolff: 17,107.

Photographs

3 Nancy Sheehan.
4 Charlie Hogg.
4 (bottom row) Nancy Sheehan.
16 Utah Winter Games.
22 © Maxfield Parrish.
28 Masterfile.
34 Pat Canova/Southern Stock.
40 Montes De Oca/Light Images.
41 Dan McCoy/Rainbow.
46-47 James Ballard.
58 P. Beney/FPG.
64 James F. Polka/Nawrocki.
70 The Cousteau Society.
76 (detail) St. Joseph Museum, St. Joseph,
Missouri.
82 (top) Luis Villota/The Stock Market.
82 (bottom) Duncan Anderson & Rachel
Wilder/Animals Animals.
83 E.R. Degginger/Bruce Coleman.
88 David Ball/Picture Cube.
94 Culver Pictures.
100 Jon Feingersh/The Stock Market.
106 Barbara Kirk/Stock Market.
112 The Bettmann Archive.
124 Alastair Black/FPG.
130 B & J McGrath/Picture Cube.
136 Hans Namuth/Photo Researchers.
141 (left) Superstock. (right) P. Madura/FPG.
142 (detail) Paul S. Taylor, courtesy of the
Dorothea Lange Collection. © The City of
Oakland, The Oakland Museum, 1990.
148 John P. Kelly/Image Bank.
160 L. Grant/FPG.
166 Wardene Weisser/Berg & Associates.
172 William Edward Smith/Stock Market.
178 The Bettmann Archive.
184 NASA.
196 Historical Pictures Service.
202 Peter Southwick/Stock Boston.
208 AP/Wide World Photos.
214 Eunice Harris/Photo Researchers.
220 Bettmann Archive.
226 Richard Weiss/Peter Arnold.
227 J. Blank/FPG.
287 R. Rowan/Photo Researchers.
299 C. Seghers/Leo de Wys, Inc.
306 J. Domke/Leo de Wys, Inc.
323 Rick Golt/Photo Researchers.